Health

7

Editorial Advisory Board

The Career Information Center includes:

Agribusiness, Environment, and Natural Resources / 1
Communications and the Arts / 2
Computers, Business, and Office / 3
Construction / 4
Consumer, Homemaking, and Personal Services / 5
Engineering, Science, and Technology / 6
Health / 7
Hospitality and Recreation / 8
Manufacturing / 9
Marketing and Distribution / 10
Public and Community Services / 11
Transportation / 12
Employment Trends and Master Index / 13

Health 7

Career Information Center

Eighth Edition

Macmillan Reference USA
an imprint of the Gale Group
New York • Detroit • San Francisco • London • Boston • Woodbridge, CT

Editorial Staff

Editorial Director: Darryl Kestler

Project Editor: Carol J. Ciaston

Researchers/Bibliographers: Christopher D. Binkley, Douglas Burton, Cheryl MacKenzie, Lauren Weber

Copyediting Supervisor: Helen H. Castro

Photo Editors: Sara Matthews, Brian Suskin

Electronic Preparation: Fiona Torphy

Acknowledgments: Many people gave their help, their time, and their experience to this project. We especially want to thank all the people at unions and trade and professional associations for their help in providing information and photographs. We also wish to thank the U.S. Department of Labor, Bureau of Labor Statistics, for providing up-to-date statistics, salary information, and employment projections for all the job profiles.

Publisher, Macmillan Reference USA: Elly Dickason

Associate Publisher, Macmillan Reference USA: Jill Lectka

Content Project Manager, Gale Group: Sheila Dow

Editor, Gale Group: Jaime E. Noce

Developed and produced by Visual Education Corporation,
Princeton, New Jersey

Macmillan Library Reference USA
1633 Broadway
New York, NY 10019

Gale Group
27500 Drake Rd.
Farmington Hills, MI 48331

ISSN 1082-703X

ISBN 0-02-865637-7 (set)

ISBN 0-02-865644-X (volume 7)

Printed in the United States of America

printing number
1 2 3 4 5 6 7 8 9 10

This paper meets the requirements of ANSI/NISO Z39.48-1992 (Permanence of Paper).

Contents

Job Summary Chart

Job	Salary	Education/ Training	Employment Outlook	Page
Job Profiles—No Specialized Training				
Admitting Clerk	Average—$355 a week	High school	Good	29
Dental Assistant	Median—$10.88 an hour	High school	Excellent	30
Dialysis Technician	Average—$18,000 to $22,200	High school	Very good	32
★ Home Health Aide	Median—$7.58 an hour	Varies—see profile	Excellent	33
Laboratory Animal Care Worker	Median—$7.12 an hour	High school	Good	35
Nurse's Aide and Orderly	Average—$8.32 an hour	None	Very good	36
★ Optometric Assistant	Starting—$15,000 Average—$18,300 to $21,000	High school	Excellent	37
★ Substance Abuse Counselor	Starting—$15,000 to $20,000	High school	Excellent	39
Ward Clerk	Average—$10.57 an hour	High school	Good	40
Job Profiles—Some Specialized Training/Experience				
AIDS Counselor	Median—$30,590	Varies—see profile	Varies—see profile	42
Ambulance Driver	Average—$9.00 an hour	License and training	Very good	44
Biomedical Equipment Technician	Average—$20,500 to $24,900	High school plus training	Very good	46
Cardiac Monitor Technician/ Perfusionist	Median—$24,360	High school plus training	Poor	48
Cardiology Technologist	Average—$17.44 an hour	High school plus training	Fair	49
★ Dental and Medical Secretary	Median—$10.88 an hour	High school plus training	Excellent	51
★ Dental Hygienist	Median—$22 an hour	2-year college; license	Excellent	53
★ Dental Laboratory Technician	Median—$10.88 an hour	High school plus training	Excellent	55
Electroneurodiagnostic Technologist	Median—$32,070	High school plus training	Fair	57
Emergency Medical Technician	Median—$20,290	High school plus training	Very good	59
Environmental Health Specialist	Average—$37,000	Varies—see profile	Good	61
Hospice Worker	Varies—see profile	Varies—see profile	Varies—see profile	63
★ Inhalation Therapist	Average—$17.14 an hour	2-year or 4-year college	Excellent	65
Licensed Practical Nurse	Median—$26,940	High school plus training; license	Good	67
★ Medical Assistant	Median—$20,680	High school plus training	Excellent	69
Medical Laboratory Worker	Average—$13.38 an hour	High school plus training	Good	71

★ High-growth job

Job Profiles—Advanced Training/Experience

★ High-growth job

Job	Salary	Education/ Training	Employment Outlook	Page
Osteopathic Physician	Average—$124,000	Varies—see profile	Very good	126
Pharmacist	Median—$66,220	College; license	Fair	128
Pharmacologist	Median—$66,220	Advanced degree	Very good	130
★ Physical Therapist	Median—$56,600	College; license	Very good	132
Physician	Varies—see profile	Advanced degree; license	Very good	133
★ Physician Assistant	Median—$47,090	Varies—see profile	Excellent	136
Podiatrist	Varies—see profile	Advanced degree; license	Good	138
★ Prosthetist and Orthotist	Average—$36,000 to $59,000	Varies—see profile	Excellent	139
Psychiatrist	Average—$131,300	Advanced degree; license	Very good	141
Psychologist	Median—$48,050	Advanced degree	Good	143
Public Health Educator	Starting—$22,000 to $25,000 Average—$28,000 to $35,000	Advanced degree	Very good	145
Recreation Therapist	Average—$13.98 an hour	College	Very good	147
Registered Nurse	Median—$40,690	Varies—see profile	Very good	149
★ Speech Pathologist and Audiologist	Median—$43,080	Advanced degree	Excellent	151
Surgeon	Median—$217,000	Advanced degree; license	Very good	153

★ High-growth job

Foreword

The eighth edition of the *Career Information Center* mirrors the ongoing changes in the job market caused by new technological and economic developments. These developments continue to change what Americans do in the workplace and how they do it. People have a critical need for up-to-date information to help them make career decisions.

The *Career Information Center* is an individualized resource for people of all ages and at all stages of career development. It has been recognized as an excellent reference for librarians, counselors, educators, and other providers of job information. It is ideally suited for use in libraries, career resource centers, and guidance offices, as well as in adult education centers and other facilities where people seek information about job opportunities, careers, and their own potential in the workforce.

This eighth edition updates many of the features that made the earlier editions so useful.

- A Job Summary Chart, a quick reference guide, appears in the front section of each volume to help readers get the basic facts and compare the jobs described in the volume. High-growth jobs are highlighted and identified with a star.
- Each volume of the *Career Information Center* begins with an overview of the job market in that field. These "Looking Into . . ." sections have been completely revised and updated. They also include new graphs, charts, and boxes providing information such as industry snapshots and the fastest-growing and top-dollar jobs in the field. A new "Global View" feature tells how the new global economy is affecting jobs in the field.
- Each volume has a section called "Getting Into . . . ," which contains useful information on entering the particular field. It offers self-evaluation tips and decision-making help; and it relates possible job choices to individual interests, abilities, and work characteristics. There is also practical information on job hunting, using the Internet and classified ads, preparing resumes, and handling interviews. "Getting Into . . ." also includes a section on employee rights.
- Each volume has a listing of all job profiles in the series and the volumes in which they appear, making access to profiles in other volumes easy.
- *Career Information Center* contains 685 job profiles in which nearly 2,000 jobs are discussed. Each profile describes work characteristics, education and training requirements, getting the job, advancement and employment outlook, working conditions, and earnings and benefits.
- Job summaries, provided for each job profile, highlight the education or training required, salary range, and employment outlook.
- Volume 13 has been revised to reflect career concerns of the new century and employment trends through the year 2008. This volume includes updated articles on benefits, employment law, health in the workplace, job search strategies, job training, job opportunities at home, adjusting to job loss, and identifying opportunities for retraining.
- More than 560 photographs appear in the *Career Information Center,* including many new photos. Profile photos provide a visual glimpse of life on the job. Photos have been selected to give the reader a sense of what it feels like to be in a specific field or job.
- Updated bibliographies in each volume include recommended readings and World Wide Web sites in specific job areas. Additional titles for the vocational counselor are included in Volume 13.
- Each volume also contains a comprehensive directory of accredited occupational education and vocational training facilities listed by occupational area and grouped by state. Directory materials are generated from the IPEDS (Integrated Postsecondary Education Data System) database of the U.S. Department of Education.

The *Career Information Center* recognizes the importance not only of job selection, but also of job holding, coping, and applying life skills. No other career information publication deals with work attitudes so comprehensively.

Using the Career Information Center

The *Career Information Center* is designed to meet the needs of many people—students, people just entering or reentering the job market, those dissatisfied with present jobs, those without jobs—anyone of any age who is not sure what to do for a living. The *Career Information Center* is for people who want help in making career choices. It combines the comprehensiveness of an encyclopedia with the format and readability of a magazine. Many professionals, including counselors, librarians, and teachers will find it a useful guidance and reference tool.

The *Career Information Center* is organized by occupational interest area rather than in alphabetical order. Jobs that have something in common are grouped together. In that way people who do not know exactly what job they want can read about a number of related jobs. The *Career Information Center* classifies jobs that have something in common into clusters. The classification system is adapted from the cluster organization used by the U.S. Department of Labor. Each volume of the *Career Information Center* explores one of 12 occupational clusters.

To use the *Career Information Center,* first select the volume that treats the occupational area that interests you most. Because there are many ways to group occupations, you may not find a particular job in the volume in which you look for it. In that case, check the central listing of all the profiles, which is located in the front of Volumes 1 through 12. This listing provides the names of all profiles and the volume number in which they appear. Volume 13 also includes a comprehensive index of all the jobs covered in the first 12 volumes.

After selecting a volume or volumes, investigate the sections that you feel would be most helpful. It isn't necessary to read these volumes from cover to cover. They are arranged so that you can go directly to the specific information you want. Here is a description of the sections included in each volume.

- **Job Summary Chart**—This chart presents in tabular form the basic data from all profiles in the volume: salary, education and training, employment outlook, and the page on which you can find the job profile. Jobs with a high growth potential are highlighted and starred.

- **Looking Into . . .**—This overview of the occupational cluster describes the opportunities, characteristics, and trends in that particular field.

- **Getting Into . . .**—This how-to guide can help you decide what jobs may be most satisfying to you and what strategies you can use to get the right job. You will learn, for example, how to write an effective resume, how to complete an application form, what to expect in an interview, how to use networking, and what to do if someone has discriminated against you.

- **Job Summary**—These summaries, located at the beginning of each profile, highlight the most important facts about the job: education and training, salary range, and employment outlook.

Education and Training indicates whether the job requires no education, high school, college, advanced degree, voc/tech school, license, or training.

Salary Range is given as an approximate yearly wage unless "a week" or "an hour" is noted. These are average salaries that may vary significantly from region to region. In a few cases, a job is listed with a median salary. The median is a middle point in a series of values. The method for calculating a median number is different from that for calculating an average number, but the results do not vary greatly.

Employment Outlook is based on several factors, including the Bureau of Labor Statistics' projections through the year 2008. The ratings are defined as follows: *poor* means there is a projected employment decrease of 1 percent or more; *fair* means there is a projected employment increase of 0 to 13 percent; *good* means there is a projected employment increase of 14 to 26 percent; *very good* means there is a projected employment increase of 27 to 40 percent; and *excellent* means there is a projected employment increase of 41 percent or more. The outlook is then determined by looking at the ratings and other employment factors. For example, a job with excellent projected employment growth in which many more people are entering the field than there are jobs available will have an outlook that is good rather than excellent.

For all categories, the phrase *Varies—see profile* means the reader must consult the profile for the information, which is too extensive to include in the Job Summary.

- **Job Profiles**—The job profiles are divided into three categories based on the level of training required to get the job. Each profile explores a number of related jobs and covers seven major topics: description of the job being profiled, the education and training requirements, ways to get the job, advancement possibilities and employment outlook, the working conditions, the earnings and benefits, and places to go for more information.

Job Profiles—No Specialized Training includes jobs that require no education or previous work experience beyond high school.

Job Profiles—Some Specialized Training/Experience includes jobs that require one, two, or three years of vocational training or college, or work experience beyond high school.

Job Profiles—Advanced Training/Experience includes jobs that require a bachelor's degree or advanced degree from a college or university and/or equivalent work experience in that field.

- **Resources—General Career Information** includes a selected bibliography of the most recent books, audiovisual materials, and web sites on general career information, how-to books on such topics as resume writing and preparing for tests, and useful computer software. In addition, there are special sections of readings for the career counselor in Volume 13.

- **Resources—**Each volume also contains a bibliography of books, audiovisual materials, and web sites for specific fields covered in that volume.

- **Directory of Institutions Offering Career Training—**This listing, organized first by career area, then by state, includes the schools that offer occupational training beyond high school. For jobs requiring a bachelor's degree or an advanced degree, check a library for college catalogs and appropriate directories.

- **Index—**This index, which is located at the end of each volume, lists every job mentioned in that volume. It serves not only to cross-reference all the jobs in the volume but also to show related jobs in the field. For example, under the entry LICENSED PRACTICAL NURSE, you will find Home Health Aide, Nurse's Aide and Orderly, and Ward Clerk. In addition, the "profile includes" part of an entry lists other jobs that are mentioned in the profile, in this case Licensed Vocational Nurse and Registered Nurse.

- **Volume 13, Employment Trends and Master Index—**This volume includes several features that will help both the job seeker and the career counselor. A useful correlation guide provides the *DOT (Dictionary of Occupational Titles)* number of most of the job profiles in the *Career Information Center.* There is also a special section on career information for Canada. The updated and revised "Employment Trends" section contains articles on health in the workplace; employment projections through the year 2008; job search strategies; employment trends for women, minorities, immigrants, older workers, and the physically challenged; employment demographics; benefits programs; training; employment opportunities at home; employment law; adjusting to job loss; identifying opportunities for retraining. All articles have been written by authorities in these fields. The articles provide job seekers and career professionals with an overview of current employment issues, career opportunities, and outlooks. Finally, there is a master index to all the jobs included in all 13 volumes.

The *Career Information Center* is exactly what it says it is—a center of the most useful and pertinent information you need to explore and choose from the wide range of job and career possibilities. The *Career Information Center* provides you with a solid foundation of information for getting a satisfying job or rewarding career.

Comprehensive Job Profile List

The following list includes job profiles and the corresponding volume number.

Looking Into Health

Every day millions of Americans turn to trained health care providers for their medical care. In private medical offices around the nation, physicians—assisted by nurses and aides—treat minor injuries such as sprained ankles and illnesses such as strep throat and childhood mumps, test patients to diagnose their ailments, and screen people for potential problems. They examine pregnant women and provide prenatal care. They also perform checkups for children and adults. For individuals at high risk for certain diseases, they administer immunizations.

In hospitals, a greater variety of health care professionals perform a wider variety of tasks. Medical professionals help individuals who have immediate, severe, or longer-term needs. Emergency room physicians examine and treat people with immediate life-threatening illnesses or those who suffer from severe bleeding or injuries. Internists diagnose and treat medical problems and provide medications that pharmacists prepare. Surgeons, with the help of anesthesiologists, nurses, and others, perform surgical operations.

Every day technicians in hospitals conduct X rays, lab analyses, and other diagnostic tests. Hospital nurses check the vital signs of patients, administer medications, and maintain charts on patient progress. Orderlies, nurse's aides, and others tend to the physical needs of patients, bathe them, and deliver their meals. Dietitians, social workers, and physical, occupational, and other therapists help patients prepare for release from the hospital. Behind the scenes, supervisors, administrators, accountants, maintenance workers, admissions clerks, patient records clerks, and other staff members keep the hospital running smoothly.

On the road, ambulance drivers rush paramedics and emergency medical technicians to people injured in car accidents, caught in fires, and endangered by other emergencies. These medical workers provide immediate first aid, set fractures, and keep injured or ill people safe until they get to the hospital. In private homes, outpatient treatment centers, and residential health care facilities, nurses, aides, and doctors tend to elderly people and people with chronic medical problems, providing more of the services traditionally delivered in hospitals.

Keeping Americans healthy requires millions of workers and billions of dollars—and the numbers keep growing. Overall, the health care industry in the United States employs more than 7 million trained workers.

FROM MAGIC TO MODERN MEDICINE

In ancient times, people knew little about what caused disease or how the human body worked. They concluded that evil spirits or angry gods caused illness. Some of their cures—boring holes in the skull to let out evil spirits, for example—did more harm than good. Nevertheless, ancient people made some important medical discoveries. More than 4,000 years ago, people in ancient Egypt were already using castor oil

As the demand for health care services rises, some of the fastest-growing occupations will be in allied health. *(The Terry Wild Studio.)*

to purge the digestive system and tannic acid to treat burns. An Egyptian text written around 2500 B.C. describes how to use compression to stop bleeding.

The man considered to be the founder of modern medicine was a Greek physician named Hippocrates, who lived in the 5th century B.C. Hippocrates and his followers wrote about 70 books describing a new philosophy of medicine, based not on folklore or magic but on careful observation of patients and detailed records of their symptoms. With this information, physicians could draw accurate conclusions about what caused disease and how it could be treated. This procedure—collecting data and using the data to draw conclusions—is the basis of what we call the scientific method.

Hippocrates made two other lasting contributions to medical science. His observations led him to conclude that disease is often the result of diet, climate, occupation, or other environmental factors. Hippocrates also established a standard of conduct for physicians that still guides the medical profession today. These standards are summarized in the Hippocratic oath, which all new physicians are still required to take. The Hippocratic oath includes this vow: "I will practice my profession with conscience and dignity; the health of my patient will be my first consideration."

The Search for Causes

Ideas like those of Hippocrates did not have a widespread impact on medicine until the Renaissance in the 16th century. The Renaissance was a period of intense intellectual awakening and scientific inquiry in all fields including medicine. The first accurate anatomy text was published in 1543, about the same time that serious research began into the cause of infectious diseases. A century later, the first precise description of blood circulation appeared, along with an explanation of how the lungs work.

Until then, no one had actually proved how disease spread. In the mid-19th century, a series of experiments by Louis Pasteur proved that microorganisms called bacteria can invade the body and cause infection and disease. More important, Pasteur discovered how to prevent this bacterial invasion through immunization. Robert Koch, considered cofounder with Pasteur of the science of bacteriology, identified the specific bacteria that cause tuberculosis and cholera.

Global View: Health

As in other career fields, opportunities for health care are expanding with the growth of the global economy and the Internet. Doctors are finding work abroad as well as in the United States. Medical students may seek training in a foreign nation. Even patients are going global, using the Internet to research everything from doctors to advances in medical treatments.

The ease of international communications has prompted several American firms to open health care facilities in foreign nations. Such operations have opened in Eastern Europe and the former Soviet Union, where traditional state-run health care systems are unable to care for the region's aging population. Other United States-run medical facilities soon may appear on foreign soil, as the World Trade Organization plans to open public health care systems around the world to private investment and competition.

With many nations (including the United States) experiencing a shortage of trained health care professionals, demand for an education in medicine is high. Some U.S. medical schools state that 10 to 20 candidates apply for every opening, and some nursing schools report a 3-year waiting period for acceptance. As a result, many students are seeking training at accredited medical schools in other nations. Programs span the globe, from the West Indies to Israel, and include training in a wide range of medical fields. Many of these schools are approved for U.S. federal financial aid.

The Internet has made it easier for students to find foreign medical schools. Many of these schools process application forms over the Internet and provide online guidance regarding financial aid. Some school web sites enable prospective students to "chat" with current students, graduates, and professors to learn about the school.

The Internet has also created a new health care field. Health information web sites, such as WebMD, are among the sites most often visited by the general public. They allow consumers far greater access to health care information than ever before-from news and warnings on drugs and updates on clinical trials, to in-depth studies of diseases and conditions. Hospitals, insurance companies, and nonprofit organizations, such as the American Heart Association, sponsor many of these sites. Thousands of health care professionals, including physicians and nurses, act as writers and consultants to the web sites.

The pace of medical progress quickened in the 19th and 20th centuries. In the 1840s, the use of ether as an anesthetic made possible many surgical operations that were previously too painful for patients to bear. The development of X rays in 1895 revolutionized the diagnostic process. Alexander Fleming's 1928 discovery of penicillin, the first antibiotic, was also a landmark achievement. For the first time a drug could kill disease-causing organisms inside the body of a person who was already ill.

Medical Science and Public Health

By the mid-19th century medical science had proved what Hippocrates had suspected: Disease is often caused by an unsafe environment. This knowledge led officials to begin massive programs to improve public health. They drained swamps to eliminate disease-carrying insects, sanitized drinking water supplies, and quarantined people with infectious diseases. They also began programs of education and vaccination, which led to the virtual eradication of diseases such as cholera, typhus, typhoid fever, and yellow fever in the United States.

Today public health agencies continue their work to keep the public safe and well informed. The United States Centers for Disease Control and Prevention (CDC), the World Health Organization (WHO), and other agencies continue to research new ways to prevent the spread of infectious diseases, promote health, and prolong life.

The CDC's mission is to keep track of diseases in the United States and help control them. Statisticians and lab workers at the agency pay close attention to epidemics, their spread, and their prevention. The role of the WHO is to oversee the public health of all members of the United Nations. The WHO helps governments to promote family planning and provide their citizens with access to primary health care. It also watches population patterns and funds public health research and development. The WHO employs researchers, primary health care providers, and others who focus on education, food and water supply, sanitation, immunization, and the prevention and control of disease.

Public health agencies also serve as educators, warning people of health hazards such as those posed by smoking, alcohol and drug abuse, occupational hazards, and environmental pollution. In recent years the fight against the deadly AIDS epidemic has been a key focus of public health agencies around the world.

THE TECHNOLOGY REVOLUTION

Technology has revolutionized the practice of medicine throughout the 20th century. The first three

Top-Dollar Jobs in Health

These are high-paying jobs described in this volume. The figures represent typical salaries or earnings for experienced workers.

$100,000–$250,000	Anesthesiologist Dentist Osteopathic Physician Physician Psychiatrist Surgeon
$50,000–$100,000	Chiropractor Health Care Administrator Hospital Administrator Medical Physicist Optometrist Physical Therapist

high-tech diagnostic tools—X-ray machines, electroencephalographs (EEGs), and electrocardiographs (EKGs or ECGs)—were all developed early in this century. X-ray machines aim X-ray beams at patients' bodies. Since X rays are better absorbed by bone and other dense structures than by soft tissue such as the lungs, their beams cast shadows of varying intensity. These shadows can be captured on X-ray film. Trained physicians and X-ray technicians can read this film to detect bone fractures and locate unexplained shadows that may be cast by tumors, infections, or foreign objects.

EEGs and EKGs use electrical impulses to diagnose physical problems. By placing electrodes on a patient's scalp or chest, medical personnel can study patterns caused by the movement of electrical impulses within the body. Certain distinct, abnormal patterns of electrical activity are signs of epilepsy, stroke, or brain tumors. These patterns may also indicate disorders in the heart muscle. Advanced EKG technology, in conjunction with imaging technology like ultrasound and nuclear-imaging equipment, works with imaging computer software to construct a three-dimensional model of the heart, showing problem areas.

Computers and the Medical Profession

In recent decades computer technology has continued to have a tremendous impact on medicine. Computerized axial tomography (CAT or CT) scanners, first used in the 1970s, process X-rays into computerized images, giving physicians even greater detailed information about tumors, cysts, and other tissue abnormalities (such as infection) within the body. Magnetic resonance imaging (MRI) scanners analyze changes in magentic fields to help diagnose disorders in tissues.

More recent types of diagnostic scanners can show the level of cell activity in certain parts of the body. These scanners can help detect cancer cells, since these cells generally grow more quickly than normal cells. Positron-emission tomography (PET) scanners can track the presence of a radioactive isotope. Physicians introduce a small amount of that isotope into the patient's body, then use the PET scanner to see where it travels. A high concentration of the isotope may indicate cancer cells or another type of disorder, such as mental illness. PET scanners are used to locate brain tumors, investigate epileptic attacks, and study brain function in various mental illnesses.

Other medical procedures employ sound technology. Ultrasound scanners use sound waves to view conditions within the body, whereas lithotripsy uses sound waves to break down large gallstones. Another new technology—magnetoencephalography—permits physicians to study the magnetic fields within the brain, providing even greater detail on brain activity than EEGs can provide. With these high-tech tools, and others such as video imaging, physicians are learning more about the body—both its functions and its malfunctions.

Computer technology also helps physicians, technicians, and nurses manage the vast amount of medical information they need to access records, make diagnoses, and decide on treatment plans. Some computer programs permit physicians to input the medical history of a patient along with information on the patient's current symptoms. The program then compares this information to databases of general medical and pharmaceutical information. After analyzing the symptoms, the program suggests several possible diagnoses, ranks their probability, and lists the tests, treatments, and drug therapies appropriate for each one. Of course, computer technology cannot replace the role of the physician, but it can save physicians and patients time and money.

Computers can also aid in patient therapy. Besides helping medical personnel design artificial bones and limbs, prosthesis software gives orthopedic surgeons the ability to customize artificial limbs to match patients' individual needs. Computer-embedded prostheses, therapeutic visors, and other space-age technologies all exist today, and they promise to help improve the lives of millions of people.

Computer-assisted training also is a major part of medical school education. Research developed from detailed CAT scans of cadavers, for example, has resulted in detailed computer-based anatomy texts, which give medical students the ability to use computers to study their subjects in color, from any angle, and with enhanced detail. Interactive diagnostic programs provide students with experience that cannot be found in ordinary textbooks. The programs allow students to practice observing and diagnosing medical problems. Computers also play an important part in helping nursing staff and records technicians keep patient records up-to-date and accessible at a keystroke.

THE PEOPLE DOING THE WORK

All the technology available today is useless without trained, educated health care workers. Inside the hospitals, in doctors' offices, and elsewhere, experts with a wide variety of skills provide medical care. Within the broad categories of doctors, nurses, and technicians are scores of specialized occupations.

Physicians

Physicians today make up about 4 percent of the health care workforce. Until after World War I, almost all doctors were general practitioners who treated anyone who came to them, young and old alike. These professionals delivered babies, set broken bones, prescribed medicines and other treatments for disease, and comforted the dying.

As medicine became more complex, medical doctors became more specialized. Nearly 70 percent of all physicians in the United States today are specialists. The majority practice near major medical centers in and around large cities. Cardiologists treat heart patients; nephrologists treat individuals with kidney problems; geriatricians work with the elderly; hematologists deal with disease of the blood; and dermatologists treat skin disease and skin problems. Occupational medicine physicians study problems caused by the workplace, such as noise-induced hearing loss, multiple chemical sensitivity, and repetitive stress injury. Today there are specialists in every field, including gynecology, ophthalmology, urology, neurology, otolaryngology, psychiatry, and dozens of others.

Although the long-standing trend has been toward specialization, there is an increasing portion of medical students preparing for a career in general practice (often called family practice). Family physicians often run private practices. They treat minor and chronic ailments; teach disease prevention, nutrition, and good health care; and screen for potential problems. This trend toward family practice has been spurred in part by federal student loan programs designed to help students who agree to work in urban and rural areas facing a shortage of primary caregivers. And although family practice has traditionally been a lower-paying field than most specialties, the current trend is toward equalization of salaries among family practitioners and specialists.

Not all doctors are M.D.s (doctors of medicine). D.O.s (doctors of osteopathy), for example, receive much the same education and training as M.D.s and employ many standard medical techniques. In fact, many osteopaths practice in a manner indistinguishable from an M.D. However, osteopaths approach medicine with a different philosophy. They take a holistic approach to medicine, looking for a connection between diet, lifestyle, and environmental factors in diagnosis and treatment. Osteopaths generally focus on the impact of the musculoskeletal system on illness and disorders and often use physical manipulation, rather than medicine or surgery, to diagnose and treat problems.

Some health care practitioners have advanced degrees and licenses but are neither M.D.s nor D.O.s. These include chiropractors, who concentrate on skeletal and muscular wellness and treat pain and problems of alignment by manipulating the bones and muscles; optometrists, who prescribe corrective lenses for sight or eye muscle problems; and psychologists, who treat mental problems.

Nurses and Nurse Practitioners

According to some estimates, the current supply of physicians (about 412,000) exceeds the demand throughout much of the country, although many urban and rural areas still suffer a shortage. In stark contrast, nurses have been in short supply for the past several decades, and the demand will continue to grow through the turn of the century. By the late 1980s, the nursing shortage climbed to 20,000 and was

Although the long-standing trend has been toward specialization in medicine, increasing numbers of medical students are preparing for careers in general practice. *(The Terry Wild Studio.)*

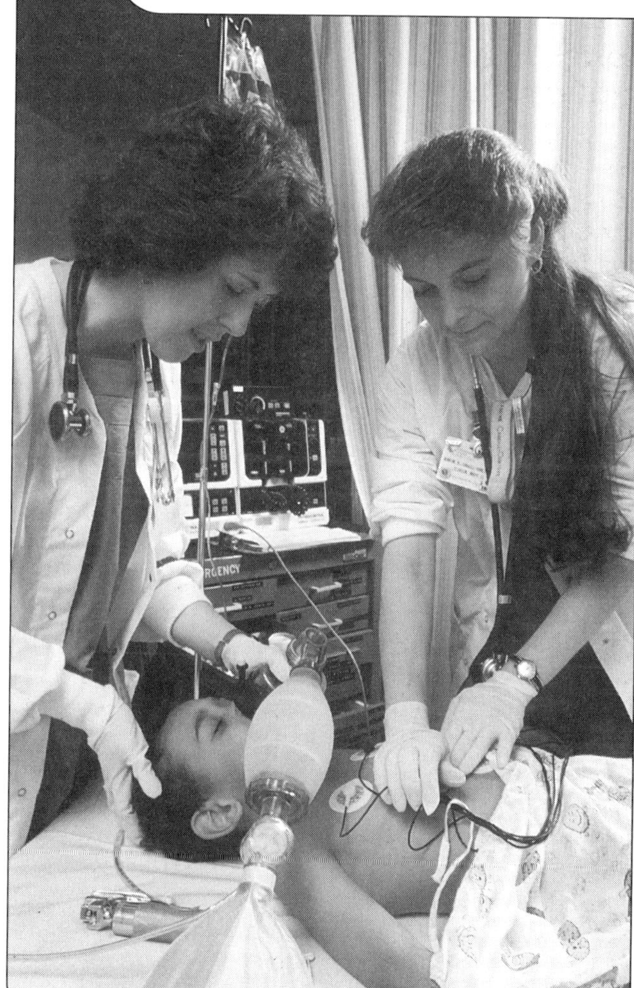

deemed so critical that some hospitals were paying signing bonuses of up to $10,000 to each new nurse hired. By the late 1990s, many hospitals were actually laying off nurses as the hospitals "downsized" staffs; this trend was counterbalanced by an increased demand for nurses in home and outpatient services.

One reason for the increased demand is that as people live longer, they need more nursing care. Also, the level of training required to operate high-tech monitoring and treatment equipment has led many hospitals and other health care facilities to require that nurses have advanced training. Like people in other medical professions, many nurses now specialize, getting additional training beyond their basic four-year degree or diploma. In hospitals and clinics, some nurses work in a particular area of care, such as cardiology, pediatrics, or psychiatry. Others become nurse anesthetists, nurse clinicians, or nurse educators. Nurse-midwives, who are qualified to provide gynecological care and obstetric care, are able to deliver babies when no medical complications exist.

Nurse practitioners are registered nurses with advanced training. Some practice alongside physicians; others work independently. Nurse practitioners perform many of the same tasks as physicians. Frequently they examine and treat patients in settings where physicians are not readily available.

Allied Health Professionals

Changes in technology and escalating health care costs combined with an increased demand for health care have all led to an increased need for workers who can provide medical services. In the mid-1990s, six of the ten fastest-growing occupations were in health care.

Medical assistants work in hospitals and doctors' offices, performing both clinical and administrative work. Physical therapists, occupational therapists, respiratory therapists, recreational therapists, speech pathologists, and other therapists help patients regain or improve their physical skills. Therapy assistants and aides work with therapists and prepare patients for therapy. Medical social workers help patients and health care providers to navigate the complex health care system to find necessary services and the means to pay for them.

Athletic trainers and sports therapists work with athletes and others to keep them physically fit and uninjured. Dietitians and nutritionists, working both inside and outside hospitals, help individuals learn how what they eat can affect their health. Physician assistants, like nurse practitioners, have some of the training of medical doctors and may examine patients alongside doctors. Physician assistants and nurse practitioners may perform laboratory tests and make preliminary diagnoses, depending on state regulations.

As health care becomes even more dependent on technology, the demand for medical technicians continues to rise. Three of the fastest-growing occupations are medical record technicians, dental hygienists, and emergency medical technicians. Skilled technicians trained to operate dialysis machines are also in demand as are biomedical technicians.

Alternative Medicine Professionals

Although many alternative medicine treatments are considered unorthodox, or even worthless, by the medical establishment, an increasing number of people are turning to these methods. In addition, more and more doctors trained in conventional medicine are incorporating these alternatives into their practices to treat certain disorders, such as chronic pain disorder. Some health insurers, in exchange for slightly higher monthly payments, cover the costs of certain alternative treatments.

Some health care practitioners specialize in one area of alternative medicine. For example, herbologists use herbs and other plants to heal and prevent disease. Homeopaths work under the theory that giving an individual a minute amount of a substance that causes a disease can cure or prevent that disease. Acupuncturists insert thin needles into certain parts of the body to ease pain and cure problems. Acupressurists use pressure and touch to help relieve patients' physical problems. These and other alternative healing methods date back centuries.

BEYOND THE MEDICAL OFFICE AND HOSPITAL

Not all health care is delivered in medical offices or hospitals. Hospitals today have diversified their services to include hospital-run convalescent units, outpatient clinics, rehabilitation centers, and treatment centers for patients suffering from substance abuse.

Ambulatory surgical centers, also known as surgicenters, and free-standing emergency centers, or urgicenters, play an important role in giving individuals greater access to medical care. Low-risk minor surgical procedures such as hernia repairs, tissue biopsies, and some forms of cosmetic surgery are performed in surgicenters. These centers can keep their costs low because they do not need sophisticated backup equipment or provisions for long hospital stays.

Urgicenters operate much like hospital emergency rooms. They are often open 7 days a week, 12 to 24 hours a day. Doctors, physician assistants, and nurse practitioners at urgicenters treat minor prob-

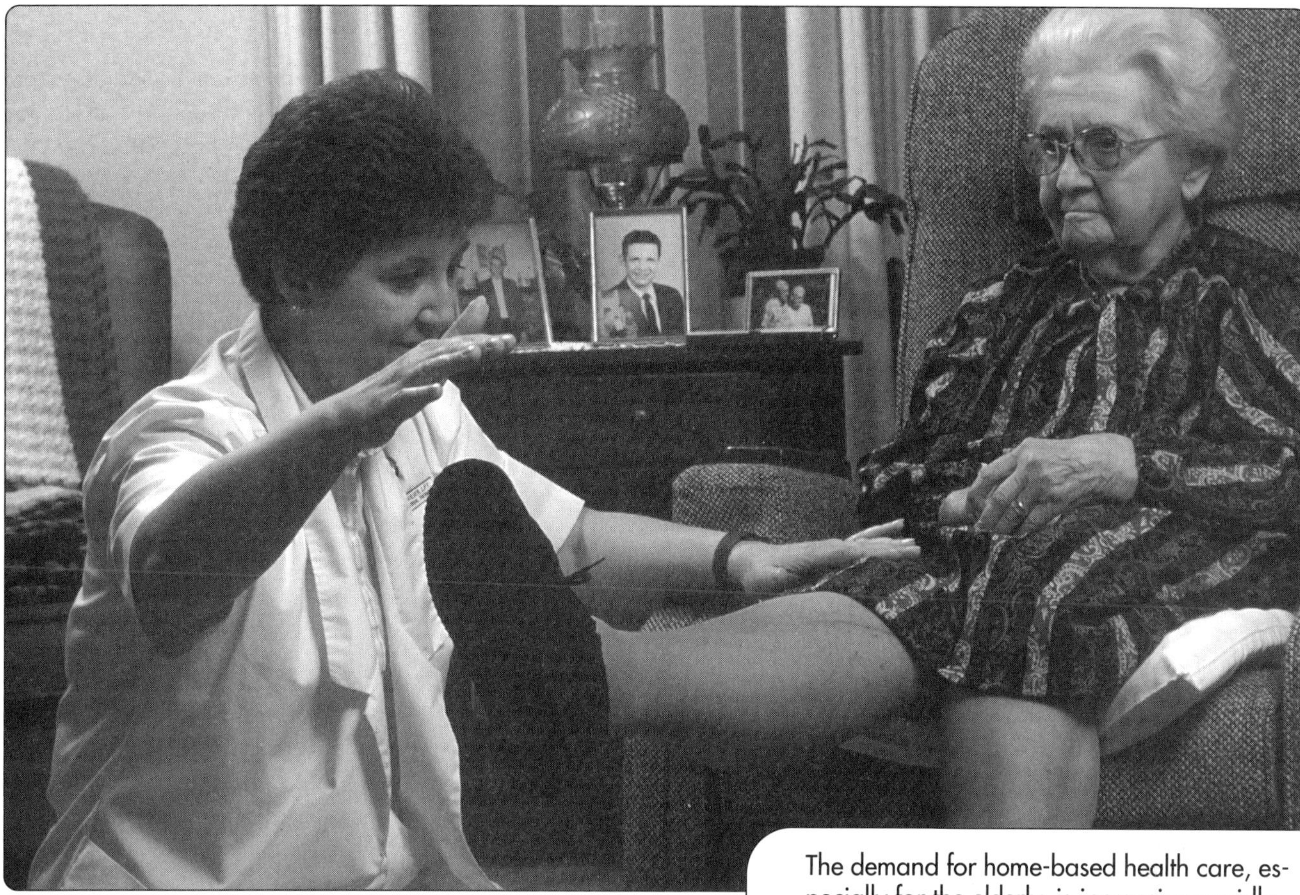

The demand for home-based health care, especially for the elderly, is increasing rapidly. One of the reasons for this is that patients are being released from hospitals more quickly than they used to be in order to reduce costs. *(The Terry Wild Studio.)*

lems such as broken bones, sprained ankles, sore throats, stomachaches, and cuts that require stitches. A visit to an urgicenter is usually more expensive than a visit to a doctor's office but less costly than a visit to a hospital emergency room.

Home-based health care is becoming another alternative to inpatient care as hospitals work to keep costs down by shortening patients' hospital stays. More patients are now sent home while still requiring full-time or frequent medical care. Thousands of agencies in this country offer home health care services for the elderly, people who are recovering after surgery, and people who are chronically ill. Some of these agencies are hospital-based, whereas others are affiliated with community health centers or religious groups. Skilled home health service agencies provide nursing, physical and occupational therapy, and speech therapy. Some agencies also provide support services such as personal care, light housekeeping, meal preparation, and transportation, which enable people to continue living independently despite their health limitations. A great number of elderly people now live on their own, with only occasional care from home health care aides who can help with chores or physical care.

Individuals who cannot live on their own without frequent medical or nursing care often move into nursing homes, rehabilitation centers, or other long-term care facilities. Here they have 24-hour access to nurses and aides and ready access to physicians. Hospices, which can be either part of residential health care facilities or home-based, are for dying individuals who want a comfortable surrounding in which to spend the last days of their lives.

The range of health care delivery options will grow even more diverse in the future, as health care delivery becomes more complex and providers look for new ways to hold down costs. The good news for health care workers is that the development of new health care delivery systems will mean more jobs. From an employment perspective, the health care industry will be a center of growth into the 21st century.

HEALTH CARE RESEARCH AND EDUCATION

A major area of health care is research and education. The current trends in federal funding are to increase spending on research in health services and health care policy issues (such as cost effectiveness studies) while maintaining or decreasing funding for scientific and medical research.

Health care researchers are constantly working to invent new technologies and improve existing technologies. Researchers and inventors continue to look for technology that will help individuals overcome or compensate for disabilities. Medical researchers, epidemiologists, and pathologists study diseases and seek cures and preventive measures. Geneticists study genes to determine how they may be used to predict or even prevent problems in patients.

The technologies currently used to diagnose illness are also being used to discover more about the human body and mind. PET scanners, for example, are being used to discover how we learn and retain language. They are also an integral part of the study of the causes of hyperactivity disorders. EEG brain wave studies are being used to learn more about depression and other mental problems. Other technologies are being developed that promise to diagnose heart and brain problems before they become acute.

Research into health care policy also is extremely active today. Health economists, for example, advise hospital administrators and public health officials on the financing of health services. Health economists are playing a role in developing reform measures for health care funding.

Health educators go to schools, public health clinics, and workplaces to teach people how to care for their own health. They teach about nutrition, exercise, alcoholism, smoking cessation, stress reduction, and ways to avoid sexually transmitted diseases. They also maintain libraries, serve as information resources for the public, and write articles for popular journals about health care.

Industry Snapshots

HEALTH CARE

The future of health care will continue to be driven by the debate over how to control costs. Regardless of the decisions made, however, the field will remain one of the strongest growth industries into the 21st century. The increasing prominence of cost-effective alternative delivery care systems, such as home-based health care, as well as technological advances requiring specialized training, will create many jobs.

HOSPITALS AND HEALTH MAINTENANCE ORGANIZATIONS

The growing cost of health insurance means that more and more individuals and employers have turned to alternative health care plans such as health maintenance organizations (HMOs) and preferred provider organizations (PPOs). Competition among hospitals and HMOs has led to widespread restructuring, with large hospital chains and HMOs coming out on top.

DOCTORS

Most physicians—nearly 80 percent of all physicians in the United States today—are specialists practicing in major medical centers in and around large cities. However, many physicians are returning to family practice. Although there is an overall surplus of doctors, many rural areas and low-income neighborhoods still suffer a shortage. As the number of insured people covered by HMOs has increased, more and more doctors are now working as salaried employees for group medical practices, clinics, or health care networks.

NURSES

The rapid growth of home health care and the high demand for nurse practitioners have made the shortage of nurses even more acute. There are currently more than 1.73 million registered nurses in the United States, and the number is expected to increase to more than 2.3 million by the year 2008. The greatest opportunities will be for those nurses trained in high-tech medical specialties.

ALLIED HEALTH WORKERS

This field includes some of the fastest-growing occupations in health care, particularly medical technicians. Medical assistants and physical therapists will also be in great demand through the next decade. As health care becomes even more technology intensive, health workers with technical and computer training will continue to be in demand.

PAYING FOR HEALTH CARE

While health care technologies and techniques continue to develop, the provision of health care has become increasingly expensive. From the point of view of many Americans, the cost of health care has reached a crisis level. Yet the nation appears to be at odds about how to solve this problem and how health care should be paid for.

The Increasing Cost of Health Care

Hippocrates could not have imagined the range of medical miracles his philosophy of medicine has made possible: heart transplants, chemotherapy, test-tube babies, artificial hip replacements, and even gene therapy. Today the nation's skilled corps of health care professionals, supported by an army of scientists and a sophisticated array of diagnostic and treatment tools, provide an unprecedented level of health care. However, the cost of this care is unprecedented as well. It now costs over $1 trillion annually—more than $3,000 per person—to meet America's health care needs.

Several factors account for the rapid growth of health care costs over the past several decades. First and foremost, Americans are now living longer. Over the years, medical advances have reduced the number of people who die young from diseases such as polio and tuberculosis. Americans take better care of themselves through better nutrition, increased workplace safety, and better preventive care. Longer life expectancy, combined with a lowered birth rate, has driven the median age of the population upward.

The number of expensive treatment and diagnostic options has also increased. Major organ transplants, coronary bypass surgery, and long-term kidney dialysis—all extremely costly procedures—have become commonplace. Technological innovations permit low-birthweight babies and individuals with serious physical impairments (such as accident victims) to survive, although at significant expense. Equipment

Summer Jobs in Health

HEALTH CARE

Summer internships are available in hospitals and health care agencies. Summer jobs are available for medical and dental assistants, nurse's aides and orderlies, therapy assistants, and laboratory assistants. Contact:

- doctors' and dentists' offices
- hospitals and clinics
- nursing homes
- health care agencies
- summer camps for the disabled

Sources of Information

American Hospital Association
1 North Franklin
Chicago, IL 60606
www.aha.org

National Association of Community Health Centers
1330 New Hampshire Avenue, NW, Suite 122
Washington, DC 20036
www.nachc.com

RELATED SERVICES

Summer jobs are available in hospitals and nursing homes for catering and housekeeping workers. Clerical workers are needed in hospital admissions and records departments and in doctors' offices. Home health care workers can assist housebound patients. Contact:

- hospitals
- nursing homes
- employment agencies
- social service agencies

Sources of Information

American Health Care Association
1201 L Street, NW
Washington, DC 20005
www.ahca.org

National Association of Health Unit Coordinators
1947 Madron Road
Rockford, IL 61107

MEDICAL RESEARCH

Summer internships are available in universities, research institutes, and hospitals. Summer jobs include research assistant, laboratory assistant, and animal care worker. Clerical workers are also needed during summer vacations. Contact:

- research institutions
- hospitals
- medical supply companies
- pharmaceutical companies
- government research agencies

Sources of Information

American Federation for Clinical Research
6900 Grove Road
Thorofare, NJ 08086-9431

Providing adequate health care in a growing and changing society involves making adaptations, such as having EMTs ride bicycles when providing emergency rescue services in crowded cities. *(Martha Tabor.)*

costs, development costs, and usage costs can be extremely high. Some technologies, such as PET scanners, can cost millions of dollars and are expensive to maintain. Developing, testing, and receiving approval for new drugs can also prove very costly.

Another factor driving up the cost of health care is malpractice suits against doctors and other medical professionals. Physicians today pay tens of thousands of dollars each year in malpractice insurance premiums.

Insurance: The Traditional Payment Method

Traditionally, Americans' health care is paid for by medical insurance, which is supplied in all or part by their employers. Under traditional indemnity insurance, patients receive medical treatment from the providers of their choice and send the bills to the insurance companies for payment. Under this system, individuals have no incentive to shop around for bargains, and providers have no incentive to limit costs.

This situation has changed in recent years. As the cost of health care increases, the cost of health care insurance also rises, causing employers to cut back on insurance coverage or to limit the options available to employees. Today, due to unemployment and reduced employer coverage, approximately 16 percent of the American population has no health care coverage. The uninsured face staggering medical bills when they become sick or injured.

Since the mid-1960s, the federal government has been paying medical costs for two groups that do not generally have employers—the elderly and the poor—through its Medicare and Medicaid plans. These plans help to make sure that everyone has access to health care. Nevertheless, increasing numbers of people are largely or even entirely uninsured and at risk of not getting the care they need in a timely and comprehensive way. Moreover, debates in Congress over how best to reduce the budget may limit the umbrella coverage that currently exists.

Cost-Saving Initiatives

In recent years the nation's health care providers have been under increasing pressure to curb spiraling costs. Hospitals that are part of chains owned by for-profit corporations have also been under pressure to increase profits.

As a result, health care providers, economists, and regulators continue to look for more cost-effective ways to deliver and pay for health care. Political leaders, insurance companies, and providers are working together to find a solution to the dilemma of rising costs. One approach is to reduce costs through new delivery systems, such as surgicenters. Another is to use less expensive providers, such as nurse practitioners, instead of doctors, whenever feasible.

Other innovations are directed at how health care is paid for. One innovation was the development of diagnostic related groups (DRGs). DRGs were first implemented by the U.S. government in its Medicare system. Under the older system, hospitals had treated Medicare patients and then billed the government. The longer patients stayed in the hospital and the more procedures they underwent, the more the hospital could charge. Under this system, the hospital had no incentive to minimize costs.

The DRG plan, initiated by Congress in 1983, put health economists to work to predetermine how much a hospital should expect to spend for each of nearly 500 categories of illnesses. The government established fees for each illness, based on the average cost of treating it, taking into account the length of a typical hospital stay, the number of diagnostic tests, and the cost of surgery and other procedures. Under this system, hospitals may charge the government only the DRG rate and no more. If the hospital's actual cost of treating a Medicare patient exceeds the set DRG rate, then the hospital loses money. On the other hand, hospitals that find ways to cut the cost of treatment are allowed to keep the overpayment amount.

Many private insurers have adopted a similar payment system. Because nearly all medical care in this country is paid for by private insurance or the government, this trend has significant implications. Specifically, it means that the control of health care is shifting from health care providers to insurance companies and others who pay for the health care. In fact, many health care providers must first obtain approval from an insurer before proceeding with a medical treatment.

In an attempt to minimize costs, HMOs emphasize the importance of preventive health care. *(The Terry Wild Studio.)*

More Innovations

Whereas the government took the lead in establishing the DRG system, private insurers and providers organized two managed health care plans in their effort to help curtail rising costs. Health maintenance organizations (HMOs) offer medical coverage in a way that is fundamentally different from standard private medical insurance. An HMO is a group of health care providers—including doctors, nurses, and other health care specialists—located at one or more of the facilities affiliated with an HMO. People join an HMO by paying a fixed monthly fee. When members become ill or need checkups, they visit physicians associated with the HMO, usually at little or no cost to the member. When necessary, HMO physicians refer patients to outside specialists and hospitals. Many employers will pay some or all of the costs for employees who join an HMO because the monthly fees are usually lower than comparable coverage under conventional medical insurance. Under an HMO system, the emphasis is on preventive care. Individuals are encouraged to visit doctors and other providers before their problems become severe.

A variation of the health maintenance organization is the preferred provider organization (PPO). A PPO is a network of physicians designated by a particular insurance company to provide medical service. The insurance company offers incentives to its subscribers for choosing a preferred provider. For example, if a patient visits a preferred provider, the insurance company may pay 100 percent of the charges, whereas it may pay only 80 percent of the bill if the patient visits a doctor who is not a member of its designated PPO network.

National Health Care Coverage Debate

Even with these new developments, the cost of health care continues to rise and access remains limited. Many political and business leaders believe that the time is ripe for a comprehensive reform of the health care system. Proposals vary, but one of the most frequently suggested alternatives to the current system is an organized delivery system based on managed competition. Under this system, consumers would obtain insurance coverage through large corporations, the federal government, or regional nonprofit health care purchasing collectives sponsored by individual states. These organizations in turn would negotiate insurance contracts with organized delivery systems, such as health maintenance organizations, most of which would be run by major insurance companies. Advocates say this plan strikes a balance between free enterprise and government regulation and would provide coverage for everyone. Many oppose such a plan, however, in part out of fear of overregulation. Moreover, the current trend in the federal government is to limit government involvement in the private sector.

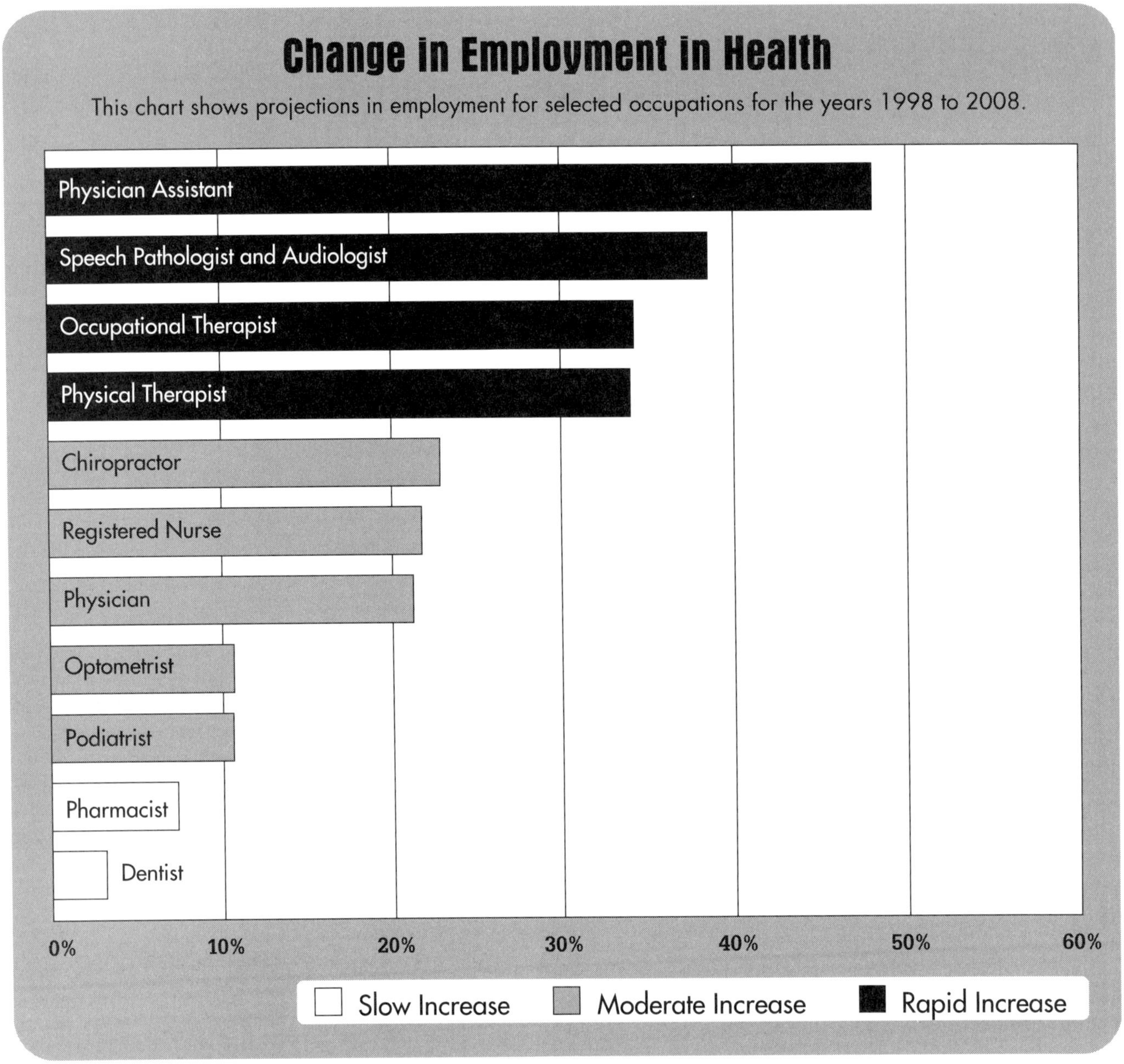

HEALTH CARE AND YOUR FUTURE

This volume describes 69 different occupations in a career field that is exciting, stimulating, and rewarding. By carefully examining each occupation and honestly evaluating your talents and interests, you can decide if one is right for you. As you look into the health field, however, remember two key trends.

First, the health care industry as a whole will continue to grow rapidly into the 21st century, creating a wealth of new and diverse opportunities and jobs. For example, as new technologies develop, opportunities for medical technicians will continue to increase. As new treatment techniques are developed, the need for physical therapists, medical assistants, and other aides and assistants will also increase. Few other industries will offer as many opportunities for employment and advancement.

Second, however, health care providers will find themselves in an increasingly competitive environment in the future. The pressure to keep costs under control may force unprofitable hospitals to close down. Doctors and those in other overstaffed professions will face stiff competition for jobs and slower salary growth. Nurses will see their roles change as they take over more responsibilities from doctors and relinquish some of their traditional duties to aides and other patient care workers. Wise job seekers will monitor these changes and evaluate their impact on employment.

Getting Into Health

Good jobs rarely, if ever, just fall out of the sky. As anybody who has ever been in the job market knows, getting the right job takes planning, perseverance, and patience. There are, however, a number of ways to make the process easier and more rewarding. This is true whether you are looking for your first job, reentering the job market, trying to get a new job, or planning a mid-career change.

This essay is designed to serve as your guide to the process of finding a job in the field of health. It starts off with the basics—helping you define your career objectives. Then it takes you through a number of steps you can use to work out a strategy to achieve these goals.

EVALUATING YOURSELF

Most people enjoy doing a job well. Apart from any praise from employers or fellow workers, there is an inner satisfaction in knowing that you've taken on a challenge and then succeeded in accomplishing something worthwhile. If you are unhappy or dissatisfied in your job and are just trying to do enough to get by, you may not be in the right job or the right field.

Making a Self-Inventory Chart

Before you make any career decisions, think about areas that interest you and things you do well. One way to go about this is to compile a self-inventory chart. Such a chart will be helpful when you decide what jobs you want to consider. It will also save time when you write cover letters and resumes, fill in applications, and prepare for job interviews.

Begin your self-inventory chart by listing all the jobs you have ever had, including summer employment, part-time jobs, volunteer work, and any freelance or short-term assignments you have done. Include the dates of employment, the names and addresses of supervisors, and the amount of money you earned. Then add a similar list of your hobbies and other activities, including any special experiences you have had, such as travel. Next, do the same for your education, listing your schools, major courses of study, grades, special honors or awards, courses you particularly enjoyed, and extracurricular activities.

In determining what you do well and what you enjoy doing, you may find a career pattern beginning to develop. If the picture still lacks detail or focus, try making a list of aptitudes, and then rate yourself *above average, average,* or *below average* for each one. Some of the qualities you might include in your list are administrative, analytic, athletic, clerical, language, leadership, managerial, manual, mathematical, mechanical, sales, and verbal abilities. You might also rate your willingness to accept responsibility and your ability to get along with people.

Compiling a Work Characteristics Checklist

Another way to choose a career path is to compile a checklist. Go through the questions in the "Work Characteristics Checklist" and then make a list of the work characteristics that are most important to you.

Do not expect a job to meet all your requirements. You have to consider which job characteristics are most important to you. If the characteristics of a job match most of your preferences, you might want to give the position serious consideration.

Work Characteristics Checklist

Do you want a job in which you can

- work outdoors?
- be physically active?
- work with your hands?
- be challenged mentally?
- work with machines?
- work independently?
- work on a team?
- follow clear instructions?
- earn a lot of money?
- have a chance for quick promotion?
- have good benefits?
- travel in your work?
- work close to home?
- work regular hours?
- have a flexible schedule?
- have a variety of tasks?
- have supervisory power?
- express your own ideas?
- be a decision maker?

Evaluating Your Career Options

It's important to evaluate yourself and your career options realistically. If you need help doing this, you can consult an experienced career counselor or take on-line aptitude tests.

Most guidance and counseling departments of high schools, vocational schools, and colleges provide vocational testing and counseling. Some local offices of the state employment services affiliated with the federal employment service offer free counseling. Career centers also offer these services.

Although vocational interest and aptitude testing can be done with paper and pencil, a variety of online programs can be used to test your interests and aptitudes. The results are measured against job skills and your personal profile is matched with potential jobs to show the training that is necessary. Some of these programs are self-administered on a personal computer whereas others must be administered and interpreted by a counselor.

Most major cities have professional career consultants and career counseling firms. You should, however, check their reputations before paying for their services. A list of counseling services in your area is available from the American Counseling Association, 5999 Stevenson Avenue, Alexandria, VA 22304 (www.counseling.org). (If you write, send a stamped, self-addressed envelope.)

You can also use the World Wide Web for services that career counselors would provide. Some sites have on-line counselors who can help you with a variety of tasks, such as obtaining information on jobs, careers, and training. They may be able to provide information on available services, including housing assistance, day care facilities, and transportation.

EVALUATING SPECIFIC JOBS

After you have taken a good look at what you do well and what you enjoy doing, you need to see how different jobs measure up to your abilities and interests. First, make a note of all the jobs in this volume that interest you. Then examine the education and training required for these jobs. Decide whether you qualify and, if not, whether you have the resources available to gain the qualifications. If possible, talk with someone who has such a job. Firsthand information can be invaluable. Also look through the appropriate trade and professional journals listed at the end of this essay and check the sections in this volume called "Resources" for books, audiovisual materials, and web sites that contain more detailed information about the job.

In addition, counselors usually have helpful information on careers in health. For more detailed information, you can write to any of the trade and professional associations listed at the end of each occupational profile.

Once you have found out all you can about a particular job, compare the features of the job with your work characteristics checklist. See how many characteristics of the job match your work preferences. By completing these steps for all the jobs that appeal to you, you should be able to come up with a list of jobs that match your interests and abilities.

WAYS TO FIND JOB OPENINGS

Once you've decided what kind of job suits you, the next step is to look for available positions. Obviously, the more openings you can find, the better your chance of landing a job. People usually apply for a number of job openings before they are finally accepted.

There are many ways to find out about job openings. A number of job-hunting techniques are explained on the pages that follow and information is given on how you can follow up on job leads.

Applying in Person

For some jobs, especially entry-level positions, your best method may be to apply directly to the company or companies for which you would like to work. If you are looking for a position as an admitting clerk or ambulance driver, for example, you might make an appointment to see the person responsible for hiring. This is a good method to use when jobs are plentiful or when a company is expanding. However, applicants for professional or supervisory positions generally need to send a cover letter and resume to the company first.

Applying in person will sharpen your interviewing techniques and give you a look at different places of employment. However, in most fields, it is not the method to use unless you are directed to do so.

Phone and Letter Campaigns

To conduct a phone campaign, use the Yellow Pages of your telephone directory to build a list of companies for which you might like to work. Call their personnel departments and find out whether they have any openings. This technique is not useful in all situations, however. If you're calling from out of town, a phone campaign can be very expensive. You may not be able to make a strong impression by phone. You also will not have a written record of your contacts.

Letter-writing campaigns can be very effective if the letters are well thought-out and carefully prepared. Your letters should always be typed. Handwritten letters and photocopied letters convey a lack of interest or motivation.

You may be able to get good lists of company addresses in your field of interest by reading the trade and professional publications listed at the end of this essay. Many of the periodicals publish directories or directory issues. Other sources you can use to compile lists of companies are the trade unions and professional organizations listed at the end of each job profile in this volume. The reference librarian at your local library can also help you find appropriate directories.

You can e-mail letters to human resource departments of companies with web sites, too. Be sure, however, that you follow all the same guidelines as you would for a letter you mail.

Your letters should be addressed to the personnel or human resources department of the organization. If possible, send it to a specific person. If you don't know who the correct person is, try to find the name of the personnel director through the directories in the library. You can also call on the phone and say, "I'm writing to ask about employment at your company. To whom should I address my letter?" If you can't find a name, use a standard salutation. It's a good idea to enclose a resume (described later in this essay) with the letter to give the employer a brief description of your education and work experience.

Keep a list of all the people you write to, along with the date each letter was mailed, or keep a photocopy of each letter. Then you can follow up by writing a brief note or calling people who do not reply within about 3 weeks.

Job Databases on the Web

The latest tool to use in looking for a job is the World Wide Web. The Internet currently has thousands of career-related sites to use to find job openings and to post your resume. Some sites, such as The Monster Board (www.monster.com), help you build a resume and post it on-line as well as allow you to search through a massive database of help-wanted listings. Others, including Job Options (joboptions.com), employ a search engine to find jobs that match your background, then post your resume on-line for employers. Another site called CareerBuilder (www.careerbuilder.com) has an interactive personal search agent that lets you key in job criteria such as location, title, and salary, and then it e-mails you when a matching position is posted in the database.

If you find a job that interests you in an ad on the web, you can respond by sending your resume and cover letter directly to the employer. Many companies even post job openings of their own in their company's human resource web pages. This allows you to target specific firms. Job hunters in many fields can also use professional associations to find jobs.

Some states, such as New Jersey, even have a home page (www.wnjpin.state.nj.us) designed to meet the needs of four groups: job seekers, students looking to make career choices, career counselors, and employers looking for workers. This one-stop career center has direct links to a variety of job listing sites on the web. You can post your resume, get information on training and education required for various jobs, read about occupations in demand, and even find out about job fairs.

Job Finder's Checklist

The following list of job-hunting tips may seem obvious, but getting all the bits and pieces in order beforehand helps when you're looking for a job.

Resume. Find out whether you will need a resume. If so, bring your resume up to date or prepare a new one. Assemble a supply of neatly typed copies or have a resume ready to e-mail to prospective employers.

References. Line up your references. Ask permission of the people whose names you would like to use. Write down their addresses, phone numbers, and job titles.

Contacts. Put the word out to everyone you know that you are looking for a job.

Job market. Find out where the jobs are. Make a list of possible employers in your field of interest.

Research. Do a little homework ahead of time—it can make a big difference in the long run. Find out as much as you can about a job—the field, the company—before you apply for it. A well-informed job applicant makes a good impression.

Organization. Keep a file on your job-hunting campaign with names and dates of employers contacted, ads answered, results, and follow-up.

Appearance. Make sure that the clothes you plan to wear to an interview are neat and clean. You may need to dress more formally than you would on the job, particularly if you are visiting a personnel office or meeting with a manager. Keep in mind that people may form an opinion of you based on their first impressions.

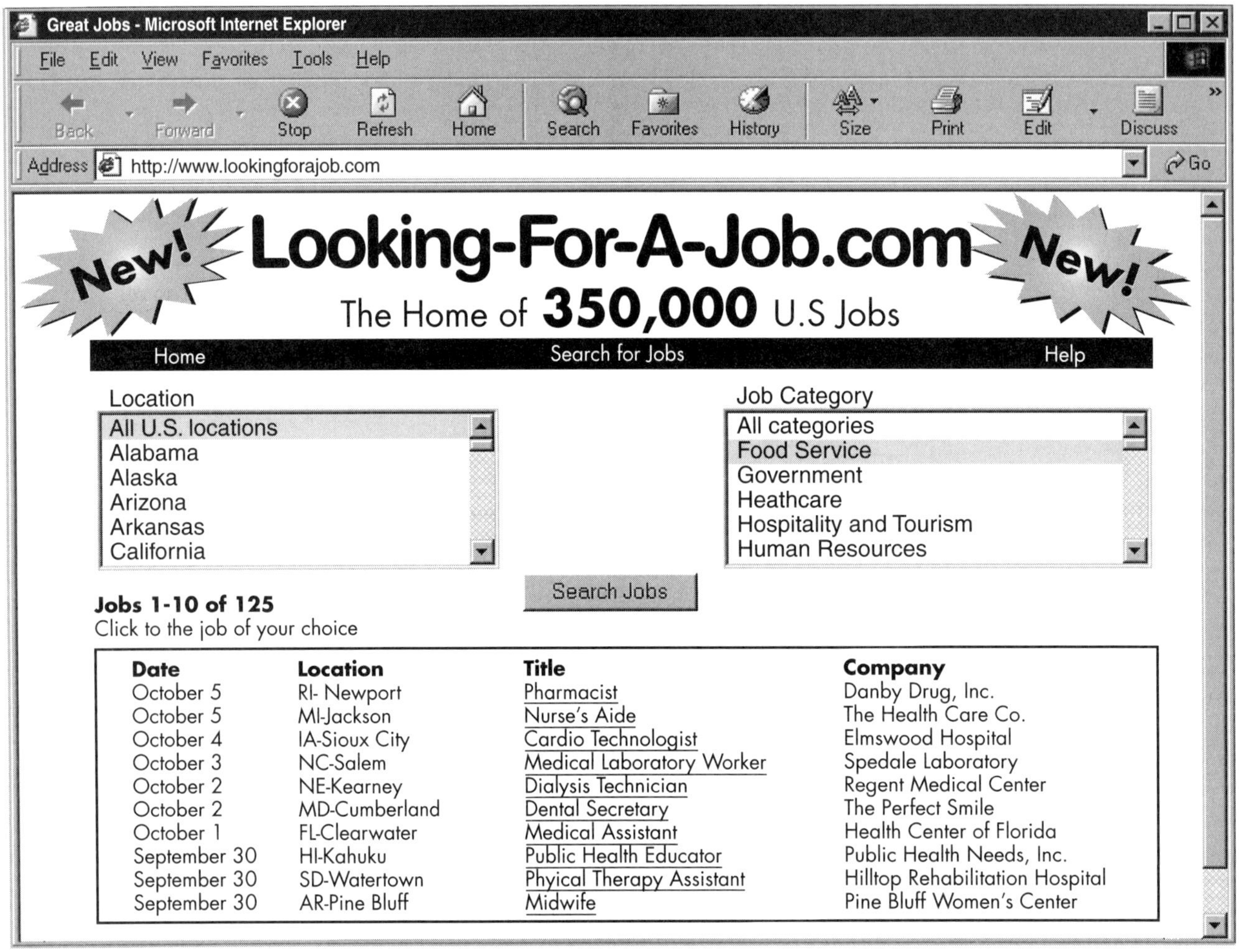

Many career-related websites can be found on the Internet. This hypothetical site (for illustrational purposes only) allows job-seekers to search for a position by location and by job description.

Help-Wanted Ads

Many people find out about job openings by reading the help-wanted sections of newspapers, trade journals, and professional magazines. Many employers and employment agencies use help-wanted classifieds to advertise available jobs.

Classified ads have their own telegraphic language. You will find some common abbreviations in the chart in this essay entitled "Reading the Classifieds." You can usually decode the abbreviations by using common sense, but if one puzzles you, call the newspaper and ask for a translation. Classified ads explain how to contact the employer, and they usually list the qualifications that are required.

As you find openings that interest you, follow up on each ad by using the method requested. You may be asked to call a specific person or send a resume. Record the date of your follow-up, and if you don't hear from the employer within 2 to 3 weeks, place another call or send a polite note asking whether the job is still open. Don't forget to include your phone number and address.

Some help-wanted ads are "blind ads." These ads give a box number but no name, phone number, or address. Employers and employment agencies may place these ads to avoid having to reply to all of the job applicants. In other words, you may not receive a response after answering a blind ad.

Situation-Wanted Ads

Another way to get the attention of potential employers is with a situation-wanted ad. You can place one of these in the classified section of your local newspaper or of a trade journal in your field of interest. Many personnel offices and employment agencies scan these columns when they're looking for new employees. The situation-wanted ad is usually most effective for people who have advanced education, training, or experience, or who are in fields that are in great demand.

A situation-wanted ad should be brief, clear, and to the point. Its main purpose is to interest the employer enough so you are contacted for an interview. It should tell exactly what kind of job you want,

Reading the Classifieds

HELP WANTED

BIOMEDICAL TECHNICIAN
Suburban hospital is seeking 2 perm f/t biomed techs to supervise medical equipment, maintenance program. For further information call 000-0000.
Pine Springs Hospital
Equal Opportunity Employer.

DENTAL ASSISTANT—Fee neg. Chair side & desk work. Exp. pfd. but not nec. Zenith Personnel, 555 Riverview, 000-0000.

LPN—Position avail. all shifts. Must have 1 yr. exp. and successful completion of formal medication course. Call Joan Philips, 000-0000. Orange County Hospital. Equal Opportunity Employer.

MEDICAL LAB. TECH.
Must have cert. Min. 3 yrs. exp., prefer emerg. lab. exp. Sal. commensurate w/exp. Ask for John, 000-0000.

MEDICAL SECRETARY F/P Avail. immed. 2 yrs. medical sec. training or equivalent exp. Gd. typ., office skls. WP exp. helpful. Top hosp., sal., gd. bnfts. MEDICAL PLACEMENTS (agency), 000-0000 ext. 24.

ORDERLY
Good oppty for person with 2-3 yrs. exp. & good refs. H.S. grad prfd. Call 000-0000. Equal Opportunity Employer.

PHYSICAL THERAPIST
PROGRESSIVE
Rehabilitation center is now accepting applications for registered physical therapists. Responsibilities incl. developmental therapy technique. Avail. Nov. 1. Call for appt. 000-0000.

RESPIRATORY THERAPIST
Afternoon shift. Immediate opening for person with AA degree in respiratory therapy & 6 months experience. Prefer registered therapist. Excellent benefits. Send resume to OAK PARK HOSPITAL.
Equal Opportunity Employer.

CLASSIFIED ABBREVIATIONS

appt.	appointment
bkgd.	background
cert.	certification, certificate
co.	company
col.	college
emerg.	emergency
eves.	evenings
exp.	experience
fee neg.	fee negotiable (fee can be worked out with employer)
f/p., f/pd.	fee paid (agency fee paid by employer)
f/t	full time
gd. bnfts.	good benefits
hosp.	hospital
K	thousand
M	thousand
mgr.	manager
min.	minimum
nec.	necessary
neg.	negotiable
oppty.	opportunity
perm.	permanent
pfd.	preferred
p/t	part time
sal.	salary
sec., secy.	secretary
techs.	technicians
temp.	temporary
typ.	typist, typing
w/	with
WP	word processing

SITUATION WANTED

DENTAL HYGIENE—Student seeking summer job. 000-0000 Eves.

DENTIST
Trained in American university. Endo & Perio oriented. Seeks to join group practice in downtown area. Call 000-0000.

LPN—12 yrs. exp., hosp. trained. F/t or p/t. Excellent refs. 000-0000.

MEDICAL ASSISTANT—Excellent skills & experience, 000-0000.

MEDICAL
RECORD
TECHNICIAN
Organized, exp. tech seeks challenging oppty. HS grad w/3 yrs exp county hosp. Knowledge of computer systems. Call 000-0000.

MEDICAL SECY—Excellent skills & experience, 000-0000.

NURSE
Student seeks position in Dr.'s office or home. Also have volunteer and office exp. Call 000-0000.

NURSE'S AIDE seeks f/t temp work. Able to work eves. Hosp. & home nursing exp. Good refs. Call 000-0000.

OPTICIAN
Exp. dispensing & shopwork. Superior customer contact, seeks position 3 days a week. Would consider Saturday work, 000-0000.

PHARMACIST
Exp. hosp. dept. supervisor, state registered. Seek hosp. position conducting training programs, upgrading personnel, 000-0000.

RADIOLOGIC
TECHNOLOGIST
Career-minded indiv. Grad. AMA approved program w/2 yrs exp. Avail immed, willing to work any shift. Call 000-0000.

---

why you qualify, and whether you are available for full-time or part-time work. Use abbreviations that are appropriate.

If you are already employed and do not want it known that you are looking for a new position, you can run a blind ad. A blind ad protects your privacy by listing a box number at the publication to which all replies can be sent. They are then forwarded to you. You do not need to give your name, address, or phone number in the ad.

Networking

A very important source of information about job openings is networking. This means talking with friends and acquaintances about jobs in your area of interest. For example, if you would like to work in dentistry, get in touch with all the people you know who work in dental offices, laboratories, or clinics. Speak with people you know who have friends or relatives in the field. It makes sense to use all the contacts you have.

There's nothing wrong with telling everyone who will listen that you are looking for a job—family, friends, counselors, and former employers. This will multiply your sources of information many times over.

You can use the web to make contacts, too. You can meet people with similar interests in news groups, which are organized by topic. Then you can write to them by e-mailing back and forth. Many fields have professional organizations that maintain web sites. You might use them to keep current on news affecting your field.

Sometimes a contact knows about a job vacancy before it is advertised. You can have an advantage, then, when you get in touch with the employer. Don't, however, use the contact's name without permission. Don't assume that a contact will go out on a limb by recommending you, either. Once you have received the inside information, rely on your own ability to get the job.

Placement Services

Most vocational schools, high schools, and colleges have a placement or career service that maintains a list of job openings and schedules visits from companies. If you are a student or recent graduate, you should check there for job leads. Many employers look first in technical or trade schools and colleges for qualified applicants for certain jobs. Recruiters often visit colleges to look for people to fill technical and scientific positions. These recruiters usually

Notes on Networking

Let people know you're looking. Tell friends, acquaintances, teachers, business associates, former employers—anyone who might know of job openings in your field.

Read newspapers and professional and trade journals. Look for news of developments in your field and for names of people and companies you might contact.

Use the World Wide Web. Make contacts through news groups, or find out information on web sites for professional organizations in your field.

Join professional or trade associations in your field. Contacts you make at meetings could provide valuable job leads. Association newsletters generally carry useful information about people and developments in the field.

Attend classes or seminars. You will meet other people in your field at job-training classes and professional development seminars.

Participate in local support groups. You can gain information about people and places to contact though support groups such as Women in Business, Job Seekers, Forty Plus, Homemakers Reentering the Job Market, as well as through alumni associations.

Be on the lookout. Always be prepared to make the most of any opportunity that comes along. Talk with anyone who can provide useful information about your field.

represent large companies. Visit your placement office regularly to check the job listings, and watch for scheduled visits by company recruiters.

State Employment Services

Another source of information about job openings is the local office of the state employment service. Many employers automatically list job openings at the local office. Whether you're looking for a job in private industry or with the state, these offices, which are affiliated with the federal employment service, are worth visiting.

State employment service offices are public agencies that do not charge for their services. They can direct you to special programs run by the government in conjunction with private industry. These programs, such as the Work Incentive Program for families on welfare, are designed to meet special needs. Some, but not all, of these offices offer vocational aptitude and interest tests and can refer interested people to vocational training centers. The state employment service can be a valuable first stop in your search for work, especially if there are special circumstances in your background. For example, if you did not finish high school, if you have had any difficulties with the law, or if you are living in a difficult home environment, your state employment service office is equipped to help you.

Private Employment Agencies

State employment services, though free, are usually very busy. If you are looking for more personal service and want a qualified employment counselor to help you find a job, you might want to approach a private employment agency.

Private employment agencies will help you get a job if they think they can place you. Most of them get paid only if they're successful in finding you a job, so you need to show them that you are a good prospect. These agencies will help you prepare a resume if you need one, and they will contact employers they think might be interested in you.

Private employment agencies are in the business of bringing together people who are looking for jobs and companies that are looking for workers. For some positions, usually middle- and higher-level jobs, the employment agency's fee is often paid by the employer. In such cases, the job seeker pays no fee. In other cases, you may be required to pay the fee, which is usually a percentage of your annual salary. Paying a fee is a worthwhile investment if it leads to a rewarding career. In addition, the fee may be tax deductible.

Some agencies may also ask for a small registration fee whether or not you get a job through them. Some agencies may demand that you pay even if you find one of the jobs they are trying to fill through your other contacts. Just be sure to read and understand the fine print of any contract you're about to sign, and ask for a copy to take home. Since the quality of these agencies varies, check to see if an agency is a certified member of a state or national association.

Some employment agencies, called staffing services, operate in a different way. They are usually paid by employers to screen and refer good candidates for job openings. They earn money when they refer a candidate who is hired by the employer. The employee pays no fee. Staffing firms, however, only spend time on candidates they think they may be able to place.

Private employment agencies are usually helping many people at one time. They may not have the time to contact you every time they find a job opening. Therefore, you may need to phone them at reasonable intervals after you have registered.

Civil Service

In your search for work, don't forget that the civil service—federal, state, and local—may have many jobs in health. You may contact the state employment office or apply directly to the appropriate state or federal agency. The armed services also train and employ civilians in many fields, including health. Don't neglect these avenues for finding jobs.

Civil service positions usually require you to take a civil service examination. Books are available to help you prepare for these examinations, and your local civil service office can give you information, too.

Unions

In certain types of jobs in the field of health, such as nursing, unions can be useful as sources of information. If you are a member of a union in your field of interest, you may be able to find out about jobs in the union periodical or through people at the union local.

If you do not belong to a union, you may contact a union in the field you are interested in for information about available employment services. You will find addresses for some unions in the job profiles in this book.

Temporary Employment

A good way to get a feel for the job market—what's available and what certain jobs are like—is to work in a temporary job. There are both private and state agencies that can help place people in short-term jobs in health. Nurses, nurse's aides, and medical technicians are examples of workers who fill temporary jobs.

Temporary employment can increase your job skills, your knowledge of a particular field, and your chances of hearing of permanent positions. In today's tight labor market, many companies are using the services of temporary workers in increasing numbers. In fact, temporary agencies may sign multimillion-dollar contracts to provide businesses with a range of temporary workers. In some cases, temporary workers are in such demand that they may receive benefits, bonuses, and the same hourly wages as equivalent full-time workers. Some temporary agencies are even joining with companies to create long-term career paths for their temporary workers.

PRESENTING YOURSELF ON PAPER

An employer's first impression of you is likely to be based on the way you present yourself on paper. Whether it is in an application form or on a resume, you will want to make a good impression so that employers will be interested in giving you a personal interview. A potential employer is likely to equate a well-written presentation that is neat with good work habits and a sloppy, poorly written one with bad work habits.

Writing an Effective Resume

When you write to follow up a lead or to ask about job openings, you should also send information about yourself. The accepted way of doing this is to send a resume with a cover letter.

The work *resume* is derived from the French word *résumer,* meaning "to summarize." A resume does just that—it briefly outlines your education, work experience, and special abilities and skills. A resume may also be called a curriculum vitae, a personal profile, or a personal data sheet. This summary can act as your introduction by mail or e-mail, as your calling card if you apply in person, and as a convenient reference for you to use when filling out an application form or when being interviewed.

A resume is a useful tool in applying for almost any job in the field of health. It is valuable, even if you use it only to keep a record of where you have worked, for whom, and the dates of employment. A resume is usually required if you are being considered for professional or executive positions in the health field. Prepare it carefully. It's well worth the effort.

The goal of a resume is to capture the interest of potential employers so they will call you for a personal interview. Since employers are busy people, the resume should be as brief and as neat as possible. You should, however, include as much relevant information about yourself as you can. This is usually presented under at least two headings: "Education" and "Experience." The latter is sometimes called "Employment History." Many people add a third section titled "Related Skills," "Professional Qualifications," or "Related Qualifications."

If you prepare a self-inventory such as the one described earlier, it will be a useful tool in preparing a resume. Go through your inventory, and select the items that show your ability to do the job or jobs in which you are interested. Plan to highlight these items on your resume. Select only those facts that point out your relevant skills and experience.

Once you have chosen the special points to include, prepare the resume. At the top, put your name, address, and phone number. After that, decide which items will be most relevant to the employer you plan to contact.

State Your Objective Some employment counselors advise that you state a job objective or describe briefly the type of position for which you are applying. The job objective usually follows your name and address. Don't be too specific if you plan to use the same resume a number of times. It's better to give a general career goal. Then, in a cover letter, you can be more specific about the position in which you are interested.

Describe What You've Done Every interested employer will check your educational background and employment history carefully. It is best to present these sections in order of importance. For instance, if you've held many relevant jobs, you should list your work experience first, followed by your educational background. On the other hand, if you are just out of school with little or no work experience,

DO YOU KNOW YOUR RIGHTS?

JOB DISCRIMINATION—WHAT IT IS

Federal and State Law

An employer cannot discriminate against you for any reason other than your ability to do the job. By federal law, an employer cannot discriminate against you because of your race, color, religion, sex, or national origin. The law applies to decisions about hiring, promotion, working conditions, and firing. The law specifically protects workers who are over the age of 40 from discrimination on the basis of age.

The law also protects workers with disabilities. Employers must make their workplaces accessible to individuals with disabilities—for example, by making them accessible to wheelchairs or by hiring readers or interpreters for blind or deaf employees.

Federal law offers additional protection to employees who work for the federal government or for employers who contract with the federal government. State law often provides protection also, for instance, by prohibiting discrimination on the basis of marital status, arrest record, political affiliations, or sexual orientation.

Affirmative Action

Affirmative action programs are set up by businesses that want to make a special effort to hire women and members of minority groups. Federal employers and many businesses that have contracts with the federal government are required by law to set up affirmative action programs. Employers with a history of discriminatory practices may also be required to establish affirmative action programs.

Discrimination Against Job Applicants

A job application form or interviewer may ask for information that can be used to discriminate against you illegally. The law prohibits such questions. If you are asked such questions and are turned down for the job, you may be a victim of discrimination. However, under federal law, employers must require you to prove that you are an American citizen or that you have a valid work permit.

Discrimination on the Job

Discrimination on the job is illegal. Being denied a promotion for which you are qualified or being paid less than coworkers are paid for the same job may be forms of illegal discrimination.

Sexual, racial, and religious harassment are forms of discrimination and are prohibited in the workplace. On-the-job harassment includes sexual, racial, or religious jokes or comments. Sexual harassment includes not only requests or demands for sexual favors but also verbal or physical conduct of a sexual nature.

JOB DISCRIMINATION—WHAT YOU CAN DO

Contact Federal or State Commissions

If you believe that your employer practices unfair discrimination, you can complain to the state civil rights commission or the federal Equal Employment Opportunity Commission (EEOC). If, after investigating your complaint, the commission finds that there has been unfair discrimination, it will take action against the employer. You may be entitled to the job or promotion you were denied or to reinstatement if you were fired. You may also receive back pay or other financial compensation.

Contact a Private Organization

There are many private organizations that can help you fight job discrimination. For example, the American Civil Liberties Union (ACLU) works to protect all people from infringement on their civil rights. The National Association for the Advancement of Colored People (NAACP), National Organization for Women (NOW), and Native American Rights Fund may negotiate with your employer, sue on your behalf,

it's probably best to list your educational background first and then, under employment history, to mention any part-time and summer jobs or volunteer work you've done.

Under educational background, list the schools you have attended in reverse chronological order, starting with your most recent training and ending with the least recent. Employers want to know at a glance your highest qualifications. For each educational experience, include years attended, name and location of the school, and degree or certificate earned, if any. If you have advanced degrees (college and beyond), it isn't necessary to include high school and elementary school education. Don't forget to highlight any special courses you took or awards you won, if they are relevant to the kind of job you are seeking.

Chronological and Functional Resume Information about your employment history can be presented in two basic ways. The most common format is the chronological resume. In a chronological re-

or start a class action suit—a lawsuit brought on behalf of all individuals in your situation.

WHAT TO DO IF YOU LOSE YOUR JOB

Being Fired and Being Laid Off

An employer usually has the right to fire an employee at any time. In many cases, however, an employer can fire you only if there is good cause, such as your inability to do the job, violation of safety rules, dishonesty, or chronic absenteeism.

Firing an employee because of that employee's race, color, religion, sex, national origin, or age (if the employee is over 40) is illegal. Firing an employee for joining a union or for reporting an employer's violation (called whistle-blowing) is also prohibited. If you believe you have been wrongfully discharged, you should contact the EEOC or the state civil rights commission.

At times, employers may need to let a number of employees go to reduce costs. This reduction in staff is called a layoff. Laying off an employee has nothing to do with the employee's job performance. Federal law requires employers who lay off large numbers of employees to give these employees at least two months' notice of the cutback.

Unemployment Compensation

Unemployment insurance is a state-run fund that provides payments to people who lose their jobs through no fault of their own. Not everyone is entitled to unemployment compensation. Those who quit their jobs or who worked only a few months before losing their jobs may not be eligible.

The amount of money you receive depends on the amount you earned at your last job. You may receive unemployment payments for only a limited period of time and only so long as you can prove that you are actively looking for a new position.

Each claim for unemployment compensation is investigated before the state makes any payments. If the state unemployment agency decides to deny you compensation, you may ask the agency for instructions on how to appeal that decision.

OTHER PROTECTIONS FOR EMPLOYEES

Honesty and Drug Testing

Many employers ask job applicants or employees to submit to lie-detector tests or drug tests. Lie-detector tests are permitted in the case of high-security positions, such as police officers. Some states prohibit or restrict the testing of applicants or employees for drug use. Aptitude and personality tests are generally permitted.

Other Federal Laws

The Fair Labor Standards Act prescribes certain minimum wages and rules about working hours and overtime payments. Workers' compensation laws provide payment for injuries that occur in the workplace and wages lost as a result of those injuries.

The Occupational Safety and Health Act sets minimum requirements for workplace safety. Any employee who discovers a workplace hazard should report it to the Occupational Safety and Health Administration (OSHA). The administration will investigate the claim and may require the employer to correct the problem or pay a fine.

Rights Guaranteed by Contract

Not every employee has a written contract. If you do, however, that contract may grant you additional rights, such as the right to severance pay in the event you are laid off. In addition, employees who are members of a union may have certain rights guaranteed through their union contract.

Before you sign any contract, make sure you understand every part of it. Read it thoroughly and ask the employer questions. Checking the details of a contract before signing it may prevent misunderstanding later on.

KEVIN LIEBERMAN

222 E. 91st Street • Apartment 2F • New York, NY 12345
222-734-4943 (home) • 222-748-3260 (work)

Work Experience

1993 to present
Physical Therapist
Pediatric Unit, Midtown General Hospital, New York, NY
Conduct in-hospital therapeutic treatment for pediatric surgical patients and victims of disabling diseases. Provide long-term outpatient care for handicapped children. One day a week, provide at-home care for housebound patients. Redesigned curriculum for after-school play therapy session.

1991 to 1993
Assistant Physical Therapist
Department of Education, Parkway Hospital, Ridgewood, NJ
Provided information and assistance for orthopedic, palsy, and stroke patients. Acted as coteacher of classes for the handicapped on mobility and returning to work.

Education

1991
Master of Science in Physical Therapy
Rutgers University, School of Public Health, New Brunswick, NJ
Wrote thesis on developing handwriting skills in stroke victims. Program included six-month hospital internship with rotations in pediatrics, geriatrics, orthopedics, and cardiac unit.

1988
Bachelor of Science
James College, University of Mic

Professional Certification

Licensed Physical Therapist, Stat

References

Available upon request.

- State your name, address, and telephone number first.
- State job objective or general career goal in a few words.
- List education and work experience in reverse chronological order, with most recent item first.

Marquicia Jackson

801 Leland Avenue
Arlington, VA 12345
(444) 893-3877

JOB OBJECTIVE

Dental assistant in clinic or private office.

EDUCATION

1998 to 1999
Diploma
Dental Assistant Program
Fairfax County Community College, Fairfax, VA
Program combined classroom instruction with clinical experience at Department of Health Dental Services Clinic. Clinical experience included performing full series of dental X rays.

1994 to 1998
Diploma
Wilson High School, Arlington, VA
Participated in Senior Tutor's program, assisting grammar school children with reading and arithmetic.

WORK EXPERIENCE

Summers, 1996 to 1999
Receptionist/Clerk Typist
Superior Temporary Personnel Services, Alexandria, VA
Completed numerous temporary office assignments for agency clients. Duties included greeting visitors, using complex telephone systems, typing, ordering office supplies, and maintaining records systems. Work required accuracy, flexibility, and ability to deal with varied situations.

Summer, 1995
Waitress
Village Chateau Restaurant, Arlington, VA

PROFESSIONAL CERTIFICATION

Certificate
Dental Assisting National Board, 1999

REFERENCES

Available upon request.

- List your work experience first if it is more important than your educational background.
- Keep descriptions of your education and work experience brief.
- List special skills and qualifications if they are relevant to the job.

sume, you summarize your work experience year by year. Begin with your current or most recent employment and then work backward. For each job, list the name and location of the company for which you worked, the years you were employed, and the position or positions you held. The order in which you present these facts will depend on what you are trying to emphasize. If you want to call attention to the type or level of job you held, for example, you should put the job title first. Regardless of the order you choose, be consistent. Summer employment or part-time work should be identified as such. If you held a job for less than a year, specify months in the dates of employment.

It is important to include a brief description of the responsibilities you had in each job. This often reveals more about your abilities than the job title. Remember, too, that you do not have to mention the names of former supervisors or how much you earned. You can discuss these points during the interview or explain them on an application form.

The functional resume, on the other hand, emphasizes *what you can do* rather than *what you have done.* It is useful for people who have large gaps in their work history or who have relevant skills that would not be properly highlighted in a chronological listing of jobs. The functional resume concentrates on qualifications—such as familiarity with hospital procedures to organizational skills or managerial experience. Specific jobs may be mentioned, but they are not the primary focus of this type of resume.

Explain Special Skills You may wish to include a third section called "Related Skills," "Professional Qualifications," or "Related Qualifications." This is useful if there are points you want to highlight that do not apply directly to educational background or work experience. Be sure these points are relevant to the kind of work you are seeking. This section is most effective if you can mention any special recognition, awards, or other evidence of excellence. It is also useful to mention if you are willing to relocate or can work unusual hours.

Have References Available Employers may also want to know whom they can contact to find out more about you. At the start of your job search, you should ask three or four people if you may use them as references. If you haven't seen these people for a while, you may want to send them a copy of your resume and let them know what kind of position you're seeking. Your references should be the kind of people your potential employer will respect, and they should be able to comment favorably on your abilities, personality, and work habits. You should indicate whether these people are personal references or former work supervisors. Avoid using any relatives. You can list the names and addresses of your references at the end of your resume or in a cover letter. Or, you can simply write, "References available upon request." Just be sure you have their names, addresses, and phone numbers ready if you are asked.

Present Yourself Concisely Tips for making your resume concise include using phrases instead of sentences and omitting unnecessary words. When appropriate, start a sentence with a verb, such as *maintained* or *coordinated.* There is no need to say "I"—that is obvious and repetitive.

Present Yourself Well Employment counselors often recommend that resumes be no longer than one page because employers won't take the time to read a second page. If you've held many positions related to your occupation, go on to the second page, but don't include beginning or irrelevant jobs. If you have a lot of work experience, limit the education section to just the essentials.

You should also concentrate on the appearance of your resume. It should be typed on a good grade of 8½" × 11" white bond paper. If you can't type, a professional typist can do it for you for a small charge. Be sure that it is neatly typed with adequate margins. The data should be spaced and indented so that each item stands out. This enables a busy executive or personnel director to see at a glance the facts of greatest interest.

You will probably need many copies of your resume during your job search. Each copy should be as neat and as clear as your original. If possible, input your resume on a computer and print copies on a good-quality printer. You may want to have your resume reproduced professionally. A photo-offset printer can make several hundred excellent copies for a moderate fee. A photocopying machine may be more economical for smaller quantities.

These suggestions for writing a resume are not hard-and-fast rules. Resumes may be adapted to special situations. For example, people with a variety of work experience often prepare several versions of their resume and use the experience that's most relevant when applying for a particular job.

If this is your first resume, show it to someone else, perhaps a guidance counselor, for constructive advice. No matter what, be truthful while emphasizing your assets. You can do that by showing the abilities, skills, and specific interests that qualify you for a particular job. Don't mention any weaknesses or deficiencies in your training. Do mention job-related aptitudes that showed up in previous employment or in school. Don't make up things about yourself; everything that's in your resume can, and sometimes will, be checked.

KEVIN LIEBERMAN

222 E. 91st Street • Apartment 2F • New York, NY 12345
222-734-4943 (home) • 222-748-3260 (work)

February 19, 2000

Mr. Johnson Tellory
Personnel Department
St. Mary's Hospital
13 E. 49th Street
New York, NY 12345

Dear Mr. Tellory:

I am writing in response to the notice for a Director of Physical Therapy posted on the employees' bulletin board at St. Mary's Hospital. The opening was brought to my attention by Dr. Wong (surgery department). I am interested in taking on responsibility for a physical therapy program and would like to learn more about the position.

I understand that the therapy division at St. Mary's is structured so that physical, occupational, and speech therapists consult weekly on each patient. I feel that this type of coordination is essential, and I would be eager to take an active role in the s
members of our department at Midtown General, and as a
training and staff supervision.

I enclose my resume and would be free to meet with you a
I would also be interested in meeting members of the phy

Very truly yours,

Kevin Lieberman

Kevin Lieberman

Enclosure

Marquicia Jackson
801 Leland Avenue
Arlington, VA 12345
(444) 893-3877

December 2, 2000

Patricia Gomez, D.M.D.
Jefferson Medical Building
Jefferson Boulevard
Arlington, VA 12345

Dear Dr. Gomez:

Henry Martin, who has recently joined your office as a dental assistant, is a former classmate of mine from the Fairfax County Dental Assistant Program. He mentioned that you are looking for a second dental assistant to work evenings and weekends. I would like to apply for the position.

During my training, I had the opportunity to participate in clinical practice on patients of all ages. I especially enjoyed working with children and adolescents. I understand that your practice specializes in orthodontics for young people. This would suit me very well. Evening and weekend hours would present no problem for me.

I enclose my resume. I am available for an interview at your convenience. I look forward to hearing from you.

Very truly yours,

Marquicia Jackson

Marquicia Jackson

Enclosure

Writing Cover Letters

When you send your resume through the mail or the Internet, you should send a cover letter with it. This is the same whether you are writing to apply for a specific job or just to find out if there are any openings.

A good cover letter should be neat, brief, and well written with no more than three or four short paragraphs. Since you may use your resume for a variety of job openings, your cover letter should be very specific. Try to get the person who reads it to think that you are an ideal candidate for a particular job. If at all possible, send the letter to a specific person, either to the personnel director or to the person for whom you would be working. If necessary, call the company and ask to whom you should write.

Start your letter by explaining why you are writing. Say that you are inquiring about possible job openings at the company, that you are responding to an advertisement in a particular publication, or that someone recommended that you should write. (Use the person's name if you have received permission to do so.)

Let your letter lead into your resume. Use it to call attention to your qualifications. Add information that shows why you are well suited for that specific job. For example, the physical therapist in the sample letter points out his interest in program management and in coordination of therapy efforts. These interests fit in well with the position in question. In the second sample letter, the applicant for a dental assistant mentions that she has experience in the type of dentistry practiced by the prospective employer. She also emphasizes her willingness to work evenings and weekends.

Completing the Application Form

Many employers ask job applicants to fill out an application form. This form usually duplicates much of the information on your resume, but it may ask some additional questions. Give complete answers to all questions except those that are discriminatory. If a question doesn't apply to you, put a dash next to it.

You may be given the application form when you arrive for an interview, or it may be sent to your home. When filling it out, print neatly in ink. Follow the instructions carefully. For instance, if the form asks you to put down your last name first, do so.

The most important sections of an application form are the education and work histories. As in your resume, many applications request that you write these in reverse chronological order, with the most recent experience first. Unlike your resume, however, the application form may request information about your earnings on previous jobs. It may also ask what rate of pay you are seeking on this job.

Be prepared to answer these and other topics not addressed on your resume. Look at the sample application form, and make note of the kinds of questions that you are likely to be asked—for example, your Social Security number, the names of previous supervisors, your salary, and your reason for leaving. If necessary, carry notes on such topics with you to an interview. You have a responsibility to tell prospective employers what they need to know to make an informed decision.

Neatness Counts Think before you write on an application form so you avoid crossing things out. An employer's opinion of you may be influenced just by the general appearance of your application form. A neat, clearly detailed form may indicate an orderly mind and the ability to think clearly, follow instructions, and organize information.

Know Your Rights Under federal and some state laws, an employer cannot demand that you answer any questions about race, color, creed, national origin, ancestry, sex, marital status, age (with certain exceptions), number of dependents, property, car ownership (unless needed for the job), or arrest record. Refer to the information on job discrimination in this essay for more information about your rights.

PRESENTING YOURSELF IN AN INTERVIEW

An interview is the climax of your job-hunting efforts. On the basis of this meeting, the prospective employer will decide whether or not to hire you, and you will decide whether or not you want the job.

Prepare in Advance

Before an interview, there are a number of things you can do to prepare. Begin by giving some more thought to why you want the job and what you have to offer. Then review your resume and any lists you made when you were evaluating yourself so that you can keep your qualifications firmly in mind.

Learn as much as you can about the organization. Check with friends who work there, read company brochures, search the Internet, or devise other information-gathering strategies. Showing that you know something about the company and what it does will indicate your interest.

Try to anticipate some of the questions the interviewer may ask and think of how you would answer. For example, you may be asked: Will you work overtime when necessary? Are you ready to go to night school to improve some of your skills? Preparing answers in advance will make the process easier for you. It is also wise to prepare any questions you may

1 Always print neatly in blue or black ink. When completing an application at home, type it, if possible.

2 Read the application carefully *before* you start to fill it out. Follow instructions precisely. Use standard abbreviations.

3 If you aren't applying for a specific job, indicate the kind of work you're willing to do.

4 You don't have to commit to a specific rate of pay. Write "open" or "negotiable" if you are uncertain.

5 Traffic violations and so on do not belong here. Nor do offenses for which you were charged but not convicted.

6 If a question doesn't apply to you, write "NA" (for not applicable) or put a dash through the space.

7 Take notes along to remind you of school names, addresses, and dates.

8 If you're short on "real" employment, mention jobs such as babysitting, lawn mowing, or any occasional work.

9 Your references should be people who can be objective about you, such as former employers, teachers, and community leaders.

10 Under the heading "Reason for Leaving," a simple answer will do. Avoid saying "better pay"—even if it's so.

APPLICATION FOR EMPLOYMENT

NAME (LAST) | (FIRST) | (MIDDLE) | SOCIAL SECURITY NO.

PRESENT ADDRESS | CITY | STATE | ZIP CODE | AREA CODE | TELEPHONE NO.

PERMANENT ADDRESS | (IF DIFFERENT FROM ABOVE) | AREA CODE | TELEPHONE NO.

POSITION APPLIED FOR | DATE AVAILABLE

SALARY OR WAGE DESIRED | WILL YOU RELOCATE? | REFERRED BY

ARE YOU A U.S. CITIZEN? YES ______ NO ______ | IF NOT A U.S. CITIZEN, LIST VISA NUMBER AND EXPIRATION DATE: NUMBER ______________ DATE ________

WITHIN THE LAST FIVE YEARS HAVE YOU BEEN CONVICTED OF A FELONY? ☐ YES ☐ NO IF YES, GIVE DETAILS ON BACK PAGE | HAVE YOU EVER BEEN EMPLOYED BY OUR COMPANY? IF YES, GIVE DETAILS ON BACK PAGE ☐ YES ☐ NO

EDUCATION	INSTITUTION NAME AND ADDRESS	DID YOU GRADUATE?	MAJOR FIELD OF STUDY	CLASS STANDING
HIGH SCHOOL				
COLLEGE OR UNIVERSITY				
GRADUATE STUDY				
OTHER				

EMPLOYMENT RECORD

PLEASE LIST ALL EMPLOYMENT STARTING WITH MOST RECENT. ACCOUNT FOR ALL PERIODS (INCLUDING U.S. ARMED FORCES, PERIODS OF UNEMPLOYMENT, AND VOLUNTARY SERVICES).

LIST YOUR MOST RECENT POSITION HELD | MAY WE CONTACT YOUR PRESENT EMPLOYER? ☐ YES ☐ NO

EMPLOYER'S NAME AND COMPLETE ADDRESS/PHONE	DATES EMPLOYED: FROM / TO; SALARY: START / FINAL	POSITION TITLE; NAME AND TITLE OF SUPERVISOR; REASON FOR LEAVING
	FROM TO	POSITION TITLE
	SALARY: START FINAL	NAME AND TITLE OF SUPERVISOR / REASON FOR LEAVING
EMPLOYER'S NAME AND COMPLETE ADDRESS/PHONE	DATES EMPLOYED FROM TO	POSITION TITLE / NAME AND TITLE OF SUPERVISOR
	SALARY START FINAL	REASON FOR LEAVING
EMPLOYER'S NAME AND COMPLETE ADDRESS/PHONE	DATES EMPLOYED FROM TO	POSITION TITLE / NAME AND TITLE OF SUPERVISOR
	SALARY START FINAL	REASON FOR LEAVING

PERSONAL REFERENCES

NAME	ADDRESS	PHONE NUMBER
1.		
2.		
3.		

have about the company or the position for which you are applying. The more information you have, the better you can evaluate both the company and the job.

Employers may want you to demonstrate specific skills for some jobs. For example, an applicant for a job as an admitting clerk might be tested on clerical skills. In the health field, you may also be asked for documents confirming that you are licensed or registered with a professional organization.

On the appointed day, dress neatly and in a style appropriate for the job you're seeking. When in doubt, it's safer to dress on the conservative side, wearing a tie rather than a turtleneck or wearing a dress or blouse and skirt rather than pants and a T-shirt. Be on time. Find out in advance exactly where the company is located and how to get there. Allow extra time in case you get lost, get caught in a traffic jam, can't find a parking spot, or encounter another type of delay.

Maintain a Balance

When your appointment begins, remember that a good interview is largely a matter of balance. Don't undersell yourself by sitting back silently. Don't oversell yourself by talking nonstop about how wonderful you are. Answer all questions directly and simply, and let the interviewer take the lead.

Instead of saying, "I'm reliable and hardworking," give the interviewer an example. Allow the interviewer to draw conclusions from your example.

It's natural to be nervous before and during a job interview. However, you need to try to relax and be yourself. You may even enjoy the conversation. Your chances of being hired and being happy if you get the job are better if the employer likes you as you are.

Avoid discussing money until the employer brings it up or until you are offered the job. Employers usually know in advance what they are willing to pay. If you are the one to begin a discussion about the salary you want, you may set an amount that's either too low or too high.

Be prepared to ask questions, but don't force them on your interviewer. Part of the purpose of the interview is for you to evaluate the company while you are being evaluated. For instance, you might want to ask about the company's training programs and its policy on promotions.

Don't stay too long. Most business people have busy schedules. It is likely that the interviewer will let you know when it's time for the interview to end.

Don't expect a definite answer at the first interview. Employers usually thank you for coming and say that you will be notified shortly. Most employers want to interview all the applicants before they make a hiring decision. If the position is offered at the time of the interview, you can ask for a little time to think about it. If the interviewer tells you that you are not suitable for the job, try to be polite. Say, "I'm sorry, but thank you for taking the time to meet with me." After all, the company may have the right job for you next week.

Follow Up After the Interview

If the job sounds interesting and you would like to be considered for it, say so as you leave. Follow up after the interview by writing a brief thank-you note to the employer. Express your continued interest in the position and thank the interviewer for taking the time to meet with you.

It's a good idea to make some notes and evaluations of the interview while it is still fresh in your mind. Write down the important facts about the job—the duties, salary, promotion prospects, and so on. Also evaluate your own performance in the interview. List the things you wish you had said and things you wish you had not said. These notes will help you make a decision later. They will also help you prepare for future interviews.

Finally, don't hesitate to contact your interviewer if you haven't heard from the company after a week or two (unless you were told it would be longer). Write a brief note or make a phone call in which you ask when a decision might be reached. Making such an effort will show the employer that you are genuinely interested in the job. Your call will remind the interviewer about you and could work to your advantage.

TAKE CHARGE

The field of health offers many job opportunities. Job hunting is primarily a matter of organizing a well-thought-out campaign. Scan the classified ads, search through online job banks, watch for trends in local industry that might be reported in the news, and check with people you know in the field.

Take the initiative. Send out well-crafted resumes and cover letters. Respond to help-wanted advertisements. Finally, in an interview, state your qualifications and experience in a straightforward and confident manner.

TRADE AND PROFESSIONAL JOURNALS

The following is a list of some of the major journals in the field of health. These journals can keep you up-to-date with what's happening in your field of interest. These publications can also lead you to jobs through their own specialized classified advertising sections.

Dentists, Dental Assistants, and Dental Technicians

Journal of the American Dental Association, ADA Publishing, 211 East Chicago Avenue, Chicago, IL 60611.
www.ada.org/

Health Administration and Education

Hospitals and Health Networks, Headquarters, 425 Market Street, 34th Floor, San Francisco, CA 94105.
www.hhnmag.com/default.asp

Nursing

Geriatric Nursing, National Geriatric Nursing Association, 7250 Parkway Drive, Suite 510, Hanover, MD 21076.
www.mosby.com/gerinurs

Journal of Practical Nursing, 1400 Spring Street, Suite 310, Silver Spring, MD 20910.

The Nurse Practitioner: The American Journal of Primary Health Care, 111 Bethlehem Pike, P.O. Box 908, Springhouse, PA 19477.

Nursing Outlook, Mosby, Inc. Subscription Services, 11830 Westline Industrial Drive, St. Louis, MO 63146-3318.
www1.mosby.com/nursoutlook/

Physicians and Specialized Practitioners

American Family Physician, 11400 Tomahawk Creek Parkway, Leawood, KS 66211-2672.
www.aafp.org

American Journal of Psychiatry, 1400 K Street, NW, Washington, DC 20005.
ajp.psychiatryonline.org

American Journal of Public Health American Public Health Association, Subscriptions Department 5037, Washington, DC 20061-5037.
www.apha.org

The Gerontologist, Duke South, Room 0508, Durham, NC 27710.
www.geron.org/journals/gerontologist.html

JAMA, Journal of the American Medical Association, Subscriber Service Center, P.O. Box 10946, Chicago, IL 60610-0946.
jama.ama-assn.org

Journal of the National Cancer Institute, Oxford University Press, 2001 Evans Road, Cary, NC 27513.
jnci.oupjournals.org

New England Journal of Medicine, 860 Winter Street, Waltham, MA 02451-1413.
www.nejm.org

Psychology and Mental Health

American Psychologist, American Psychological Association, 750 First Street, NE, Washington, DC 20002-4242.
www.apa.org/journals/amp.html

Monitor on Psychology, American Psychological Association, 750 First Street, NE, Washington, DC 20002-4242.
www.apa.org

Community Mental Health Journal, 233 Spring Street, New York, NY 10013-1578.

Psychology Today, 49 East 21st Street, 11th Floor, New York, NY 10010.

Therapists

American Journal of Occupational Therapy, ATOA Products, P.O. Box 64949, Baltimore, MD 21264-4949.
www.aota.org

Journal of Speech, Language, and Hearing Research, 10801 Rockville Pike, Rockville, MD 20852.
www.asha.org

Physical Therapy, 1111 North Fairfax Street, Alexandria, VA 22314-1488.
www.apta.org

Admitting Clerk

Definition and Nature of the Work

Admitting clerks are usually the first employees that patients meet when entering a hospital. Admitting clerks interview new patients and sign them in to the hospital. They explain the hospital's rates, policies, and procedures to patients and to those who bring patients to the hospital. Admitting clerks arrange for new patients to be taken to their rooms. They type the admitting forms and keep careful records for each patient.

Education and Training
High school

Salary Range
Average—$355 a week

Employment Outlook
Good

Education and Training Requirements

Applicants should have a high school diploma. Courses in math, business, and typing are important. Experience in other clerical jobs is useful. Job applicants who have worked as volunteers in a hospital may also be preferred. Admitting clerks generally learn about hospital forms and procedures on the job.

Getting the Job

You can apply directly to hospital personnel offices. You can also check newspaper want ads and job banks on the Internet. Private employment agencies or your state employment office may list openings.

Advancement Possibilities and Employment Outlook

With further education and experience, admitting clerks can advance to the position of admitting officer. Admitting officers supervise the work of admitting clerks.

The outlook for admitting clerks is good through the year 2008. Employment is expected to increase as fast as the average due to the increasing demand for health services. The turnover is high, and many new job openings will be created.

Working Conditions

Admitting clerks come into contact with all types of people. Aside from patients, relatives, and visitors, they deal with doctors, nurses, and other hospital workers. The atmosphere is usually quiet and friendly. At times, however, admitting clerks must deal with patients and relatives who are upset. Admitting clerks need to be tactful when asking personal questions. They should be able to handle tense situations. Admitting clerks usually work 40 hours a week. They may work weekends and night shifts. Part-time positions are often available as well.

Earnings and Benefits

Earnings vary depending on location and experience. Currently, admitting clerks earn an average salary of $355 a week. Benefits generally include paid vacations and holidays and health insurance.

Where to Go for More Information

American Hospital Association
1 North Franklin
Chicago, IL 60606
(312) 422-3000
www.aaha.org

National Health Council
1730 M Street, NW, Suite 500
Washington, DC 20036
(202) 785-3910
www.nhcouncil.org

Dental Assistant

Education and Training
High school

Salary Range
Median—$10.88 an hour

Employment Outlook
Excellent

Definition and Nature of the Work

Dental assistants perform a number of duties in a dentist's office. Many of their tasks are clerical. In addition, they perform chairside duties when a dentist examines his or her patients. Chairside duties involve direct contact with patients. Dental assistants work under the strict supervision of dentists.

Dental assistants schedule appointments, keep records, receive payments from patients, and order supplies. When patients come to the office, dental assistants locate their medical records for the dentist's use. Dental assistants guide patients to the chair and prepare them for the examination.

Dental assistants often operate X-ray machines. During treatment, they hand the dentist the proper materials and tools. They operate the suction hose that keeps the patient's mouth dry so the dentist can work on it. Sometimes dental assistants make an impression of a patient's mouth or teeth. They may also sterilize instruments, develop X rays, and mix compounds for cleaning or filling teeth.

Most dental assistants work in private offices for one or more dentists. Other assistants work in public health departments, clinics, hospitals, and dental schools.

Education and Training Requirements

Dental assistants need a high school diploma. Courses in biology, English, mathematics, bookkeeping, and typing are helpful. Many dental assistants learn their skills on the job.

An increasing number of dental assistants attend colleges, vocational schools, and technical institutes to enroll in dental assisting programs. Students are given classroom, laboratory, and preclinical instruction. There are currently more than 240 training programs approved by the American Dental Association Commission on Dental Accreditation. These are generally 1- or 2-year programs that lead to a certificate or to an associate degree. Also, the American Dental Association has accredited a correspondence course. Graduates of accredited programs can become certified dental assistants if they pass a test.

Getting the Job

If you go to school to learn to be a dental assistant, the placement office can help you find a job. You can also apply directly to dentists' offices, hospitals, and private clinics. To get a job with the government, apply to take the necessary civil service test. Check with state and private employment agencies. Also check newspaper want ads and job banks on the Internet.

Advancement Possibilities and Employment Outlook

Dental assistants can advance with experience and further training. In a large dental office, they may become supervisors of other assistants. By taking further dental courses, they can qualify to become dental hygienists or dental laboratory technicians.

The outlook is excellent through the year 2008, with employment expected to grow much faster than the average. More assistants should be needed as the field

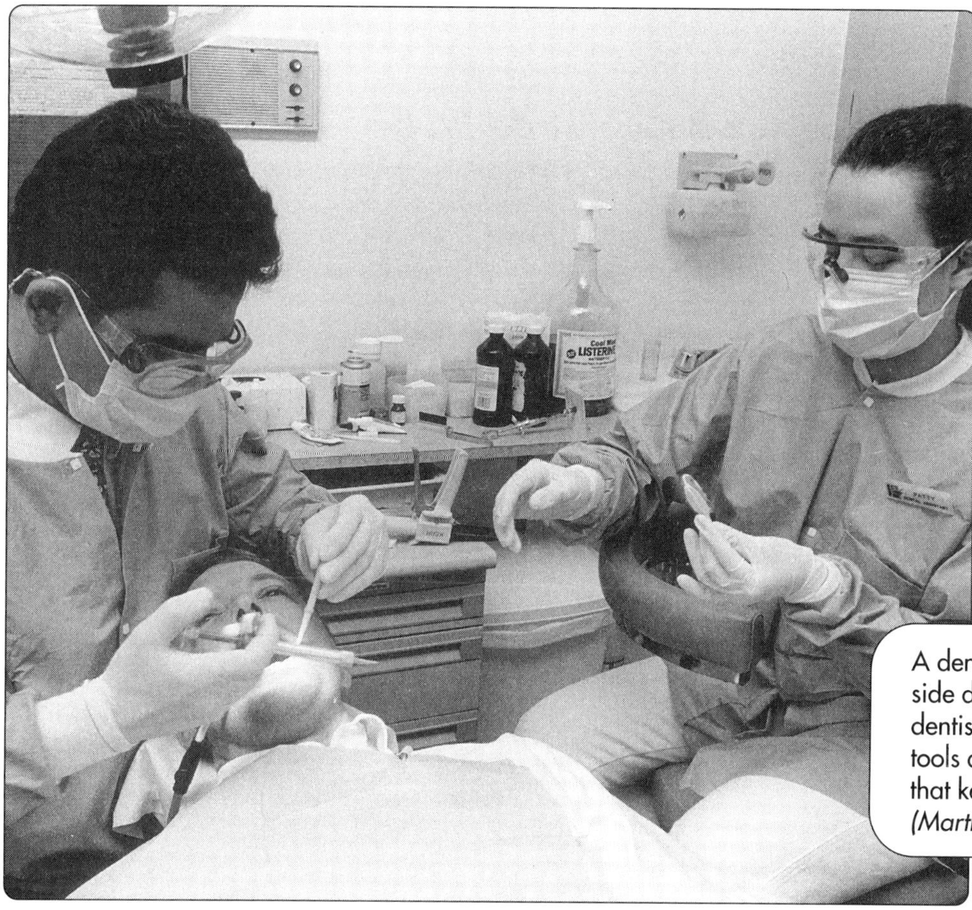

A dental assistant performs chair-side duties that include handing the dentist the proper materials and tools and operating the suction hose that keeps the patient's mouth dry. *(Martha Tabor.)*

of dental care continues to grow. In addition to jobs made available by expansion in the field, more assistants will be needed to replace those who retire. Expanding population, the growing awareness of the importance of dental care, and increasing availability of dental insurance should also add to the demand for dental assistants.

Working Conditions

Most dental offices are comfortable and clean. Dental assistants deal with many kinds of people. They may have to comfort frightened children or calm worried parents. They must also be careful in their work, especially when handling X-ray and dental equipment.

Dental assistants generally work 40 hours a week. Some work part-time. Assistants are often expected to work on Saturdays.

Earnings and Benefits

Dental assistants earn a median salary of $10.88 an hour. Benefits usually include paid holidays and vacations. Other benefits vary, depending on the employer. Publicly employed dental assistants generally receive the same benefits as other hospital or health agency workers.

Where to Go for More Information

American Dental Assistants Association
203 North LaSalle Street, Suite 1320
Chicago, IL 60601-1210
(312) 541-1550

American Dental Association
211 East Chicago Avenue
Chicago, IL 60611-2678
(312) 440-2500
www.ada.org

National Association of Dental Assistants
900 South Washington Street, Suite G13
Falls Church, VA 22046-4020
(703) 237-8616

Dialysis Technician

Education and Training
High school

Salary Range
Average—$18,000 to $22,200

Employment Outlook
Very good

Definition and Nature of the Work

Dialysis technicians work with people who have kidney problems. These technicians, who are sometimes called hemodialysis technicians, operate machines that act as a patient's kidneys by cleaning poisons out of the blood. Dialysis patients generally use the machine for 5 to 6 hours, three times a week. The technicians help patients feel comfortable during the procedure and stay with them while the machine is working. They must also keep the machine in good working condition.

Most dialysis technicians work in hospitals under the supervision of a head nurse. Others work in dialysis units run by private companies.

Education and Training Requirements

You need a high school diploma to become a dialysis technician. You should also have an interest in caring for people. Courses in science and health are useful, as is volunteer or part-time work in a hospital. Mechanical ability is also important in this job.

Dialysis technicians train on the job. In a hospital they are taught how to operate the machine by a head nurse. Companies that have dialysis units may also offer training.

Getting the Job

You can apply directly to hospitals or companies that have dialysis units. In addition, check state and private employment services for job listings and information.

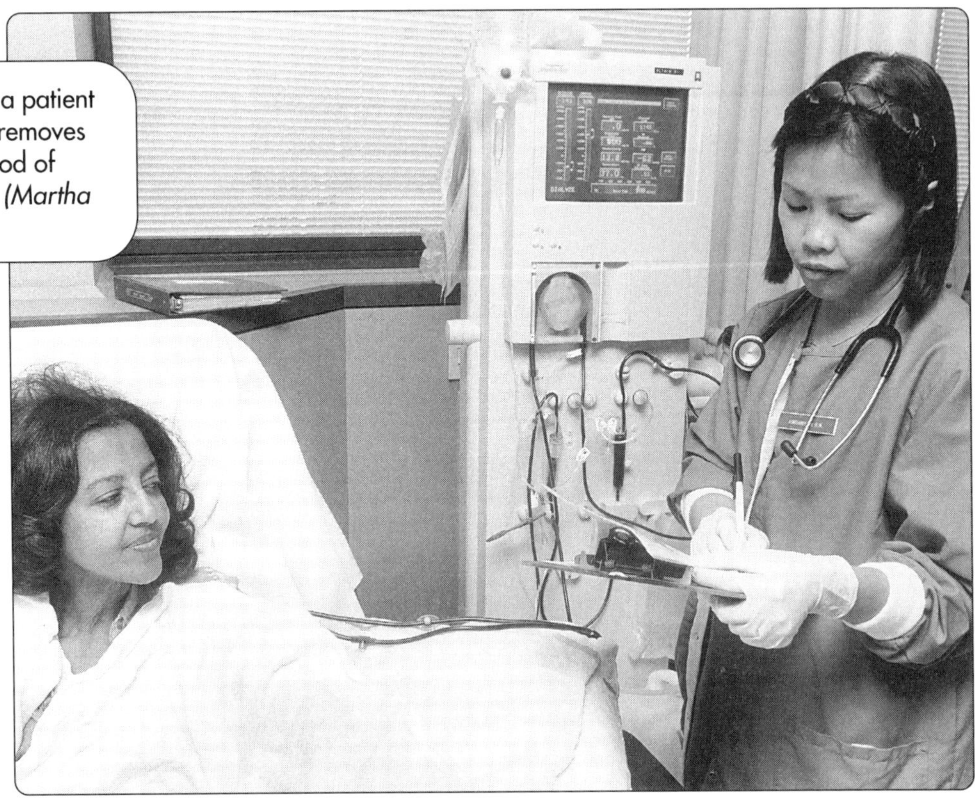

A dialysis technician monitors a patient on a dialysis machine, which removes waste substances from the blood of people with kidney problems. *(Martha Tabor.)*

Advancement Possibilities and Employment Outlook

Advancement is possible with education and experience. Technicians working in large dialysis units may become chief technicians. With further training, some dialysis technicians become biomedical equipment technicians.

The employment outlook is very good through the year 2008. The field is growing steadily and there is a need for qualified workers.

Working Conditions

Technicians work 40 hours a week. They often work with people who need understanding and encouragement. They must be careful workers who can keep calm in a medical emergency.

Earnings and Benefits

Salaries vary with experience. Starting salaries for dialysis technicians range from $16,500 to $17,800 a year. Technicians with more experience earn $18,000 to $22,200 a year. Benefits include paid holidays and vacations, sick leave, and health insurance.

Where to Go for More Information

American Hospital Association
1 North Franklin
Chicago, IL 60606
(312) 422-3000
www.aaha.org

National Health Council
1730 M Street, NW, Suite 500
Washington, DC 20036
(202) 785-3910
www.nhcouncil.org

National Kidney Foundation
30 East 33rd Street, 11th Floor
New York, NY 10016
(800) 622-9010
www.kidney.org

Home Health Aide

Education and Training
Varies—see profile

Salary Range
Median—$7.58 an hour

Employment Outlook
Excellent

Definition and Nature of the Work

Home health aides provide services in the home for people who cannot care for themselves. Their clients include the elderly or people with long-term illnesses or disabilities. Home health aides work for hospitals and health care agencies.

Health aides provide a variety of services for their clients. They give them baths and massages and change bandages if necessary. Sometimes they help them to get dressed, do exercises, and get in and out of bed. Aides see that their clients take their medicine, although they cannot prescribe drugs themselves.

Aides often help with household chores. They may change bed linens and do some light laundry or cleaning. Sometimes they take clients for walks or rides. They may read to them or just keep them company.

In some cases, home health aides instruct clients and their families in health care. For example, they may teach a new mother how to care for her baby, or they may show parents how to help a handicapped child. Sometimes aides move into a client's home for a period of time.

Education and Training Requirements

Some employers prefer to hire high school graduates, but a high school diploma is not necessary to enter this field. Volunteer work and part-time or summer jobs in hospitals are good experience. Training courses for home health aides are generally about 2 to 3 weeks long. Hospitals, adult education schools, health

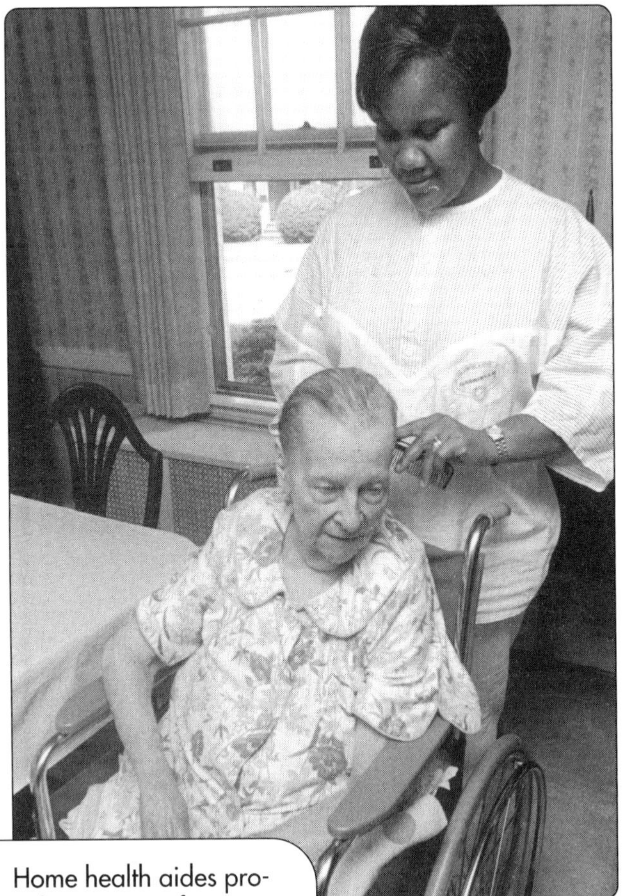

Home health aides provide a variety of services to people who cannot care for themselves. *(Martha Tabor.)*

departments, and volunteer agencies offer these courses. Many home health aides receive on-the-job training under the supervision of a registered nurse. Federal law suggests 75 hours of both classroom and practical training. Some states require home health aides to be certified. The federal government also has guidelines for home health aides whose employers receive reimbursement from Medicare. They must pass a competency test covering 12 areas that include reading and recording vital signs, basic nutrition, personal hygiene and grooming, and knowledge of emergency procedures. Aides must be in good health. They should also be patient, understanding, and cheerful.

Getting the Job

Apply to local health care agencies or to hospitals for jobs. You can also check newspaper want ads and job banks on the Internet. State and private employment agencies may also list openings for home health aides.

Advancement Possibilities and Employment Outlook

With further education, a home health aide can become a teaching health aide or a licensed practical nurse. The employment outlook for home health aides is excellent through the year 2008. In fact, it is expected to be one of the fastest growing occupations. This trend reflects several developments. First, hospitals are making an increased effort to contain costs by moving patients out of hospitals quickly without compromising their health. Second, studies have shown that patient treatment often proves to be more effective in familiar rather than clinical surroundings. Third, improvements in portable medical technology have made in-home treatment a feasible alternative to hospitalization. Finally, an increase in the elderly population is certain in the years ahead. This should provide many openings in this field and a shortage of workers.

Working Conditions

Home health aides generally work a 40-hour week. They might spend 4 hours at one home in the morning and 4 hours at another in the afternoon. Part-time work is sometimes available. Aides are sometimes needed on weekends and overnight. Aides work with many different kinds of people and in many different kinds of homes. Some aides might live with a client for a period of time to provide round-the-clock care.

Earnings and Benefits

Earnings vary depending on experience and location. The median income for aides who work for Medicare-certified agencies is $7.58 an hour. Some aides are paid on a per-visit basis. Aides typically earn higher wages in the Northeast and the West. Most employers supply no benefits. Also, aides are not normally paid for their travel time because they go from one client to another.

Where to Go for More Information

American Hospital Association
1 North Franklin
Chicago, IL 60606
(312) 422-3000
www.aaha.org

National HomeCaring Council
513 C Street, NE
Washington, DC 20002
(202) 547-7424

Laboratory Animal Care Worker

Education and Training
High school

Salary Range
Median—$7.12 an hour

Employment Outlook
Good

Definition and Nature of the Work

Laboratory animal care workers take care of animals that are used in scientific research. Laboratory animal care workers include assistant laboratory animal technicians, laboratory animal technicians, and laboratory animal technologists. Scientists do experiments for drug companies, medical schools, and research centers. They use animals to learn about animal and human diseases and treatments. They study animals to learn about animal behavior and intelligence. Animal care workers help the scientists and carry out their instructions.

Laboratory animal care workers look after a wide variety of animals, including mice, guinea pigs, rats, rabbits, monkeys, dogs, or even birds, insects, and fish. Animal care workers provide food and water for the animals and keep their cages clean. They check for signs of illness, injury, or disease. They also maintain careful records on each animal regarding such things as diet, weight, medication, and behavior. They may also order food and supplies for the animals. Sometimes they take samples from the animals and help scientists or medical doctors perform experiments.

Some laboratory animal care workers are *veterinarian's assistants.* They may administer medication orally or by injection, treat minor wounds, and prepare animals for surgery.

Education and Training Requirements

A high school education is usually required for unskilled jobs in laboratories. Courses in science are helpful. Some laboratories will give you on-the-job training. You can also take a 2-year program in animal care at a college or technical school. Certification is available from the American Association for Laboratory Animal Science (AALAS), but it is not required for work. There are three levels of certification: assistant laboratory animal technician, laboratory animal technician, and laboratory animal technologist. For each level of certification there are age, education, experience, and examination requirements.

Laboratory animal care workers need a knowledge of animals' eating and sleeping habits. They should enjoy working with animals and be able to follow directions carefully.

Getting the Job

You can apply directly to medical schools, drug companies, research centers, or animal hospitals. Your school placement office may also have a list of openings. Some laboratories place want ads in the newspapers or in job banks on the Internet.

Advancement Possibilities and Employment Outlook

With training and experience, laboratory animal care workers can become supervisors, research assistants, or animal breeders. The employment outlook is good through the year 2008. Drug companies, medical schools, and research centers are employing increasing numbers of technicians to help them with experiments. However, with the growing concern over animal rights, many commercial product companies are limiting or eliminating their animal-testing activities.

Where to Go for More Information

American Association for Laboratory Animal Science
9190 Crestwyn Hills Drive
Memphis, TN 38125-8538
(901) 754-8620
www.aalas.org

American College of Laboratory Animal Medicine
96 Chester Street
Chester, NH 03036
(603) 887-2467
www.aclam.org

Working Conditions

Laboratory animal care workers usually work 40 hours a week. Sometimes they must work nights and weekends. Working areas are usually well lighted and pleasant. However, animal care workers are exposed to unpleasant smells. They spend most of their time working with animals rather than with people.

Earnings and Benefits

Salaries vary depending on education and experience. The median salary for laboratory animal care workers is $7.12 an hour. Benefits include paid holidays and vacations, health insurance, sick leave, and sometimes pension plans and free tuition.

Nurse's Aide and Orderly

Education and Training
None

Salary Range
Average—$8.32 an hour

Employment Outlook
Very good

Definition and Nature of the Work

Nurse's aides and orderlies help nurses care for patients. They help to keep patients comfortable and tend to their basic needs. Aides and orderlies generally spend most of their time with patients, carrying meal trays to them, answering call lights when patients signal for help, and helping to move them when necessary. Aides and orderlies make beds, give baths and massages, and fill water pitchers and ice bags. They may also perform routine tests, such as taking a patient's temperature, pulse, and blood pressure. Sometimes aides and orderlies do light cleaning, distribute linens, set up equipment, deliver messages, and assemble meal trays for patients who are on special diets.

Many nurse's aides and orderlies work in hospitals. An increasing number work in nursing homes and long-term care facilities for elderly people. Some work with psychiatric patients and are called psychiatric aides.

Education and Training Requirements

There are no specific education requirements for these jobs. Aides and orderlies are usually trained on the job under the supervision of a registered nurse or a licensed practical nurse. Training generally lasts from 1 week to 3 months. Some high schools also offer courses that give students credit for on-the-job experience. Volunteer jobs in hospitals are good experience, as are courses in home nursing and first aid.

Getting the Job

Apply directly to the hospitals or nursing homes in which you want to work. You can also check newspaper want ads and job banks on the Internet. State and private employment agencies sometimes list openings for nurse's aides and orderlies.

Advancement Possibilities and Employment Outlook

Aides and orderlies can advance with further education. Some train to be licensed practical nurses while working part-time as aides or orderlies. Others may learn to operate specialized equipment, such as electrocardiograph machines.

The employment outlook is very good and is expected to continue to expand with the growing demand for health services. There is fast growth and high turnover in this occupation. An increase in the elderly population will also contribute to this demand. Nurse's aides and orderlies will remain an important part of the health care team.

Working Conditions

Nurse's aides and orderlies generally work 40 hours a week. This usually includes some night or weekend work. The surroundings are generally quiet and clean. Aides may spend much of their day standing and walking, and performing many tasks. They often have unpleasant duties and may have to deal with uncooperative patients. However, helping others can be a rewarding experience.

Since they work with sick people, aides and orderlies need to be patient and understanding. They should be healthy and responsible. They should also be able to stay calm in emergencies.

Earnings and Benefits

Salaries vary with experience and place of employment. Salaries for nursing home aides average $8.32 an hour. Benefits usually include paid holidays and vacations and health insurance.

Where to Go for More Information

American Nurses Association
600 Maryland Avenue, SW
Washington, DC 20024-2517
(800) 274-4262
www.ana.org

National League for Nursing
61 Broadway
New York, NY 10014
(800) 669-9656
www.nln.org

Optometric Assistant

Education and Training

High school

Salary Range

Starting—$15,000
Average—$18,300 to $21,000

Employment Outlook

Excellent

Definition and Nature of the Work

Optometric assistants perform routine tasks in optometrists' offices. Their work enables optometrists to devote their time to patient care that requires specialized training. Optometric assistants do clerical work, such as bookkeeping and scheduling appointments. They also help the optometrist during eye examinations.

Optometrists give their patients eye examinations for vision, color blindness, and eye pressure. When the tests are completed, an optometrist can prescribe the necessary eyeglasses for the patient. Optometric assistants often prepare patients for the tests. They may put drops in patients' eyes or direct and seat patients at eye-testing machines.

Assistants may explain eye exercises to patients or teach them how to use contact lenses. In some offices, optometric assistants help people choose the frames for their glasses. When the eyeglasses are made, optometric assistants adjust them for a proper fit.

Some assistants work in laboratories that fill prescriptions for eyeglasses. They put lenses into frames or repair broken frames. Most optometric assistants work in private offices. Some work in health clinics or for government agencies. Others are employed by companies that make optical instruments.

Education and Training Requirements

Optometric assistants should have a high school diploma or its equivalent. Most are trained on the job. Optometrists prefer applicants who are accurate and able to work well with delicate and breakable tools and materials.

There are also formal training programs for this work. Some technical schools, community colleges, and colleges of optometry offer 1-year programs. Training for optometric assistants generally includes secretarial and office skills as well as medical procedures.

Getting the Job

If you attend a training program, your school placement office can give you job information. If you do not have training, contact optometrists in your community and ask about on-the-job training. To get a government job, apply to take the necessary civil service test. State and private employment offices can also provide information about employment opportunities. You should also check newspaper want ads and job banks on the Internet for listings.

Advancement Possibilities and Employment Outlook

An assistant may train with an optometrist who specializes in a field such as contact lenses. Learning a specialty will enable the assistant to get a better-paying job.

The employment outlook is excellent through the year 2008. Job openings will be created by the coverage of eyecare services through public and private insurance programs and the new, more economical eyecare chains. Also, the growth of the older population is certain to assure the need for qualified optometric assistants. Opportunities will be best for people who have completed a formal training program.

Working Conditions

Most optometric assistants work in modern, well-lighted offices and laboratories. Offices can be very busy at times. However, the work area is usually quiet and clean. Optometric assistants work under the direct supervision of an optometrist. They must enjoy working with people because they usually have a lot of contact with patients. Work hours vary, but assistants typically work about 40 hours a week. They may also be required to work on evenings and Saturdays. Many optometric assistants work part-time.

Earnings and Benefits

Beginning optometric assistants earn a salary of about $15,000 a year. Optometric assistants with experience may average $18,300 to $21,000 a year. Benefits generally include paid holidays and vacations and health insurance.

Where to Go for More Information

American Optometric Association
243 North Lindbergh Boulevard
St. Louis, MO 63141-7851
(800) 365-2219
www.aoanet.org

Substance Abuse Counselor

Education and Training
High school

Salary Range
Starting—$15,000 to $20,000

Employment Outlook
Excellent

Definition and Nature of the Work

Substance abuse counselors help people who have problems related to alcohol and other drugs. They counsel addicts as well as those who are afraid they might become addicts. They also help former addicts. Sometimes they counsel the families, friends, and loved ones of addicts, whose lives are inevitably affected by the problem as well.

Addiction counselors, as they are sometimes called, usually help with practical problems. For example, a counselor might help a former addict find a job. Counselors do not prescribe medicine or provide medical or psychological therapy. Substance abuse counselors are often supervised by doctors, psychologists, or social workers.

Some of these counselors work in halfway houses, where addicts live while they are under treatment. Counselors may also work in outpatient clinics where people come in on a regular basis for treatment. Other counselors work in hospitals, treatment centers, or human service agencies. Sometimes these counselors are former substance users themselves who have learned from their mistakes and want to help others. Substance abuse counselors hold counseling sessions for one person or for a group of people. At these sessions counselors try to help addicts talk about, understand, and cope with their problems.

Education and Training Requirements

A high school diploma is usually required for this field of work. Counselors generally are trained on the job. Training programs vary in length from 6 weeks to 2 years. Some colleges also offer training programs for counselors. These programs usually last 2 years and include courses on the effects of alcohol and other drugs. Students may also learn crisis intervention—a way of handling emergency situations. Emergencies may involve emotional or medical problems. Graduates of these programs usually receive an associate degree. Certification is also available by the National Board for Certified Counselors. For some positions, a bachelor's

Substance abuse counselors help people who have alcohol or drug problems talk about, understand, and cope with their problems. *(Martha Tabor.)*

degree or higher in sociology, psychology, or a related field may be required. An increasing number of substance abuse counselors are getting their master's degrees in mental health counseling.

Getting the Job

You can apply for a job at a halfway house, treatment center, hospital, or clinic that offers substance abuse counseling. Your school placement office may be able to give you job information. Also check state and private employment agencies. Newspaper want ads and job banks on the Internet sometimes list jobs for substance abuse counselors.

Advancement Possibilities and Employment Outlook

Substance abuse counselors who have a high school diploma or an associate degree can advance to the position of director of a halfway house. However, most other advanced jobs in the field of substance abuse, such as rehabilitation counselors or social workers, require at least a bachelor's degree. For other jobs, such as psychologist, the minimum education requirement is a master's degree. The employment outlook is excellent for counselors through the year 2008.

Working Conditions

Most substance abuse counselors work a 40-hour week. Some live in halfway houses. The work can be tense and sometimes frustrating. Counselors work closely with other people and should enjoy helping others.

Earnings and Benefits

Salaries vary depending on education, experience, and level of responsibility. Substance abuse counselors entering the field earn between $15,000 and $20,000 a year. Those with a master's degree average $25,000 to $35,000 annually. Benefits usually include paid holidays and vacations, health insurance, and pension plans.

Where to Go for More Information

National Association of Alcoholism and Drug Abuse Counselors
1911 North Fort Myer Drive, Suite 900
Arlington, VA 22209
(800) 548-0497
www.naadac.org

Ward Clerk

Education and Training
High school

Salary Range
Average—$10.57 an hour

Employment Outlook
Good

Definition and Nature of the Work

Ward clerks perform clerical work at the nurse's station of a hospital or nursing unit. Ward clerks are usually supervised by a registered nurse. Their work allows nurses to spend more time on patient care.

Ward clerks do most of the paperwork for their nursing unit. They keep records on the patients and on the ward's hospital staff. They may perform other routine clerical duties. Clerks also act as receptionists for their ward. They answer the telephone and direct visitors to patients' rooms. Sometimes ward clerks also do other jobs, such as ordering supplies or taking mail or flowers to patients.

Education and Training Requirements

Most hospitals prefer ward clerks who have a high school diploma. Courses in mathematics, typing, and other business subjects are helpful. Computer skills

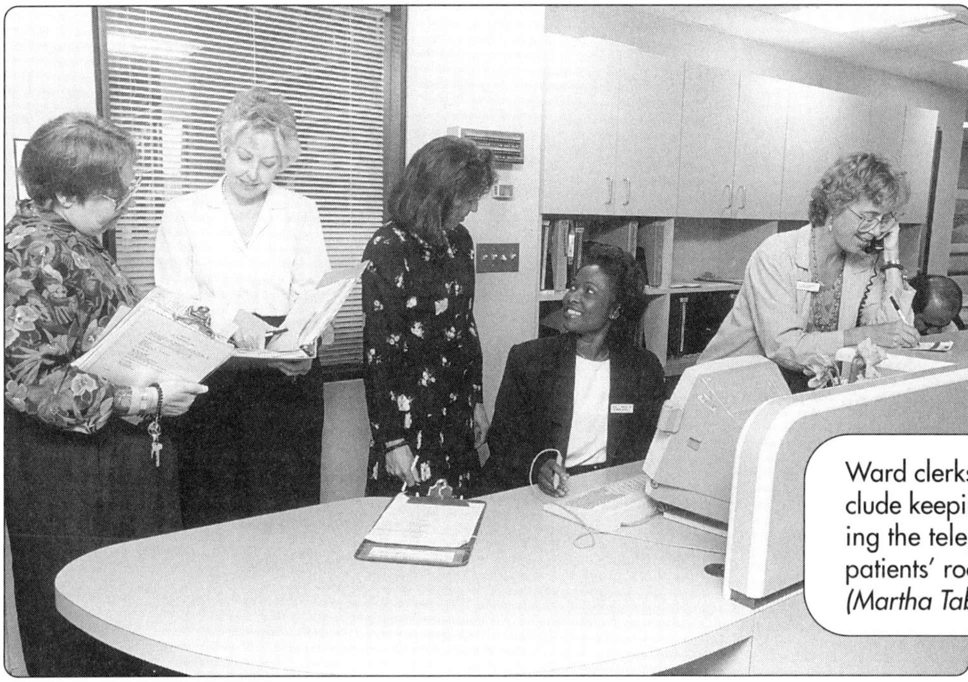

Ward clerks perform clerical tasks that include keeping records of patients, answering the telephone, directing visitors to patients' rooms, and ordering supplies. *(Martha Tabor.)*

are a plus. Volunteer or part-time work in a hospital is also useful experience. Ward clerks are usually trained on the job.

Getting the Job

You can apply directly to the hospital in which you want to work. Check newspaper want ads and job banks on the Internet. State and private employment agencies also list openings for ward clerks.

Advancement Possibilities and Employment Outlook

Advancement is possible with further education and experience. Ward clerks can become ward managers, who are in charge of all nonnursing duties in their wards. If they increase their clerical skills, they can become secretaries. Some ward clerks work part-time while training to become licensed practical nurses.

The employment outlook is good through the year 2008. Hospitals are using more ward clerks to take care of routine tasks so that nurses are free to perform other duties.

Working Conditions

Ward clerks work 40 hours a week, often on weekends and at night. They usually work in clean and comfortable surroundings. Ward clerks have contact with patients, visitors, doctors, nurses, and other hospital workers. They should be friendly and enjoy working with people. Ward clerks should also be responsible, efficient workers.

Earnings and Benefits

Salaries vary depending on experience, location, and level of responsibility. Ward Clerks earn an average of $10.57 an hour. Benefits include paid holidays and vacations, health insurance, and pension plans.

Where to Go for More Information

American Hospital Association
1 North Franklin
Chicago, IL 60606
(312) 422-3000
www.aaha.org

National Health Council
1730 M Street, NW, Suite 500
Washington, DC 20036
(202) 785-3910
www.nhcouncil.org

AIDS Counselor

Education and Training
Varies—see profile

Salary Range
Median—$30,590

Employment Outlook
Varies—see profile

Definition and Nature of the Work

AIDS (acquired immunodeficiency syndrome) is a disorder of the immune system that has no cure or vaccine. Contrary to what many believe, all groups of people are at risk of contracting HIV (human immunodeficiency virus), which leads to the disease. Heterosexuals and homosexuals have an equally high chance of being infected by the virus. Intravenous drug have similar chances of being infected. AIDS counselors provide support and assistance for those suffering from AIDS. They also provide instructions for AIDS prevention and information to the public.

Some AIDS counselors talk to people who are about to have an AIDS test. If the test is positive, they provide advice and counseling. Others lead individual and family counseling sessions for those who have been diagnosed as having AIDS. Still others lead support groups for patients, for those who have lost friends and family to the disease, and for those who feel they are at risk.

One of the responsibilities of an AIDS counselor is to provide practical advice to people with AIDS on how to cope with their daily lives and the problems they may encounter. This may include finding housing, medical services, and legal advisers.

Volunteers play an important part in assisting organizations that counsel people with AIDS. They may become "buddies," visiting AIDS patients in their homes and assisting with household tasks. Others work for telephone hotlines and provide information about AIDS testing. Many are involved in administrative tasks that help these organizations operate.

AIDS counselors may also spend time writing and talking to the general public. They provide information about the disease and its prevention through brochures, discussion groups, and training sessions. They may supply information to employers about AIDS in the workplace.

Education and Training Requirements

Because the AIDS epidemic is a fairly recent development in this country, there is no formal training to become an AIDS counselor. Experience is often more important than education. The best way to gain experience is to become a volunteer with an organization that cares for people with AIDS. Most organizations provide initial training for volunteers, and many provide follow-up sessions. Paid positions are usually filled by people with master's degrees in the field of mental health or social work. These people often have counseling experience in substance abuse.

Getting the Job

Organizations that work with people who have AIDS rely on volunteers. The best way to get a job in this field is to apply directly to these organizations as a volunteer. Your school placement office may be able to give you information about

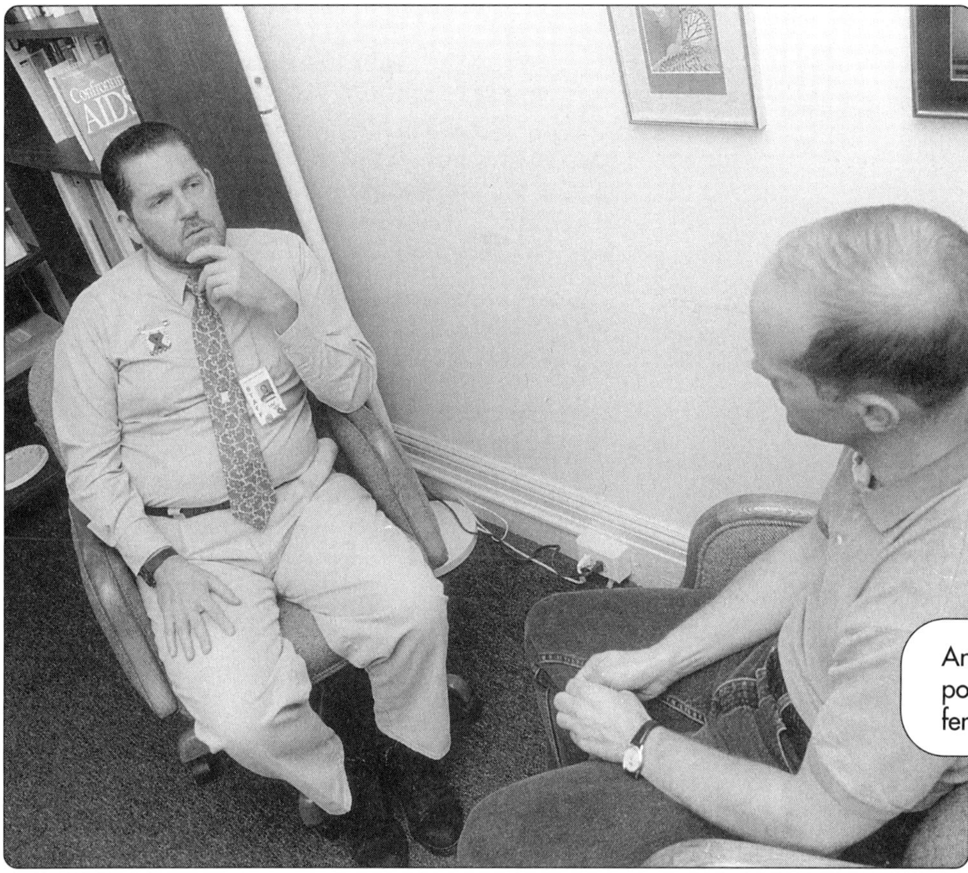

An AIDS counselor provides support and assistance to a man suffering from AIDS. *(Martha Tabor.)*

paid positions. You can also apply to hospitals and hospices in areas where there are large numbers of AIDS patients.

Advancement Possibilities and Employment Outlook

Experienced AIDS counselors with master's degrees can advance to administrative positions. Some may become AIDS educators who write, organize, and deliver information to the public. Others become training specialists and design training programs for volunteers and professionals. Within organizations counselors may become project coordinators, project directors, or regional directors.

Although the number of AIDS cases will increase steadily in the future, the outlook for paid employment is uncertain. The demand for volunteers will remain high, but paid positions will depend on the level of private and government funding. Job opportunities will be most plentiful for those with master's degrees and experience in a related field.

Working Conditions

AIDS counselors in paid positions usually work a 40-hour week. Some work in clean hospital environments and mental health clinics. Those who work in hospices work in pleasant surroundings. Many volunteers and counselors also visit AIDS patients in their homes, which may be in poor inner-city areas.

People suffering from AIDS are under severe emotional and physical stress, which often affects their interaction with AIDS counselors. Therefore, AIDS counselors must be able to work with people who are very ill and severely depressed due to the effects of the disease.

Where to Go for More Information

American Psychological Association
750 First Street, NE
Washington, DC 20002-4242
(800) 374-2721
www.apa.org

American Public Health Association
800 First Street, NW
Washington, DC 20001
(202) 777-2500
www.apha.org

Earnings and Benefits

Many AIDS counselors are volunteers and do not receive a salary. For those in paid positions, salaries are very similar to those of other social workers. The median salary of social workers is $30,590 annually. Salaries are generally higher for private practitioners, administrators, and researchers. Benefits for those working for hospitals and public health departments generally include paid vacations and holidays, health insurance, and retirement plans.

Ambulance Driver

Education and Training
License and training

Salary Range
Average—$9.00 an hour

Employment Outlook
Very good

Definition and Nature of the Work

Ambulance drivers are often the first members of the medical team to reach a person in need of medical attention. They drive vehicles that carry sick people and accident victims to hospitals—people who are too ill or too badly hurt to get to the hospital by themselves. Ambulance drivers work for hospitals and for police, fire, and community first aid squads. They also work for private ambulance companies that provide emergency or invalid carrier service. Invalid carrier service is provided when, for example, a recovering patient is moved from a hospital to a nursing home. In some communities, a large percentage of the ambulance drivers are volunteers. Some drivers, however, are salaried.

Ambulance drivers are generally trained to serve as *emergency medical technicians-ambulance.* They are trained to give certain kinds of emergency care, which is called basic life support, when they reach a patient. The best known emergency medical technicians (EMTs) are called *paramedics.* They are trained to give advanced life support. They work under the direct supervision of medical professionals. When they reach a patient, they notify professionals at the hospital by two-way radio, explain the situation, and carry out the physician's instructions. Paramedics also are trained to carry out a limited number of procedures at their own discretion.

Dispatchers receive calls for ambulance service and relay information to ambulance drivers. The level of training required to become a dispatcher has been raised in recent years. Highly trained dispatchers are called telecommunicators or C-Meds.

Education and Training Requirements

Ambulance drivers must be at least 18 years old, with a driver's license and a good driving record. The must also be trained in emergency medical care. Some are required to have the Red Cross first-aid training certificate. The U.S. Department of Transportation has designed a 110-hour program to train emergency medical technicians-ambulance. In this course, students learn how to handle common emergencies as well as how to use equipment. All states offer this or an equivalent program. Police, fire, and health departments offer this course. It is also taught in hospitals, medical schools, colleges, and universities.

After taking the course, you can become a registered EMT-ambulance. To do that, you must pass a written and a practical exam given by the National Registry of Emergency Medical Technicians.

Training programs for paramedics last from 3 to 5 months. To become registered as an EMT-paramedic, you must complete the course, have 6 months of field training, and pass a written and a practical exam.

A third type of registration, called EMT-intermediate, is offered. It is a level above EMT-ambulance and a step below EMT-paramedic. Registration is not required to get a job, but registered EMTs may have a better chance of getting higher-paying jobs. All states have certification requirements, which vary from state to state. EMTs must re-register every 2 years.

Ambulance drivers are trained to give basic life support to ill or injured people. Paramedics, such as the one pictured here, can give advanced life support under the direct supervision of medical professionals. *(The Terry Wild Studio.)*

Getting the Job

You can apply directly to your local ambulance service or hospital for a job. If you are in school, ask the placement office for help in finding a job.

Advancement Possibilities and Employment Outlook

Emergency medical technicians can take training courses that lead to higher levels within the job. With further training, some become emergency medical technician-administrators.

The employment outlook is very good through the year 2008. An increased demand for medical services will result in much faster than average job growth, and emergency medical services are expected to experience average growth. There may be greater competition for EMT jobs. Municipal government and private ambulance services will provide the best opportunities for qualified ambulance drivers.

Working Conditions

Ambulance drivers usually work 40 hours a week. They work irregular hours including nights, weekends, and holidays. Since many ambulance calls involve matters of life and death, drivers work under intense pressure. Ambulance drivers bend and lift and perform other physically strenuous duties. The work is demanding and requires a high degree of commitment.

Earnings and Benefits

Ambulance drivers earn an average salary of $9.00 an hour. Benefits usually include paid holidays and vacations, health insurance, and pension plans.

Where to Go for More Information

American Ambulance Association
1255 Twenty-third Street, NW, Suite 200
Washington, DC 20037
(800) 523-4447
www.the-aaa.org

National Association of Emergency Medical Technicians
408 Monroe Street
Clinton, MS 39056
(800) 346-2368

Biomedical Equipment Technician

Education and Training
High school plus training

Salary Range
Average—$20,500 to $24,900

Employment Outlook
Very good

Definition and Nature of the Work

Biomedical equipment technicians specialize in the use and maintenance of medical equipment such as heart-lung machines, dialysis machines, and equipment used for measuring blood pressure and brain waves. Unlike electrocardiograph and electroencephalograph technicians, who specialize in one type of equipment, biomedical equipment technicians are familiar with many different kinds of machines. Biomedical equipment technicians work in hospitals and research organizations. They also work for manufacturers' sales departments and research and development departments. Most technicians work under the direction of biomedical engineers.

In hospitals, biomedical equipment technicians may become experts at using certain pieces of equipment. Some technicians work in several departments with many different kinds of equipment. Technicians teach nurses, therapists, and other members of the hospital staff to operate the machines. They inspect new equipment to make sure that the machinery received is the same as what was ordered. They also see that it operates properly.

Technicians make minor repairs on equipment at the hospital. When equipment must be sent back to the manufacturer for major repairs, they write an analysis of the problem so the manufacturer can fix and return the equipment quickly. Technicians also maintain detailed records on the use and condition of all equipment.

Education and Training Requirements

You need 1 to 3 years of training after high school to become a biomedical equipment technician. Training courses are available at junior and community colleges. These colleges generally work closely with local hospitals and manufacturers. During the training period, students learn how to operate many different kinds of medical instruments. Even after they have completed their formal training, technicians must keep up with new developments in the field.

The Association for the Advancement of Medical Instrumentation issues certification for biomedical equipment technicians. In order to qualify, technicians must pass a test given by the association. Many employers prefer to hire technicians who have certification.

Getting the Job

Your school placement office can help you find a job. You can also apply directly to hospitals, biomedical equipment manufacturers, and research organizations. Your state employment office may list openings. Also check newspaper want ads and job banks on the Internet for employment opportunities.

Advancement Possibilities and Employment Outlook

With further education, technicians can hold research and teaching positions. To become a biomedical engineer, at least a bachelor's degree and specialized biomedical training are required.

The employment outlook is very good through the year 2008. New jobs are expected to open in the future. Research and development expenditures are expected to increase. The rapid development and wide use of biomedical equip-

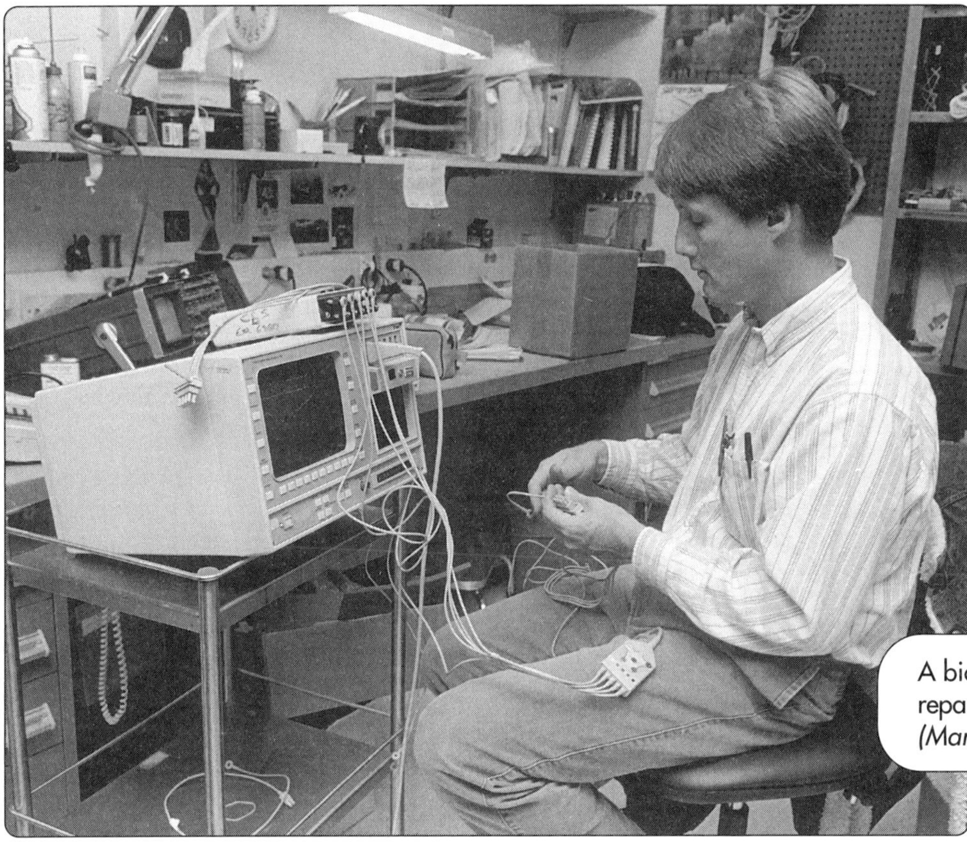

A biomedical equipment technician repairs a heart monitor at a hospital. *(Martha Tabor.)*

ment along with accelerated growth in the output of technical products should increase the need for biomedical equipment technicians. The companies that make the equipment have the greatest need for these technicians. Trained workers are also needed in hospitals and research organizations.

Working Conditions

Technicians work with highly trained doctors and engineers. They must be able to communicate their mechanical knowledge to others. Most technicians work in or near large cities where medical facilities and companies are located.

Hours vary for technicians depending on where they work. Hospital technicians generally work 8-hour shifts. They may have to work at night or on weekends. Those employed by research organizations or manufacturing companies usually work regular hours.

Earnings and Benefits

Earnings vary depending on the type of work done and the specific employer. The average salary for technicians who service equipment is $20,500 to $24,900 a year. Technicians in advanced positions can make from $30,000 to $35,000 a year. Benefits include paid holidays and vacations, health insurance, and pension plans.

Where to Go for More Information

American Hospital Association
1 North Franklin
Chicago, IL 60606
(312) 422-3000
www.aaha.org

Association for the Advancement of Medical Instrumentation
3330 Washington Boulevard, Suite 400
Arlington, VA 22201-4598
(800) 332-2264
www.aami.org

Biomedical Engineering Society
8401 Corporate Drive, Suite 110
Landover, MD 20785-2224
(310) 459-1999
www.bmes.org

Cardiac Monitor Technician/Perfusionist

Education and Training
High school plus training

Salary Range
Median—$24,360

Employment Outlook
Poor

Definition and Nature of the Work

Cardiac monitor technicians check the heart rhythm patterns of patients to detect abnormal pattern variations. They usually work in the intensive care or cardiac care units of hospitals. These technicians are responsible for reviewing patients' records to determine normal heart rhythms. They monitor current patterns and note any deviations. To do this, technicians use instruments called calipers to measure the length and height of a patient's heart rhythm pattern on graphic tape readouts. Cardiac monitor technicians observe the cardiac monitor screen and listen for an alarm to identify any abnormal heart rhythm variation. They notify nurses and doctors when medical attention is needed.

Perfusionists are closely related to cardiac monitor technicians in the type of work they do. They set up and operate a heart-lung machine that takes over the functions of a patient's heart and lungs. These machines are used during operations or at times when respiratory failure occurs. Perfusionists must review a patient's medical history and current status, and set up and test the heart-lung machine and related equipment. They operate the machine to regulate blood circulation and composition, control body temperature, and administer any necessary drugs.

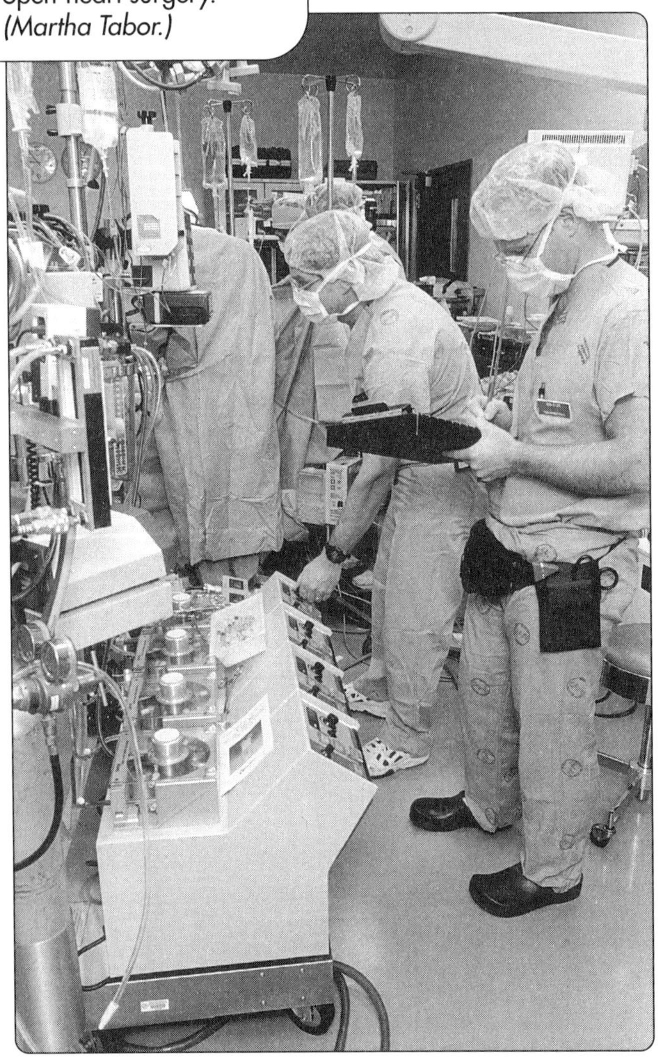

Cardiac perfusionists operate heart-hung machines to regulate blood circulation and composition during open-heart surgery. *(Martha Tabor.)*

Education and Training Requirements

Most cardiac monitor technicians and perfusionists are trained on the job in hospital programs that last from 1 month to a year. A high school diploma or its equivalent is required for acceptance into a hospital's training program. Courses in health, biology, and English are recommended. Some vocational/technical schools and community colleges offer 1- to 2-year training programs in cardiac technology.

Getting the Job

You can consult high school guidance counselors for information on job openings at hospitals, or you can contact hospitals directly. Those who graduate from a formal 1- or 2-year program can find out about job openings through the school's placement office. Students who have participated in field internships may be hired upon graduation by the hospital where they trained.

Advancement Possibilities and Employment Outlook

Cardiac technicians advance by learning to perform more complex specialty procedures. With additional training, education, and experience, cardiac monitor technicians and perfusionists can become cardiovascular or cardiopulmonary technicians or cardiology technologists. Advancement to supervisory or training positions is also possible.

Job openings for cardiac monitor technicians and perfusionists are expected to decline through the year 2008. This decline is due primarily to the increased efficiency of the machines and equipment used, which require fewer technicians to perform an increasing number of tests. Those with the most training and experience will have the best opportunities.

Working Conditions

Technicians usually work a standard 5-day, 40-hour week, in clean and quiet surroundings. Occasionally they are expected to work weekends and evenings, and those in smaller hospitals may be on 24-hour call for emergencies.

Because they work with people who are ill or anxious about their health, technicians must be patient, reassuring, alert to emergencies, and able to cope with responsibility. Most of all, they must be able to remain calm under pressure.

Earnings and Benefits

The starting salary for cardiac monitor technicians and perfusionists is about $15,000 a year. The median salary for experienced technicians is $24,360 a year. Those with previous formal training earn more than those who have been trained on the job. Technicians working in hospitals usually receive benefits that include hospitalization insurance, paid sick leave, and paid vacations. Some hospitals also provide pension plans, uniform allowances, and tuition assistance for further education.

Where to Go for More Information

American College of Cardiology
9111 Old Georgetown Road
Bethesda, MD 20814-1699
(800) 253-4636
www.acc.org

Alliance of Cardiovascular Professionals
910 Charles Street, Suite A
Fredericksburg, VA 22401-5810
(540) 370-0102
www.acp-online.org

Cardiology Technologist

Education and Training
High school plus training

Salary Range
Average—$17.44 an hour

Employment Outlook
Fair

Definition and Nature of the Work

Cardiology technologists use advanced monitoring equipment to measure one of the most crucial indicators of a person's health—the heartbeat. Once a procedure reserved for patients with suspected heart problems, electrocardiograph (EKG) testing is now a common practice in hospitals. Most doctors order EKGs for their patients before surgery and as part of routine physical exams, especially for those who are middle-aged. EKG machines record the electrical impulses that occur during and between heartbeats. The machines print graphs called electrocardiograms (EKGs), which doctors study to learn about the condition of their patients' hearts. Cardiology technologists operate the EKG machines and make sure they are working properly.

To take an EKG, a cardiology technologist fastens disclike electrodes to the patient's chest, arms, and legs. During this process, the technologist explains the procedure to the patient and tries to make the patient feel as comfortable as possible. This helps to limit faulty readings, which can be caused by stress, among other things. Once the patient is hooked up and settled, the technologist operates the controls on the EKG machine, allowing the electrodes to pick up electronic signals from the heart and transmit them to the machine. The machine is equipped with a special pen, or stylus, that records the heartbeat patterns on graph paper.

Experienced cardiology technologists sometimes administer more advanced types of cardiovascular tests. Holter monitoring involves a 24- to 48-hour surveillance of a patient going about a normal daily routine—sitting, standing, eating,

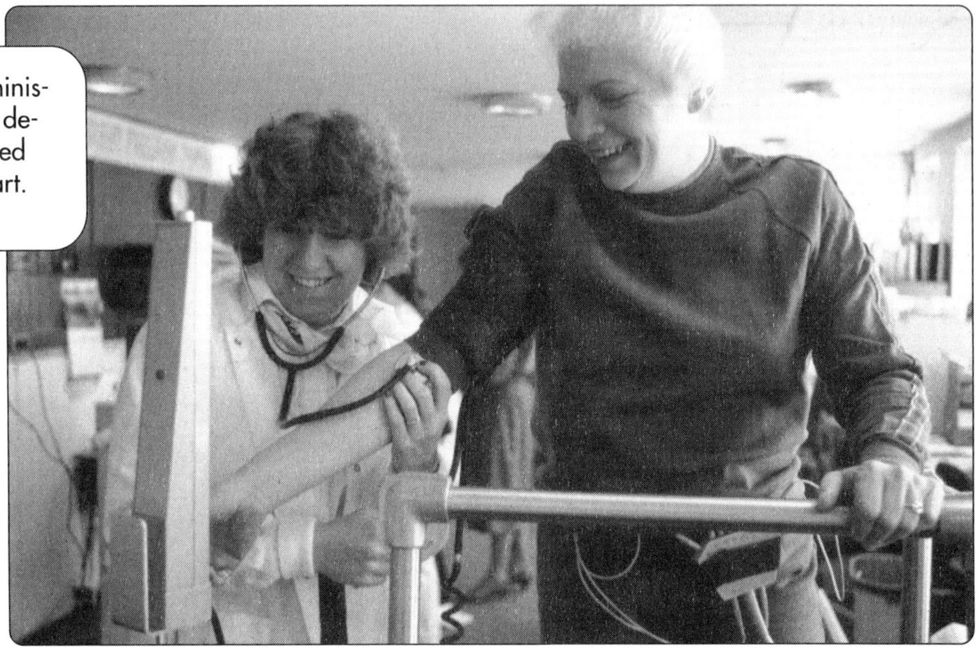

A cardiology technologist administers a treadmill stress test. This determines the effect that increased exertion has on a patient's heart. *(The Terry Wild Studio.)*

and sleeping. Electrodes are placed on the patient's chest, and a portable cassette monitor is strapped to the patient's waist. At the end of the testing period, the cassette is scanned and printed for a physician to interpret.

Cardiology technologists may also administer the treadmill stress test. After taking a patient's medical history and resting heartbeat and blood pressure, the technologist asks the patient to start walking slowly on a treadmill. The technologist gradually increases the treadmill's speed while monitoring the performance of the patient's heart. The treadmill stress test is a way of determining the effect of increased exertion on a patient's heart.

After cardiology technologists remove an EKG from a machine, they may edit it or make notes on it before giving it to a physician. Technologists are trained to detect and highlight false readings, which can occur due to the sensitivity of the EKG machine to other electrical impulses. Cardiology technologists can also identify unusual patterns emerging on the graphs. However, they do not interpret EKGs or diagnose ailments. That is the job of the physician. Cardiology technologists work in hospital cardiology departments, cardiac rehabilitation centers, clinics, doctors' offices, or medical schools.

Education and Training Requirements

You must have a high school diploma to become a cardiology technologist, although more employers are beginning to favor those who have completed formal training. Recommended high school courses include health, biology, anatomy, and mathematics. Most hospitals provide on-the-job training lasting from 8 to 16 weeks. Trainees are supervised by a cardiologist or an EKG supervisor. Technical schools and community colleges also offer 2-year training programs. Certification is offered by the American Cardiology Technologists Association.

Getting the Job

You can apply directly to hospitals for job openings. If you have some college training, you may have an advantage in finding employment. Check with your school placement office. Also check state and private employment services for openings for cardiology technologists.

Advancement Possibilities and Employment Outlook

Doctors are using EKGs more frequently as part of routine physical examinations. In large hospitals, cardiology technologists can become supervisors of other technologists. As they gain more experience and training, they can move into better paying jobs as skilled technicians. Opportunities are best for cardiology technologists who learn how to do more complex procedures.

The employment outlook for cardiology technologists is fair, with job growth expected to be slower than the average through the year 2008. The occupation is small, and there will only be a few openings each year. Most jobs will be in hospitals, but growth is fastest in the offices and clinics of cardiologists. Although EKGs are administered more than ever, registered nurses and other office personnel in hospitals are being trained to perform basic EKG procedures. This is because the newer equipment is more efficient and easier to use. Opportunities will be best for technologists who have training in the more advanced tests such as Holter monitoring and stress testing.

Working Conditions

Cardiology technologists generally work 40 hours a week and sometimes weekends. They may also be on call at night and on weekends. They usually work in clean, pleasant surroundings and are recognized as an important part of the medical team. They work closely with doctors and nurses as well as with patients. An important part of a cardiology technologist's job is putting patients at ease before and during the procedure. A technologist should be calm, confident, and sympathetic.

Earnings and Benefits

Salaries vary with education and experience. Registered cardiology technologists earn an average of $17.44 an hour. Those with more experience and those who are trained to perform more advanced tests can make more. Most employers offer paid vacations, sick leave, pensions, and health insurance.

Where to Go for More Information

American Society of Extra-Corporeal Technology
503 Carlisle Drive, Suite 125
Herndon, VA 20170
(703) 435-8556
www.amsect.org

Association for the Advancement of Medical Instrumentation
3330 Washington Boulevard, Suite 400
Arlington, VA 22201-4598
(800) 332-2264
www.aami.org

National Health Council
1730 M Street, NW, Suite 500
Washington, DC 20036
(202) 785-3910
www.nhcouncil.org

Dental and Medical Secretary

Education and Training

High school plus training

Salary Range

Median—$10.88 an hour

Employment Outlook

Excellent

Definition and Nature of the Work

Dental secretaries and medical secretaries perform clerical and secretarial duties for dentists and physicians, respectively. They take shorthand, type, and file patients' records. To do their job, they must have an understanding of the procedures and terms that physicians and dentists use. Secretaries may also keep track of patients' payments, so they need to be familiar with insurance rules and billing practices.

Secretaries sometimes take a patient's medical history before the physician or dentist sees the patient. Secretaries may also ask what the patient's symptoms are and how long a condition has lasted. If this information is collected

Dental and medical secretaries talk to patients on the phone and arrange appointments for them. They make sure that patients who need immediate care see the dentist or doctor with minimal delay. *(Martha Tabor.)*

in advance, physicians and dentists can devote their time to diagnosing and treating patients.

Medical and dental secretaries also arrange appointments for patients. They make sure that people who need immediate care are able to see the doctor or dentist without much delay. When there are emergencies that make the physician or dentist late, secretaries must tactfully explain the delay to patients who are waiting.

Most secretaries work in the private offices of physicians and dentists. Some work in hospitals and clinics. Secretaries with a knowledge of medical terms are also employed by the medical information and medical emergency departments of large companies. Other dental and medical secretaries work in the research laboratories of drug companies. They may also work for health organizations and government agencies.

Education and Training Requirements

Most medical and dental secretarial positions require a high school education. Candidates need skills in shorthand, typing, filing, and bookkeeping. Some employers hire secretaries and provide on-the-job training in medical or dental language. However, most employers prefer to hire candidates who have secretarial training. Computer and word processing skills have become increasingly important in this field as part of secretarial training. Training courses are given in business and vocational schools and in junior and community colleges. Courses last from a few months to 2 years.

Getting the Job

Check with your school placement office. Physicians, dentists, hospitals, and clinics often advertise jobs in local newspapers or job banks on the Internet. For a government job, apply to take the necessary civil service test.

Advancement Possibilities and Employment Outlook

Advancement is possible with further education and experience. Secretaries may go on to become medical or dental assistants or technicians.

The employment outlook is good through the year 2008. As the health services industries continue to expand, there will be faster than average employment growth for medical secretaries. Also, as the population grows, physicians and dentists will acquire more patients, and they will need secretaries with some medical knowledge. More secretaries will be needed to handle the increase in medical insurance paperwork as well.

Working Conditions

Medical and dental secretaries work in clean and comfortable offices. Much of their time is spent at a desk. They have a great deal of contact with a variety of people both in person and on the telephone. Sometimes their days are hectic. They must be prepared to move quickly from one situation to another. Medical and dental secretaries must be calm and capable of dealing with all kinds of problems. They should also be responsible, organized, and efficient.

Medical and dental secretaries work 35 to 40 hours a week. Because their hours match those of physicians and dentists, many secretaries have some evening and weekend work.

Earnings and Benefits

Salaries vary greatly depending on education, experience, and location. Medical and dental secretaries earn a median income of $10.88 an hour. Benefits may include paid vacations, holidays, health insurance, and sick leave.

Where to Go for More Information

American Association of Medical Assistants
20 North Wacker Drive, Number 1575
Chicago, IL 60606-2903
(312) 899-1500
www.aama-ntl.org

National Health Council
1730 M Street, NW, Suite 500
Washington, DC 20036
(202) 785-3910
www.nhcouncil.org

International Association of Administrative Professionals
10502 Northwest Ambassador Drive
P.O. Box 20404
Kansas City, MO 64195-0404
(816) 891-6600
www.iaap-hq.org

Dental Hygienist

Education and Training
2-year college; license

Salary Range
Median—$22 an hour

Employment Outlook
Excellent

Definition and Nature of the Work

Dental hygienists are licensed professionals who help dentists provide treatment and care of the mouth, teeth, and gums. State laws limit the duties that hygienists may perform. In some states, hygienists can perform some tasks for which dentists have traditionally been responsible. These tasks may include taking dental impressions and administering local anesthetics.

Generally, hygienists keep records of patients' dental histories and take X rays for the dentist's evaluation. Hygienists may also be responsible for informing the dentist of the condition of a patient's mouth so that the dentist can quickly locate problem areas. In most states, hygienists are licensed to remove stains and deposits from the teeth. Cleaning, combined with the application of fluorides to the teeth, helps prevent diseases of the gums and further tooth decay.

Hygienists also teach patients how to prevent dental problems. Patients who do not care for their teeth between visits can undo everything the dentist has accomplished. Therefore, hygienists emphasize the importance of good nutrition, proper brushing, and regular dental checkups.

In small dental offices, hygienists may also act as the office assistant or the laboratory technician. They may schedule appointments and do some laboratory work, such as polishing gold inlays and making models from dental impressions. However, not all dental hygienists work in dental offices. There are also job opportunities in clinics and public health agencies.

Education and Training Requirements

To practice, dental hygienists must be licensed by the state in which they wish to work. To qualify for licensure, hygienists must pass both a written and a clinical

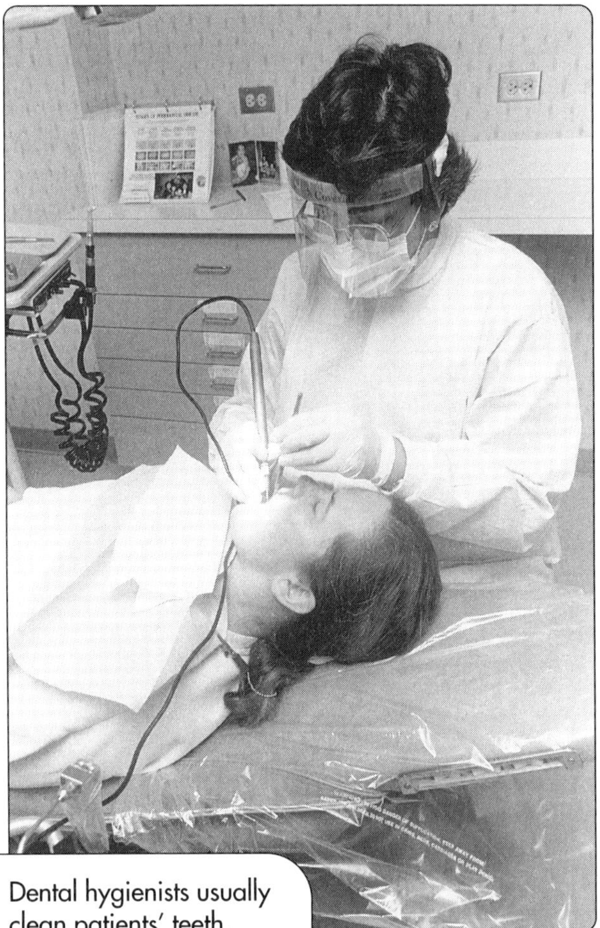

Dental hygienists usually clean patients' teeth, teach patients how to prevent dental problems, and inform the dentist about possible problem areas in patients' mouths. *(Martha Tabor.)*

examination administered by the state. They must also be a graduate of a school of dental hygiene accredited by the Commission on Dental Accreditation. To enter such a school, you must have at least a high school education. To get into some bachelor's degree programs, you must have 2 years of college. Many schools require that you take an aptitude test given by the American Dental Hygienists Association. Two-year associate degree programs qualify you to work in a private office. Four-year bachelor's degree programs qualify you to do research, teach, or work in public or school health programs.

Getting the Job

Your school placement office can help you find a job. Check the want ads in trade and professional journals, as well as in local newspapers or job banks on the Internet. Apply directly to dentists' offices or clinics in which you would like to work. If you want to work for a school or public health program, apply to take the necessary civil service test.

Advancement Possibilities and Employment Outlook

Advancement possibilities are best for dental hygienists who work in public, hospital, or school health programs. Those who have a bachelor's or master's degree may take on supervisory or administrative jobs. Hygienists with a master's degree may teach in dental hygiene schools.

The employment outlook for dental hygienists is excellent. It is projected to be one of the fastest growing occupations through the year 2008. Employment prospects should be favorable as the demand for dental care increases with public awareness of the importance of oral health.

Working Conditions

Most dental hygienists work in dentists' offices. These offices are generally clean, pleasant, and well lighted. Dental hygienists work with a small staff and usually enjoy a close relationship with their fellow workers. Hygienists often attend to a number of different patients in the course of a day. The work is especially varied in schools and in public health positions.

In general, hygienists work between 35 and 40 hours a week. Part-time employment is also common. Hygienists who work in dentists' offices may work some evenings and Saturdays. School hygienists work during school hours.

Earnings and Benefits

Salaries vary depending on education, experience, and geographical location. The median income for dental hygienists is $22 an hour. Benefits generally include paid holidays and vacations. Hygienists who work for government health agencies receive the same benefits that other government workers receive.

Where to Go for More Information

American Dental Association
211 East Chicago Avenue
Chicago, IL 60611-2678
(312) 440-2500
www.ada.org

American Dental Hygienists Association
444 North Michigan Avenue, Suite 3400
Chicago, IL 60611
(312) 440-8900
www.adha.org

National Health Council
1730 M Street, NW, Suite 500
Washington, DC 20036
(202) 785-3910
www.nhcouncil.org

Dental Laboratory Technician

Definition and Nature of the Work

Dental laboratory technicians construct and repair dentures (false teeth), bridges, crowns, and other devices that dentists order for patients. They work from the dentist's written instructions and from plastic or wax impressions of the patient's mouth.

Dental laboratory technicians work with plaster, wax, ceramics, and plastic, as well as with gold and other metals. They use many different kinds of tools and equipment. They use hand tools for carving and shaping. Then they use electric drills, presses, lathes, and high-heat furnaces for completing each dental piece.

Some dental laboratory technicians specialize. They may work chiefly on crowns and bridges or with ceramics. Generally these specialists work in large laboratories. Workers in smaller laboratories or in dentists' offices usually perform all stages of the dental work.

Education and Training
High school plus training

Salary Range
Median—$10.88 an hour

Employment Outlook
Excellent

Education and Training Requirements

You usually need a high school diploma to become a dental laboratory technician. High school courses in art, ceramics, metalwork, and chemistry are helpful. Many technicians are trained on the job or in apprenticeship programs. Dental laboratory trainees work under the supervision of experienced technicians. They start by doing simple jobs, such as mixing plaster and pouring it into molds. Apprentices also receive classroom training. The training period generally lasts 3 or 4 years.

Dental lab technicians use hand tools to carve and shape dentures, bridges, crowns, and other dental devices. *(Martha Tabor.)*

An increasing number of technicians are entering formal training programs after high school. These programs usually last 2 years and are followed by about 3 years of practical experience. Technicians can become certified dental technicians by passing tests given by the National Board for Certification.

Dental laboratory technicians should have good vision and color sense. They also need manual dexterity for handling the tiny pieces of material they use in their work. Because the work demands precision, technicians should have patience and should enjoy detailed work.

Getting the Job

You can apply directly to dentists' offices and laboratories for jobs and training. If you attend school, ask your placement office for help in finding a job. Private and state employment agencies sometimes list openings for dental laboratory technicians. You should also check the newspaper want ads and job banks on the Internet.

Advancement Possibilities and Employment Outlook

Dental laboratory technicians can advance as they gain experience. They can become experts in a specialized kind of laboratory work. In large laboratories, some technicians become managers or supervisors. Some technicians start their own laboratories. To do this, they need capital or financing to buy equipment. They also need knowledge about running a business.

Employment opportunities are expected to be excellent through the year 2008.

Working Conditions

Dental laboratories are found mostly in large cities and heavily populated states. Most are very small, but a few employ more than 200 technicians. Technicians usually work 40 hours a week. Those who are self-employed may work longer hours.

Technicians generally work independently. Since each job in a laboratory is different, the work is diverse and interesting. It is not strenuous work, but it does require close attention to detail. Dental laboratories are generally pleasant places in which to work, although there is sometimes pressure when deadlines must be met.

Earnings and Benefits

Salaries vary depending on technicians' experience and area of specialization. Trainees in dental laboratories average only slightly above the minimum wage. However, earnings in this field increase greatly with experience. The median salary for dental technicians is $10.88 an hour. Self-employed technicians can earn more.

Benefits usually include paid holidays and vacations, as well as health insurance and pension plans. Self-employed dental laboratory technicians must provide their own benefits.

Where to Go for More Information

American Dental Association
211 East Chicago Avenue
Chicago, IL 60611-2678
(312) 440-2500
www.ada.org

National Association of Dental Laboratories
8201 Greensboro Drive, Suite 300
McLean, VA 22102-3810
(800) 950-1150
www.adal.org

National Dental Association
3517 Sixteenth Street, NW
Washington, DC 20010
(202) 588-1697
www.ada.org

Electroneurodiagnostic Technologist

Education and Training
High school plus training

Salary Range
Median—$32,070

Employment Outlook
Fair

Definition and Nature of the Work

Electroneurodiagnostic (END) technology enables health care professionals to record and study the electrical activity of the brain and nervous system. END technologists use a variety of techniques and instruments to record electrical activity arising from a patient's brain, spinal cord, peripheral nerves, and other parts of the nervous system. END technologists work with specially trained physicians who interpret the data and determine treatment based on the information. Data gathered with END technology are used for medical research and to diagnose health problems such as brain tumors, strokes, toxic/metabolic disorders, epilepsy, sleep disorders, and organic impairment such as Alzheimer's disease.

END technologists maintain END equipment, obtain medical histories, prepare patients for procedures, record patients' electric potentials, and calculate results. A major part of the job is interacting with patients undergoing END procedures.

END technologists apply electrodes to a patient's head, and must choose the most appropriate combination of instrument controls and electrodes to receive accurate data. Many END technologists work in operating rooms; they must also understand the effects of anesthesia on a patient's responses.

END technologists may perform a variety of common procedures in the course of their work. The electroencephalogram (EEG) is a recording of the ongoing activity in the brain. It is the most well-known END procedure, and many END departments still carry the title "EEG Lab."

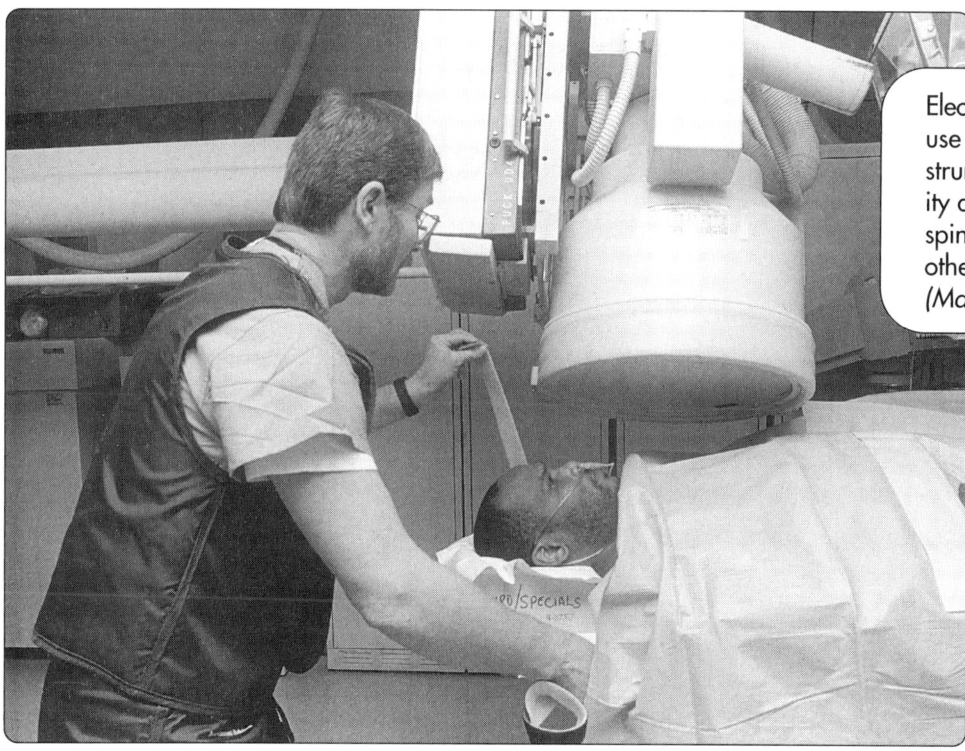

Electroneurodiagnostic technologists use a variety of techniques and instruments to record electrical activity arising from a patient's brain, spinal cord, peripheral nerves, and other parts of the nervous system. *(Martha Tabor.)*

Another common END procedure is the evoked potential (EP) test, which records electrical activity from the nervous system occurring in direct response to an outside stimulus. END technologists evaluate sleep disorders with the polysomnogram (PSG) test; they evaluate electric potentials from the eyes through a procedure called the electronystagmogram (ENG) and from the peripheral nerves through nerve conduction studies (NCS).

Senior END technologists may have supervisory duties in addition to their regular jobs. They may manage an END lab, keep records, set work schedules, train other END technologists, and schedule patients' appointments. END technologists must have above-average intelligence, inquiring minds, the desire to learn, manual dexterity, and a sympathetic personality.

Education and Training Requirements

Generally, END technologists have a high school diploma and many have postsecondary training in the field. Many current END technologists learned their skills while on the job, but the trend is toward hiring candidates with some formal training. High school students interested in the field should study biology, anatomy, mathematics, and English.

Many 2-year colleges offer training in END technology, as do some hospitals and vocational schools. Courses provide instruction in human anatomy and physiology, neurology, neuroanatomy, neurophysiology, medical terminology, computer technology, and electronics and instrumentation. Interested students should seek out programs accredited by the Commission on Accreditation of Allied Health Education Programs. Another professional group, the American Board of Registration of Electroencephalographic and Evoked Potential Technologists, awards the credentials "registered EEG technologist" and "registered evoked response technologist" to qualified applicants.

Getting the Job

Local hospitals are the best source of information for training and employment opportunities. High school students interested in pursuing a career in END technology should work as volunteers at their local hospitals to become familiar with hospital procedures.

Advancement Possibilities and Employment Outlook

There are a relatively small number of END technologists employed—recent statistics from the Bureau of Labor Statistics place the number at about 5,400 technologists. Employment of END technologists is expected to grow slower than the average through the year 2008. New technologies and cross-trained employees will limit employment growth.

An experienced END technologist can work toward a position managing a hospital or clinic's END department as chief technologist. Typically, a chief technologist reports directly to a neurologist, neurosurgeon, electroencephalographer, or some other physician.

Working Conditions

END technologists work in hospitals, neurology clinics, health maintenance organizations, and psychiatric facilities. Their surroundings are clean and well lighted. Some technologists work in specific designated rooms, whereas others move equipment to perform tests in patients' rooms. Technologists work standard 40-hour workweeks and spend about half of their time on their feet. Technologists working in a hospital may be on call during evenings, weekends, and holidays.

Since END technologists often work with critically ill patients, they need great tact and emotional strength. The job also may require physical strength in helping to move patients who are unable to move on their own.

Earnings and Benefits

Salaries vary according to an END technologist's education and experience. The median income for END technologists is $32,070 a year.

Where to Go for More Information

American Board of Registration of Electroencephalographic and Evoked Potential Technologists
P.O. Box 916633
Longwood, FL 32791
(407) 788-6308

American Medical Electroencephalographic Association
P.O. Box 757
Pewaukee, WI 53072-0757
(414) 784-3435

American Society of Electroneurodiagnostic Technologists
204 West Seventh Street
Carroll, IA 51401-2317
(712) 792-2978
www.aset.org

Emergency Medical Technician

Education and Training
High school plus training

Salary Range
Median—$20,290

Employment Outlook
Very good

Definition and Nature of the Work

Emergency medical technicians (EMTs) offer immediate aid to victims of accidents or critical illnesses. They may provide their services at the scene of the crisis, en route to the hospital, or in the emergency room. Usually an EMT's first contact with a victim is at the scene of the crisis. EMTs work on-call and are dispatched to an emergency site when needed. Since they are frequently the victim's first source of medical assistance, emergency medical technicians must be able to quickly yet accurately determine the nature and extent of the problem and decide how it should be treated. In many cases, they must treat the victim instantly if his or her life is to be saved. After giving the appropriate emergency care at the site, EMTs usually transport victims to proper medical facilities. They report their observations and care given, and often stay on hand to provide any additional assistance.

The duties and capabilities of an emergency medical technician depend on the training acquired. However, all EMTs are qualified to give cardiopulmonary resuscitation (CPR) to a person suffering cardiac arrest, control the bleeding of an accident victim, and administer oxygen to someone who has stopped breathing. Emergency medical technicians are also trained to deliver babies, subdue people who are displaying violent behavior, treat allergic reactions, apply splints and antishock suits, and treat wounds.

There are four levels of registration for technicians. *Emergency medical technicians-nonambulance* are qualified to give basic emergency care in settings other than ambulances, such as hospitals, nursing homes, and medical facilities. Many are nurses, nurse's aides, or hospital orderlies. *Emergency medical technicians-ambulance* perform basic emergency care and rescue work and operate and maintain ambulances. *Emergency medical technicians-intermediate* have

Emergency medical technicians must arrive quickly at the scene of a crisis, diagnose the problem, and decide how it should be treated. Some EMTs in major cities ride bicycles to avoid delays caused by traffic. *(Martha Tabor.)*

taken additional training courses that enable them to provide more advanced forms of treatment, such as trauma assessment and airway management. *Emergency medical technicians-paramedic* are the most highly trained. They generally work on mobile intensive care units and are in voice contact with a physician. They are authorized to give medication and intravenous fluids under a doctor's guidance. Paramedics are also qualified to use defibrillators on heart attack victims to restore a regular heartbeat. Emergency medical technicians work for fire and police departments, hospitals, and private and public ambulance services.

Education and Training Requirements

Completion of a standard training program is mandatory for each level of registration. To enter the basic emergency care program, you must be at least 18 years old, with a high school diploma and a driver's license. For the paramedic course, you need to be 21 years old. Each state has its own program requirements, but most require nonambulance and ambulance technicians to complete approximately 110 hours of classroom training in basic emergency care. Some practical training in an ambulance or emergency room is also required. For instance, ambulance technicians must complete 6 months of ambulance rescue service. Both intermediate and paramedic candidates must have an ambulance technician's training plus 6 months of field experience before they can enter their respective courses. EMT intermediate training typically includes 35 to 55 hours of additional instruction beyond basic emergency care. Paramedic training and testing, which involves 750 to 2,000 hours of instruction, may take more than a year to complete.

Hospitals, police and fire departments, colleges, universities, and medical schools offer EMT courses. Certification involves both written and practical tests. Technicians at all levels must be recertified every 2 years. Refresher courses for EMTs are available at all levels.

Getting the Job

Volunteer technicians are always needed, and this is an excellent way to find out if you are suited to the work. To volunteer, you must take the training courses and pass the tests. For a job, check with your local police or fire department, or apply directly to the first aid squad in your area. You can also apply to hospitals and private ambulance services.

Advancement Possibilities and Employment Outlook

Competent technicians can advance fairly quickly to the paramedic level if they are willing to meet training requirements mandated by their states. The employment outlook is very good through the year 2008. As the population ages, the need for more emergency medical services should increase. Opportunities for paramedics will be best in communities that are just setting up advanced rescue teams. Although job stress and turnover will produce many openings, keen competition is expected for those jobs.

Working Conditions

The work is demanding and unpredictable, requiring physical stamina, manual dexterity, emotional stability, compassion, good judgment, and the ability to react quickly under stressful conditions. Some EMTs work on rotating shifts, working a 24-hour shift for 1 day and then having 2 days off. Others work a single shift each day, totaling anywhere from 40 to more than 55 hours a week. Night and weekend work is often required, and many EMTs are on call for emergencies.

Earnings and Benefits

The median salary for EMTs is $20,290 a year. Those with more experience can earn up to $34,480 a year.

Benefits for EMTs employed by city or local governments include paid vacations and holidays, pension plans, and health insurance. Benefits for EMTs working for private companies vary and may not include pension plans.

Where to Go for More Information

National Association of Emergency Medical Technicians
408 Monroe Street
Clinton, MS 39056
(800) 346-2368

Environmental Health Specialist

Education and Training
Varies—see profile

Salary Range
Average—$37,000

Employment Outlook
Good

Definition and Nature of the Work

Environmental health specialists monitor health and safety conditions in residential, industrial, commercial, and recreational settings. A person who works as an environmental health specialist may also be called an *environmental health* or *safety inspector,* or a *health and safety specialist.* The main responsibilities of the position are to determine the existence of possible health hazards and to take steps to correct them.

Most environmental safety specialists work for government agencies that monitor local, state, and federal safety and environmental regulations. This includes checking plants and factories for pollution or industrial waste; inspecting restaurants for cleanliness; and inspecting schools, day care centers, and nursing homes for harmful substances such as radon or lead paint. Environmental safety specialists also monitor how hospitals handle biological waste and ensure that swimming pools and other recreational facilities are safe for public use. Government-employed environmental safety specialists issue permits and certificates stating that a particular residence, place of business, or recreational facility has met minimum acceptable health and safety standards.

As part of the inspection process, environmental health specialists may collect samples of soil, air, water, and possible pollutants from the places they inspect. They then test the samples to determine whether there are dangerous levels of any hazardous substances. If possible health problems are discovered, the specialists draw up a plan to monitor the facility to determine the source and nature of the hazard. This may involve setting up equipment at the inspection site to monitor air or water quality, and checking the records periodically to ensure that health and quality standards are met. The environmental health specialist then evaluates the success of any steps taken to resolve the problem, and finds alternative solutions if necessary.

Environmental health specialists who work for private companies are responsible for keeping the firm's facilities up to government standards. They need to make sure that government inspectors who monitor the company find no problems or violations. Because the job is preventative in nature, the environmental health specialist must be aware of all the areas in which health or safety problems are likely to arise and develop plans to help employees reduce the possibility of violations. For this reason, they must be familiar with current government and industry regulations.

Education and Training Requirements

Most positions for environmental health specialists require at least an associate's degree in science, but many call for a bachelor's degree. Significant course work in chemistry, biology, public health, physical sciences, or a related field is highly desirable. Those who want to work for the government have to complete a certification course administered by the appropriate local, state, or federal agency. Most states have licensing boards that examine potential candidates and grant certification to qualified applicants. The type of training and certification needed depends on the types of facilities being inspected. It is possible to receive specialist certification for dealing with certain types of hazardous materials.

Getting the Job

Private companies post openings for environmental health specialists in newspaper classified sections and on Internet job search sites. Government agencies may also have job listings at local government offices.

Advancement Possibilities and Employment Outlook

Environmental health specialists who work for government agencies typically advance along a specified career ladder in which they receive salary increases according to a set schedule. When the top salary level is reached, further advancement leads to supervisory positions. There is a good deal of competition for these positions, which are based on the needs of the agency as well as the qualifications of the candidate.

Increasing concern for environmental health and safety is balanced by public concern for reductions in the size and regulatory power of the government. For this reason, the employment outlook for government-employed environmental safety inspectors is about average. Most job openings in government work will come as a result of retirement of existing employees or their transfer to other fields of work. The demand for environmental health specialists in private industry should grow as more companies turn toward self-enforcement of regulations to avoid government sanctions.

Working Conditions

Environmental health specialists work in a very wide range of settings. The inspection work may take place in modern homes and offices, industrial plants, private businesses, and even parks and wildlife refuges. Analysis of materials collected during inspections occurs in a laboratory setting. The job may entail exposure to potentially dangerous materials including industrial pollution, medical and nuclear waste, airborne and waterborne germs or other contaminants, and substances such as lead and asbestos.

Earnings and Benefits

Inspectors working for the federal government begin at salaries between $25,000 and $31,000. The average annual salary of environmental health specialists as a group is $37,000. The highest 10 percent earn more than $72,000 a year, based on experience. Both government positions and jobs in private industry offer paid vacation, medical, and retirement benefits.

Where to Go for More Information

Institute of Environmental Sciences and Technology
940 East Northwest Highway
Mount Prospect, IL 60056
(847)255-1561

Hospice Worker

Education and Training
Varies—see profile

Salary Range
Varies—see profile

Employment Outlook
Varies—see profile

Definition and Nature of the Work

Hospice workers specialize in caring for people who are terminally ill and in helping their families adjust to the loss of a loved one. Most hospice programs offer patients both at-home assistance and residential facilities. Patients remain in their own homes whenever possible. The aim of a hospice program is to make the final weeks or months comfortable for a patient. For many patients, this entails medication to control pain, visits with family and friends, counseling, and assistance with practical matters, such as housekeeping and shopping.

Hospice workers include nurses, doctors, counselors, social workers, clergy members, homemakers, and health aides. These professionals work as a team to ensure that the physical, emotional, and practical needs of each patient are met and that the family receives comfort and support.

Education and Training Requirements

In addition to the training and education required for the discipline you choose, hospice work necessitates specialized instruction in caring for terminally ill patients. Even if you want to work as a volunteer, you generally must participate in training sessions offered by the hospice to become acquainted with the hospice philosophy, the methods of caring for a terminally ill patient, and the emotional effects of the illness on both the patient and the family.

Getting the Job

Volunteer work is an excellent way to break into the field because hospices need people who will donate their time to care for patients either in their homes or at an inpatient facility. This will provide you with training and practical experience.

Hospice workers take care of the needs of terminally ill patients. *(The Terry Wild Studio.)*

Advancement Possibilities and Employment Outlook

Volunteer workers can be promoted to paying positions as health aides, but advancement to professional positions will generally depend on level of education. Those who have a degree in social work, nursing, psychology, or medicine should have the best advancement opportunities. They can become directors or coordinators of hospice programs.

The employment picture is uncertain because hospice care remains somewhat controversial due to its emphasis on preparing for death rather than sustaining life. However, the hospice movement is gaining momentum and is seen by many as a humane and cost-effective way of caring for terminally ill patients. An increasing number of hospice programs are covered by Medicare or Medicaid. The future of hospices will depend on the amount of federal support they receive.

Working Conditions

Hospices are staffed 24 hours a day. Many employees work nights or weekends, remaining on call to patients who are home. The work is emotionally demanding and often very diverse. It requires patience, sensitivity, good judgment, and excellent communication and listening skills.

Where to Go for More Information

National Hospice and Palliative Care Organization
1700 Diagonal Road, Suite 300
Alexandria, VA 22314-2848
(800) 658-8898
www.nhpco.org

Earnings and Benefits

Many hospice workers are volunteers and do not receive a salary. Paid hospice workers earn salaries similar to those of their counterparts in regular hospitals. Doctors may earn $100,000 a year or more. Nurses earn a median salary of $40,000 a year, whereas orderlies earn from $13,800 to $17,900 a year. Benefits for hospice employees usually include paid holidays and vacations, health insurance, and pension plans.

Inhalation Therapist

Education and Training
2-year or 4-year college

Salary Range
Average—$17.14 an hour

Employment Outlook
Excellent

Definition and Nature of the Work

Inhalation therapists treat patients who have difficulty breathing. They work with all types of patients, from premature infants to stroke victims to elderly patients with lung disease. They operate such equipment as respirators, ventilators, and oxygen tents. Inhalation therapists are also called respiratory therapists. Most inhalation therapists work in hospitals under the supervision of physicians, but a growing number are contracted outside of hospitals in home health agencies and nursing homes.

Inhalation therapists often work in emergency situations resulting from injury or illness. They also work in ongoing treatment programs for patients with breathing disorders, such as emphysema.

Inhalation therapists operate machines that provide oxygen. Some kinds of equipment provide medicine in the form of a mist or gas. Usually physicians give inhalation therapists prescriptions stating the medicine and dosage to be given to the patient. It is generally up to the therapist to decide what equipment should be used. Inhalation therapists must be aware of the dangers and hazards involved in each kind of treatment. They observe patients during treatment and report any adverse reactions to the doctor.

In most hospitals, inhalation therapists are responsible for having faulty equipment repaired. They may make small repairs themselves. Inhalation therapists are often called on to explain the equipment to nurses. Therapists must also know how to work in a sterile environment.

Education and Training Requirements

Training programs vary in length from 21 months to 4 years. Technical schools and community and junior colleges offer 2-year programs leading to an associate degree. Four-year colleges offer bachelor's degrees. Hospitals, medical schools,

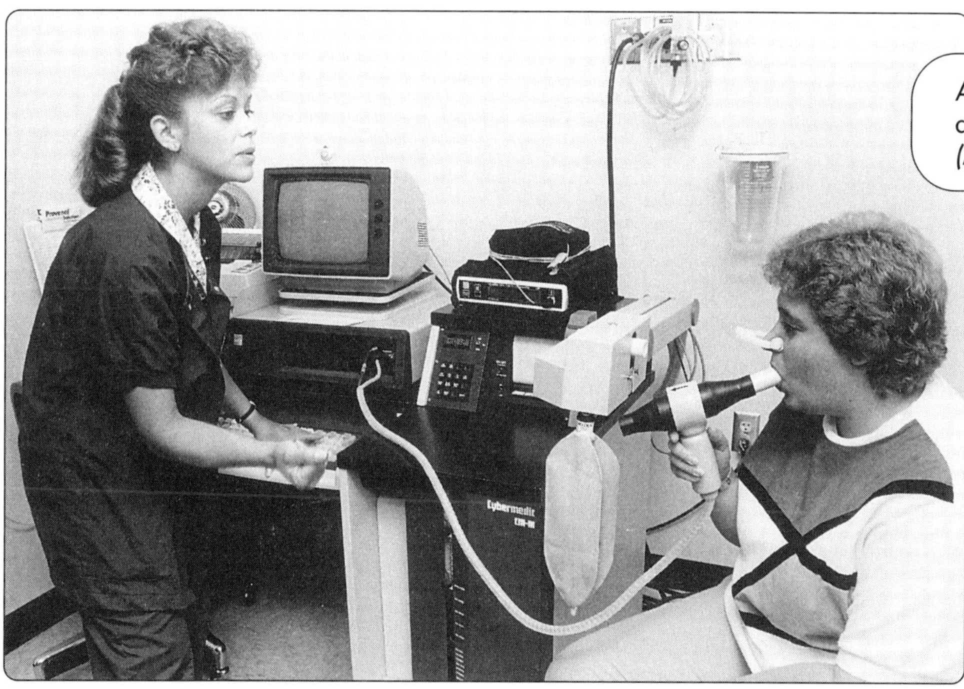

An inhalation therapist conducts a lung function test on a patient. *(Martha Tabor.)*

and the armed forces also offer training. To get into a program, you must be a high school graduate with a background in mathematics and science. A good background in English is also helpful because inhalation therapists must keep very detailed records of the treatment they administer.

The National Board for Respiratory Therapy certifies and registers inhalation therapists. To become a certified respiratory therapy technician (CRTT), you must graduate from a program approved by the Committee on Allied Health Education and Accreditation of the American Medical Association. Most employers require therapists to hold the CRTT or at least be eligible to take the certification exam. You must also have 1 year of work experience and pass a written test. To become a registered respiratory therapist (RRT), you must graduate from an approved program, have 62 semester hours of college credit and 1 year of experience, and pass both a written and a practical test. An increasing number of therapists receive on-the-job training to administer electrocardiograms and stress tests.

Getting the Job

Your school placement office may be able to help you find a job. If you receive your training in a hospital, it is likely you will be hired by that hospital. Trade and professional journals often carry listings for inhalation therapists. You can also check newspaper want ads and job banks on the Internet.

Advancement Possibilities and Employment Outlook

Inhalation therapists may advance to supervisory positions. Those who have advanced degrees may get teaching positions. Advancement depends on training, personal qualifications, and performance.

The outlook for inhalation therapists is excellent through the year 2008, with employment expected to increase much faster than the average. The projected growth of the middle-aged and elderly populations is expected to increase the risk of heart disease, and more inhalation therapists will be needed to provide services for these individuals. Also, as respiratory therapists are required to perform a greater variety of duties, this could mean more jobs for inhalation therapists than currently expected. Opportunities will be best for inhalation therapists who work with newborns or infants.

Working Conditions

Inhalation therapists do most of their work in hospitals. In emergencies they may work in ambulances. However, because most therapy work can be scheduled in advance, inhalation therapists have fairly regular hours.

Therapists generally work 40 hours a week. They may be expected to work some evenings and weekends. Many therapists work part-time.

Earnings and Benefits

Salaries vary with education and place of employment. The average income for experienced therapists is $17.14 an hour. Benefits include paid holidays and vacations, health insurance, and pension plans.

Where to Go for More Information

American Association for Respiratory Care
11030 Ables Lane
Dallas, TX 75229
(972) 243-2272
www.aarc.org

American Lung Association
1740 Broadway, 14th Floor
New York, NY 10019-4374
(212) 315-8700
www.lungusa.org

Licensed Practical Nurse

Education and Training
High school plus training; license

Salary Range
Median—$26,940

Employment Outlook
Good

Definition and Nature of the Work

Licensed practical nurses (LPNs) help physicians and registered nurses (RNs) care for patients. They have the technical knowledge to perform routine nursing duties, but they may also make appointments, maintain patient records, and perform basic clerical duties. Their work allows doctors and registered nurses to devote their time to patient care that requires specialized knowledge. Most licensed practical nurses work in hospitals, nursing homes, other health care institutions, and private homes. Some are employed in doctors' offices, clinics, and public health agencies. Still others work in large businesses. They care for workers who have accidents or become ill on the job. Licensed practical nurses are also called licensed vocational nurses.

Licensed practical nurses have a great deal of contact with their patients. It is important that nurses keep patients in good spirits. They also take patients' blood pressures, check temperatures, and apply bandages. In some cases, practical nurses may give their patients drugs that doctors have prescribed. Licensed practical nurses watch for changes in their patients' condition. If there is a change, they report it to the doctors immediately.

Licensed practical nurses sometimes work in special units of a hospital. These include cardiac, burn, and maternity units. LPNs may be trained to use special equipment and may direct nurse's aides.

On occasion, patients who are recovering from an illness hire licensed practical nurses to work in their homes. The nurses provide basic bedside care as well as follow the specific instructions of a patient's doctor. For example, they may give drugs on schedule or change bandages. In addition, they may take over some homemaking chores.

Education and Training Requirements

Many schools that train licensed practical nurses prefer to admit high school graduates. Admission requirements usually include passing an aptitude test and taking a physical exam.

Training programs currently take 1 year to complete and include both classroom study and supervised patient care. Junior and community colleges, technical and vocational schools, and hospitals offer these programs. The armed services also offer state-approved courses. However, there is a move to two levels of nursing. Technical nurses, such as LPNs, will be required to have an associate degree. Professional nurses, such as RNs, will be required to have a bachelor's degree. Those interested in careers in nursing should check current state regulations. All LPNs must be licensed. To qualify for a license, you must complete a state-approved course and pass a written test.

Getting the Job

Your school placement office may be able to help you find a job. You can apply directly to hospitals, clinics, and other institutions in which you would like to work. Check with private employment agencies that specialize in medical job placements. Newspaper want ads and job banks on the Internet often carry listings for licensed practical nurses.

To get a job in home health care, contact local hospitals and clinics. They usually maintain lists of practical nurses. When a patient needs private care, hospitals suggest someone from their lists.

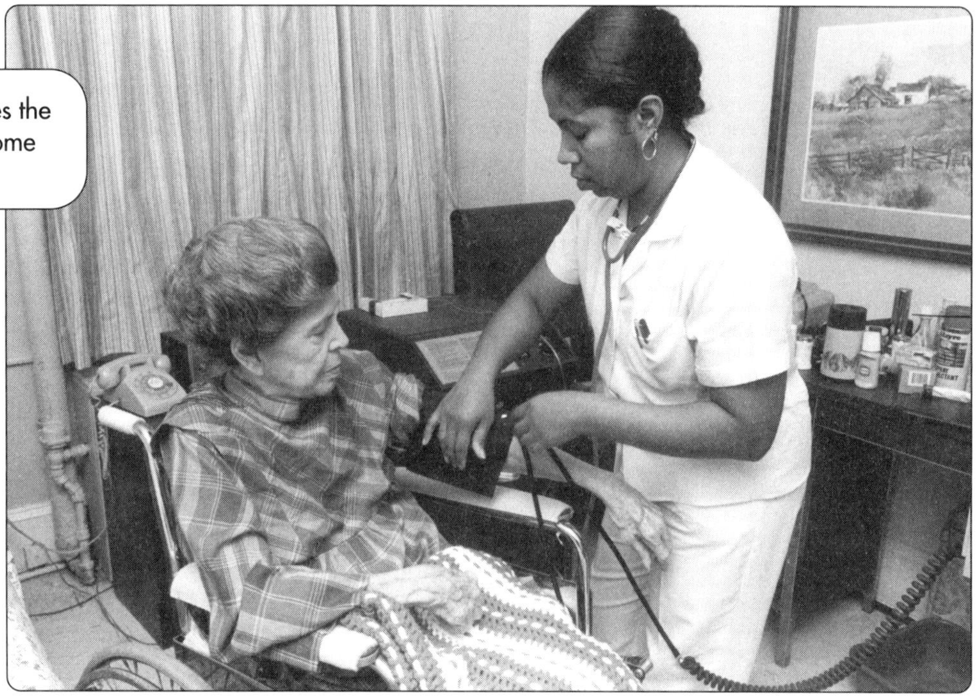

A licensed practical nurse takes the blood pressure of a nursing home resident. *(Martha Tabor.)*

Advancement Possibilities and Employment Outlook

Licensed practical nurses can take extra courses to specialize in one field, such as the care of newborn infants. With further training, they may become registered nurses. However, this training may be extensive.

The outlook for licensed practical nurses is good, with employment expected to increase as fast as the average through the year 2008. These jobs will be concentrated in clinics, rehabilitation hospitals, and long-term care facilities. There will also be increasing demand for skilled LPNs to work in home health care.

Working Conditions

Licensed practical nurses can usually choose where they work, from hospitals to private homes. LPNs must keep an even temper, especially when caring for difficult and unhappy patients. They must stand for long periods and often have to help patients move in bed, stand, walk, or dress. Licensed practical nurses always work under the direction of registered nurses or doctors.

Practical nurses work 40 hours a week. Sometimes they work at night and on weekends. They generally earn premium pay for these shifts. Jobs in private homes often involve longer hours. Each case places different demands on the practical nurse's time.

Earnings and Benefits

Salaries vary with experience and place of employment. Most full-time licensed practical nurses earn an average salary of $26,940 a year. In most hospitals, salary increases are given at regular intervals. Benefits include paid holidays and vacations, health insurance, and pension plans.

Where to Go for More Information

National Association for Practical Nurse Education and Service
1400 Spring Street, Suite 330
Silver Spring, MD 20910
(301) 588-2491

National Federation of Licensed Practical Nurses
893 U.S. Highway 70 West, Suite 202
Garner, NC 27592-4547
(800) 948-2511
www.nflpn.org

National League for Nursing
61 Broadway
New York, NY 10014
(800) 669-9656
www.nln.org

Medical Assistant

Education and Training
High school plus training

Salary Range
Median—$20,680

Employment Outlook
Excellent

Definition and Nature of the Work

Medical assistants aid physicians by performing administrative duties and handling basic clinical tasks. They work in doctors' offices, hospitals, and medical clinics, helping to keep operations running smoothly and efficiently. The job description of a medical assistant varies from office to office. Some assistants do patient and laboratory work exclusively. Others are responsible for medical records, bookkeeping, and answering phones. In most small offices, medical assistants may handle all these tasks.

Most medical assistants work in private offices. They help doctors examine and treat patients. They check the height, weight, temperature, and blood pressure of each patient. Assistants write down patients' medical histories and run simple laboratory tests. Sometimes they answer patients' questions about medicines and treatment at home. Assistants may also give injections, apply bandages, and take X rays. Many assistants take electrocardiograms, which measure the electrical impulses of the heart.

Medical assistants are sometimes in charge of buying and maintaining medical equipment and furniture for the doctor's office. They may also act as office managers. They plan the doctor's schedule, greet patients, file records and correspondence, and type letters and bills. Assistants keep medical records up to date and handle tax and insurance forms. At the doctor's request, they arrange for laboratory tests or for a patient's admission to the hospital. In a large group practice or in a hospital clinic, the duties of the medical assistant may be divided among several assistants.

Education and Training Requirements

A high school diploma is required to enter this field. Although medical assistants can be trained on the job, most employers prefer to hire graduates of formal training programs. Vocational schools offer 1-year programs resulting in a certificate or diploma. Community colleges offer 2-year programs leading to an

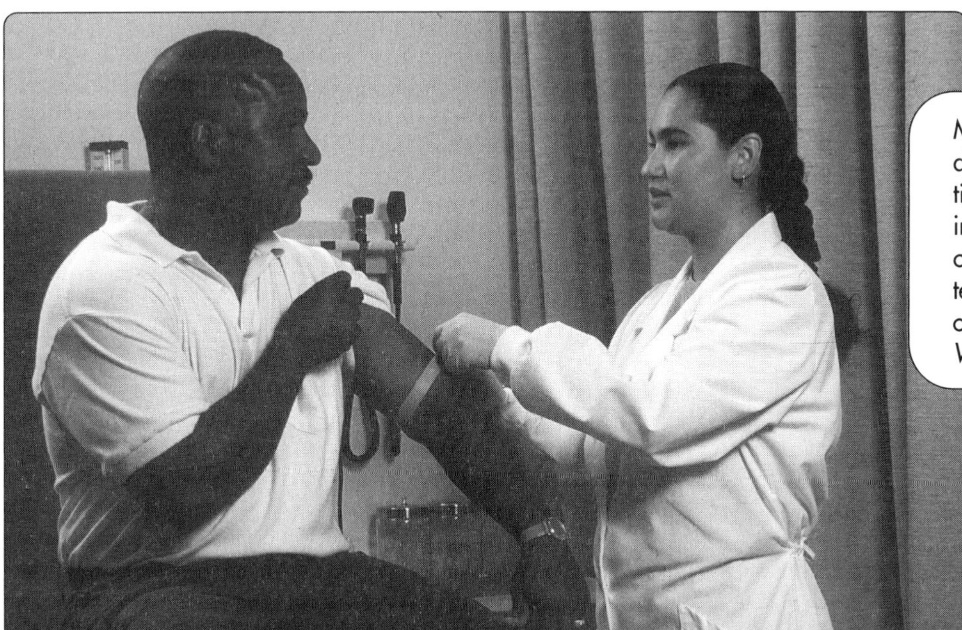

Most medical assistants help doctors examine and treat patients. Their duties include drawing blood, giving injections, and checking the height, weight, temperature, and blood pressure of each patient. *(The Terry Wild Studio.)*

associate degree. Students study anatomy, physiology, ethics, and medical terminology. They learn laboratory techniques, clinical procedures, and first aid. They are also given practical training in typing, accounting, and insurance processing. More than 350 programs have been approved by the Commission on Accreditation of Allied Health Education Programs (CAAHEP).

A medical assistant can become certified or registered by various associations such as the American Association of Medical Assistants or the American Medical Technologists. This involves meeting certain training and experience requirements, as well as passing a national test. Certification and registration are not necessary for employment, but they give you professional standing.

Getting the Job

Your high school placement office may be able to help you find a job. State employment offices and private employment agencies that specialize in medical job placements often list openings. In many communities, a local medical assisting association handles job openings throughout the country. Often, the local medical society serves as a clearinghouse for employment possibilities in doctors' offices. The want ads in newspapers and professional journals also list job opportunities.

Advancement Possibilities and Employment Outlook

Advancement can come with experience and further training. Additional skills, such as shorthand and the ability to use a transcribing machine, are often useful. These skills make jobs in laboratories, pharmaceutical houses, public health departments, and private industry possible. Medical assistants who show leadership qualities can become supervisors.

The employment outlook for medical assistants is excellent. Medical assisting is projected to grow much faster than average through the year 2008. The best job prospects are for medical assistants with formal training, experience, or both. Medical assistants with word processing and computer skills will also have an advantage. The growing needs of an aging population combined with an increase in the number of doctors contribute to a greater demand for medical assistants. Also, more diagnostic testing and a heavier, more complex volume of paperwork will cause employment growth. Many doctors need at least one assistant, and large group practices, clinics, and hospitals need many. As the total number of jobs for medical assistants continues to grow, the high turnover rate in the occupation will also create many openings each year.

Working Conditions

Doctors' offices, hospitals, and clinics are busy and challenging places in which to work. Medical assistants come into contact with all kinds of people. The duties are generally varied. Medical assistants typically work 40 hours a week. Those who work in private offices may work some evenings and Saturdays.

Earnings and Benefits

Earnings depend on training, experience, size of practice, and geographic location. Medical assistants who have an associate degree generally earn more than those who have little or no training. The median income for medical assistants is $20,680 a year. Wages are typically higher in the Northeast and the West. Benefits usually include paid holidays and vacations. Medical assistants who work for clinics, hospitals, and group practices also receive health insurance and pension plans.

Where to Go for More Information

American Association of Medical Assistants
20 North Wacker Drive, Number 1575
Chicago, IL 60606-2903
(312) 899-1500
www.aama-ntl.org

American Medical Technologists
710 Higgins Road
Park Ridge, IL 60068
(800) 275-1268
www.amt1.com

Medical Laboratory Worker

Definition and Nature of the Work

Medical laboratory workers conduct laboratory tests that aid in the detection, diagnosis, and treatment of disease. Medical laboratory workers include medical laboratory assistants, medical laboratory technicians, histologic technicians, and cytotechnologists. Medical laboratory workers are supervised by medical laboratory technologists and physicians, such as pathologists. Most medical laboratory workers work in hospitals. Some work in research institutes and clinics. Others are employed in commercial medical laboratories that run tests for doctors and hospitals on a fee basis.

Medical laboratory assistants perform routine tasks in the laboratory. For example, they collect examples of blood and urine, label them, and conduct simple tests on them. They sterilize instruments; prepare, stain, and label slides; and keep records of tests. *Medical laboratory technicians* perform tasks that require more technical knowledge than assistants have. Technicians must have 2 years of training after high school, whereas assistants generally need only 1 year. Medical laboratory technicians perform tests involved in blood banking. For example, they may help to determine a donor's blood type. They also do analyses of blood and urine and perform tests that require a knowledge of microbiology and chemistry.

Histologic technicians prepare slides of body tissue for examination by medical technologists and pathologists. They freeze tissue so that it can be cut into paper-thin slices. They also stain the slides so that the tissue can be seen clearly under a microscope.

Cytotechnologists look for signs of cancer in body cells. Unusual cell formation may be a sign of disease. Cytotechnologists look at slides of body tissue through a microscope. They usually work under the supervision of a pathologist.

Education and Training
High school plus training

Salary Range
Average—$13.38 an hour

Employment Outlook
Good

Education and Training Requirements

You must have a high school diploma or its equivalent to be a medical laboratory worker. High school courses in science and math offer good preparation. You generally need specialized training after high school. Certification is not required to work. However, it can be an advantage in finding a job or advancing in the field. Manual dexterity and normal color vision are generally required.

In the past, most medical laboratory assistants were trained on the job. However, formal training is now becoming important for new workers. You can attend a 12-month training program in a hospital, vocational school, or community college. The Committee on Allied Health Education and Accreditation has certified training programs for medical laboratory assistants. The programs include classroom instruction as well as practical experience. Courses for medical laboratory assistants include bacteriology, hematology, urinalysis, blood banking, and serology.

The best way to acquire training as a medical laboratory technician is to take a 2-year accredited training program offered in community and junior colleges, 4-year colleges, and universities. The Committee on Allied Health Education and Accreditation has accredited more than 100 of these programs. Several organizations also offer certification for technicians.

In some states, technicians must be licensed to work. The requirements vary, but usually include a written examination. Accredited training programs are also available for histologic technicians and for cytotechnologists.

It is very important that medical laboratory workers carefully research training programs before choosing one. Selecting the right program can help during job hunting because certain areas of medicine have different training requirements.

Getting the Job

Your school placement office can help you find a job. You can also apply directly to hospitals, clinics, laboratories, and research institutions for which you would like to work. Check newspaper want ads, job banks on the Internet, and professional journals as well.

Advancement Possibilities and Employment Outlook

Additional training is usually required to advance. Medical laboratory assistants may become technicians. Technicians may study to become technologists. A master's degree is generally required for teaching and research positions.

The outlook for medical laboratory workers is good through the year 2008, with employment expected to increase as fast as the average. As the older population grows, so will the volume of testing and the number of clinical laboratories. The probability of new and more powerful diagnostic tests and research laboratories working to find the cause, treatment, and cure for AIDS (acquired immunodeficiency syndrome) also should create jobs.

Working Conditions

Working conditions for medical laboratory workers vary depending on their specialty. However, in all cases the work is very detailed. Medical laboratory assistants sit for much of the day. They rarely have contact with patients. Their tasks are generally routine. Medical laboratory technicians, however, perform a wide range of tests.

Cytotechnologists' work seldom varies from one day to the next. They are not closely supervised. Histologic technicians, on the other hand, perform many different tasks. Generally, they work under the supervision of several people. Histologic technicians may be under pressure to work quickly. At times, tissue samples of a person who is being operated on are sent to the technicians, and they must prepare the slides immediately.

Medical laboratory workers usually work 40 hours a week. Those who work in hospitals may be required to work some evenings and weekends. Medical laboratory workers may be required to wear uniforms and protective clothing.

Earnings and Benefits

Medical laboratory workers earn an average salary of $13.38 an hour. Experienced workers can earn more. Benefits generally include paid holidays and vacations. Some workers have pension plans.

Where to Go for More Information

American Medical Technologists
710 Higgins Road
Park Ridge, IL 60068
9800) 275-1768
www.amt1.com

American Society of Clinical Pathologists
2100 West Harrison Street
Chicago, IL 60612-3798
(800) 621-4142
www.ascp.org

Medical Record Technician and Clerk

Education and Training
Varies—see profile

Salary Range
Average—$10.57 an hour

Employment Outlook
Excellent

Definition and Nature of the Work

Medical record technicians and clerks maintain hospital reports on patients. They keep track of patients' medical histories and charts, ensure that all the proper forms are present and signed, and make certain that the medical information is correct and accessible to doctors and nurses. They are sometimes called health information technicians. Technicians and clerks work in the record department of hospitals and clinics. Although they perform duties similar to clerks, technicians are typically needed for more specialized work. In large hospitals, technicians and clerks work under the direction of a medical record administrator. In small hospitals and clinics, highly experienced technicians may head the medical record department.

Medical record technicians and clerks check each patient's chart before the patient leaves the hospital. They make sure that all necessary information about the patient's illness is on record. These records must be maintained for insurance purposes and in the event the patient returns to the hospital. In addition, technicians and clerks sometimes collect information, such as the kinds of diseases treated in a hospital. The statistics that are gathered from this information can help both doctors and scientists in their research.

Technicians also put medical information into code. This code makes it easier to use the information in the files. Codes also make it easier to cross-index the files. Cross-indexing is an important part of a technician's job. In a cross-indexed system, information on a particular treatment might be available not only under the name of the patient, but also under the name of the disease or under the names of the doctors involved in the case.

Most medical record technicians and clerks work in hospitals, clinics, and nursing homes. In large institutions, they may work with computerized record systems. Some government agencies hire people who have experience working with medical records. Health and property-liability insurance companies sometimes need technicians and clerks. These workers help insurance companies collect information to settle medical claims.

Education and Training Requirements

A high school diploma is necessary to be a medical record clerk. Clerks must have basic secretarial skills. They usually receive 1 month of on-the-job training. Completion of a correspondence course in medical transcription offered by the American Medical Record Association is helpful in getting a job.

Medical record technicians need more advanced training. Junior and community colleges offer 2-year training programs that lead to an associate degree. These programs usually include courses in biology, record keeping, and data processing. After training, technicians are eligible to take a test to become an accredited record technician (ART). Although all technicians do not have to be accredited, many hospitals require it, especially for promotion to jobs with more responsibilities. Medical record technicians and clerks should be organized and accurate, and should demonstrate attention to detail.

Getting the Job

If you attend a training program, your school placement office may be able to help you find a job. You can apply directly to hospitals, clinics, and medical

Medical record technicians ensure that all the information about patients is correct and accessible to doctors and nurses. Good records are important for insurance reasons, for research, and in case the patient returns to the hospital. *(Martha Tabor.)*

centers. Check with private employment agencies and your state employment office for available positions. Newspaper want ads and job banks on the Internet sometimes carry listings for medical record technicians and clerks.

Advancement Possibilities and Employment Outlook

With further education, medical record clerks may become medical record technicians. A few technicians become supervisors. With additional study, a technician can qualify as a medical record administrator. Many hospitals encourage clerks and technicians to continue their schooling by giving them time off from work to attend classes. Technicians who work for the government may take civil service tests to advance.

The employment outlook for medical record technicians and clerks is excellent through the year 2008, with projections indicating this to be one of the fastest growing occupations. While hospitals will continue to employ the largest number of medical record technicians and clerks, job growth will be faster in the offices and clinics of physicians, nursing homes, and home health agencies. One of the biggest tasks of the health care industry will be to keep track of the increasing number of medical records necessary for insurance claims, Medicare reimbursement, and legal actions. The rapid growth of medical tests and procedures, plus an increasing volume in medical records, will require more workers to keep patients' records up to date. Increasingly, information is being processed by automation, so technicians and clerks with strong computer skills will have an advantage.

Where to Go for More Information

American Health Information Management Association
233 North Michigan Avenue, Suite 2510
Chicago, IL 60611-1683
(312) 787-2672
www.ahima.org

American Hospital Association
1 North Franklin
Chicago, IL 60606
(312) 422-3000
www.aaha.org

National Health Council
1730 M Street, NW, Suite 500
Washington, DC 20036
(202) 785-3910
www.nhcouncil.org

Working Conditions

The record departments of hospitals are usually pleasant places in which to work. Medical record technicians and clerks usually have little to no contact with patients. Most technicians and clerks work 40 hours a week. However, since records are needed in hospitals 24 hours a day, 7 days a week, there is some night and weekend work. Part-time work may also be available.

Earnings and Benefits

Salaries vary depending on geographical location and experience. The average salary for accredited medical record technicians is $10.57 an hour. Benefits include paid holidays and vacations, health insurance, and pension plans.

Nuclear Medicine Technologist

Definition and Nature of the Work

Education and Training
Varies—see profile

Salary Range
Median—$39,610

Employment Outlook
Good

Nuclear medicine technologists help in the diagnosis and treatment of certain diseases. They administer radiopharmaceuticals (radioactive drugs) to patients and monitor the concentration levels of the drugs in the patient's body. Technologists work directly with patients under the supervision of a physician.

Technologists perform several specific duties. First they explain the test procedures to patients. Then they prepare a dosage of the radiopharmaceutical, following set safety procedures. After administering the drug, the technologists operate a gamma scintillation camera, or scanner, which creates pictures of the drug as it passes through parts of the patient's body. Abnormal areas show higher or lower concentrations of radioactivity than normal. The images are produced on a computer screen or photographic film for a physician to examine. Nuclear medicine technologists must also keep records of patient treatments, equipment use and maintenance, and the amount and type of radiopharmaceuticals received, used, and disposed of.

Education and Training Requirements

Individuals interested in pursuing a career in nuclear medicine technology must complete one of the following: a 2-year certification program, which is offered in many hospitals and some technical schools; a 2-year associate degree program at a community college; or a bachelor's degree program from a 4-year college or university. One-year certificate programs are also available

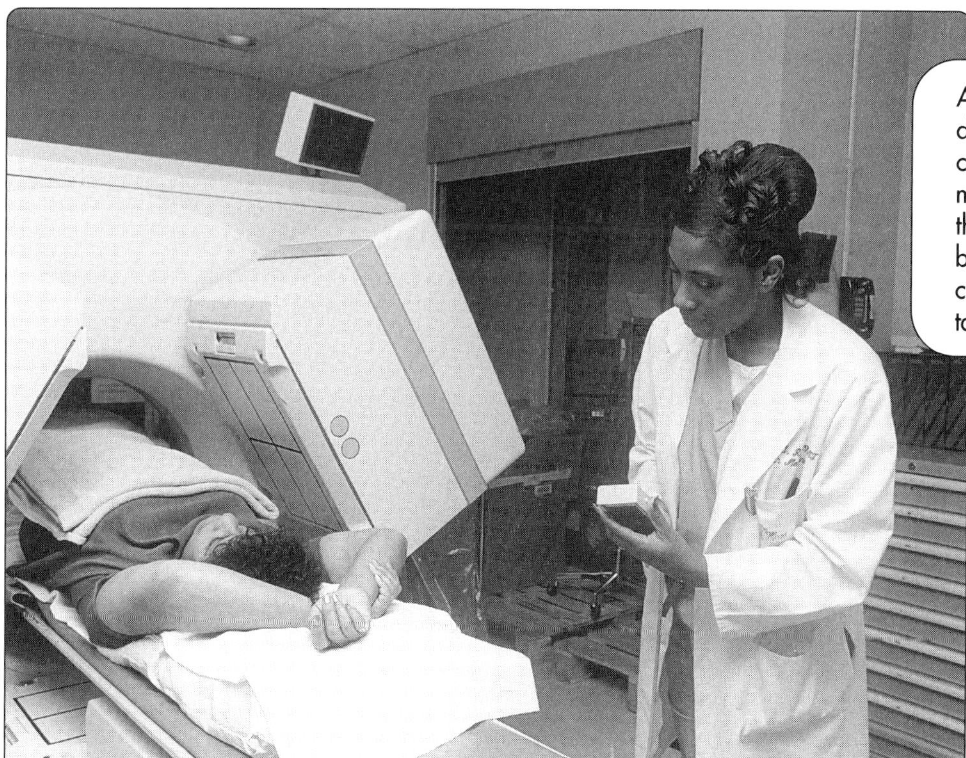

After administering radioactive drugs to patients, nuclear medicine technologists operate machines to create pictures of the drug in parts of the patients' bodies. These images help physicians to diagnose and treat certain diseases. *(Martha Tabor.)*

for health professionals, especially those wishing to specialize. Recommended courses include the physical sciences, radiation biology, radiopharmaceuticals, imaging techniques, and computer science. There are currently more than 100 formal training programs accredited by the Joint Review Committee on Education Programs in Nuclear Medicine Technology.

About half of all states require technologists to be licensed. Most employers prefer to hire certified or registered technologists, so many technologists obtain a voluntary professional certification or registration from the Nuclear Medicine Technology Certification Board or the American Registry of Radiologic Technologists.

Getting the Job

Most nuclear medicine technologists work in hospitals, which hire only certified or registered technologists. Sometimes individuals with a bachelor's degree in an accepted specialty or those who have completed an accredited training program can obtain entry-level positions in doctors' offices or clinics.

Advancement Possibilities and Employment Outlook

Nuclear medicine technologists can advance to supervisory positions such as chief technologist or department administrator. Some technologists advance through specialization, such as nuclear cardiology, or move on to work in research laboratories. Those technologists with advanced degrees may become teachers in nuclear medicine technology programs.

Employment of nuclear medicine technologists is expected to grow about as fast as the average through the year 2008. Technological innovations may increase the diagnostic use of nuclear medicine, especially for the nation's aging population. However, the occupation is small, and only a few openings each year are expected in this field. Opportunities will be best for technologists trained in both nuclear medicine and radiologic procedures.

Working Conditions

Nuclear medicine technologists usually work in clean, well-lighted environments. They generally work a 40-hour week, although evening and weekend hours, on-call duty, and shift work may be expected. Technologists must possess strong physical stamina, since they stand most of the day and may have to lift or position patients.

Earnings and Benefits

The median annual salary for nuclear medicine technologists is $39,610. Those with more experience and training can earn more. Full-time technologists usually receive benefits that include health insurance and paid vacation time.

Where to Go for More Information

American College of Nuclear Medicine
P.O. Box 175
Landisville, PA 17538-0175
(717) 898-5008

The Society of Nuclear Medicine
1850 Samuel Morse Drive
Reston, VA 20190-5316
(703) 708-9000
www.snm.org

Occupational Therapy Assistant

Definition and Nature of the Work

Occupational therapy assistants provide rehabilitative services to people with mental, emotional, physical, or developmental impairments. They work under the supervision of occupational therapists. Many occupational therapy assistants work in hospitals. Others work in homes for the aged, clinics, special schools, or occupational workshops.

Assistants may work with paralyzed or crippled people or with people who have just been fitted with an artificial limb. They help them work through rehabilitative exercises and activities outlined in a treatment plan by an occupational therapist. They also work with people who have emotional or mental problems. Assistants may teach patients how to feed and dress themselves. Assistants may also teach patients crafts that are fun and require patients to use their minds and bodies. Assistants may help teach job skills, such as typing or electrical repair, that will help patients to earn a living.

Occupational therapy assistants may be responsible for ordering supplies and taking care of the equipment used in therapy. They may write up observation and progress reports on the patients and do other paperwork. Sometimes they may handle clerical duties.

Education and Training
Varies—see profile

Salary Range
Median—$28,690

Employment Outlook
Excellent

Education and Training Requirements

To enter a training program for occupational therapy assistants, you must have a high school diploma or its equivalent. Courses in crafts, health, science, and typing are helpful. Work experience in summer camps or hospitals is useful.

Training for occupational therapy assistants is given in community colleges and vocational and technical schools. Most programs last 2 years and lead to an associate degree. Courses may include basic medical terminology, anatomy, mental health, and pediatrics. If you graduate from a program approved by the American Occupational Therapy Association and pass a test, you can become a certified occupational therapy assistant (COTA).

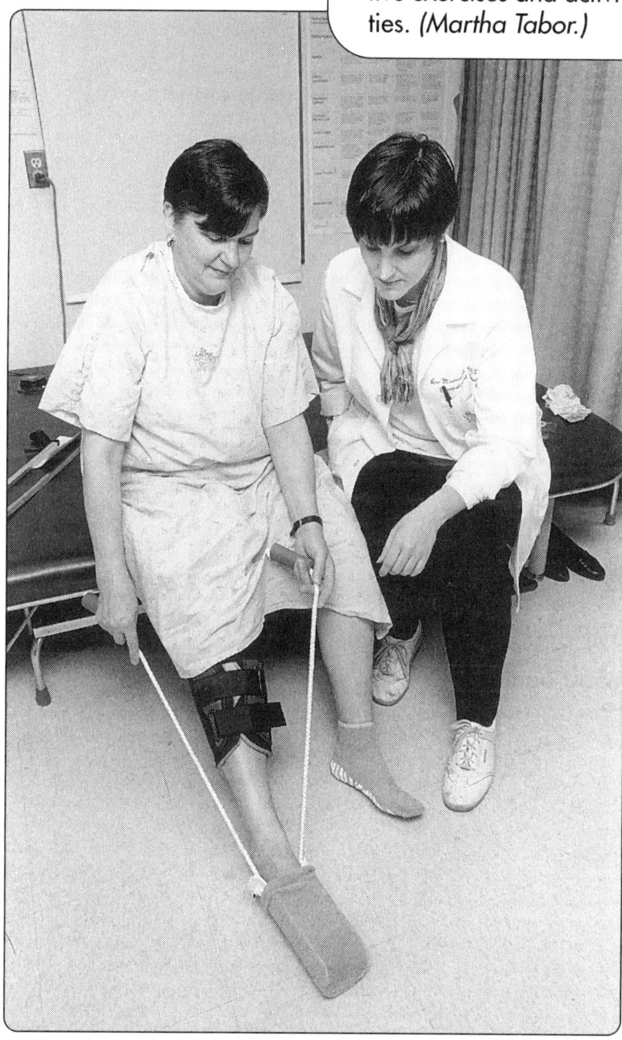

An occupational therapy assistant helps a patient work through rehabilitative exercises and activities. *(Martha Tabor.)*

Getting the Job

You can apply directly to hospitals or clinics for a job. Job openings are sometimes listed in newspaper want ads or job banks on the Internet. School placement offices can also help you to find a job. Also check state and private employment agencies.

Advancement Possibilities and Employment Outlook

In large hospitals and clinics, assistants can become supervisors. With further training and experience, a certified occupational therapy assistant can become a registered occupational therapist (OTR).

The employment outlook for occupational therapy assistants is excellent through the year 2008. It is projected to be one of the fastest growing occupations, but because the field is so small, only a few job openings will result. Due to a growing public interest in the rehabilitation of disabled people, there will be a demand for rehabilitation services and long-term care. These programs have had great success. Also, there is an anticipated high rate of turnover among occupational therapy assistants, which should result in openings. The employment outlook is best for graduates of approved programs.

Where to Go for More Information

The American Occupational Therapy Association
4720 Montgomery Lane
P.O. Box 31220
Bethesda, MD 20824-1220
(800) 668-8255
www.aota.org

American Society of Hand Therapists
401 North Michigan Avenue, Suite 2400
Chicago, IL 60611-4267
(312) 321-6866
www.asht.org

Working Conditions

Occupational therapy assistants usually work 40 hours a week. Some weekend or evening hours may be required. Most occupational workshops are nicely decorated. Assistants should be friendly and understanding. They often work with people who are in pain or who need to be cheered up. Assistants should be good at working with their hands and should enjoy helping others.

Earnings and Benefits

Salaries vary with education and experience. The median salary for occupational therapy assistants is $28,690 a year. Benefits include paid holidays and vacations, health insurance, and pension plans.

Operating Room Technician

Education and Training
Voc/tech school

Salary Range
Median—$12.76 an hour

Employment Outlook
Excellent

Definition and Nature of the Work

Operating room technicians are part of the surgical team. They assist the doctors, nurses, and other operating room workers. They help prepare patients for surgery by washing, shaving, and disinfecting the intended areas of operation. They clean and set up the surgical equipment. They also transport patients to the operating room, position them on the operating table, and cover them with surgical drapes. Operating room technicians are sometimes called surgical technicians.

Operating room technicians set up the operating room with instruments and supplies. They help the surgical team scrub in and put on their gowns, gloves, and masks. During surgery, they hand instruments and supplies to the proper surgeons. They may also monitor a patient's vital signs. Technicians help keep track of equipment. They may also help to prepare samples of tissues or organs that will be tested in a laboratory. At times they operate some of the machines in the operating room.

After an operation, technicians take patients to the recovery room. They help to clean and restock the operating room and get it ready for the next operation.

Education and Training Requirements

Operating room technicians usually need a high school diploma. Courses in health and science are helpful. Summer or volunteer work in a hospital is also good experience.

Most operating room technicians receive formal training in vocational and technical schools, hospitals, and community colleges. These training programs, which provide both classroom training and supervised clinical experience, last from 9 months to 2 years. Students take a variety of courses including anatomy, medical terminology, and professional ethics. They also learn procedures such as how to sterilize instruments, handle drugs, and control infections. Some technicians train on the job in programs lasting from 6 weeks to 1 year. Operating room technicians who pass a national exam can become certified as surgical technologists. Certification is not required to get a job, but an increasing number of employers prefer to hire certified surgical technologists.

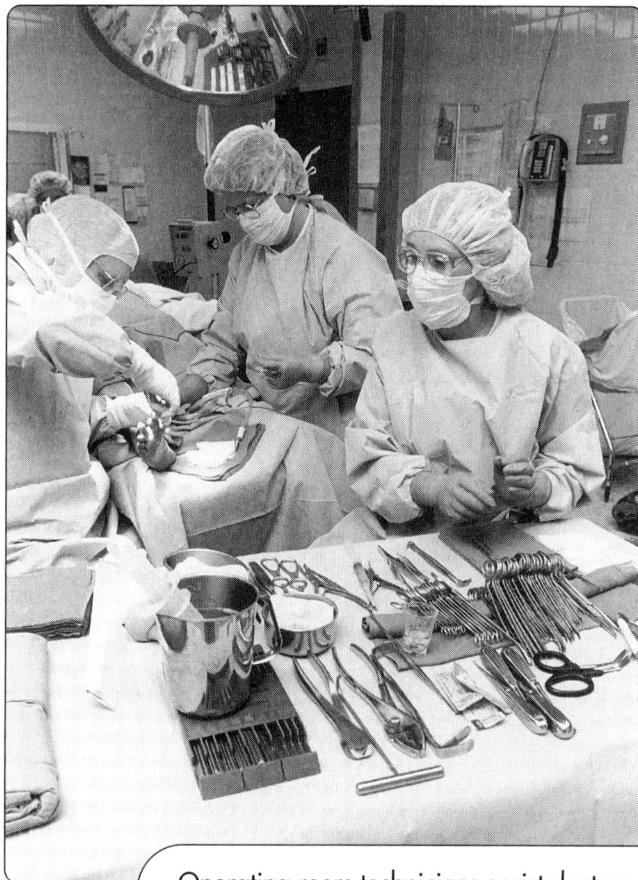

Operating room technicians assist doctors, nurses, and other operating room workers before, during, and after surgery. *(Martha Tabor.)*

Getting the Job

You can apply directly to the hospital in which you want to work. Also check job listings at state or private employment offices. Newspaper want ads and job banks on the Internet sometimes list jobs for operating room technicians.

Advancement Possibilities and Employment Outlook

Operating room technicians can advance to jobs with more responsibility as they gain experience. They can also specialize in a particular area of surgery such as neurosurgery. With further education they can also move into other health care jobs.

The employment outlook is excellent through the year 2008. Growth and aging of the population, advances in surgical techniques, and widespread insurance coverage are expected to increase the number of operations performed. Graduates of postsecondary school training programs will have the best opportunities.

Working Conditions

Operating room technicians generally work 40 hours a week. Sometimes they must be on call for night and weekend work. They work with doctors, nurses, and other hospital workers. Operating rooms are well-lighted, quiet places. Sometimes tense situations arise, however. Operating room technicians need to be careful workers. They must remain calm in emergencies. They should also be in good health.

Earnings and Benefits

Salaries vary depending on education, experience, and location. Operating room technicians earn a median salary of $12.76 an hour. Benefits include paid holidays and vacations, health insurance, and pension plans.

Where to Go for More Information

American Hospital Association
1 North Franklin
Chicago, IL 60606
(312) 422-3000
www.aaha.org

Association of Surgical Technologists
7108 South Alton Way, Building C
Englewood, CO 80112-2106
(303) 694-9130
www.ast.org

National Health Council
1730 M Street, NW, Suite 500
Washington, DC 20036
(202) 785-3910
www.nhcouncil.org

Optician

Education and Training
High school plus training

Salary Range
Median—$22,440

Employment Outlook
Good

Definition and Nature of the Work

Opticians fill doctors' prescriptions for eyeglasses. They prepare the lenses by grinding the glass to fit the prescription of each patient. Then they put the lenses into frames. Opticians also make sure that the lenses and frames fit the patient properly.

There are two kinds of opticians: *dispensing opticians*, who are sometimes called prescription opticians or ophthalmic dispensers, and *optical laboratory technicians*, who are also called optical mechanics. Most dispensing opticians work in stores that sell eyeglasses. Optical laboratory technicians generally work in laboratories that fill orders from dispensing opticians. Some retail stores have laboratories on their premises. These stores employ both kinds of opticians. Some opticians work for optometrists and ophthalmologists. Others work for firms that make precision lenses for cameras, microscopes, telescopes, and military equipment.

Dispensing opticians help patients select the size, color, and shape of their frames. They measure each patient's face to decide exactly where the lenses should be placed. Then they send information on the size, color, shape, and prescription of the lenses to the optical laboratory. When the eyeglasses have been made, the dispensing optician measures and adjusts the glasses for the patient until they fit properly. Dispensing opticians also fit patients for contact lenses. Some specialize in this kind of work.

Optical laboratory technicians actually make the eyeglasses. They receive doctors' prescriptions and the measurements made by dispensing opticians. Technicians use power machines to grind and polish the lenses. In large laboratories they specialize in different parts of the job. *Optical surfacers* take flat pieces of

A dispensing optician helps a patient select the size, color, and shape of her frames. *(Sara Matthews.)*

glass and grind them according to prescription. Then they polish the lenses. *Optical finishers*, or *bench technicians*, cut the lenses so they fit into the frames. Some optical laboratory technicians make contact lenses. *Contact lens technicians* grind pieces of plastic to the right prescription. They use power equipment, such as jewelers' lathes, and also polish by hand. Contact lens technicians generally work in large laboratories. They usually specialize in one phase of the work.

Education and Training Requirements

The training requirements for dispensing opticians and for optical laboratory technicians are similar. Employers generally prefer high school graduates. You should take courses in algebra, geometry, physics, mechanical drawing, and shop.

Most opticians are trained on the job. However, formal training is increasingly preferred. On-the-job training generally lasts several years. There are also apprenticeship programs, which usually take 2 to 4 years to complete. Two-year colleges also offer training programs that lead to an associate degree.

Some states require opticians to be licensed. Licensing requirements usually include meeting educational and training standards and passing a written or practical test. In some states you must pass both tests.

Getting the Job

Your school placement office can help you find a job. You can apply directly to companies and private dispensing opticians for on-the-job training. In addition, you can apply to companies that operate apprenticeship programs.

Advancement Possibilities and Employment Outlook

Dispensing opticians may advance by becoming the managers of their stores. Some open up their own businesses. Optical laboratory technicians may become supervisors.

The outlook for opticians is good through the year 2008, with employment expected to increase as fast as the average. The anticipated growth of the middle-aged and elderly populations requiring health and vision care will create a need for opticians. Also, as more customers buy contact lenses or more than one pair of glasses, the number of jobs for opticians is expected to increase.

Working Conditions

Dispensing opticians work in clean, quiet offices. Optical laboratory technicians work with power machines. Their work is somewhat dirty, and laboratories are generally noisy. All opticians must be precise and exacting. In addition, dispensing opticians must have a talent for sales and enjoy working with people. Opticians generally work 40 hours a week. Dispensing opticians may work some evenings and Saturdays.

Earnings and Benefits

Earnings vary depending on education, experience, and place of employment. The median annual salary of an optician is $22,440. Owners, managers, and certified graduates of opticianry schools can earn more. Benefits for salaried opticians generally include paid holidays and vacations, health insurance, and pension plans.

Where to Go for More Information

National Academy of Opticianry
8401 Corporate Drive, Suite 603
Landover, MD 20785
(800) 229-4828
www.nao.org

Optical Society of America
2010 Massachusetts Avenue, NW
Washington, DC 20036
(202) 223-8130
www.osa.org

Opticians Association of America
10341 Democracy Lane
Fairfax, VA 22030-2505
(703) 691-8355
www.opticians.org

Orthoptist

Education and Training
2-year college plus training

Salary Range
Average—$23,400 to $25,200

Employment Outlook
Good

Definition and Nature of the Work

Orthoptists work in the field of eye care. They specialize in the treatment of patients who are suffering from problems of muscle imbalance of the eye. The most common of these problems is crossed eyes. Cross-eyed patients do not have binocular vision; that is, both eyes do not work together as they should. Orthoptists use diagnostic instruments and procedures to test patients. They teach them how to strengthen their eye muscles through exercise. Orthoptists work mainly with children because crossed eyes are easier to correct when a patient is young. They teach their patients eye exercises to do at home. They meet regularly with their patients to check their progress. Orthoptists usually work under the supervision of ophthalmologists, who are medical doctors specializing in diseases of the eye. Orthoptists work in hospitals, clinics, private doctors' offices, and medical centers.

Education and Training Requirements

To be trained as an orthoptist, you first need 2 to 4 years of college. Then you must enroll in a special school that offers courses in orthoptics. These programs usually last about 24 months and include both classroom and clinical training. You must complete an approved program and pass an exam to become a certified orthoptist.

Getting the Job

Your school placement office can help you to find a job as an orthoptist. The American Association of Certified Orthoptists also keeps a file of job openings.

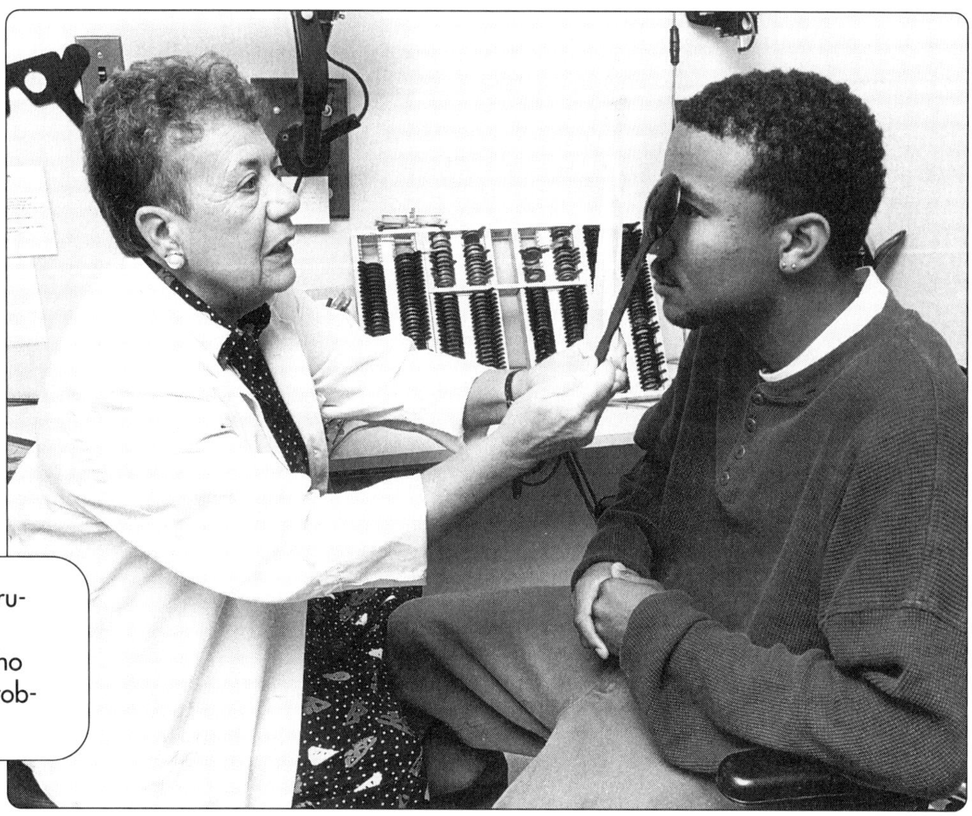

Orthoptists use diagnostic instruments and procedures to test patients. They treat patients who have eye muscle imbalance problems. *(Martha Tabor.)*

You can also apply directly to an ophthalmologist for employment. Newspaper want ads and job banks on the Internet may be other sources of job information.

Advancement Possibilities and Employment Outlook

Orthoptists are important members of the eyecare team. As they gain experience, they often take on more responsibility in the care of patients with crossed eyes and related vision problems. Sometimes they also help in the training of new orthoptists. There are now many more openings than there are qualified orthoptists. The job future also looks promising. More ophthalmologists are making use of the special training of orthoptists.

Working Conditions

Because this is a very specialized field, most jobs are located in or around major cities. The offices are generally pleasant places in which to work. Orthoptists work with a variety of people. Usually orthoptists work during ophthalmologists' office hours. This is generally a 40-hour week, which often includes evenings or Saturdays. Part-time work is sometimes available.

Orthoptists deal with people who have a handicap that can be emotionally upsetting. They should therefore be understanding, enthusiastic, and encouraging with their patients. Orthoptists should be good teachers who can explain eye exercises clearly, especially to children.

Earnings and Benefits

Salaries vary depending on experience, position, and location. Beginning orthoptists earn an average of $17,000 to $18,200 a year. Experienced orthoptists average $23,400 to $25,200 a year. Benefits generally include paid holidays and vacations and health insurance.

Where to Go for More Information

National Health Council
1730 M Street, NW, Suite 500
Washington, DC 20036
(202) 785-3910
www.nhcouncil.org

Pharmaceutical Detail Representative

Education and Training
2-year or 4-year college

Salary Range
Starting—$25,000 to $35,000 Average—$35,000 to $50,000

Employment Outlook
Varies—see profile

Definition and Nature of the Work

Pharmaceutical detail representatives are employed by drug companies. They distribute information about their companies' products to physicians, hospital nurses, and medical technicians.

Detail representatives are salespeople, but not in the usual sense. They do not take orders from doctors. They try to persuade doctors to prescribe more of their companies' drugs. Patients then buy the drugs. Most doctors are very busy. Detail representatives usually have no more than 5 or 6 minutes to talk with a doctor. In that time they must describe their company's newest products. They outline what a drug is designed to do and how it works. They also explain its advantages over older drugs, attempting to convince doctors as to why their product is better than others.

Detail representatives must have a basic knowledge of how the human body works. They must also have some understanding of disease and pharmacology. Doctors question detail persons about drugs and their side effects. Detail persons must know which drugs will be of interest to doctors in different specialties.

A pharmaceutical detail representative distributes information about a new drug to a doctor's office. Detail representatives must speak clearly and concisely under pressure, because they only spend a few minutes at each medical office. *(The Terry Wild Studio.)*

Detail representatives are assigned territories based on postal zip codes. They make up their own itineraries. They concentrate on the doctors who write the most prescriptions. This information is available from surveys of pharmacists. Detail persons may leave samples of new drugs with doctors. They must keep careful records concerning samples.

Detail representatives must be able to talk clearly and concisely under pressure. They must have pleasant personalities. Building long-lasting relationships with doctors is part of the job. They must be able to accept rejection. About 40 percent of doctors refuse to see detail persons at all. Others will not see them when they are very busy.

Education and Training Requirements

To become a detail person, you must have a high school diploma. Most employers prefer to hire college graduates, preferably with a bachelor of science degree. However, 2 years of college should be sufficient to qualify for most jobs. The drug companies provide on-the-job training. They select trainees on the basis of the trainees' verbal and social skills. The training consists of intensive study followed by supervised field work.

Representatives must keep abreast of current medical and product knowledge throughout their careers. They attend regular meetings to get product information. They must maintain a general knowledge of advances in medicine. Correspondence courses are available through the Certified Medical Representatives Institute, which offers certification.

Getting the Job

If you are a college student, ask your college placement office for information about applying to become a pharmaceutical detail representative trainee. Representatives of drug companies may also visit your campus. Otherwise, you should write to major drug companies and request interviews. Once you are selected as a trainee, a job is guaranteed.

Advancement Possibilities and Employment Outlook

Some representatives prefer to stay in the field. Some advance to supervisory and training positions. A few advance to administrative and planning posts. Occasionally a detail person will transfer to another department in the company or move into a related health occupation.

The job outlook for detail persons is fair to good. Some companies are expanding rapidly and will need to hire additional representatives.

Working Conditions

Pharmaceutical detail representatives set their own hours to fit doctors' schedules. They may have to spend much time traveling. They often have to wait to see doctors despite appointments. The general atmosphere in the drug industry is becoming increasingly competitive. Pharmaceutical detail representatives must be able to cope with stressful situations. These will be caused by competition with other detail representatives for access to doctors during their limited free time.

Earnings and Benefits

Commissions account for a large proportion of earnings for detail representatives. Depending on the company, roughly 10 to 20 percent of their earnings is derived from commissions based on the drugs ordered by doctors. Beginners' earnings average $25,000 to $35,000 a year. The average for the occupation is $35,000 to $50,000 a year. Top earnings are $60,000 a year. Detail persons receive health insurance and paid vacations and holidays. They also receive free cars and some travel expenses.

Where to Go for More Information

The Certified Medical Representatives Institute, Inc.
4950 Brambleton Avenue
Roanoke, VA 24018
(703) 989-4596

Physical Therapy Assistant

Education and Training
Varies—see profile

Salary Range
Median—$21,870

Employment Outlook
Excellent

Definition and Nature of the Work

Physical therapy assistants work under the supervision of physical therapists. They use physical treatment procedures to help people cope with pain and disability caused by disease or injury. Physical therapists and their assistants usually work in hospitals, nursing homes, or clinics. They are part of a health care team that includes doctors, occupational therapists, and social workers.

Physical therapy assistants work with people of all ages. Some work with elderly patients who have trouble moving about. Some work with handicapped children. Others work with patients who have lost an arm or a leg, have arthritis problems, or are paralyzed. Physical therapy assistants use many different types of equipment and procedures. They treat patients by using massage, exercise, heat, cold, and light. Assistants help teach patients how to use and care for wheelchairs, braces, and artificial limbs.

Assistants have other duties that give physical therapists more time to put their special training to use. Assistants may do some office work, for example, or they may get equipment ready for the therapist. They may also prepare a patient for a therapy session.

Education and Training Requirements

If you want to be a physical therapy assistant, a high school diploma or its equivalent is required. You should take courses in mathematics and science in high school. You can also get experience by volunteering part-time in a hospital or clinic, or working with handicapped children in summer camps.

Training requirements vary. Most states require that you take an accredited 2-year associate degree program. Many states also require that you be licensed.

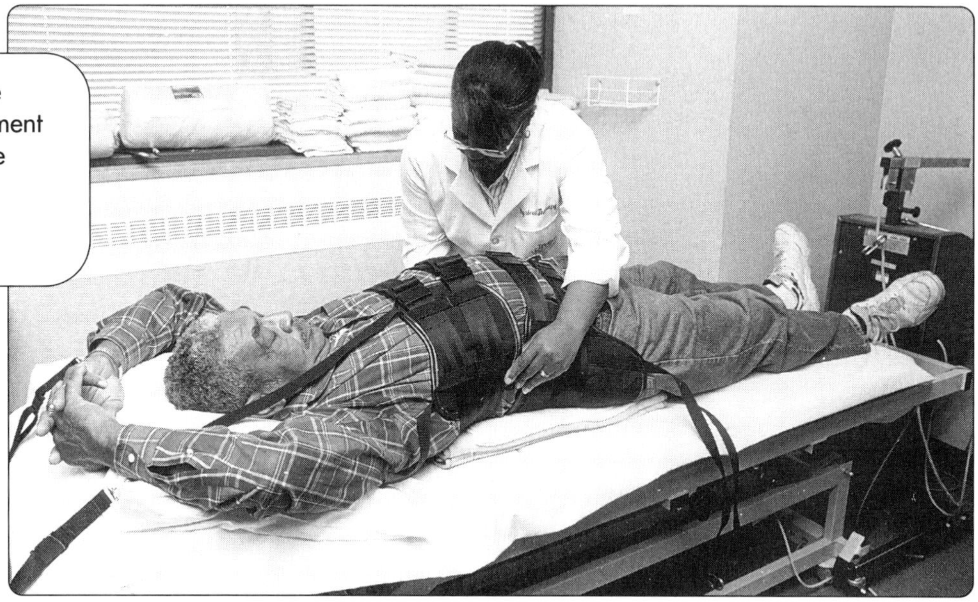

Physical therapy assistants use many different types of equipment and procedures to help people cope with pain and disability caused by disease or injury. *(Martha Tabor.)*

Getting the Job

If you receive training, your college placement office can help you find a job as a physical therapy assistant. You can also apply directly to hospitals or clinics. Another good source of job openings is newspaper want ads.

Advancement Possibilities and Employment Outlook

As physical therapy assistants gain experience, they are often given more responsibility and salary increases. Some assistants continue their education to become physical therapists.

The employment outlook for physical therapy assistants is excellent through the year 2008. It is projected to be among the fastest growing occupations in the economy. Opportunities will be best for graduates of accredited training programs. The expansion of rehabilitation services for people with physical disabilities will create many new jobs. The need for physical therapy is expected to grow as the number of people over the age of 75 increases. Advances in rehabilitation medicine and therapeutic techniques are likely to create additional demands.

Where to Go for More Information

American Physical Therapy Association
1111 North Fairfax Street
Alexandria, VA 22314-1488
(800) 999-2782
www.apta.org

National Association of Rehabilitation Instructors
P.O. Box 405
Huntsville, AL 35801
(800) 671-6840

National Rehabilitation Association
633 South Washington Street
Alexandria, VA 22314-4109
(703) 836-0850
www.nationalrehab.org

Working Conditions

Physical therapy assistants usually work in clean, pleasant places. Their patients may sometimes be depressed by their disabilities. Assistants can help them by being cheerful and encouraging. Physical therapy assistants should also be healthy and able to work well with their hands. Most physical therapy assistants work 40 hours a week. Some work part-time.

Earnings and Benefits

Salaries vary with experience and place of employment. The median yearly salary for physical therapy assistants is $21,870. Benefits include paid holidays and vacations and health insurance.

Psychiatric Aide/Technician

Education and Training
Varies—see profile

Salary Range
Median—$10.66 an hour

Employment Outlook
Good

Definition and Nature of the Work

Psychiatric aides/technicians provide routine care for mentally impaired or emotionally disturbed patients. Psychiatric aides are also called *mental health assistants, clinical attendants, psychiatric nursing assistants, ward attendants*, or *rehabilitation technicians*. They work under the supervision of a mental health team that may include psychiatrists, psychologists, and social workers.

Aides help patients bathe, dress, and eat. They escort patients to examinations, treatments, therapy, and recreation. Aides also spend a great deal of time socializing with patients. They may play cards or games with patients, watch television with them, or lead group outings. Since psychiatric aides spend so much time interacting with patients, their observations on patient behavior are very valuable to the rest of the staff.

Education and Training Requirements

There are no formal educational requirements to become a psychiatric aide, although many employers prefer to hire high school graduates. High school courses in the social and biological sciences are beneficial.

Some employers, especially hospitals, require job applicants to have previous training or experience. Other employers provide informal on-the-job training. Some states require psychiatric aides to complete a formal training program and obtain certification.

Getting the Job

School placement officers or counselors can offer assistance in finding job openings. The local office of the state employment agency can provide current listings of available jobs. You also can apply directly to the personnel offices of mental health facilities or hospitals.

Psychiatric aids/technicians spend a great deal of time socializing with patients. Their observations on patient behavior are very valuable to the rest of the psychiatric staff. *(Earl Dotter.)*

Advancement Possibilities and Employment Outlook

Advancement opportunities for psychiatric aides/technicians are somewhat limited. After gaining experience, psychiatric aides may become senior aides, helping to train new workers. Most advancement, however, requires additional formal training and education.

Employment of psychiatric aides/technicians is expected to grow more slowly than the average through the year 2008. However, employment will rise due to the increase in the number of older people, who often require mental health services, and to a more accepting attitude toward those needing mental health care. Employment for psychiatric aides is likely to decline in hospitals, due to attempts to cut costs by limiting in-patient treatment. As a result, job growth should increase in private psychiatric facilities and community health clinics that will take in patients for treatment.

Working Conditions

Most psychiatric aides/technicians work in the psychiatric units of hospitals, private psychiatric facilities, state or county mental institutions, or community mental health clinics. They generally work a 40-hour week, but often must be available to work night, weekend, and holiday shifts. Many aides work only on a part-time basis.

Work as a psychiatric aide can be physically and emotionally demanding. Aides stand for long hours and may have to lift or move patients. Sometimes they must deal with disoriented, disturbed, or even violent patients. It is important for aides to be calm, patient, and caring.

Where to Go for More Information

American Association of Psychiatric Technicians
P.O. Box 928
Orem, UT 94059-0928
(800) 391-7589
www.aapt.com

American Health Care Association
1201 L Street, NW
Washington, DC 20005
(202) 842-4444
www.ahca.org

Earnings and Benefits

Salaries vary depending on the type of employer and the geographic location. Earnings for full-time psychiatric aides average $10.66 an hour. Aides who work night or weekend shifts generally earn more than those on day shifts. Most full-time aides employed by hospitals or state facilities receive medical benefits, paid holidays, sick leave, and paid vacation time.

Radiologic Technologist

Education and Training
2-year or 4-year college

Salary Range
Median—$32,880

Employment Outlook
Good

Definition and Nature of the Work

Radiologic technologists use X rays to help physicians diagnose and treat illness and injury. They usually work under the direction of radiologists, who are medical doctors specializing in X rays. Most radiologic technologists work in hospitals, but some work in medical laboratories, clinics, or doctors' or dentists' offices. Others help to staff mobile X-ray units or work in private industry. Radiologic technologists are usually responsible for writing reports, developing X-ray film, and maintaining their equipment.

There are three types of radiologic technologists. *Diagnostic X-ray technologists* take X rays that help doctors locate tumors, ulcers, broken bones, and other abnormal conditions. Sometimes diagnostic X-ray technologists have patients drink chemical mixtures to make organs show up on X-ray film or on a fluoroscope. *Radiation therapy technologists* help doctors to diagnose and treat disease by exposing certain parts of the patient's body to X rays or other forms of radiation. *Nuclear medicine technologists* help doctors to diagnose and treat disease by using radioactive materials. These radioactive substances are given to patients through the mouth or by injection into the veins. Nuclear medicine technologists use special equipment to trace the progress and concentration of the radioactive materials in various parts of the body.

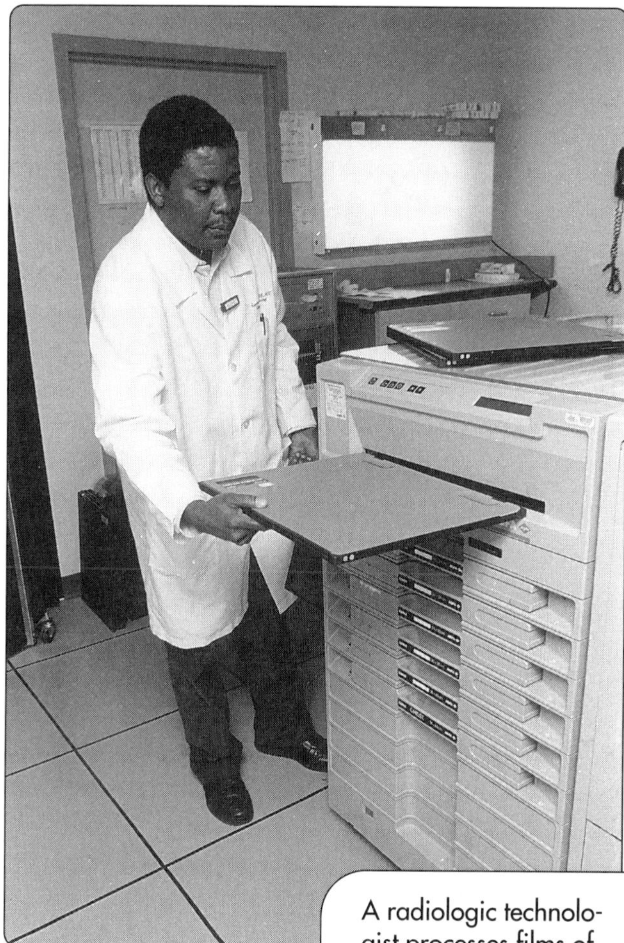

A radiologic technologist processes films of patient X rays at a hospital. Radiologic technologists are also responsible for writing reports and maintaining equipment. *(Martha Tabor.)*

Education and Training Requirements

You can become a radiologic technologist by enrolling in a 2- to 4-year program in radiography that leads to a certificate, associate degree, or bachelor's degree. A high school diploma or its equivalent is needed to enter a program. Hospitals, colleges, medical schools, and vocational and technical schools offer these programs. After graduating from an approved program, you can take an exam leading to registration by the American Registry of Radiologic Technologists. With further training and experience, registered technologists can become certified in radiation therapy technology or nuclear medicine technology.

Getting the Job

Many hospitals will hire students that they have helped to train. School placement offices can also help you find a job. The want ads in newspapers and professional journals are another good source of job leads.

Advancement Possibilities and Employment Outlook

Experienced radiologic technologists can become supervisors of other workers in large X-ray departments. They can also learn to operate other types of hospital equipment. Technologists who have a bachelor's degree can become instructors or administrators. Some technologists advance by getting jobs with the manufacturers of X-ray equipment. They may sell or service this equipment.

The employment outlook for the field of radiologic technology is good through the year 2008. However, the number of candidates going into the field is also increasing. Also, more hospitals are merging their radiologic and nuclear medicine departments in an effort to cut costs. Radiographers who are also trained in more than one type of imaging technology will have the best prospects. In the years ahead, a growing number of radiologic technologists will find jobs in offices of physicians, health maintenance organizations, diagnostic imaging centers, and freestanding cancer clinics.

Working Conditions

Radiologic technologists generally work 40 hours a week. Sometimes they must work night and weekend shifts. Part-time work is often available.

Where to Go for More Information

American Association for Women Radiologists
1891 Preston White Drive
Reston, VA 20191
(703) 648-8939
www.aawr.org

American Society of Radiologic Technologists
15000 Central Avenue, Southeast
Albuquerque, NM 87123-3917
(800) 444-2778
www.asrt.org

Radiological Society of North America
820 Jorie Boulevard
Oak Brook, IL 60523
(630) 571-2670
www.rsna.org

Radiologic technologists need manual dexterity and mechanical ability. They come in contact with a wide variety of people and should be sympathetic and friendly. Their working environment is usually clean and pleasant. Technologists should be in good health and must always work carefully to avoid exposing themselves and others to harmful radiation.

Earnings and Benefits

Salaries depend on education, experience, and location. Experienced technologists earn a median income of $32,880 a year. Benefits include paid holidays and vacations, health insurance, and pension plans.

Acupuncturist

Education and Training
Varies—see profile

Salary Range
Average—$40,000

Employment Outlook
Varies—see profile

Definition and Nature of the Work

Acupuncturists practice an ancient Chinese medical therapy. They insert very fine stainless steel needles into a patient's body at specific points. Acupuncturists believe that the body is divided into a number of complicated pathways, or meridians. They contend that energy, or "ch'i," should flow smoothly along these meridians, and blocked or stagnant "ch'i" results in illness and pain.

They use needles to regulate the flow of energy, which they believe promotes the smooth functioning of hormones, nerves, blood supply, and vital organs. Acupuncture may also be used in place of anesthetics.

Recent medical research has confirmed some of the basic assumptions of acupuncture. It seems that electromagnetic energy flows through the body in patterns like meridians. Stimulation by needles at acupuncture points releases hormones called endorphins in the brain, which block pain.

Many people visit acupuncturists for the treatment of headache pain, asthma, or arthritis. Acupuncturists question clients about their state of health. Then they evaluate pulse rates at 12 different points of the body and make a diagnosis.

Taking various factors into account, they decide which size needles to use and where to insert them (there are 365 acupuncture points on the body). Sometimes the needles are rotated. Several sessions may be necessary to achieve the desired result. The treatment is not painful.

Acupuncturists must be skillful and competent with their hands. They must accurately insert and manipulate needles because needles used incorrectly can potentially damage vital organs. They must sterilize the needles carefully to avoid infection. They need great patience to perfect their skill and must relate well to other people.

Many acupuncturists are qualified in such fields as medicine, nursing, and physical therapy. A number of them offer acupuncture as an additional service while continuing in their original professions.

Education and Training Requirements

Acupuncture is a new profession in this country. Before you receive your training, you must first check whether acupuncture is allowed in the state where you want to live.

Available training varies from apprenticeship to 3-year postgraduate programs. State regulations and minimum training requirements also vary and are subject to change. In some states, you must first be a doctor of medicine (M.D.) or a chiropractor. However, in other areas, a master's of acupuncture (C.A.) at an accredited postgraduate school may provide the qualifications necessary for certification. This degree usually consists of 2 years of study plus a year of supervised practice.

There are at least five types of acupuncture used in this country. A student should be thoroughly grounded in one type of acupuncture before learning another. There are about 15 accredited schools; each specializes in one type of acupuncture. You must read enough basic material to decide which tradition most appeals to you. Introductory literature and information about schools are available from the National Council of Acupuncture Schools and Colleges.

You should contact the schools that teach the type of acupuncture that you prefer. Ask for their entry requirements. Most schools will only consider students who have a degree with certain science and social science courses.

Clinical experience with the sick is also required. Midcareer applicants from fields such as nursing usually meet these requirements. High school students can ask for advice on the best preparation.

Finally, you also need to determine whether it would be possible to establish a private practice or if you need to work under supervision after receiving your training. A state employment counselor may be able to help you with this information.

Getting the Job

Most acupuncturists are self-employed. Only a small percentage are affiliated with hospitals. Until recently, nearly all students in acupuncture schools came from careers in the medical field. Upon graduation, they were advised to continue their previous work and develop their acupuncture practices as second jobs.

There is no established route for graduates to enter practice. A system of associates may be developed; graduates could then spend the first years working with experienced acupuncturists.

Advancement Possibilities and Employment Outlook

Public acceptance of acupuncture is growing rapidly. About two-thirds of the states now regulate acupuncture. Treatments are increasingly covered by insurance.

Several joint studies with the medical profession are examining specific uses of acupuncture, such as drug detoxification and control of chronic pain. However, the total number in the profession is still very small.

As with doctors, advancement comes with building a practice. However, most people (and most doctors) know little about acupuncture. The process of building a practice can therefore be very slow.

Where to Go for More Information

American Academy of Medical Acupuncture
5820 Wilshire Boulevard, Suite 500
Los Angeles, CA 90036
(213) 937-5514

American Acupuncture Association
4262 Kissena Boulevard
Flushing, NY 11355
(718) 886-4431

Working Conditions

Acupuncturists work in comfortable offices that must be kept quiet and clean. They can usually set their own hours. Some work late on certain evenings for the convenience of their patients. A few work in hospitals or clinics.

Earnings and Benefits

Those who have worked in the profession for several years earn an average of $40,000 a year. Acupuncturists in private practice must provide their own benefits.

Anesthesiologist

Definition and Nature of the Work

Education and Training
Advanced degree

Salary Range
Median—$220,000

Employment Outlook
Very Good

Anesthesiologists are physicians responsible for the physical well-being of patients undergoing surgical procedures. They accomplish this by administering anesthetics, which are medicines to prevent patients from feeling pain and sensations; by closely monitoring a patient's vital signs during surgery and adjusting anesthetics accordingly; and by monitoring the patient through the first recovery stages after the operation and administering appropriate medications during recovery. In addition to helping patients through surgery, anesthesiologists may also help to treat patients with conditions causing chronic pain. Many specialize in specific types of problems, such as respiratory or neurological illness.

Anesthesiologists are responsible for one of the cornerstones of the health care industry. Each year, approximately 25 million anesthetics are administered to patients in the United States, with more than 90 percent administered by or under the direct supervision of an anesthesiologist.

An anesthesiologist's first contact with a patient is usually during a "preoperative interview" during which the anesthesiologist reviews the patient's complete medical history and any medications currently used by the patient. At that time, the anesthesiologist discusses the upcoming surgery with the patient and reviews the options for anesthesia and pain-killing drugs to be used in recovery. The anesthesiologist also becomes familiar with the patient's preexisting medical conditions, such as diabetes or heart disease, and plans how to control those problems during surgery.

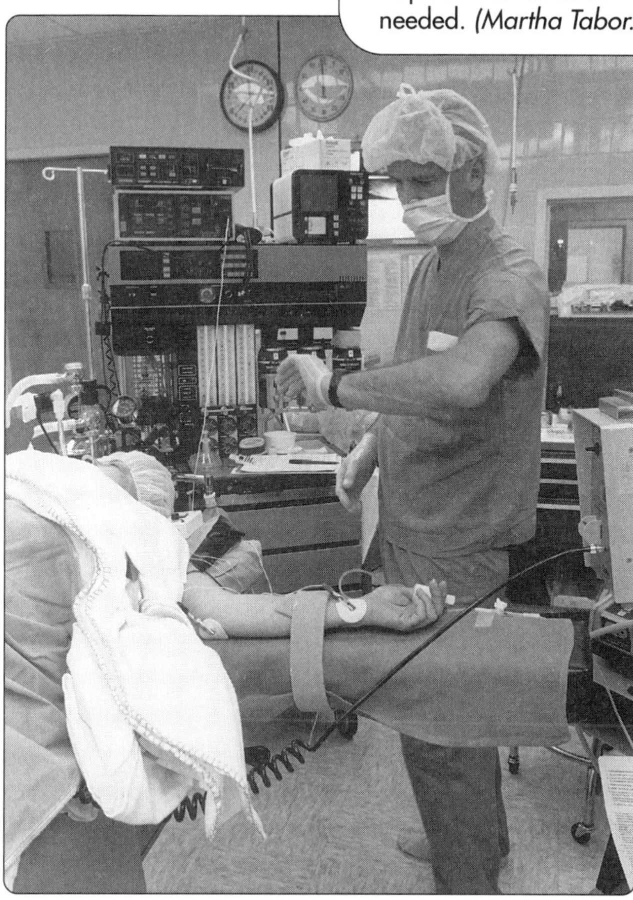

During surgery, an anesthesiologist carefully monitors the patient's vital signs—including heart rate and rhythm, blood pressure, breathing, and brain and kidney function—and adjusts anesthetics as needed. *(Martha Tabor.)*

During surgery, the anesthesiologist is responsible for the patient's well-being as the surgeon and other members of the medical team perform the medical operation. In the first phase of surgery, the anesthesiologist applies the anesthesia. During the middle phase, as the surgery actually takes place, the anesthesiologist uses sophisticated electronic equipment to carefully monitor the patient's vital signs, including heart rate and rhythm, blood pressure, breathing, and brain and kidney functions. As the surgical procedure progresses, the anesthesiologist may have to adjust the patient's anesthesia to compensate for changes in the patient's physical state.

When surgery is finished, the recovery phase begins. The anesthesiologist administers medications to reverse the effects of the anesthetic, returning the patient to consciousness if a general anesthetic has been used. After surgery, patients are moved to a recovery room, where the anesthesiologist is still responsible for their well-being. In recovery, the patient is closely monitored by nurses and other specially trained staff under the supervision of the anesthesiologist. Eventually, the anesthesiologist determines when the patient has recovered sufficiently to leave the recovery room.

There are three main types of anesthesia administered during surgery: general, regional, and local. General anesthesia renders the patient unconscious and unable to feel pain or any other sensation. Many general anesthetics are gases or vapors administered through a mask or breathing tube, whereas others are liquid medicines introduced through a vein. Regional anesthesia numbs an entire area of the body requiring surgery. Local anesthesia is used to numb a specific part of the body (such as the foot or hand). Both regional and local anesthetics are administered via injections. In addition to anesthetics, patients requiring regional and local anesthetics often are given sedatives to help them relax during surgery.

Anesthesiologists work in hospitals or outpatient medical facilities where surgery is performed. Some work in emergency rooms, where they handle victims of heart attacks, shock, drug overdoses, traumatic injuries, and other serious health problems requiring immediate care.

Anesthesiologists operate as part of a team. In surgery, the team includes the surgeons performing the operation and nurses supporting them. Anesthesiologists often work directly with a nurse anesthetist who helps administer medications to the patient during surgery.

The job of anesthesiologist requires intelligence, perseverance, and years of sophisticated training. Besides great technical skills, an anesthesiologist needs a good bedside manner, especially during the preoperative interview when the anesthesiologist must be able to calm the patient while eliciting vital information. Anesthesiologists must themselves keep calm during high-stress situations, and they need to be able to maintain peak levels of concentration during long surgical procedures.

Education and Training Requirements

Anesthesiologists are highly educated medical professionals. They must undergo extensive training in addition to their basic medical education.

Like any other physician, an anesthesiologist must successfully complete a 4-year undergraduate degree and a 4-year medical school program. After medical school, an anesthesiologist takes an additional 4 years of specialized training.

During the first year of specialized training, an anesthesiologist serves a general internship and is trained in diagnosis or treatment in other areas of medicine. This is followed by an intensive 3-year residency program on the technology and medical aspects of anesthesiology. Besides anesthesiology, an anesthesiologist must also study cardiology, critical care medicine, internal medicine, pharmacology, and surgery. An anesthesiologist may choose to specialize in a particular field, such as neurosurgical anesthesiology, and undergo additional training in that field.

Once an anesthesiologist has completed college, medical school, and residency and specialized training, his or her education is by no means finished. New developments in the field of anesthesiology require anesthesiologists to continually update their knowledge and skills through professional seminars and special continuing education course work. All students interested in pursuing anesthesiology need a strong background in physics, chemistry, biology, and mathematics.

Getting the Job

Like all physicians, anesthesiologists must be driven, self-motivated individuals willing to work long hours under intense pressure. In addition, a medical education is extremely costly and requires a huge financial commitment. An estimated 80 percent of all medical students borrow money to cover their education expenses.

Anyone interested in pursuing a career in medicine should consider volunteer work at a local hospital or health clinic. That is a good way to gain firsthand experience in working with patients, doctors, nurses, and health care managers.

Advancement Possibilities and Employment Outlook

Anyone who has made it through medical school and residency training to become a fully licensed and practicing anesthesiologist has already made it to the top of his or her chosen field. He or she may decide to pursue a position as the anesthesiology department head within a specific hospital or health care facility. Individuals wishing to quit their medical practice can often find work as teachers.

At present, anesthesiologists account for approximately 5 percent of the 560,000 physicians in the United States. The growing and aging population will increase demand for physicians' services in the coming years. However, escalating health care costs will tend to limit the number of expensive treatments, including surgery. Competition for jobs at hospitals, including anesthesiologists' positions, is expected to be intense.

Working Conditions

Anesthesiologists work in hospitals and medical facilities offering outpatient surgery. They divide their time between patients' rooms, operating theaters, and post-operation recovery rooms. The job can be extremely stressful and may demand long hours. Anesthesiologists are often "on call," during which time they must be prepared to show up for emergency procedures at all hours of the day and night.

Earnings and Benefits

Anesthesiologists are near the top of the pay scale among all physicians. The median annual income for anesthesiologists is $220,000.

Where to Go for More Information

American Medical Association
515 North State Street
Chicago, IL 60610-4320
(312) 464-5000
www.ama-assn.org

Association of American Medical Colleges
Section for Student Services
2450 N Street, NW
Washington, DC 20037-1127
(202) 828-0400
www.aamc.org

Art and Music Therapist

Education and Training
Varies—see profile

Salary Range
Average—$25,000 to $35,000

Employment Outlook
Very good

Definition and Nature of the Work

Art and music therapists are practicing artists and musicians who combine their talents with professional training in health and psychology. They devise programs to help prevent or alleviate physical, mental, and social problems.

Therapists often work as members of a larger health care team serving a number of patients. Together, they discuss their cases and decide on the best form of treatment. Art and music therapists may carry on their work with individuals or in groups.

Art and music therapists work to improve self-confidence and self-control and to relieve depression and anger. Patients are encouraged to deal with these problems by expressing themselves through music and art. For example, with the help of an art therapist, aggressive children may be able to channel their aggression into painting rather than into other forms of detrimental behavior. A music

Art and music therapists devise programs to help patients deal with their problems by expressing themselves through music and art. *(Martha Tabor.)*

therapist may help people who have difficulty in relating to others by having them play and move to music with other people.

Art therapists are often involved in diagnosing mental illness, particularly in children. They use art in various ways as a diagnostic tool. For example, the use of shapes, colors, details, or lack of fine points in a drawing or painting can reveal certain emotions and other problems. Therapists also work in schools and in centers for elderly people to prevent depression and other forms of mental illnesses.

Education and Training Requirements

A master's degree from an accredited college is usually required in order to practice as an art therapist. To become a certified music therapist, you must complete an accredited 4-year bachelor's degree program in music therapy. A liberal arts degree with training in music as well as a strong background in psychology and the biological, social, and behavioral sciences is also sufficient for music therapists. Students in these programs must complete an internship to graduate and receive certification. Those who wish to work in public schools must complete further courses to be eligible for a teaching certificate.

Getting the Job

Your college placement office is probably the best source of job information. Art and music therapists can also apply to state employment offices and federal agencies. Professional organizations, such as the American Art Therapy Association or the National Association for Music Therapy, assist their members in finding positions.

Advancement Possibilities and Employment Outlook

In private practice, music and art therapists can work to expand their number of clients. Those in hospitals and clinics may advance to supervisory positions. Many positions for these therapists are in government-supported institutions. Here advancement is in the form of increases in pay and rank following successful reviews. However, promotion may involve leaving clinical practice and becoming an administrator.

Art and music therapy are growing occupations. More and more hospitals and institutions are employing therapists of all types. Schools and nursing homes are also recognizing the value of art and music as preventive and remedial therapies. The outlook for employment is very good through the year 2008.

Working Conditions

Art and music therapists work in a number of different settings. They work in hospitals and mental health facilities, schools, and private offices. The surroundings are generally cheerful and pleasant. Most therapists work a 40-hour week. Those in private practice may have irregular hours to accommodate their patients' schedules.

Earnings and Benefits

Average salaries for experienced therapists are between $25,000 and $35,000 a year. Therapists with a doctoral degree who teach in universities can earn $50,000 a year or more. Benefits usually include paid holidays and vacations, health insurance, and pension plans. Some therapists receive tuition assistance for further study. Art and music therapists in private practice must provide their own benefits.

Where to Go for More Information

American Art Therapy Association
1202 Allanson Road
Mundelein, IL 60060-3808
(847) 949-6064
e-mail: estygarlll@aol.com

National Association of Schools of Music
11250 Roger Bacon Drive, Suite 21
Reston, VA 20190-5202
(703) 437-0700
www.arts-accredit.org

Blood Bank Technologist

Education and Training
College

Salary Range
Median—$32,440

Employment Outlook
Good

Definition and Nature of the Work

Medical technologists, also known as clinical laboratory technologists, perform laboratory tests that are crucial to the detection, diagnosis, and treatment of disease. Blood bank technologists, or immunohematologists, are specialized medical technologists. They collect, type, and prepare blood and its components for transfusions.

Blood bank technologists perform other types of blood tests as well, and may also be responsible for interpreting data and reporting test results to the attending physicians. The duties of blood bank technologists may include purchasing, maintaining, and repairing the specialized equipment and instruments used in blood analysis. Blood bank technologists also conduct research, design new laboratory procedures, and establish or continue the training and education of other laboratory employees. Blood bank technologists usually are employed in large laboratories.

Education and Training Requirements

To be a blood bank technologist, you need a bachelor's degree with a major in medical technology or one of the life sciences. Recommended courses include chemistry, biology, microbiology, mathematics, and specialized courses in clinical laboratory skills. Courses in computers and business management are also important.

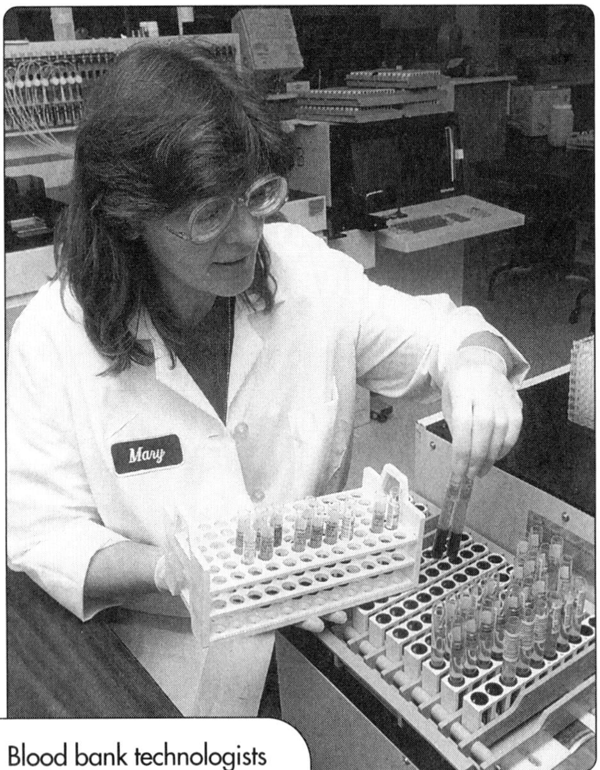

Blood bank technologists perform tests on blood that are crucial to the detection, diagnosis, and treatment of disease. *(Martha Tabor.)*

Many employers require blood bank technologists to be certified by a professional society or certifying agency. To become certified, a technologist must pass a written exam. Some states, including Florida, California, and Hawaii, require all laboratory personnel to be licensed or registered.

Blood bank technologists must have strong analytical, problem-solving, and communication skills, as well as the ability to work well under pressure. They also need manual dexterity and must pay close attention to detail.

Getting the Job

The placement services of colleges and schools of medical technology offer assistance in finding a first job as a blood bank technologist. Registries of medical technologists, newspaper want ads, job banks on the Internet, and commercial placement agencies are also good sources of employment opportunities.

Advancement Possibilities and Employment Outlook

With experience and the successful completion of a certification program, blood bank technologists can advance to supervisory positions, laboratory management, or the position of chief medical technologist. Positions in research and teaching require graduate training, and the position of laboratory director requires a doctorate. Experienced technologists can also work in product development, marketing, or sales with manufacturers of home diagnostic-testing kits, laboratory equipment, or laboratory supplies.

The employment outlook for blood bank technologists is good through the year 2008. However, many independent medical laboratories and hospitals have consolidated, which has increased competition for jobs. Technological developments will encourage the use of diagnostic testing and spur employment. On the other hand, increased automation will limit growth, since fewer workers will be required to perform tests.

Working Conditions

Blood bank technologists usually work in hospitals, clinics, public health agencies, research institutions, or independent medical laboratories. Some technologists work in Veterans Administration hospitals and the U.S. Public Health Service. Technologists usually work a 35- to 40-hour week with night, weekend, holiday, and shift work often required, especially in hospitals. Blood bank technologists must stand for long periods. They must be extremely careful in handling specimens and solutions to avoid contaminating test samples or exposing themselves to disease.

Earnings and Benefits

Although salaries vary with the place of employment, the average annual salary for medical technologists in hospitals or large medical centers is $32,500 to $37,900. Benefits include paid holidays and vacations, health insurance, and a pension plan.

Where to Go for More Information

American Association of Blood Banks
8101 Glenbrook Road
Bethesda, MD 20814-2749
(301) 907-6977
www.aabb.org

American Medical Technologists
710 Higgins Road
Park Ridge, IL 60068
(800) 275-1268
www.amt1.org

Chiropractor

Education and Training
Advanced degree; license

Salary Range
Median—$63,930

Employment Outlook
Very good

Definition and Nature of the Work

Chiropractors practice a special system of health care known as chiropractic. Chiropractic is based on the belief that physical health is associated with the nervous system, and interference with the nervous system impairs normal functions and lowers resistance to disease. Chiropractors treat patients chiefly by manipulating parts of the body, especially the spinal column. The spinal column is important because the spinal cord, the fundamental part of the nervous system, passes through it. Chiropractors try to correct any disorders of the skeleton or spine that may interrupt the flow of nerve impulses to various parts of the body. They do not use drugs or surgery to treat patients.

Chiropractors use a variety of methods to learn about a patient's condition. They ask the patient questions and examine the patient carefully. They usually look to see and feel whether body structures are out of place. They often use X rays to get a picture of the patient's bone structure. In addition, chiropractors use laboratory tests, such as urinalysis or blood tests, as well as instruments, such as stethoscopes, to diagnose disorders. However, some patients need drugs, surgery, psychiatry, and other types of treatment that chiropractors do not use. Chiropractors refer these patients to physicians who can give them the proper treatment.

Chiropractors use several kinds of treatment. They usually manipulate the affected part of the body. They also treat patients with light, heat, cold, water, exercise, or other forms of physical therapy. In addition, chiropractors often advise their patients about diet and mental outlook to help promote good health.

Most chiropractors have their own private practices or share ownership with other chiropractors. Some teach chiropractic or do research in hospitals, clinics, health agencies, or private industry. Many chiropractors specialize in such areas as athletic injuries, diseases of children and women, and X-ray diagnoses.

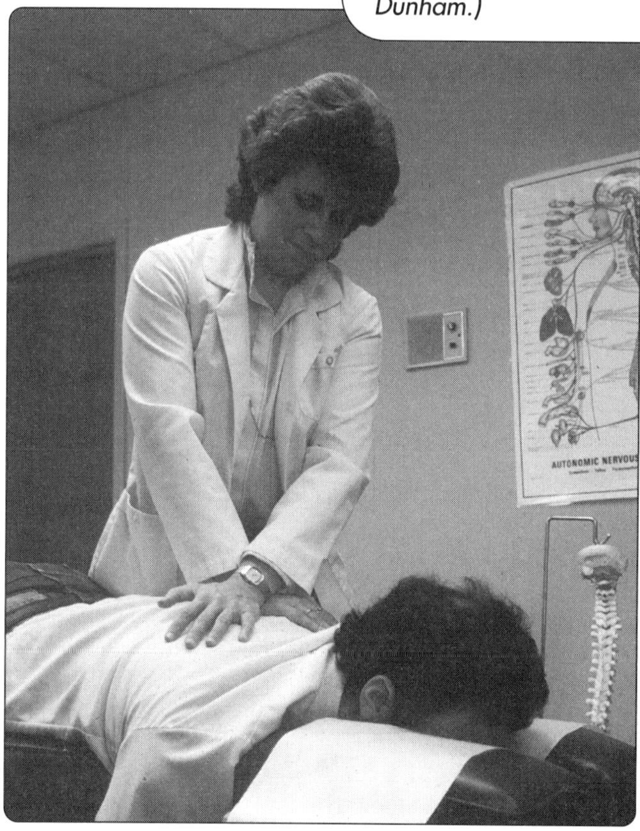

Chiropractors manipulate the spinal column in order to correct disorders of the skeleton or spine that interrupt the flow of nerve impulses to various parts of the body. *(Tom Dunham.)*

Education and Training Requirements

Students usually need 2 years of college before they can enroll in a special chiropractic college. They should take courses in science and other subjects required by the chiropractic college that they want to attend. After completing a 4-year program in a chiropractic college, graduates receive the degree of doctor of chiropractic (D.C.). All states require that chiropractors be licensed. Requirements vary, however, from state to state. In all states chiropractors must pass a state board examination. In some states they must also pass a test in basic science.

Getting the Job

Nearly all newly licensed chiropractors enter private practice. Some of them open their own offices right away. Others buy an established practice from a chiropractor who is retiring. Still others join the office of a practicing chiropractor to get experience. Chiropractic colleges can provide information about setting up a practice.

Some chiropractors have salaried jobs that are usually in clinics, chiropractic colleges, or private industry. Job openings of this kind can be found through the want ads of newspapers, Internet job banks, or in professional publications.

Advancement Possibilities and Employment Outlook

Chiropractors usually advance by building their practices. The degree of their success depends on their skill and location as well as other factors. Some chiropractors advance by moving into high-level jobs in teaching, research, or administration.

The employment outlook is very good through the year 2008 due to growing use of chiropractic services. Demand for chiropractors is related to the ability of patients to pay, either directly or through health insurance, and to public acceptance of the profession, which is growing. However, more people are going into this field. There may be competition for jobs in some geographical areas.

Where to Go for More Information

American Chiropractic Association
1701 Clarendon Boulevard
Arlington, VA 22209
(800) 986-4636
www.amerchiro.org

International Chiropractors Association
1110 North Glebe Road, Suite 1000
Arlington, VA 22201
(703) 528-5000
www.chiropractic.org

Working Conditions

Chiropractors usually work in pleasant offices. If they are in private practice, they can set their own hours. To be successful, they need to have good business sense and self-discipline. They should be able to work with all kinds of people. Chiropractors must also be able to work well with their hands.

Earnings and Benefits

The earnings of chiropractors vary greatly. The median annual salary is $63,930. Since chiropractors are usually self-employed, they must provide their own benefits, such as pension funds and insurance policies.

Dentist

Education and Training

Advanced degree; license

Salary Range

Median—$110,160

Employment Outlook

Fair

Definition and Nature of the Work

Dentists are health professionals who take care of the teeth, gums, and supporting bones of the mouth. They help their patients keep their teeth and gums healthy. They also treat diseased teeth and gums. Dentists sometimes detect general diseases of the body that can affect the condition of a patient's mouth.

Most dentists work as general practitioners in their own office or with a group of dentists. They often have dental assistants and dental hygienists working for them. Under the dentist's direction, these helpers sometimes take X rays, clean patients' teeth, and teach patients how to care for their teeth and gums at home. Dentists may take X rays themselves. They examine patients' mouths for cavities, sores, swelling, or other signs of disease. They may fill cavities, pull teeth that cannot be saved, or replace missing teeth. Dentists use both hand and power tools. They may use a local or general anesthetic to keep patients comfortable during treatment. Some dentists do their own laboratory work. Others send this work out to dental laboratories. Sometimes general practitioners refer patients to specialists.

There are eight areas of specialization for dentists. Orthodontists straighten teeth by fitting them with wires or braces. Oral surgeons operate on the mouth

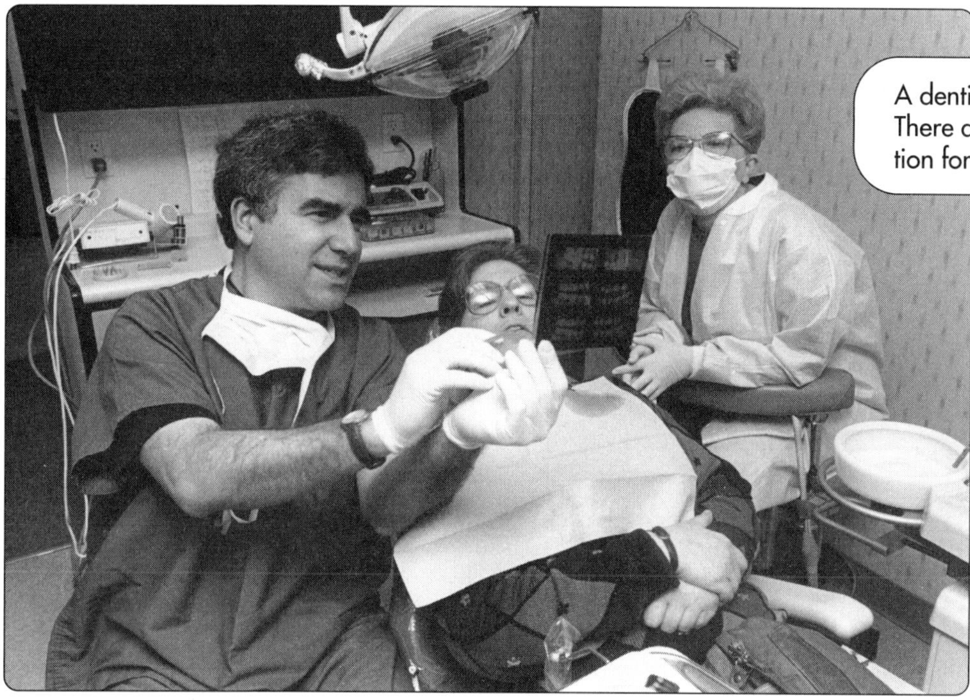

A dentist shows X-rays to a patient. There are several areas of specialization for dentists. *(Martha Tabor.)*

and jaws. Endodontists treat diseases of the soft pulp inside the teeth. Oral pathologists diagnose and sometimes treat diseases of the mouth. Pedodontists specialize in dentistry for children and teenagers. Periodontists are concerned with problems of the gums. Prosthodontists replace missing teeth with artificial teeth. Public health dentists develop care programs. A small percentage of dentists also work in teaching, research, or administration jobs.

Education and Training Requirements

You need 6 to 8 years of training after high school before you can work as a dentist. You must complete 2 to 4 years of college before entering a dental college. Most students have at least a bachelor's degree when they begin dental college. The 4-year program at a dental college leads to either a doctor of dental surgery (D.D.S.) or a doctor of dental medicine (D.D.M.) degree. Dentists who decide to specialize need from 2 to 4 years of further training.

All states require dentists to be licensed. They must graduate from an approved dental college and then pass a state board examination.

Getting the Job

Most newly licensed dentists enter private practice. Since it is becoming more difficult to open new practices, many dentists start out by working with a dentist who is already established. Other dentists find salaried positions in hospitals or government agencies. Your dental college placement office can give you information on how to begin a practice.

Advancement Possibilities and Employment Outlook

Dentists usually advance by building their practices. Some become specialists. Others may go into high-level teaching, research, or administration jobs. Employment is expected to grow slower than the average for all occupations through the year 2008. Most jobs will result from the need to replace the large number of dentists projected to retire. The demand will continue to grow because members of the baby boom generation will need maintenance on dental work, and more elderly people are likely to retain their original teeth. In addition, the provision of dental insurance is expected to create some new jobs for dentists. However, despite increases in demand for dental services, dentists are more likely to hire dental hygienists and dental assistants to handle services they perform themselves, rather than hiring more dentists.

Working Conditions

Dentists must spend long hours on their feet. They must take precautions against infectious diseases and must be able to deal with tense patients. They are rewarded, however, by the prestige of their profession. Because they often have several helpers, dentists must be able to supervise the work of others. They should also have good business sense. They must be responsible and careful professionals who can work well with their hands.

Dentists usually set their own schedules. Many choose to work more than 40 hours a week. These often include some evening and Saturday hours. Some dentists prefer a part-time schedule.

Earnings and Benefits

Earnings for dentists vary widely. They depend on the dentist's experience, skill, and willingness to work long hours. Earnings also depend on location and on the type of practice. The median income for dentists is $110,160 a year. Since most dentists are self-employed, they must provide their own benefits.

Where to Go for More Information

American Association of Dental Schools
1625 Massachusetts Avenue, NW, Sixth Floor
Washington, DC 20036-2212
(202) 667-9433
www.aads.jhu.edu

American Dental Association
211 East Chicago Avenue
Chicago, IL 60611-2678
(312) 440-2500
www.ada.org

Epidemiologist

Education and Training
Advanced degree

Salary Range
Varies—see profile

Employment Outlook
Good

Definition and Nature of the Work

Epidemiologists study infectious and noninfectious diseases that afflict large segments of the population. They work to find the causes of diseases and to develop new treatments. Epidemiology, which was once limited to the study of communicable diseases, such as cholera and tuberculosis, now also encompasses the study of noninfectious diseases, such as cancer and heart disease. However, much of epidemiologists' work concerns the study of AIDS.

In conducting their studies, epidemiologists carefully count the number of affected people and categorize them according to characteristics such as gender, race, social class, and marital status. They also record the number of new cases of a particular disease and try to determine when and how these people became ill. These studies are repeated regularly to detect any changes, new symptoms, or previously unrecorded causes of a disease.

To identify factors that contribute to a disease, epidemiologists may compare a group of people afflicted by the disease with a group that is not afflicted. Epidemiologists often work with other types of medical detectives, such as pathologists, who deal with the world's deadliest viruses.

Education and Training Requirements

Epidemiologists must have a medical degree. In addition, many have a master's degree or doctoral degree in one of the sciences, such as biochemistry or microbiology. Many epidemiologists were practicing physicians before they pursued graduate degrees, and most had researching experience or advanced clinical training before they became epidemiologists. In-depth knowledge of medicine, scientific methods, and research techniques is essential.

As an epidemiologist, you should be prepared to continue studying throughout your career to stay up to date on the most current knowledge and advances. You must also be detail oriented and precise in your work habits.

Getting the Job

The placement officers of medical and graduate schools will have information on available positions. Qualified individuals can also contact research facilities directly to inquire about research openings.

Advancement Possibilities and Employment Outlook

After gaining experience in this area of medical research, individuals can become supervisors of epidemiology departments or even directors of an entire research facility.

The need for epidemiologists will grow through the beginning of the 21st century, as new diseases infect the population, and as diseases that were thought to be under control reappear. Epidemiologists will be needed to track the diseases, uncover symptoms and causes, and point the way to possible containment or cures.

Working Conditions

Epidemiologists generally work in clean, well-lighted offices and laboratories. They usually work for research institutes or privately funded research groups. Many work for the Centers for Disease Control and Prevention in Atlanta, Georgia, or for other government agencies. A 40-hour, 5-day week is the standard; however, although as with most professions in the medical field, a flexible schedule is often required.

Earnings and Benefits

Earnings vary depending on the type of employer and the experience and qualifications of the epidemiologist. Most are paid according to the general scale for physicians. The average income for all physicians is between $115,000 and $238,000 a year. Epidemiologists in research positions are provided with medical insurance, paid vacations and holidays, and pension plans.

Where to Go for More Information

American Medical Association
515 North State Street
Chicago, IL 60610-4377
(312) 464-5000
www.ama-assn.org

Geriatric Social Worker

Education and Training
Varies—see profile

Salary Range
Varies—see profile

Employment Outlook
Excellent

Definition and Nature of the Work

Geriatric social workers constitute a division of social work that is concerned with the welfare of the elderly. They try to improve the quality of life for senior citizens and help to alleviate some of the negative aspects of aging. They help senior citizens to enjoy happier, more productive lives.

Geriatric social workers are employed in a variety of settings and have a wide range of duties. Most geriatric social workers specialize in one of three areas. Many work in the area that involves the primary function of geriatric social workers-to assess the needs of senior citizens. These workers are often associated with community organizations, such as family service agencies or day care centers (many of which have outreach programs). The workers may help to decide which senior citizens need home health aides, special transportation, or similar services. With the help of such services, some elderly people may be able to stay out of nursing homes. Geriatric social workers are trained to recognize normal and abnormal aging patterns. They can suggest when an elderly client needs to see a doctor and can arrange for a visit. They can help a family decide whether it would be best to place the client in an institution.

Geriatric social workers also work in the area whose function is to help the elderly deal with their problems. Many older adults are lonely. Social workers encourage clients to participate in group activities. Many workers are skilled in leading these activities or in arranging for others to lead. Some have a background in mental health. They may provide therapy for clients suffering from depression or anxiety (both common conditions among the elderly). Most social workers act as a link between their clients and the numerous confusing public and private programs designed for the aging. Social workers help their clients to apply for appropriate services. They help sort out any problems in the delivery of these services. Social workers providing direct services can be found in many types of institutions, including retirement communities, nursing homes, hospitals, and employment programs for older adults.

A small number of geriatric social workers work in the area where they plan and organize services for the elderly. Every program or agency has an executive director or its equivalent. Large organizations may have many administrators. State and county long-range-planning bodies have no clients; their function is to estimate future needs and plan how these needs can best be met.

Geriatric social workers must enjoy working with older people and respect them. The reward of the occupation is having a strong rapport with the clients. Workers should be emotionally mature, objective, and sensitive to the needs of others. They must also be well-organized and keep careful records.

Education and Training Requirements

Training in social work with a specialty in gerontology is available at the associate, bachelor's, and master's degree levels. A postgraduate degree with a specialization in aging is recommended. Some of the better jobs require advanced degrees. Training requirements may vary with geographic region; they tend to be higher in metropolitan versus rural areas. Consult your local guidance counselor.

Getting the Job

Your college placement office may be able to help you find a job. Consult the job listings in your local newspapers and on the Internet. You can also contact the

Geriatric social workers help senior citizens to enjoy happier, more productive lives. They help the elderly deal with their problems and alleviate some of the pain of aging. *(Martha Tabor.)*

organizations providing services for senior citizens in your area and ask for information interviews.

Advancement Possibilities and Employment Outlook

Geriatric social workers can advance to supervisory and administrative positions. The director of a small program may go on to run a larger organization.

The outlook for geriatric social workers is excellent, especially for those with advanced degrees. The number of senior citizens is increasing rapidly. The need for geriatric social workers will also rise.

Working Conditions

Geriatric social workers are employed in a variety of settings. Their services may be needed at retirement communities, nursing homes, state and government agencies, or hospices. Since the locations of employment may differ, the social worker might be providing service in a modern, well-lighted building one day and a poorly maintained inner city setting the next.

Earnings and Benefits

Earnings vary widely. Some of the factors that affect salaries are type of institution, level of training, and region. Beginning salaries are about $15,000 to $24,000 a year. Experienced workers generally earn between $20,000 and $30,000 a year. Those with an advanced degree might earn $36,000 or more in some positions. Benefits usually include medical insurance, life insurance, and paid vacations.

Where to Go for More Information

Association for Gerontology in Higher Education
1030 15th Street, NW, Suite 240
Washington, DC 20005-1503
(202) 289-9806
www.aghe.org

National Association of Social Workers
750 First Street, NE, Suite 700
Washington, DC 20002-4241
(800) 638-8799
www.socialworkers.org

Health Care Administrator

Education and Training
College

Salary Range
Varies—see profile

Employment Outlook
Very good

Definition and Nature of the Work

Health care is one of the largest sectors of the American economy, and it is undergoing radical changes in order to meet the needs of a growing and aging population. Like other sophisticated businesses, health care requires skilled managers. The especially fluid nature of the health care industry has created a great demand for qualified managers and administrators.

Currently, more than one-half of health care administrators are employed by hospitals. Other health care administrators work for health maintenance organizations (HMOs), long-term facilities (e.g., nursing homes), mental health institutions, outpatient facilities, home health care agencies, and independent group practices. As health care trends such as managed care and preventive medicine become more common, relatively fewer administrators will be employed by hospitals. Other trends affecting health care administration include integrating health care delivery, ever-evolving technology, and the rapidly aging American population.

There are many different types of health care administrators. Generalists set the overall direction of the health care facility that they manage and do not specialize in any one facet of health care. Top administrators or chief executive officers and assistant administrators without specific titles are usually generalists. They must combine a basic understanding of clinical issues with business management expertise. Top managers are also often called on to represent their health care facility to the general public and/or investors.

Specialist managers generally fall into one of two categories: clinical and nonclinical. Nonclinical managers are responsible for such nonhealth functions as finance, housekeeping, and human resources. Clinical managers specialize in functions unique to the health care industry, such as nursing, surgery, therapy, medical records, and outpatient services. Clinical managers usually have more narrowly defined responsibilities than generalists or nonclinical managers.

The ever-evolving health care industry requires skilled managers and administrators to make difficult decisions and face complex situations on a daily basis. *(Earl Dotter.)*

Governments and insurance companies also employ health care administrators. Those employing administrators include public health departments, health planning agencies, and the Veteran's Administration (VA) health care system. Insurance companies need administrators to help manage medical records and claims.

Certain tasks are common to most health care administrators and managers, regardless of their specialty or employer. Most managers evaluate personnel and their job performance; develop budgets; and implement policies, objectives, and procedures established for their various departments. All managers must also be able to coordinate their efforts with those of other managers and administrators in the best interests of their health care facility, its doctors, nurses, and patients.

The number of administrators employed by a given health care facility is determined by the size of the facility. A large hospital or HMO may employ dozens of managers, whereas a small group of physicians in a group practice may hire a single administrator to handle billing and other administrative duties.

Health care administrators often face difficult decisions and complex situations on a daily basis. The job requires good leadership and management skills, excellent problem-solving abilities, and the capacity to work long hours under stress.

Education and Training Requirements

A college degree is almost always a prerequisite for finding employment as a health care administrator. Candidates with a bachelor's degree can expect to compete for jobs as administrative assistants or assistant department heads. Department managers usually will have at least a master's degree. In addition, many clinical managers also have practical experience in their field (e.g., as nurses or therapists) in addition to management training and experience.

In 1997, accredited programs leading to a master's degree in health services administration were offered at 67 schools in the United States. Competition for entry in these programs is keen. Typically, the programs last 2 to 3 years and provide course work in hospital organization and management, marketing, accounting and budgeting, and human resources. Some programs offer students the chance to specialize in one type of health care facility or one aspect of health care management, while others offer a general education in health care administration.

Top administrators, independent health care management consultants, and researchers often have earned doctoral degrees en route to achieving their positions.

Getting the Job

High school students interested in preparing for a career in health care administration should study sciences related to health care, such as biology, chemistry, and physics. In addition, they should take available courses in business management, accounting, and marketing. Volunteering at hospitals, nursing homes, and other health care facilities also provides important exposure to the field.

Upon earning a college degree in health care management, candidates can apply directly to health care facilities for entry-level positions. As mentioned previously, graduate degrees are almost always a prerequisite for top management jobs, so many low-level health care managers participate in continuing education programs in order to advance their careers to the next level.

Advancement Possibilities and Employment Outlook

Health care managers and administrators advance their careers by moving into more responsible and higher-paying positions. They may advance within their place of employment or by moving on to larger facilities.

Employment of health service managers is expected to grow faster than average for all occupations through 2008, due to expansion and diversification in the health services industry. Expect to find relatively fewer positions in hospitals, and more positions in HMOs, home health care agencies, group practices, and long-term facilities.

Working Conditions

Health care managers and administrators work long hours in modern facilities. Hospitals, nursing homes, and other health care facilities never "close," and managers are needed at all times to solve problems and handle day-to-day operations. Health care management is a high-stress occupation because managers must make decisions balancing the health of patients with the fiscal health of their facility.

Where to Go for More Information

Healthcare Financial Management Association
2 Westbrook Corporate Center, Suite 700
Westchester, IL 60154-5700
(708) 531-9600
www.hfma.org

Healthcare Resource Management Society
P.O. Box 29253
Cincinnati, OH 45229-0253
(513) 520-1058

Earnings and Benefits

Earnings of health care administrators vary according to their responsibilities and the size of the facility they manage. In a recent survey by Modern Healthcare magazine, clinical heads at a typical hospital earned median annual salaries ranging from $57,700 (for respiratory therapy) to $100,200 (for nursing services), with most salaries falling within the $62,000 to $75,000 range. That same survey found that half of all hospital CEOs earned total compensation of at least $190,500. According to a survey conducted by the American Health Care Association, the median annual compensation of nursing home administrators was $52,800, with assistant administrators earning an average of $35,000 a year.

Hospital Administrator

Education and Training

Advanced degree

Salary Range

Average—$56,000 to $77,000

Employment Outlook

Very good

Definition and Nature of the Work

Hospital administrators manage or help to manage hospitals and clinics. They make sure that every patient receives the best possible care. A hospital often contains more than 30 departments. Large hospitals generally have several administrators, each of whom specializes in one department. Departments run by individual administrators include the X-ray department, patient services, and building maintenance. The department heads organize the day-to-day activities of their departments. They report regularly to the chief administrator. Chief administrators coordinate the work of all the members of the health care team. They usually report directly to a board of trustees. Chief administrators manage the financial operations at a facility and develop plans for personnel, space, equipment, and supplies. They also make sure that long-range plans are carried out.

Hospital administrators perform many varied tasks. Some are responsible for providing hospital workers with continuing education programs. They make sure that the skills of nurses, physicians, and technicians are upgraded regularly. Other hospital administrators develop programs that make the public aware of good health habits. They promote and market the hospital in the community by making sure that people know about the services that the hospital provides. Often they raise funds for the hospital.

A hospital administrator in charge of the ambulatory care department coordinates the work of all department personnel, manages the finances, and develops long-range plans. *(Martha Tabor.)*

Education and Training Requirements

You should begin to plan for a career as a hospital administrator by taking college preparatory courses in high school. You can gain valuable experience by working in a hospital part-time or during the summer as a volunteer, aide, or receptionist. You should obtain a bachelor's degree in liberal arts, business administration, or health.

You generally need a master's degree to become a hospital administrator. Most hospitals prefer people with a master's degree in health or hospital administration. You can earn this degree in special 2-year graduate programs that include supervised practical experience. Other hospitals prefer administrators with formal training in a field such as business, social science, or industrial engineering. However, this training must usually be combined with practical experience in the health field.

A few specialized hospitals require that their administrators be physicians. These administrators, called physician executives, generally have a master's degree in business administration in addition to their medical training. A doctoral degree in hospital administration is recommended for those who want to do research or teach in a university or for those who want high-level positions in large health organizations.

Getting the Job

Your college placement office can help you to find a job as a hospital administrator. The want ads in newspapers and job listings on the Internet are also useful. You can apply directly for jobs with hospitals, clinics, or health agencies.

Advancement Possibilities and Employment Outlook

Most hospital administrators begin as assistants to experienced administrators. Advancement is based on performance and experience. Those with ability can become senior or chief administrators. Advancement opportunities are especially good at the middle-management level.

The number of hospital administrator positions is expected to increase faster than the average through the year 2008. There will be competition for jobs due to the consolidation and centralization of hospitals. Those with advanced degrees will do best. Owing to the aging of the population, there is an increasing emphasis on long-term health care facilities and community mental health centers. Qualified administrators will be needed to plan programs for these facilities.

Working Conditions

Although comfortable, hospital offices are often hectic. Hospital administrators must be calm and able to withstand the pressure and stress of their demanding job. They are often called on to make difficult decisions quickly. They must be able to work well with other hospital workers and with the public. They must be able to take suggestions as well as to give orders. Hospital administrators usually work more than 40 hours a week. Since hospitals are open around the clock, administrators may be called in during emergencies. They may have to work overtime to solve pressing problems, to travel, or to attend community or professional meetings.

Where to Go for More Information

American College of Healthcare Executives
1 North Franklin, Suite 1700
Chicago, IL 60606-3491
(312) 424-2800
www.ache.org

Association of University Programs in Health Administration
730 11th Street, NW, Fourth Floor
Washington, DC 20001
(202) 638-1448
www.aupha.com

Earnings and Benefits

Salaries vary widely depending on education and experience and on the location and size of the hospital in which the administrators work. Experienced hospital administrators earn salaries ranging from $56,000 to $77,000. Benefits include paid holidays and vacations, health insurance, and pension plans.

Medical Illustrator

Education and Training
College plus training

Salary Range
Average—$25,000 to $50,000

Employment Outlook
Very good

Definition and Nature of the Work

Medical illustrators are artists who work in the field of medicine. They make detailed drawings for textbooks and medical journals that are used by physicians and medical students. Some make graphs or charts for research projects. Medical illustrators also build models of parts of the human body for use in lectures or seminars. They sometimes illustrate the steps that a surgeon uses during an operation or show new ways of operating. They also draw pictures of normal and diseased body conditions. Some medical illustrators help to prepare television programs and films. In some cases they help to create artificial parts, such as ears or eyes, for patients who need them.

The work of medical illustrators is very important to physicians and medical students. Illustrations point out significant details that are difficult to find in the actual body or in photographs of the body. Illustrations often show the relationship of one body structure to another. Such drawings give students a better understanding of how these structures are related. Illustrations that simplify body systems and structures can also help medical students to learn about the body before they do laboratory work or treat patients.

Medical illustrators use many techniques and media in their work. Each technique is used to achieve a specific purpose. Illustrators use drawings, paintings, and prints, for example, to simplify and coordinate related information. They create sculptures and models to show a body system in three dimensions. They use cameras to record details in a realistic way. Sometimes they make drawings or models from photographs. Medical illustrators use many different materials, including paint, pencil, ink, charcoal, and chalk. When sculpting or making models, they use clay, wax, plaster, wood, plastic, or metal.

The training of medical illustrators includes both art and science. They are usually taught to work in all branches of medicine. However, many specialize in one branch, such as in cardiology, which concerns the heart, or in neurology, which deals with the nervous system.

Some medical illustrators are employed by publishers of medical textbooks. Others work for the publishers of scientific journals. Many medical illustrators are staff members of universities, hospitals, and research institutions where they also sometimes teach. Some work for museums, drug companies, and commercial art studios. Some medical illustrators work as freelance artists-they are self-employed and receive a fee for each project that they complete.

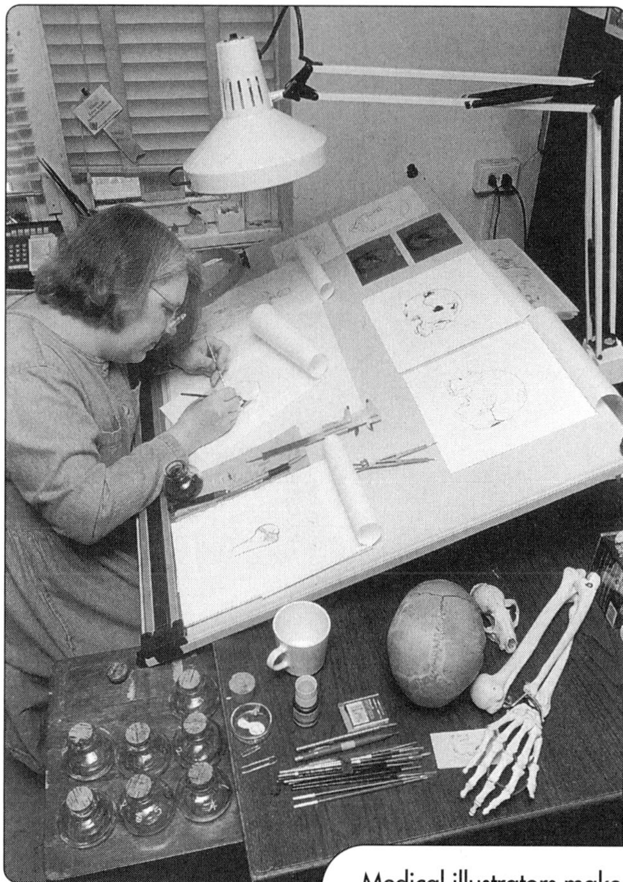

Medical illustrators make detailed drawings for textbooks and medical journals that are used by physicians and medical students. *(Martha Tabor.)*

Education and Training Requirements

Most schools of medical illustration require that students first complete 4 years of college. Requirements for entrance vary, but students usually need courses in the biological sciences and in art. Students must also show samples of their art work. The medical illustration training program lasts 2 or 3 years. Students may receive a certificate, an associate degree, a bachelor's degree, or a master's degree after completing the program.

Getting the Job

Your college placement office can help you to find a job as a medical illustrator. Professional associations can give you information about getting a job or finding work as a freelance illustrator. You can also check the want ads in newspapers, job banks on the Internet, or apply directly to hospitals, publishers, or drug companies.

Advancement Possibilities and Employment Outlook

Medical illustrators usually advance by improving their skills. They may specialize in one particular field. If they are freelance artists, they can build a reputation that will enable them to work on many assignments. Some medical illustrators move into high-level teaching jobs in medical colleges. Medical illustrators who work for publishing companies can direct the art work for a large-scale project, such as a textbook. Those working in hospitals can become senior illustrators and supervise the work of other artists.

The employment outlook is very good through the year 2008. Medical illustrators will be needed to help illustrate new developments in medicine. However, this is a small field, and there may be competition for any openings.

Working Conditions

Medical illustrators do much of their work in art studios, laboratories, and offices. These are usually quiet and well-lighted places. Sometimes illustrators must sketch in operating rooms. Although they often work alone, medical illustrators must also be able to cooperate and to work closely with medical staffs, scientists, and publishers. In addition to artistic talent, they need the ability to do exact and detailed work.

Medical illustrators who work for hospitals, universities, and drug or publishing companies generally work 40 hours a week. Freelance illustrators set their own schedules. All medical illustrators face the pressure of meeting deadlines from time to time.

Earnings and Benefits

Earnings vary widely depending on skill, experience, and place of employment. The average starting salary for medical illustrators is between $20,000 and $26,000 a year. Those medical illustrators with more experience earn between $25,000 and $50,000 a year. Benefits for salaried workers include paid holidays and vacations and health insurance. Self-employed illustrators provide their own benefits.

Where to Go for More Information

Association of Medical Illustrators
2965 Flowers Road South, Suite 105
Atlanta, GA 30341-5520
(770) 454-7933
www.medical-illustrators.org

Medical Laboratory Technologist

Education and Training
Varies—see profile

Salary Range
Average—$18.36 an hour

Employment Outlook
Good

Definition and Nature of the Work

Medical laboratory technologists assist doctors and other scientists by performing tests and research in the laboratory. They look for evidence of the presence of illnesses and parasites, identify allergic reactions and changes in body chemistry, and type and cross-match blood. They prepare vaccines and serums. Technologists perform exacting microscopic chemical and bacteriological tests. They also work as supervisors, teachers, and administrators.

Medical laboratory technologists test blood, urine, other body fluids, and tissue samples that doctors send to the laboratory. For example, technologists analyze blood and urine to look for signs of diseases, such as hemophilia or diabetes. They are also responsible for matching blood samples so that patients are given the correct type of blood during transfusions. Medical laboratory technologists identify parasites and bacteria through their tests. The technologist's work is increasingly important, because doctors are depending more on complex tests to diagnose and determine treatment for patients' illnesses.

Technologists may specialize in such areas as blood banking, virology (the study of viruses), cytology (analysis of body cells), and histology (tissue preparation and examination). In large hospitals most technologists specialize in one area. In smaller laboratories they usually perform a variety of duties.

Medical technologists work in large hospital laboratories, laboratories of private physicians, public health laboratories, and in medical research institutes. Technologists also work in colleges and universities, companies that manufacture drugs and laboratory test equipment, and the armed services.

Education and Training Requirements

Technologists must have at least 4 years of training after high school. High school courses in math and science are very helpful. The training after high school includes 3 years of college with emphasis on courses in chemistry, biological sciences, and mathematics. A 12-month clinical training session follows. Hospitals and schools offer programs accredited by the Committee on Allied Health Education and Accreditation. Many of these programs offer bachelor's degrees.

Recent graduates who pass the appropriate examinations can become certified. Several organizations offer this certification. Certification is important for technologists, because it indicates that they have met recognized standards of competence. Some states require that technologists be licensed. Requirements for licensing vary but usually include a written examination.

Many universities offer graduate programs in medical technology and related subjects for technologists who want to do certain types of laboratory work or for those who want to work in teaching, administration, or research.

Getting the Job

The placement office of your school can give you job information. You may find employment where you received your clinical training. Newspaper want ads, Internet job banks, and medical journals sometimes list openings. It is a good idea to apply directly to hospitals and laboratories. You can also apply for a position with federal, state, and local health departments.

Advancement Possibilities and Employment Outlook

Technologists can advance with further training. They may choose to specialize in one form of laboratory work or do research. Technologists can also advance to positions as teachers or administrators. A master's degree is generally required for these jobs.

The employment outlook is good through the year 2008 because of increased volume of medical testing due to population growth and an increase in disease and disability among the older population. New, more powerful and accurate diagnostic tests and advances in biotechnology should create a need for qualified medical technologists. Workers will be needed to fill supervisory positions in all laboratories. However, because of advances in equipment, technicians can now do tests that once required the expertise of a technologist.

Working Conditions

Working conditions for medical technologists are generally pleasant. Most laboratories are clean and well lighted. With careful training and proper handling of materials, technologists can keep hazards to a minimum. The hours are generally regular and the work steady. There are many opportunities for part-time work. Hospital workers may be on emergency call 24 hours a day at least once a month. Most technologists work a 40-hour week.

Earnings and Benefits

Salaries vary depending on experience, location, and the type of laboratory. Salaries for medical laboratory technologists average $18.36 an hour. Benefits include paid holidays and vacations and health insurance.

Where to Go for More Information

American Society for Clinical Laboratory Science
7910 Woodmont Avenue, Suite 530
Bethesda, MD 20814-3015
(301) 657-2768
www.ascls.org

American Society of Clinical Pathologists
2100 West Harrison Street
Chicago, IL 60612-3798
(800) 621-4142
www.ascp.org

Medical Physicist

Education and Training
Advanced degree

Salary Range
Starting—$34,700
Average—$55,000 to $73,000

Employment Outlook
Fair

Definition and Nature of the Work

Medical physicists apply the principles and theories of physics to all aspects of medicine. In the clinical setting of a hospital, medical physicists provide many important services. They help plan radiation treatment for cancer patients using external radiation beams or internal radioactive sources. They are responsible for accurately measuring the radiation administered. They also consult with physicians and may work with specific patients.

Medical physicists who specialize in nuclear medicine work with physicians in procedures that provide images of the internal organs and determine metabolic rates and blood flow. The images provide physicians with important information that allows them to make a diagnosis.

Medical physicists ensure that the extremely complex equipment used in diagnostic and treatment procedures functions properly. They also design radiation installations for hospitals and are responsible for safety precautions against the hazards of radiation.

Many medical physicists are involved in the research and design of new medical equipment. They work on new applications for high-energy machines, such as linear accelerators to treat cancer. Diagnostic imaging is constantly being improved with such new techniques as magnetic resonance imaging. Medical physicists are also engaged in research to develop imaging procedures using infrared and ultrasound sources.

There are also general areas of research for the medical physicist. They involve the use of computers in diagnosis and treatment and the accurate measurement of blood flow and oxygenation in the treatment of heart disease.

Many hospitals that employ medical physicists are medical schools, and the physicists are members of the faculty. Here they help to teach future medical physicists, medical students, and radiographic technologists. In colleges and universities they may teach medical physics, biophysics, and radiobiology to graduate and undergraduate students.

Education and Training Requirements

Graduate training in medical physics is required for all jobs in this field. Medical physicists spend 4 years earning a bachelor's degree and another 1 or 2 years earning a master's degree. Most then go on to study for doctoral degrees. Because of the nature of the work, it is important that medical physicists have good knowledge of physics and basic medical sciences, such as anatomy, physiology, genetics, and biochemistry.

Getting the Job

Your best sources for job openings are your college professors and advisers. The placement office may also be able to help you find a job as a medical physicist. In addition, you can apply directly to hospitals, universities, and government agencies. Other good sources of information are professional associations and publications.

Advancement Possibilities and Employment Outlook

Advancement opportunities are good for medical physicists with a doctoral degree. Medical physicists in hospitals and research centers can advance by taking on more responsibility and heading project teams. Those in teaching positions can advance by moving through the ranks from instructor to full professor.

The employment outlook for medical physicists is fair through the year 2008. There are more doctorates being granted than the number of openings for physicists. There will be keen competition for jobs, and those candidates with doctoral degrees have the best outlook for finding work. Job prospects will pick up as more workers retire.

Working Conditions

Most medical physicists work in hospitals and universities. Their laboratories and classrooms are clean and well lighted. Medical physicists generally work at least 40 hours a week. Overtime is often necessary for medical emergencies and special projects. To study and keep up with new developments in the field, medical physicists may work long hours on a regular basis. Medical physicists may conduct research independently or as part of a team. They are often members of a patient's medical team and must be able to communicate their ideas to doctors, students, and sometimes patients both orally and in writing.

Where to Go for More Information

American Association of Physicists in Medicine
1 Physics Ellipse
College Park, MD 20740-3846
(301) 209-3350
www.aapm.org

Earnings and Benefits

Salaries for medical physicists are similar to those of other physicists. The starting salary for physicists with a doctoral degree in private industry averages $34,700 a year. The average salary for those with a master's degree is $55,000 a year. Those with a doctoral degree earn an average of $73,000 a year.

Medical Record Administrator

Education and Training
College

Salary Range
Average—$10.57 an hour

Employment Outlook
Excellent

Definition and Nature of the Work

Medical record administrators, formerly called medical record librarians, prepare and keep records of hospital and clinic patients. These records include medicine given to the patient, surgical operations performed, the patient's diet, and the results of tests. Notes made by physicians and nurses who examine a patient are also part of these records. Medical record administrators are responsible for making sure that these records are complete. They develop systems for keeping the needed information in a usable form. Many systems are computerized. Administrators usually supervise other workers, such as medical record technicians, who take care of the technical and clerical details of medical record keeping.

Medical record administrators often prepare reports on the number of admissions, births, deaths, transfers, and discharges that occur in their hospitals. This information helps hospitals in planning for community health care. Medical record administrators may help physicians find information they need about a patient or a type of treatment. They sometimes release information to insurance companies or to research institutes. They may testify in court if their records are used as evidence in a trial.

Medical record administrators develop and maintain record-keeping systems for hospitals and clinics. *(Martha Tabor.)*

Most medical record administrators work in hospitals. Some work in nursing homes, clinics, public health agencies, medical research centers, or insurance companies. Others work for firms that make machinery or forms used to keep medical records. A small number work as consultants for institutions that do not need a full-time medical record administrator.

Education and Training Requirements

Medical record administrators need 4 years of college. You can receive special training leading to a bachelor's degree in medical record administration. You can also earn a degree in another field and then enroll in a 1-year certificate program in medical record administration. When you have completed your training, you are eligible to take an examination given by the American Medical Record Association. If you pass, you become a registered record administrator (RRA).

Getting the Job

The best place to look for your first job is at the placement office of the college where you received your training in medical record administration. The American Medical Record Association can also provide lists of job openings. Newspaper want ads and job banks on the Internet often include opportunities in the medical record field. You can also apply directly to hospitals, clinics, research centers, or health agencies.

Advancement Possibilities and Employment Outlook

Advancement in medical record work generally comes with experience. Medical record administrators can become heads of large departments where they supervise many workers. They can also move into other jobs in hospital administration or become consultants for the medical record departments of a number of small hospitals. They can teach medical record administration courses in colleges and universities.

The employment outlook is excellent through the year 2008, especially for experienced technicians who have completed a formal training program. The demand for medical care is growing. The need for accurate record keeping, especially for insurance purposes and abstracting data, should create opportunities for qualified professionals in this field.

Working Conditions

Medical record departments are usually pleasant places in which to work. Administrators do a good deal of paperwork. They interact with other hospital staff members in addition to their own helpers. They generally work 36 to 40 hours a week.

Medical record administration is a demanding job that requires organizational skills and careful work habits. Administrators must be able to communicate information to others. They are also responsible for seeing that medical information is revealed only to the proper people and organizations.

Earnings and Benefits

Salaries vary depending on the size and type of the place of employment, and on the duties and experience of the worker. Medical record administrators earn an average of $10.57 an hour. Experienced workers can earn up to $35,000 a year. Benefits include paid holidays and vacations, health insurance, and pension plans.

Where to Go for More Information

American Health Information Management Association
233 North Michigan Avenue, Suite 2150
Chicago, IL 60611-1683
(312) 787-2672
www.ahima.org

Nurse Anesthetist

Education and Training

Varies—see profile

Salary Range

Average—$54,200 to $69,200

Employment Outlook

Very good

Definition and Nature of the Work

Nurse anesthetists are registered nurses (RNs) who have received special training in anesthetics. Anesthetics are drugs that produce anesthesia (a state of painlessness or unconsciousness). Nurse anesthetists work under the supervision of an anesthesiologist (a physician specializing in anesthesia) or another physician. Most work in hospitals and in operating rooms during surgery. Anesthetists also administer anesthetics in delivery rooms, emergency rooms, or to dental or psychiatric patients. In small hospitals, nurse anesthetists may also administer oxygen in the inhalation therapy department.

Nurse anesthetists generally give anesthetics in the form of a gas or a fluid. They regulate the flow of the anesthetic and watch the patient carefully for the duration of its effect. They may also give the patient oxygen to prevent shock or other unwanted conditions. Anesthetists keep the physician informed of the patient's condition during an operation. They record the patient's progress. Sometimes nurse anesthetists help to care for the patient during recovery from anesthesia.

Education and Training Requirements

To become a nurse anesthetist, while in high school you should take college preparatory courses in mathematics, science, and the social sciences. Volunteer or part-time work in a hospital is a valuable experience. After high school you will need to earn a bachelor's degree in nursing (B.S.N.) or a bachelor's degree in a related field, with either a diploma or associate degree in nursing. You should have at least 1 year of experience working in acute care nursing before enrolling in a school of anesthesia. Schools of anesthesia are affiliated with hospitals and offer training programs lasting about 2 years. There is also a trend to incorporate this training into a bachelor's or master's degree program. Once you have graduated from an approved school of anesthesia, you are eligible to take the national certifying exam that is given by the Council on Certification of Nurse Anesthetists.

Getting the Job

The American Association of Nurse Anesthetists lists classified ads in its bulletin. Your school placement office can also help you find a job. Sometimes openings for nurse anesthetists are listed in newspaper want ads and Internet job banks.

Advancement Possibilities and Employment Outlook

Experienced and skilled nurse anesthetists can expect steady increases in responsibility and income. Some move from smaller hospitals to those offering greater opportunities and rewards. Anesthetists can become supervisors or can specialize in certain difficult types of surgery. Others become teachers.

The employment outlook for nurse anesthetists is very good through the year 2008. Technological advances in patient care permit a greater number of medical problems to be treated. In addition, the number of older people, who generally need more care than other members of the population, are expected to continue to increase. However, employment in hospitals is expected to grow more slowly than in other health care sectors. While more nurses per patient are needed, the number of inpatients (patients who stay overnight) is not likely to increase significantly. More patients are being released earlier and more procedures are being done on an outpatient basis. The most rapid growth is expected to increase in hospitals' outpatient facilities such as same-day surgery, rehabilitation, and chemotherapy.

Working Conditions

Nurse anesthetists are members of a highly trained medical care team. They must be very careful and responsible in their work. One of their rewards is knowing the importance of their contributions. Although the regularly scheduled workweek of many nurse anesthetists is only 35 hours long, they are also on call for additional hours in case of emergency.

Where to Go for More Information

American Association of Nurse Anesthetists
222 South Prospect Avenue
Park Ridge, IL 60068
(847) 692-7050
www.aana.com

Earnings and Benefits

Salaries vary depending on experience and place of employment. Nurse anesthetists usually earn salaries at the top end of the scale for all nurses. Experienced nurse anesthetists generally earn between $54,200 and $69,200 a year. Benefits include paid vacations and holidays, health insurance, and pension plans.

Nurse-Midwife

Education and Training
College plus training

Salary Range
Median—$40,690

Employment Outlook
Very good

Definition and Nature of the Work

Nurse-midwives provide routine health care for women. They may also provide counseling and information on childbirth and the care of newborns.

Nurse-midwives perform regular checkups during pregnancy. They evaluate the growth and well-being of the baby and the condition of the mother. While they discuss any problems with a physician, nurse-midwives provide routine treatment to patients. If the pregnancy continues without complication, nurse-midwives provide all prenatal care, assist the mother during labor, and deliver the baby. Following the birth, nurse-midwives make sure that the mother and baby are well and provide follow-up care. If an emergency occurs, nurse-midwives are trained to provide assistance until a doctor arrives.

Nurse-midwives also provide a variety of other services for expectant and new parents. They may lead classes in childbirth instruction, sibling preparation, and care of newborns. In addition, nurse-midwives counsel parents about the effects a new baby can have on a family.

Nurse-midwives may also provide care and perform routine examinations for babies and women who are not pregnant. They often offer counseling in health maintenance, fitness, and family nutrition. They may supply birth control information to their patients. In many areas, nurse-midwives supervise well-baby and family planning clinics.

Some midwives are known as lay midwives. They usually receive their training from another midwife and are not trained nurses. Lay midwifery varies in acceptance throughout the country. Many states do not allow lay midwives to practice, whereas in some communities, lay midwifery is a traditional practice.

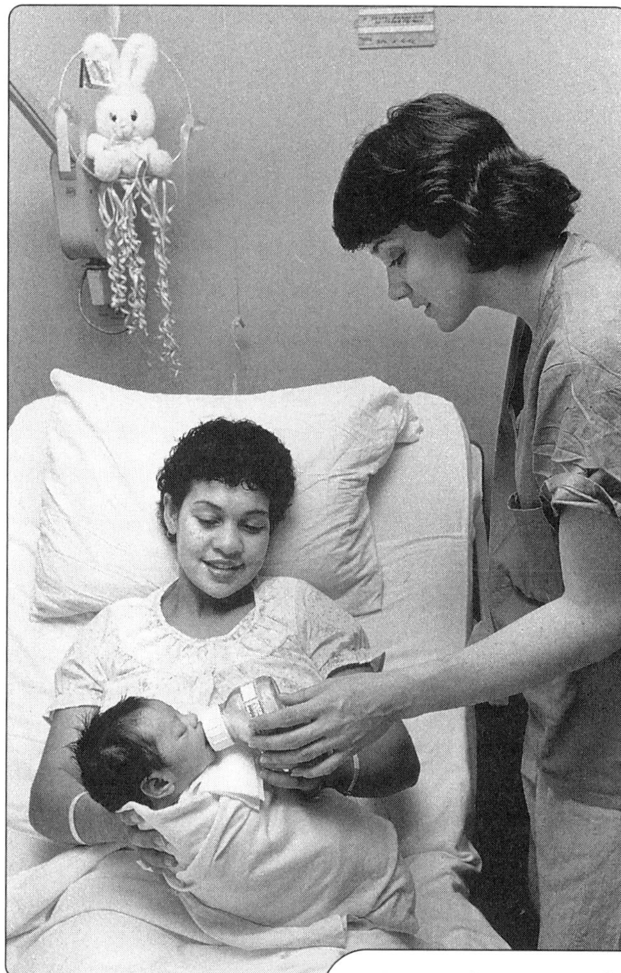

Nurse-midwives provide routine health care for women before, during, and after their pregnancy. *(Earl Dotter.)*

Education and Training Requirements

To be a certified nurse-midwife, you must first become a registered nurse. High school students should take college preparatory courses in science and mathematics. Other useful courses are English, psychology, sociology, and health. Because entry into nurse-midwife programs is competitive, it is advisable for students to choose a 4-year nursing program that leads to a bachelor's degree. It may soon be necessary for all registered nurses to have 4-year degrees.

Once you are qualified as a registered nurse, an additional 8 to 24 months of training are necessary to become a nurse-midwife. Those with bachelor's degrees may apply for master's degree programs in midwifery. These programs last for 12 to 24 months. Those who have graduated from programs approved by the American College of Nurse-Midwives may then take the national certification exam. Once certified, nurse-midwives may have to meet further requirements in the state where they want to practice.

Getting the Job

The placement office of your nursing school or college may help you find a position. Check the job listings in want ads of newspapers, on the Internet, and in nursing journals. Professional organizations, state employment offices, and health-related employment agencies may also have information about job openings. You may apply directly to hospitals, birth centers, public health departments, and health maintenance organizations. The armed services also employ nurse-midwives.

Advancement Possibilities and Employment Outlook

Nurse-midwives are highly trained practitioners and may advance to supervisory and administrative jobs in hospitals, health clinics, public health agencies, family planning clinics, and birth centers. With further education they may teach and do research in universities. Acceptance by the medical community and continued growth in the demand for nurse-midwife services will ensure an increase in the number of jobs for nurse-midwives.

The employment outlook is very good through the year 2008. A large number of jobs will be created within health maintenance organizations. Currently the number of job openings is greater than the number of qualified nurse-midwives.

Working Conditions

Working conditions vary according to the area and type of facility in which a nurse-midwife works. Some work in modern, well-equipped hospitals and clinics; others work in the pleasant homelike surroundings of a birth center. In rural areas where there are fewer medical facilities, nurse-midwives may have to travel between several small clinics. In inner-city and rural areas, nurse-midwives may also travel to visit mothers and babies in their homes. Midwives working in hospitals and clinics usually work a 40-hour week. Those in private practice and working in areas with few medical facilities often work long and irregular hours. Shift work and weekend work are often required.

Earnings and Benefits

Earnings and benefits vary widely. Nurse-midwives with experience earn a median salary of $40,690 a year. Earnings for those working in private practice depend on the number of patients seen and on the contract the nurse-midwife has negotiated. Benefits for those working for hospitals or other organizations usually include paid holidays and vacations, health insurance, and retirement plans.

Where to Go for More Information

American College of Nurse-Midwives
818 Connecticut Ave. NW Suite 900
Washington, DC 20006
202-728-9860
www.birth.org

American Nurses Association
600 Maryland Avenue, SW, 100 West
Washington, DC 20024-2571
(202) 651-7000
www.ana.org

National League for Nursing
61 Broadway
New York, New York 10014
(800) 669-9656
www.nln.org

Occupational Therapist

Education and Training
Varies—see profile

Salary Range
Median—$48,230

Employment Outlook
Very good

Definition and Nature of the Work

Occupational therapists plan therapy programs that help patients overcome physical, mental, or emotional disabilities and become as self-sufficient as possible. Most occupational therapists work in hospitals. Others work in schools, rehabilitation centers, clinics, and nursing homes. Some are consultants to government and private agencies.

Occupational therapists are part of a health team that includes physicians, physical therapists, and other specialists. This team determines the needs of each patient. For example, a doctor may tell an occupational therapist which muscles a stroke patient should relearn to use first. The therapist then decides which activities are best to rehabilitate the particular muscles. In addition, the therapist attempts to make the program interesting for the patient. For some patients, an exercise may be as simple as grasping a ball. Other patients need to practice very basic skills, such as dressing and feeding themselves. Still others can benefit most from learning job skills, such as word processing or working with power tools.

Sometimes occupational therapists use recreational therapy to enable patients to help themselves. For example, therapists may teach crafts, such as basket weaving, woodworking, or knitting, to encourage patients to use their muscles and minds in beneficial ways. They often instill in patients an interest for mu-

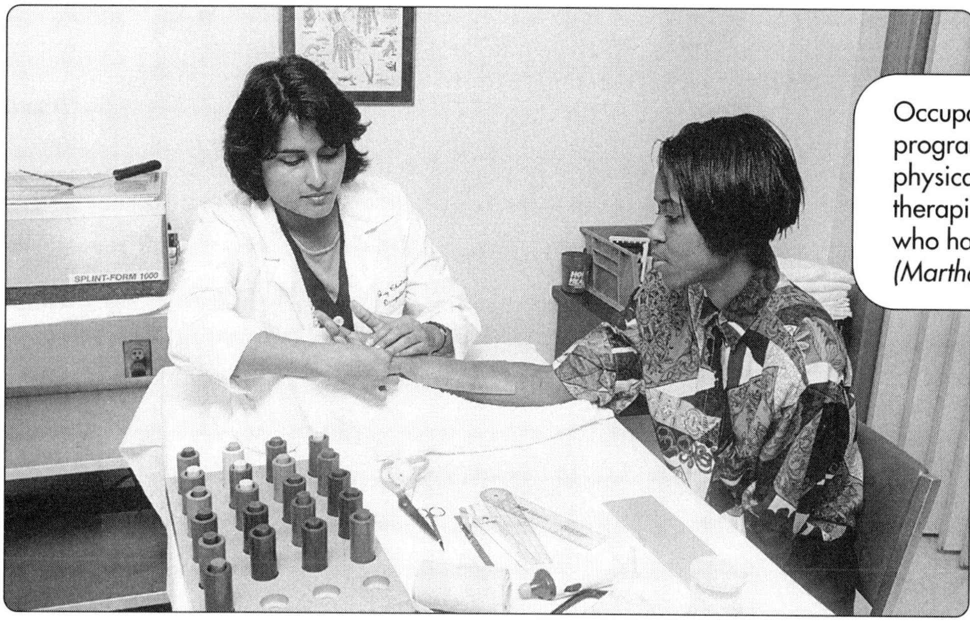

Occupational therapists plan therapy programs that help patients overcome physical disabilities. This occupational therapist makes a splint for a patient who has carpal tunnel syndrome. *(Martha Tabor.)*

sic, drama, or art to help them find ways to express their feelings. Therapists also direct games, sports, and group discussions. These recreational activities are often an important step in encouraging patients to cope with their disabilities. Recreational therapy can help patients to relax, to communicate with other people, and to gain a sense of accomplishment.

Occupational therapists plan programs that set realistic goals for each patient. They work with people of all ages and all backgrounds. They must evaluate each patient's unique set of problems. Therapists often have assistants who help them to carry out these programs.

Education and Training Requirements

To become an occupational therapist, you need a high school education. Then you can follow several paths. You can go to a 4-year college and earn a bachelor's degree in occupational therapy. You can also take a 14- to 24-month course in occupational therapy, leading to certification, after completing 4 years of college work in another field.

Occupational therapists can become registered after graduation from an approved program. If they pass an exam given by the American Occupational Therapy Association, they become registered occupational therapists (ORTs). Most states require that therapists be licensed.

Getting the Job

Your school placement office can help you to find a job. You can also apply directly to hospitals and clinics. The want ads in newspapers, job banks on the Internet, and professional publications are other sources of job leads.

Advancement Possibilities and Employment Outlook

There are several ways for occupational therapists to advance. Therapists working in hospitals or clinics can become senior therapists after several years of experience. Therapists can also become teachers or directors of occupational therapy programs. They can work as consultants, too.

The employment outlook is very good through the year 2008 due to an anticipated demand in the areas of rehabilitation and long-term care. The number of people who need rehabilitative services will rise as advances in medical technology continue to save lives and increase life expectancy. Also, as the baby boom generation begins to move into middle age, demand for cardiac rehabilitation programs is expected to increase.

Where to Go for More Information

The American Occupational Therapy Association
4720 Montgomery Lane
P.O. Box 31220
Bethesda, MD 20824-1220
(800) 668-8225
www.aota.org

American Rehabilitation Counseling Association
1835 Rohwling Road, Suite E
Rolling Meadows, IL 60008
(847) 788-0848

Working Conditions

Most occupational therapists work 40 hours a week. Sometimes evening and weekend work is required. Part-time jobs are also available.

Occupational therapists should be warm and creative people. They work closely with patients and other members of the health care team. They must be able to use their own initiative in planning and carrying out programs.

Earnings and Benefits

Salaries vary depending on education and experience. Experienced therapists earn a median income of $48,230 a year. Benefits include paid holidays and vacations, health insurance, and pension plans.

Ophthalmologist

Education and Training
Varies—see profile

Salary Range
Varies—see profile

Employment Outlook
Very good

Definition and Nature of the Work

Ophthalmologists are physicians who specialize in the care of the eye. They treat people with vision problems, eye injuries, and diseases, such as nearsightedness, glaucoma, and cataracts. Optometrists and family doctors often refer patients with serious eye conditions to ophthalmologists. Ophthalmologists can often link eye problems to disorders occurring in other parts of the body. For example, ophthalmologists are sometimes the first to detect brain tumors, diabetes, or multiple sclerosis.

Ophthalmologists use a variety of instruments to examine the eye including ophthalmoscopes, which enable them to see the inner part of the eye. Ophthalmologists can prescribe medicine, contact lenses, and eyeglasses. Sometimes they recommend eye exercises. They perform surgery when necessary. Eye surgery may involve removing a piece of glass embedded in the eye or transplanting a cornea (the transparent covering of the eye). Because the eye is so small, ophthalmologists usually operate with the help of operating microscopes and magnifying lenses. They must work with great care.

Most ophthalmologists have private practices, and some work in hospitals, health agencies, and medical colleges. Some teach, do research, and write about their special field.

Education and Training Requirements

Ophthalmologists need extensive training after high school. Most have 4 years of college and 4 years of medical school. Some medical schools accept students with

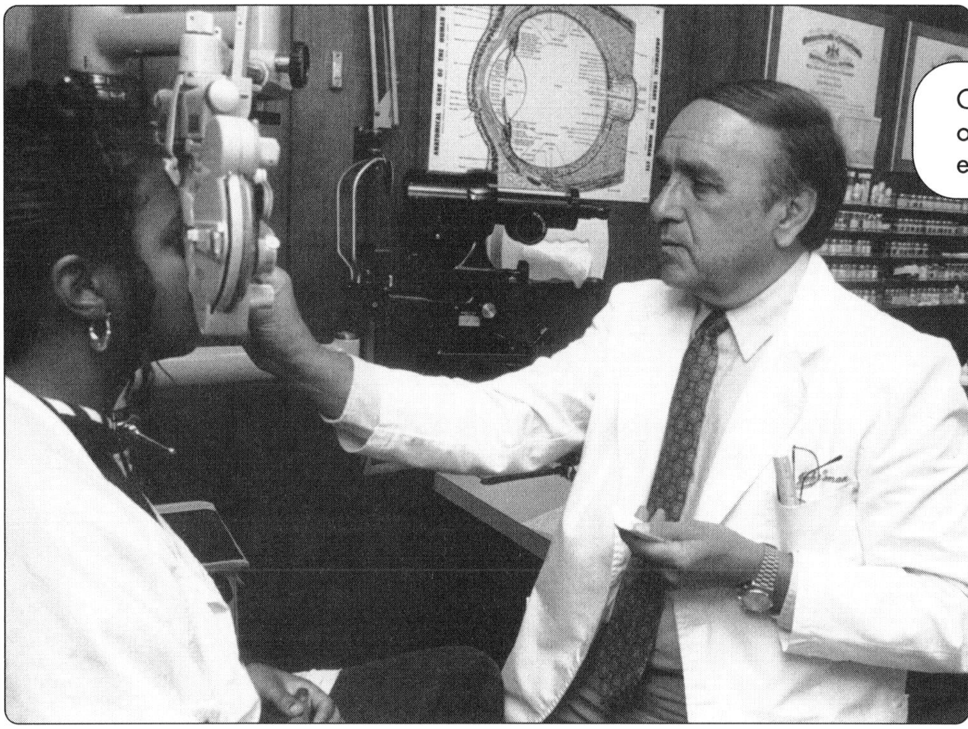

Ophthalmologists use a variety of instruments to examine the eyes. *(Martha Tabor.)*

3 years of college. After medical school, students begin about 3 years of training as hospital residents in ophthalmology (the study of the structure, function, and diseases of the eye). Usually after 1 or 2 years, residents take the test to obtain a license, which all states require. Ophthalmologists must also take an exam for specialty board certification and satisfy other specialty board requirements.

Getting the Job

The placement service at your medical school can help you find a job or refer you to doctors who are hiring associates. Many graduates begin by working as associates, and others begin as salaried employees on the staffs of hospitals or in government agencies. You can inquire directly at agencies and hospitals about possible openings. Professional organizations can also give you job information.

Advancement Possibilities and Employment Outlook

Ophthalmologists usually advance by expanding their practices. Some may specialize in one disease or disorder, such as the detachment of the retina, or in one kind of eye care, such as ophthalmology for children or elderly people. Others teach or do research at colleges and universities.

Employment of ophthalmologists is expected to increase at a rate faster than the average for all occupations. There will be a continuing need for ophthalmologists due to a larger elderly population and extended health care benefits. There may be an oversupply of ophthalmologists in the future. Although this may not affect the ability of ophthalmologists to find employment, it may reduce the number of hours they work and their earnings.

Working Conditions

Most ophthalmologists are in private practice. They generally spend regular scheduled hours in their offices and in operating rooms. Because emergencies

Where to Go for More Information

American Academy of Ophthalmology
P.O. Box 7424
San Francisco, CA 94109
(415) 561-8500
www.eyenet.org

American Medical Association
515 North State Street
Chicago, IL 60610-4320
(312) 464-5000
www.ama-assn.org

Society of Eye Surgeons
7801 Norfolk Avenue
Bethesda, MD 20814
(301) 986-1830

are unusual, ophthalmologists keep more regular hours than general practitioners. Ophthalmologists must often spend long hours, however, in meetings, study, and research. They must keep up with new developments in their field.

Ophthalmology is an important and respected profession. It requires high intelligence, good depth perception, and excellent coordination.

Earnings and Benefits

Earnings vary with experience, skill, and location. Salaries of medical residents average $32,800 for those in their first year of residency to $40,800 for those in their sixth year. Ophthalmologists with established private practices, however, can earn up to $160,000 a year. Those in private practice must provide their own benefits. Benefits for salaried ophthalmologists include paid holidays and vacations, health insurance, and pension plans.

Optometrist

Education and Training

Varies—see profile

Salary Range

Starting—$55,000
Median—$92,000

Employment Outlook

Good

Definition and Nature of the Work

Optometrists examine eyes and treat vision problems and eye disease. They prescribe eyeglasses and contact lenses, and provide vision therapy and rehabilitation programs. For example, optometrists give patients exercises to correct problems such as crossed eyes. They also prescribe drugs to treat some eye diseases and allergies.

In an examination, optometrists first talk with patients to find out the history of their eye problems. Then they carefully examine patients' eyes with the help of several instruments. Retinoscopes, for example, help optometrists to see how patients react to lenses of different strengths. Ophthalmoscopes allow them to see the inside of the eye. After the examination, they analyze the results and make the diagnosis, such as nearsightedness or farsightedness. Then optometrists prescribe lenses or other treatment, or if they diagnose eye diseases that need surgery, they refer patients to ophthalmologists (physicians who specialize in the care of the eye). Sometimes optometrists discover eye conditions due to systemic problems such as diabetes or high blood pressure. They refer patients with these diseases to other medical doctors.

Most optometrists have their own practices. Some practice with a group of optometrists. Others are employed in hospitals, clinics, and health or government agencies. Still others work for insurance companies; for manufacturers of eyeglasses, contact lenses, and other optical equipment; or for large eyewear chains. Some jobs involve the designing and testing of new products.

Education and Training Requirements

To become an optometrist, you must study for at least 6 years after high school. First you need to complete at least 2 or 3 years of college. Your courses should include laboratory sciences and other subjects required by the optometry school that you want to attend. Many students complete 4 years of college before en-

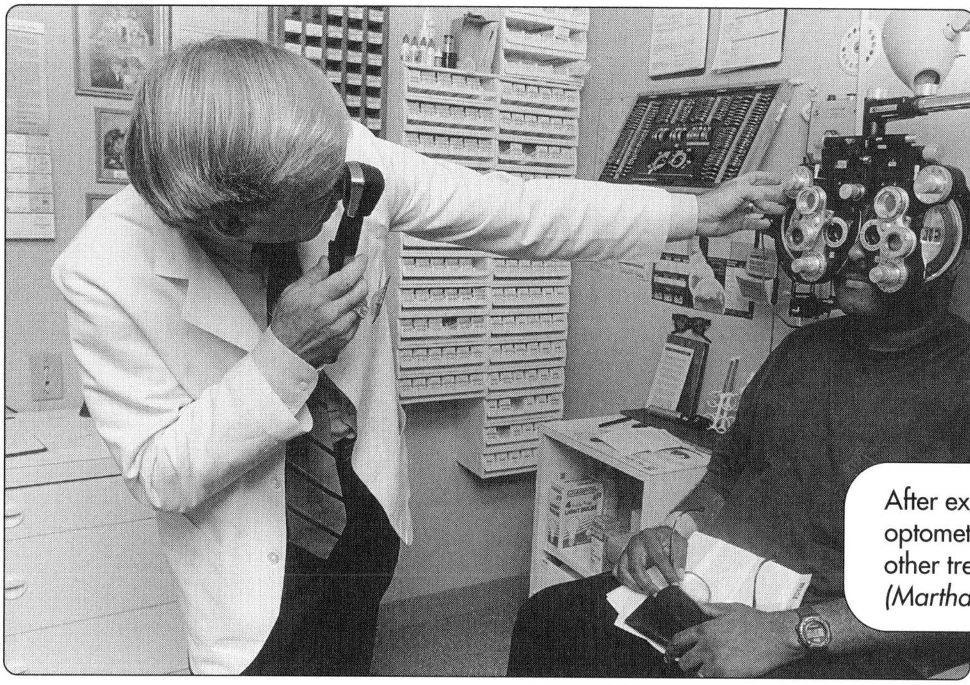

After examining a patient's eyes, an optometrist usually prescribes lenses or other treatment for vision problems. *(Martha Tabor.)*

rolling in an optometry school. In optometry school you will take a 4-year program leading to a doctor of optometry (O.D.) degree. Some optometrists may want to specialize in work with the elderly, with children, with the partially sighted, or in vision therapy. These optometrists can go on to study for a master's or doctoral degree, or they may enter a 1-year residency program that is offered for certain optometric specialties.

Optometrists must be licensed before they can work. Each state requires that optometrists graduate from an approved optometry school and pass the state licensing examinations.

Getting the Job

There are a number of ways to enter this field. Some optometrists choose to set up their own practices. Others begin by working with established optometrists. Jobs are also available in clinics, private industry, and in health or government agencies. You can apply directly for a job. You can also get advice from your school placement office or from the American Optometric Association.

Advancement Possibilities and Employment Outlook

Many optometrists become self-employed after some years as a salaried worker or as an associate in a group practice. Other optometrists specialize. For example, some specialize in the treatment of children or the elderly, in contact lenses, and in the prescription of aids for the partially sighted. Optometrists who have the additional education and experience can move into jobs in teaching, research, or administration.

The employment outlook for optometrists is good through the year 2008. The maturing of the large baby boom generation, together with rapid growth in the elderly population in the years ahead, should increase the demand for qualified optometrists. The growth of large eyewear chains will also create a need for additional optometrists. However, increased use of optometric assistants and more sophisticated equipment may lessen the demand for new optometrists.

Working Conditions

Optometrists usually work in pleasant surroundings. Those in private practice may supervise assistants. In large offices, clinics, and health and government agencies, optometrists work as members of professional health care teams. Most optometrists work 40 hours a week, often including some evening and Saturday hours. Optometrists in private practice can set their own schedules.

Optometrists have responsible jobs that require close contact with the public. They need manual dexterity and the ability to deal with a wide variety of people. Optometrists in private practice should also have business ability and self-discipline.

Where to Go for More Information

American Optometric Association
243 North Lindbergh Boulevard
St. Louis, MO 63141-7851
(314) 991-4100

National Association of Optometrists and Opticians
18903 South Miles Road
Cleveland, OH 44128
(216) 475-8929
www.aoanet.org

Earnings and Benefits

Earnings depend on experience, location, and area of specialization. Beginning optometrists earn an average of $55,000 a year. Experienced optometrists earn a median income of $92,000 a year. Optometrists in private practice must provide their own benefits. Benefits for salaried optometrists usually include paid holidays, sick days, and vacations and health insurance.

Osteopathic Physician

Education and Training
Varies—see profile

Salary Range
Average—$124,000

Employment Outlook
Very good

Definition and Nature of the Work

Osteopathic physicians practice a system of health care known as osteopathy. Osteopathy is based on the idea that health is closely related to the structure of the body. Osteopathic physicians study disorders in relation to their effect on the entire body. They specialize in a treatment called manipulative therapy in which they use their hands to move parts of the patient's body, especially the muscles and bones, into the proper positions. This therapy continues until the patient's body systems are all brought back into their correct relationship to one another.

Osteopathic physicians use the same methods that medical doctors use to diagnose and treat illness and injury. They prescribe drugs, perform surgery, and recommend the proper diet and other kinds of therapy. More than 45 percent of all osteopathic physicians are general practitioners or family doctors. As with medical doctors, osteopaths have office practices and work in hospitals. Almost 15 percent of all osteopathic physicians are specialists in fields including surgery, obstetrics and gynecology, pediatrics, psychiatry and neurology, and internal medicine. A small number of osteopathic physicians have salaried positions in osteopathic hospitals and colleges, private industry, and government agencies.

Education and Training Requirements

To become an osteopathic physician, you need extensive training after high school. You should take college courses in science and other subjects required by the osteopathic college that you want to attend. A few students start osteopathic college after only 3 years at a preprofessional college, but most students earn a bachelor's degree first. The 3- to 4-year program in an osteopathic college

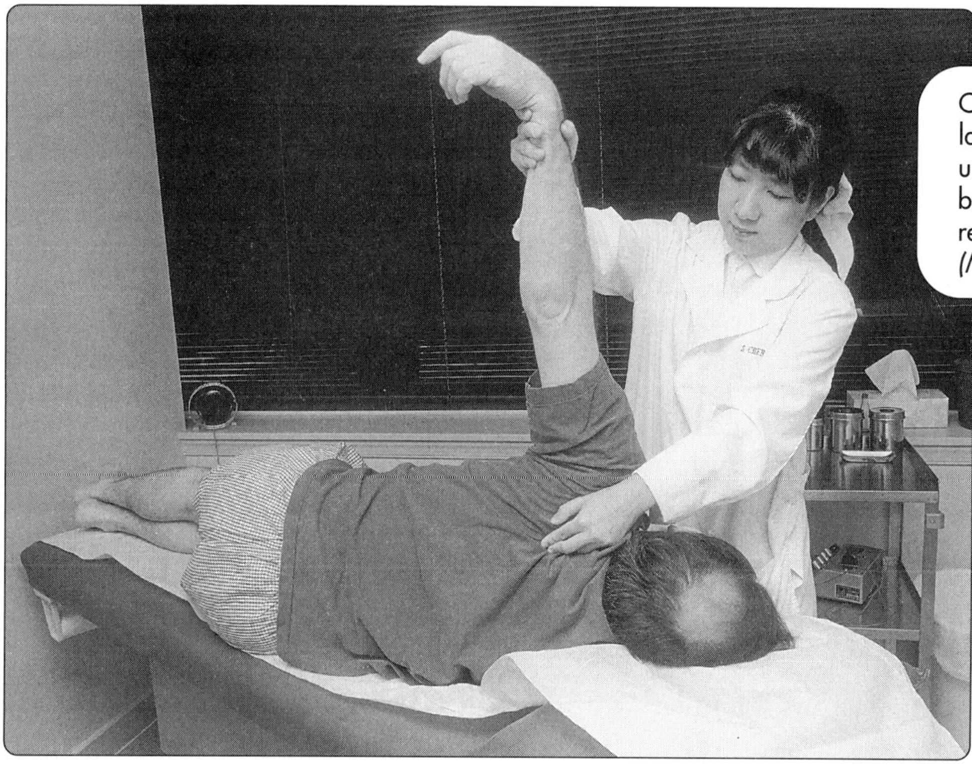

Osteopathic physicians manipulate patients' bones and muscles until all the body systems are brought back into their correct relationship to one another. *(Martha Tabor.)*

leads to the degree of doctor of osteopathy (D.O.). The training is similar to that given to doctors of medicine (M.D.'s). However, osteopathy puts more emphasis on anatomy and on the relationship between the structure of the body and its functions. Nearly all new graduates of osteopathic colleges spend a year as an intern in an osteopathic hospital. Those who want to specialize must take another 2 to 5 years of training in such areas as surgery or radiology.

In every state osteopathic physicians must be licensed before they can practice. Licensing requirements vary, but in all states, osteopathic physicians must graduate from an approved osteopathic college and pass a state board examination.

Getting the Job

Nearly all osteopathic physicians go into private practice. Some open their own practices, and others work for some time as an assistant in the office of an established osteopathic physician. Still others join group practices with other osteopathic physicians or staffs at osteopathic hospitals. Professional associations and colleges or hospitals of osteopathy can provide information about opening a practice or finding a salaried position.

Advancement Possibilities and Employment Outlook

Most osteopathic physicians advance by building their practices. Some become specialists. A small number move into positions as teachers, researchers, or administrators. Others write or edit scientific books or journals.

The federal government and most states grant osteopathic physicians the same responsibilities and privileges as medical doctors. Some osteopathic physicians serve on the staffs of nonosteopathic hospitals or practice with medical doctors. Most set up their practices in areas where there are osteopathic hospitals or clinics.

The employment outlook for osteopathic physicians is very good through the year 2008. The growing and aging population will drive overall growth in the number of physicians. New technologies permit more tests and more procedures, and allow physicians to treat conditions that were once considered untreatable. General and primary care practitioners will have the best prospects, while competition will be keen for specialists in some areas because managed health care organizations limit the use of specialists. There may be an oversupply of physicians, which would reduce their number of working hours and earnings but not necessarily job openings.

Where to Go for More Information

American Academy of Osteopathy
3500 DePauw Boulevard, Suite 1080
Indianapolis, IN 46286-1136
(317) 879-1881
www.academyofosteopathy.org

American Osteopathic Association
142 East Ontario Street
Chicago, IL 60611-2864
(800) 621-1773
www.AOA-NET.org

American Osteopathic Healthcare Association
5550 Friendship Boulevard, Suite 300
Chevy Chase, MD 20815
(301) 968-2642
www.aoha.org

Working Conditions

Most osteopathic physicians have their own practices and are able to set their own working conditions. Many work more than 50 or 60 hours a week. Some of this time is spent studying the latest advances in osteopathic medicine. Osteopathic physicians who are family doctors usually work longer and more irregular hours than specialists.

Osteopathic physicians need good business sense and self-discipline. They should be intelligent and able to deal with a wide variety of people. Good health and stamina are also important if they are to meet the demands of their profession.

Earnings and Benefits

Osteopathic physicians in private practice earn about $124,000 a year. Osteopathic physicians in private practice must provide their own benefits, such as health insurance and pension funds.

Pharmacist

Education and Training
College; license

Salary Range
Median—$66,220

Employment Outlook
Fair

Definition and Nature of the Work

Pharmacists are public health professionals who specialize in the science of drugs. They must understand the use, composition, and effects of all kinds of medicines, as well as the laws that regulate the making and selling of drugs. They dispense prescription and nonprescription drugs. Pharmacists often advise people about the use of the medicines that they supply. They order and store drugs and make sure that they remain safe, pure, and effective. They must also keep careful records of the drugs that they handle.

Most pharmacists work in community pharmacies. These are retail stores that may be owned by the pharmacist or may be part of a chain of drugstores. Community pharmacies may be large or small. They may sell just medical and sickroom needs, or they may carry a wide range of items for the health, grooming, and comfort of their customers. The pharmacist in a community pharmacy may concentrate only on the dispensing of drugs or may manage other areas of the store. Work in a community pharmacy can provide a combined professional and business management career.

Some pharmacists work in hospital or nursing home pharmacies, which also vary in size. Hospital pharmacists buy, inspect, store, and distribute drugs. They

Pharmacists work in pharmacies, hospitals, or nursing homes, dispensing drugs that require a doctor's prescription. *(Martha Tabor.)*

often keep a drug information library and advise the medical and nursing staffs about new drugs.

Other pharmacists work in the pharmaceutical industry, which includes firms that research, manufacture, or sell drugs. Pharmacists are also employed by government agencies and as teachers in colleges and universities. A small number work in specialized areas, such as in the writing or editing of books, articles, or advertisements about drugs.

Education and Training Requirements

To become a pharmacist, you must have at least 5 years of education beyond high school. In most cases you can go to any accredited college that offers the appropriate courses for your first or second year and then transfer to a college of pharmacy. Check the requirements of the college of pharmacy that you want to attend because requirements vary from college to college. Most colleges of pharmacy award a bachelor's degree at the completion of a 5-year program. Some students go on to obtain a master's or a doctoral degree in a specialized area of pharmacy. At a few schools, students earn a doctor of pharmacy (Pharm. D.) degree after 6 or 7 years of study.

All states require pharmacists to be licensed before they can practice. You need to graduate from an approved college of pharmacy and pass a state licensing board examination. You must also serve an internship or have practical experience under the supervision of a licensed pharmacist.

Getting the Job

Most pharmacists begin their careers as employees in community or hospital pharmacies. The placement service of your college of pharmacy can give you information about these job openings. You can also apply directly to pharmacies or to firms that make drugs. In addition, professional associations can provide information to help you get a job or open a pharmacy of your own.

Advancement Possibilities and Employment Outlook

Advancement depends on many factors, including location, type of work, business skill, and ambition of the pharmacist. About 60 percent of all pharmacists work in community pharmacies. Some go on to open their own pharmacies. Pharmacists who work for chain-owned drugstores can become managers. Pharmacists in hospitals can become directors of pharmacy services. Some pharmacists become administrators in government agencies. Pharmacists working for drug manufacturers can move into executive positions. If they have the necessary education, pharmacists can also advance to high-level positions in teaching or research.

The employment outlook is fair through the year 2008. Although the population continues to grow both larger and older, increased automation of drug dispensing and an increased reliance on pharmaceutical technicians will lessen the need for pharmacists. Also, managed care encourages low-cost distributors, such as mail order firms, for certain medications.

Working Conditions

Pharmacists work in clean, pleasant surroundings. Most salaried employees work about 44 hours a week. Self-employed pharmacists usually work longer hours. These usually include some evening and weekend work. Part-time schedules can often be arranged.

Pharmacists are usually on their feet for long hours. They should be in good health and be able to deal with other professional workers as well as with the public. They must be responsible people who can do careful and detailed work. Management skills are also an asset.

Earnings and Benefits

Earnings vary depending on experience, skills, and place of employment. Experienced pharmacists earn a median salary of $66,220 a year. Owners of pharmacies, managers of chain drugstores, and high-level administrators often earn much more.

Self-employed pharmacists must provide their own benefits. Benefits for salaried pharmacists generally include paid holidays and vacations, health insurance, and pension plans.

Where to Go for More Information

American Pharmaceutical Association
2215 Constitution Avenue, NW
Washington, DC 20037-2985
(800) 237-2742
www.aphanet.org

National Association of Chain Drug Stores
413 North Lee Street
P.O. Box 1417-1480
Alexandria, VA 22313-1480
(703) 549-3001
www.nacds.org

Pharmacologist

Education and Training
Advanced degree

Salary Range
Median—$66,220

Employment Outlook
Very good

Definition and Nature of the Work

Pharmacologists are scientists who develop and test drugs. Pharmacology is the medical science that is concerned with the effects of drugs on living things. Pharmacologists also test substances, such as gases, dusts, or food colorings, to determine if they are harmful to living things. They study substances to see if they promote healing. They often study the effects of these substances on laboratory animals, such as guinea pigs or monkeys.

There are several areas of specialization in pharmacology. Clinical pharmacologists test drugs on human beings. Toxicologists study poisonous drugs and other substances, such as chemicals and air pollutants that have harmful effects on living things. Molecular pharmacologists concentrate on how the molecules of drugs interact with the molecules of living things. Neuropharmacologists study the effect of drugs on the nervous system. Chemotherapists test drugs that can kill cancer cells, germs, or viruses without destroying healthy cells. Other areas that pharmacologists specialize in are biochemical pharmacology, cardiovascular pharmacology, behavioral pharmacology, and endocrine pharmacology.

The majority of pharmacologists spend most of their time in laboratories. They do careful work with scientific instruments. Many also teach and communicate their findings to other scientists. Pharmacologists work in private industry, hospitals, universities, and government agencies.

Education and Training Requirements

To become a pharmacologist, you must first obtain a bachelor's degree. Your 4-year college program should include courses in science and mathematics, as well as in other areas that will give you a broad general background. Check the requirements of the college of medicine or pharmacy that you want to attend. You will receive your specialized training in a graduate program that includes theoretical courses and laboratory research. You can earn a doctoral degree in pharmacology or in a related science or the degree of doctor of medicine (M.D.). Some medical schools have special programs that offer both degrees. You need the doctor of medicine degree in order to conduct clinical testing on humans.

Getting the Job

The placement office at your graduate school can help you find a job. You can also obtain information from professional associations or apply directly to the drug company, university, hospital, or government agency for which you want to work.

Advancement Possibilities and Employment Outlook

Most pharmacologists advance by improving their skills. Some continue to take courses throughout their careers. They often become experts in one special area of pharmacology. A pharmacologist can become head of a research team or of a university department.

The employment outlook is very good through the year 2008, especially for pharmacologists with advanced degrees. The projected increase in the middle-aged and elderly populations will increase the demand for trained professionals in all of the life sciences. Also, scientific advances that make more drug products available for the prevention, diagnosis, and treatment of diseases should create many new jobs for pharmacologists.

Working Conditions

Pharmacologists generally work in pleasant surroundings. However, they must often spend long hours in the laboratory and in the research library. They must continue to study new findings in their field. Since their work is very exacting, they must be both careful and patient. They should also be able to communicate their discoveries to others. Pharmacologists usually find great personal satisfaction in their demanding and important work.

Earnings and Benefits

Salaries vary depending on education, experience, and type of employment. Beginning pharmacologists with a doctoral degree earn salaries that range from $40,000 to $50,000 a year. Experienced pharmacologists earn a median salary of $66,220 or more a year. Benefits include paid vacations and holidays, health insurance, and pension plans.

Where to Go for More Information

American Society for Pharmacology and Experimental Therapeutics
9650 Rockville Pike
Bethesda, MD 20814-3995
(301) 530-7060
www.faseb.org/aspet

Physical Therapist

Education and Training
College; license

Salary Range
Median—$56,600

Employment Outlook
Very g51ood

Definition and Nature of the Work

Physical therapists use physical means to help people cope with pain and disability caused by disease or injury. They usually work in hospitals, nursing homes, or rehabilitation centers. Physical therapists are part of a health care team that includes physicians, occupational therapists, and psychologists.

Physical therapists test each patient and design individual programs of treatment. Therapists may use massage to improve muscle condition. They may use cold to reduce swelling or heat to relieve pain. Therapists also teach patients how to do exercises with such equipment as pulleys and weights, stationary bicycles, parallel bars, or on inclined surfaces. In addition, they use therapeutic equipment and machines including whirlpool baths, ultrasonic machines, and ultraviolet and infrared lamps. They teach patients and their families how to use and care for wheelchairs, braces, canes and crutches, and artificial limbs.

Physical therapists often supervise and instruct aides and assistants who help carry out programs of treatment. Therapists must also keep records and write reports on the progress of each patient.

Education and Training Requirements

You need a college education to become a physical therapist. The shortest route to this career is a 4-year college program leading to a bachelor's degree in physical therapy. If you have a bachelor's degree in another field, you can enroll in an 18-month program that leads to a certificate in physical therapy or in a program that offers a master's degree in physical therapy. To practice as a physical therapist, you must be licensed. Graduation from an approved program and a passing grade on a state board examination will qualify you for a license.

A physical therapist massages the scar tissue on a patient's leg before the patient begins leg-strengthening exercises. *(Martha Tabor.)*

Getting the Job

You can gain useful experience while in high school or college by doing volunteer or part-time work in the physical therapy department of a hospital. Your college placement office can help you find a job. The American Physical Therapy Association may also provide useful job information. You may want to apply directly to hospitals and rehabilitation centers. The want ads in newspapers and Internet job banks may be other sources for possible job openings.

Advancement Possibilities and Employment Outlook

Experienced therapists can become supervisors of hospital departments. In most cases they need a master's degree to move into administrative, research, or teaching positions.

The job outlook is very good through the year 2008 due to the rapidly growing need for rehabilitation and long-term care services, particularly for the growing elderly population. Advances in rehabilitation and therapeutic techniques are likely to increase the demand for qualified physical therapists. Future medical developments will permit a higher percentage of trauma victims and newborns with birth defects to survive, creating additional demand for rehabilitative care.

Although many people are training to become physical therapists, the supply of these workers is expected to fall short of the demand. Employment growth is slightly restricted by the continuing emphasis on controlling health care costs by limiting the use of some therapeutic services.

Working Conditions

Physical therapists usually work in clean, pleasant, and spacious areas. Some therapists treat patients who are confined to bed or home. Because they treat patients who may be depressed by their disabilities, physical therapists should be patient and encouraging. They need to be in good health and should be able to work well with their hands.

Most physical therapists work 40 hours a week. Those who prefer flexible hours can usually find part-time or consulting work.

Earnings and Benefits

Salaries vary with education, experience, and place of employment. Experienced physical therapists earn a median salary of $56,600 a year. Benefits for salaried physical therapists include paid holidays and vacations, health insurance, and pension plans. Self-employed therapists must provide their own benefits.

Where to Go for More Information

American Physical Therapy Association
1111 North Fairfax Street
Alexandria, VA 22314-1488
(800) 999-2782
www.apta.org

National Association of Rehabilitation Instructors
P.O. Box 405
Huntsville, AL 35801
(800) 671-6840

National Rehabilitation Association
633 South Washington Street
Alexandria, VA 22314-4109
(703) 836-0850
www.nationalrehab.org

Physician

Education and Training
Advanced degree; license

Salary Range
Varies—see profile

Employment Outlook
Very good

Definition and Nature of the Work

Physicians, or medical doctors, diagnose and treat diseases, injuries, and other disorders. They also try to promote good health and prevent illness. Physicians often supervise other health care workers, such as assistants, nurses, and technicians.

Most American physicians are involved directly in patient care. Only about one-tenth of all physicians in the United States work in areas other than patient care, such as administration or research. The majority of the physicians who provide patient care have their own or group office practices. Others work full-time in hospitals.

About one-third of the physicians providing patient care are general practitioners. They treat a wide variety of the more common health problems. When general practitioners discover illnesses or injuries that need special care, they refer patients to specialists. The other two-thirds of the physicians providing patient care are specialists who work in one particular branch of medicine. There are about 35 major fields of specialization with over 50 different subspecialties. Advances in technology have caused this specialization to increase. New procedures and diagnostic equipment require extensive skills and training. For exam-

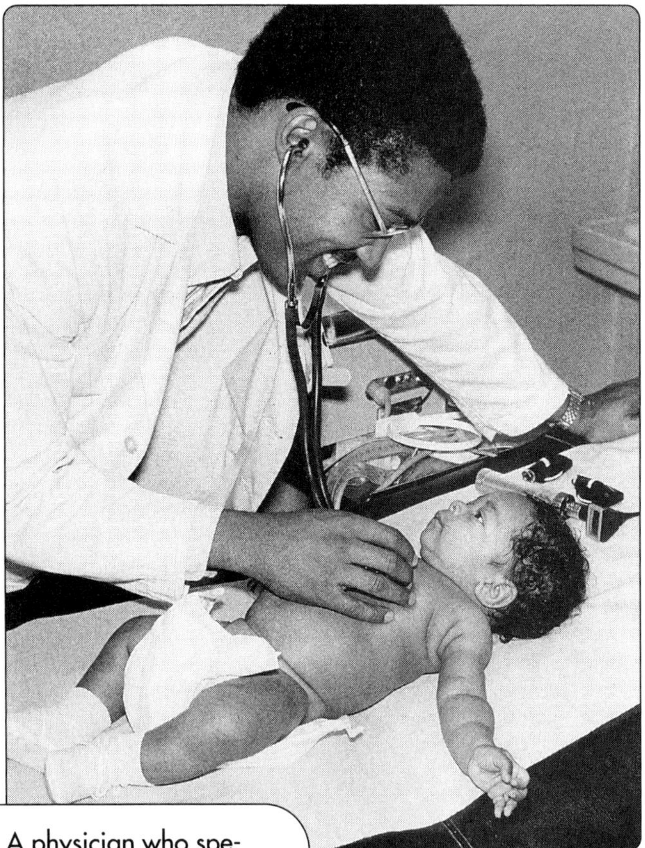

A physician who specializes in providing health care for infants and children is called a pediatrician. *(Earl Dotter.)*

ple, doctors specializing in nuclear medicine have to understand the functions of complex nuclear magnetic resonance imaging machines. These machines are used to help other physicians make diagnoses. They produce images that allow the internal organs of the body to be examined without surgery.

Other specialists include surgeons, who perform operations on patients and who often specialize further in certain kinds of surgery. For example, there are orthopedic surgeons, who operate on diseases and disorders of the joints and bones, and neurosurgeons, who treat problems of the brain and nervous system. Plastic surgeons perform operations that repair or restore damaged parts of the face or body. They use such methods as skin grafts and tissue transplants. There are also surgeons who specialize in colon and rectal surgery or in thoracic surgery, which is surgery of the chest.

Other specialists include internists, who diagnose and use medicine to treat problems of internal organs, such as the liver, heart, and lungs. Pediatricians provide health care for children. Geriatricians treat problems and diseases of the elderly. Obstetricians care for women during pregnancy and childbirth. Gynecologists treat diseases of the female reproductive organs. Psychiatrists specialize in emotional problems, and neurologists treat disorders of the nervous system. Family practitioners concentrate on primary health care for the entire family. Their special training includes surgery, internal medicine, pediatrics, obstetrics and gynecology, psychiatry, and family medicine.

Some other specialists are anesthesiologists, who administer anesthetic drugs during surgery or diagnosis, and dermatologists, who diagnose and treat diseases of the skin. Radiologists use X rays and other forms of radiant energy as tools for diagnosis and treatment. Ophthalmologists specialize in the care of the eye. Orthopedists deal with problems of the muscles, joints, and bones, and cardiologists concentrate on the heart and circulatory system. Urologists specialize in the urinary systems of both sexes and in the male reproductive organs. Otolaryngologists care for the ears, nose, and throat.

Some physicians are medical pathologists, who study changes that disease causes in body chemistry and in organs, tissues, and cells. Others specialize in preventive medicine, which includes public health and occupational medicine. Physiatrists work in rehabilitation, a special field in which physical therapy is used to help victims of disabling injuries and diseases, such as arthritis, cerebral palsy, and polio. Other specialists work with allergies and in a wide variety of other special fields.

Education and Training Requirements

Physicians must have extensive training after high school. They usually begin by going to college for 4 years to earn a bachelor's degree. However, some medical schools will accept students after they have completed only 3 years of college. Students who want to be physicians usually major in a science, such as chemistry or biology. Medical schools look for students who are well-rounded, so other courses and activities are important. Medical schools are accepting more humanities majors with strong science backgrounds. Most medical colleges have

4-year programs that lead to the degree of doctor of medicine (M.D.). Some medical colleges have experimented with programs that shorten the total time needed to obtain the M.D. degree. If a student chooses this option, then additional time as a resident is required. Residency is on-the-job medical training in a specialty at a hospital, and lasts from 3 to 7 years.

In every state, physicians need to be licensed before they can practice medicine. Requirements for licensing vary from state to state. Minimal requirements include graduating from an approved medical college and passing a licensing examination. In most states M.D.'s must also serve 1 or 2 years of residency in a hospital before they can be licensed.

Physicians who want to work as general practitioners serve a 3-year residency in a field such as general internal medicine. Those who want to become specialists must spend about 3 years as residents in their field. Specialists also need additional practice in their field before they can become certified by the appropriate specialty board. Some physicians who want to go into teaching or research go on to earn a master's or a doctoral degree in a science, such as biochemistry or microbiology.

Getting the Job

Some newly licensed physicians have their own practices and work alone. Others share offices with other doctors in a group practice or join health maintenance organizations (HMOs). A small percentage have salaried jobs in hospitals, clinics, government agencies, or private industry. Professional associations and medical colleges can provide information about going into private practice or finding a salaried position.

Advancement Possibilities and Employment Outlook

Most physicians advance by expanding their practices. They can improve their skills in general medicine or in a special field. Some physicians advance by teaching or doing research. Others study business administration and become physician executives. These doctors then become hospital administrators.

The employment outlook for physicians is very good through the year 2008. The growing and aging population will generate a demand for physicians. New technologies permit more tests, more procedures, and new treatments for patients with conditions that were previously untreatable. Those in greatest demand will be in family practice, pediatrics, geriatrics, preventive care, and internal medicine. There is evidence of an oversupply of M.D.'s., which could result in physicians reducing their working hours and earnings, but this would not necessarily reduce employment opportunities. Opportunities will be good in rural and low income areas, because physicians find these areas unattractive due to lower earnings potential and other reasons.

Working Conditions

Physicians generally work in clean, comfortable offices, clinics, or hospitals. Those who have their own practices can control some of their working conditions. Many physicians work long and irregular hours. They must be available to handle emergencies. Some physicians limit their hours or work in specialties that have few emergencies.

Physicians need high intelligence, good health, and self-discipline. They must have good business sense and the ability to organize the work of others. They should be able to deal with many different kinds of people. They should also be careful and responsible workers. Their profession demands that they continue to study new developments in medicine throughout their career.

Where to Go for More Information

American College of Physicians
Independence Mall West
Philadelphia, PA 19106
(800) 523-1546
www.acponline.org

The American Medical Association
515 North State Street
Chicago, IL 60610-4320
(312) 464-5000
www.ama-assn.org

Earnings and Benefits

Earnings vary widely depending on experience, skill, location, field of specialization, and other factors. Currently, M.D.'s serving as hospital residents earn a median income of $34,100 in their first year. By their sixth year residents earn a median income of $42,100. After they complete their training, physicians usually increase their income considerably. General practitioners currently earn about $132,000; internists, $147,000; and radiologists, $260,000.

Self-employed physicians arrange their own benefits. For those who are salaried, benefits generally include paid holidays and vacations, health insurance, and pension plans.

Physician Assistant

Education and Training
Varies—see profile

Salary Range
Median—$47,090

Employment Outlook
Excellent

Definition and Nature of the Work

Physician assistants (PAs) relieve doctors of routine chores and allow doctors to devote more of their time to patient care that requires highly specialized training. Although they are not doctors, physician assistants can do many of the jobs doctors do. Generally, they are permitted to perform many tasks that nurses are not trained to handle. Physician assistants work only under the supervision of doctors. They work with doctors and nurses in hospitals, clinics, and private offices. Physician assistants are also called physician extenders and physician associates. Physician assistant is a new profession, which is recognized in most states.

Physician assistants have varied duties. They take patients' medical histories, give first aid, and operate diagnostic and therapeutic equipment. They also perform laboratory and blood tests, comprehensive physical exams, and minor surgical procedures. Their duties depend largely on state laws that regulate their activities.

Education and Training Requirements

You need at least a high school education to be admitted to a physician assistant training program. Two years of college and health care experience are common requirements. Many applicants have bachelor's or master's degrees. Programs are taught in medical schools, colleges, community colleges, and teaching hospitals. The programs combine classroom and clinical study and last about 2 years.

Physician assistants' activities are regulated in almost all states. Many states require certification. Most states require registration with the state medical board.

Getting the Job

Your school placement office can help you find a job. You can also apply directly to hospitals, clinics, and doctors' offices in which you would like to work.

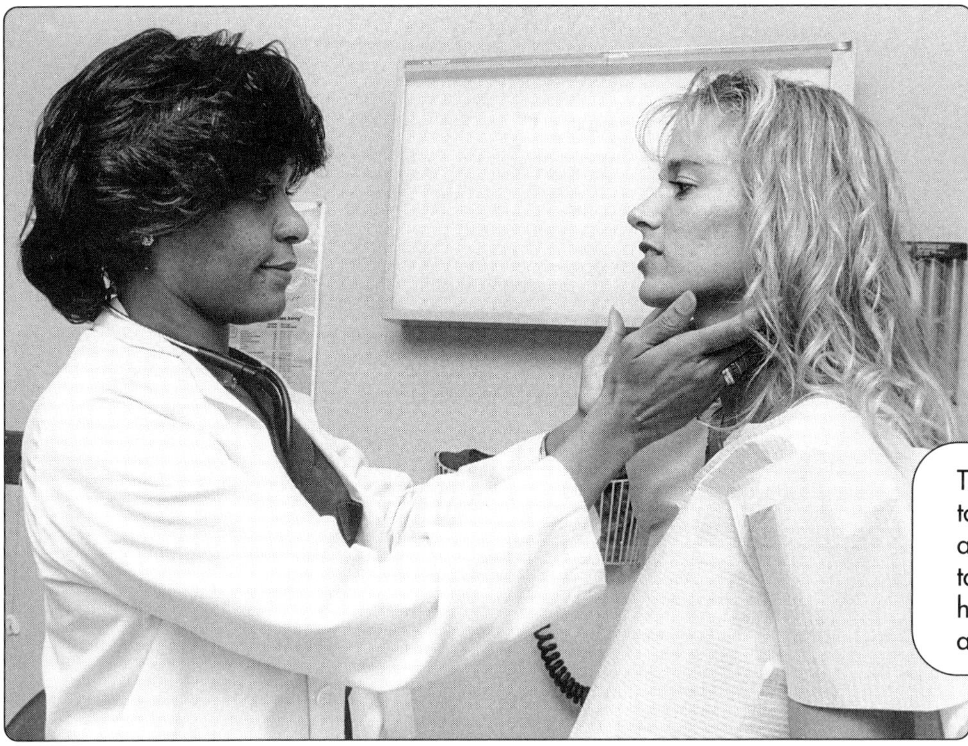

The work of a physician assistant often resembles the work of a doctor. This physician assistant performs a respiratory, head, and chest examination on a patient. *(Martha Tabor.)*

Advancement Possibilities and Employment Outlook

Physician assistants advance by accepting more responsibility or by moving into jobs that present a greater challenge. Some become specialists.

The employment outlook for physician assistants is excellent through the year 2008. Anticipated expansion of the health service industry is expected to increase the demand for qualified physician assistants. Physicians and institutions are expected to employ more physician assistants to provide primary care and assist with medical and surgical procedures. Job prospects will be particularly good in areas that have difficulty attracting physicians, such as inner city and rural clinics. In addition to office-based settings, there should be a growing number of jobs in hospitals, academic medical centers, public clinics, and prisons.

Working Conditions

The job is very demanding and requires a high degree of commitment. Physician assistants, like doctors, are always on call and generally work 40 to 60 hours a week. Physician assistants constantly interact with people, so they must be able to work well with patients and other members of the health care team.

Earnings and Benefits

Salaries vary depending on education, experience, and location. Experienced physician assistants earn a median income of $47,090 a year. Benefits generally include paid holidays and vacations, health insurance, and pension plans.

Where to Go for More Information

American Academy of Physician Assistants
950 North Washington Street
Alexandria, VA 22314
(703) 836-2272
www.aapa.org

American Association of Medical Assistants
20 North Wacker Drive, Number 1575
Chicago, IL 60606
(312) 899-1500
www.aama-ntl.org

Association of Physician Assistant Programs
950 North Washington Street
Alexandria, VA 22314-1552
(703) 548-5538
www.aapa.org/apaplist.html

Podiatrist

Education and Training
Advanced degree; license

Salary Range
Varies—see profile

Employment Outlook
Good

Definition and Nature of the Work

Podiatrists are medical practitioners who specialize in the care of the feet. Podiatrists were formerly called chiropodists. They treat people who have sore or badly shaped feet and those who have diseases or injuries of the feet. Podiatrists order X rays and laboratory tests to diagnose the patient's foot problem. They treat foot problems by manipulating or massaging the foot and by using forms of physical therapy, such as whirlpool or paraffin baths. Sometimes they provide the patient with bandages, pads, braces, splints, or other supports. They can prescribe drugs, exercise, or special shoes. Podiatrists can also perform foot surgery, either in their offices or at a hospital. Sometimes foot problems are signs of a general body illness, such as diabetes or heart trouble. When podiatrists find signs of these diseases, they refer the patient to a physician for treatment.

Most podiatrists treat all kinds of foot problems. Some specialize in fields such as foot surgery and orthopedics, which involve the treatment of deformities of foot muscles, joints, or bones. Others specialize in podopediatrics, the care of children's feet, and in podogeriatrics, the treatment of foot problems of the elderly.

Most podiatrists are in private practice. Others work in hospitals, podiatric colleges, government agencies, or private clinics.

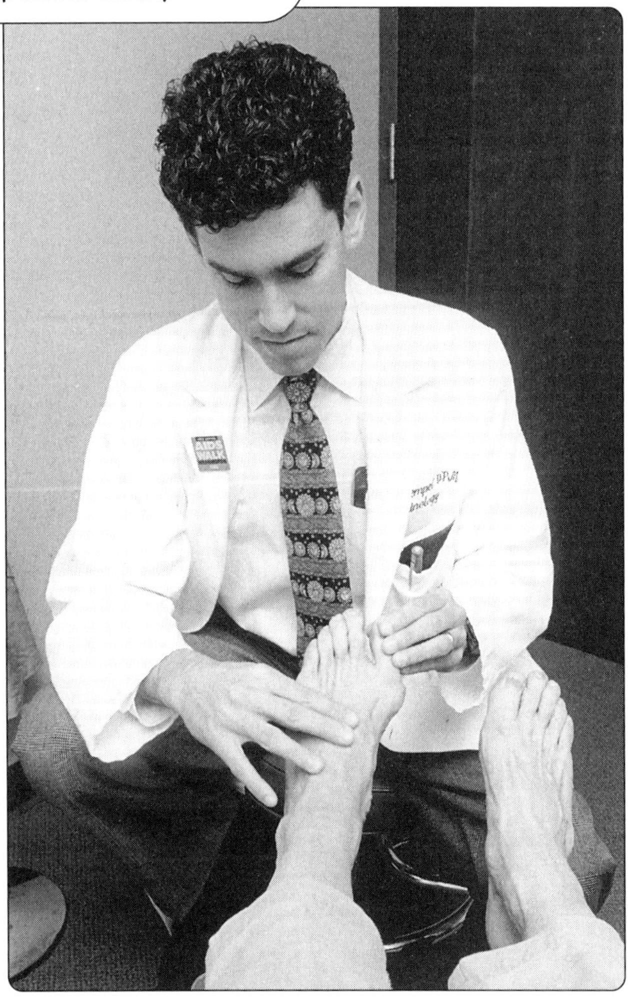

Podiatrists treat foot problems by manipulating or massaging the foot and by using forms of physical therapy. *(Martha Tabor.)*

Education and Training Requirements

Admission into a school of podiatry requires at least 3 years of college. Most applicants have a bachelor's degree. In colleges of podiatry, students take a 4-year program leading to the degree of doctor of podiatric medicine (D.P.M.). All states require that podiatrists be licensed. Requirements for licensing vary, but in all states podiatrists must at least graduate from an approved college of podiatry and pass a state board exam. A few states also require a 1-year residency.

Getting the Job

Most podiatrists go into private practice. Some newly licensed podiatrists start their own practices, or they buy established practices. Others start by working as assistants in the offices of established podiatrists. Still others take salaried positions until they have the money and experience to open their own practices. Professional associations and colleges of podiatry can provide information about getting started in this field.

Advancement Possibilities and Employment Outlook

Most podiatrists advance by expanding their practices while others may specialize. A small number of podiatrists move into teaching, research, or administrative positions in hospitals or colleges of podiatry.

The employment outlook is good through the year 2008. The anticipated growth in the elderly population requiring treatment of foot problems should continue to create openings for qualified podiatrists. Also, the popularity of fast-moving sports, such as jogging, tennis, and racquetball, is expected to increase demand in the specialty of podiatric sports medicine. Employment is hindered by the continued emphasis by insurers on controlling the costs of specialty health care.

Working Conditions

Podiatrists generally set their own working conditions. Most work about 40 hours a week, often including some evening and Saturday hours. Schedules are flexible, and some podiatrists work part-time.

Podiatrists need good vision and steady nerves. They must work well with their hands. They must have an aptitude for scientific and technical activities. They should have good business sense and the ability to deal with all kinds of people.

Earnings and Benefits

Earnings vary with experience, skill, and place of work. Podiatrists that work on salary earn a median income of $79,530 a year, while podiatrists in private practice earn a median income of $116,000 a year. Since most podiatrists are self-employed, they must provide their own health insurance and other benefits.

Where to Go for More Information

American Association of Colleges of Podiatric Medicine
1350 Piccard Drive, Suite 322
Rockville, MD 20850-4307
(800) 922-9266
www.aacpm.org

American Podiatric Medical Association
9312 Old Georgetown Road
Bethesda, MD 20814-1698
(301) 571-9200
www.apma.org

National Podiatric Medical Association
1706 East 87th Street
Chicago, IL 60617-2740
(773) 374-1616

Prosthetist and Orthotist

Education and Training
Varies—see profile

Salary Range
Average—$36,000 to $59,000

Employment Outlook
Excellent

Definition and Nature of the Work

Prosthetists and orthotists work with physicians and with physical and occupational therapists to enable patients to use damaged parts of the body or to replace parts that were lost because of an accident or illness. Prosthetists make and fit artificial limbs. Orthotists make and fit braces to help support parts of the body or to correct malformations.

Working with a doctor's prescription, orthotists and prosthetists examine the patient. They must measure the patient so that the brace or artificial limb will fit exactly. They must design each device to suit the unique needs of its wearer. Orthotists and prosthetists make braces and artificial limbs from various materials, such as wood, steel, aluminum, leather, cloth, rubber, and plastic.

Once the device is made, the prosthetist or orthotist must fit the patient very carefully, often with the help of a doctor and a physical therapist. This team checks to be sure that the device is working as it should. Physical therapists then teach the patient how to use the brace or artificial limb. If the device needs adjustments, the prosthetist or orthotist makes the necessary changes or repairs.

Orthotists make and fit braces to help support parts of the body or to correct malformations. They must design each device to suit the unique needs of its wearer. *(Sara Matthews.)*

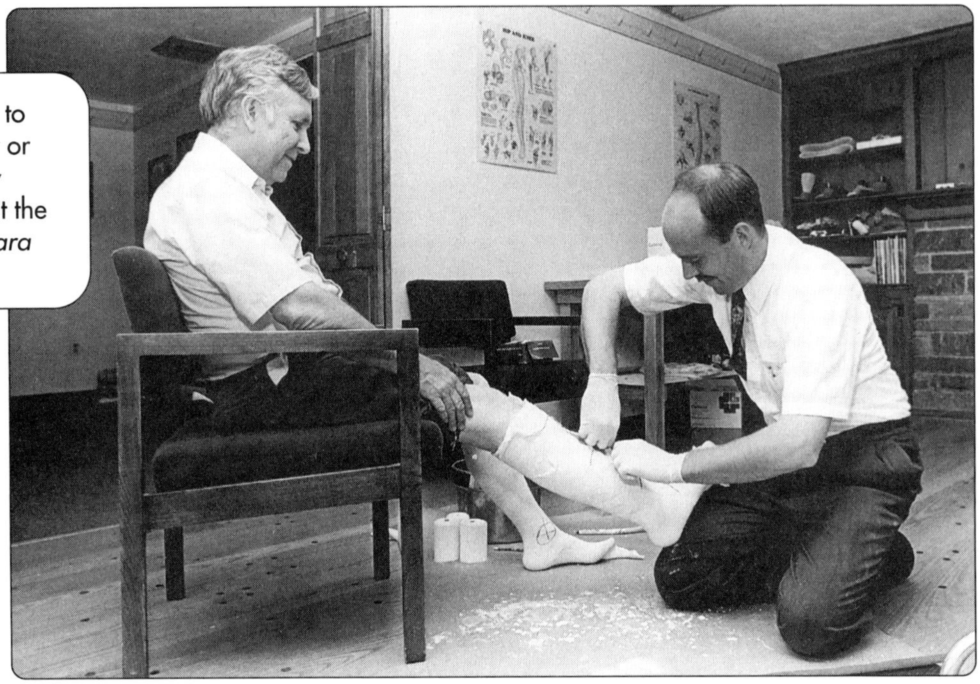

Education and Training Requirements

A bachelor's degree in prosthetics or orthotics is usually required if you want to work as a fully certified practitioner in this field. After a period of supervised clinical practice, college graduates are eligible to take an exam given by the American Board for Certification in Orthotics and Prosthetics. You can also enter this field by earning an associate degree in any field, completing a certificate program in prosthetics/orthotics, and having 4 years of experience in orthotics or prosthetics. One year of this experience in each specialty must be obtained after the certificate program is completed. After passing the proper exams, you can become a certified orthotist (CO), a certified prosthetist (CP), or a certified prosthetist-orthotist (CPO).

Getting the Job

You can apply directly to the places that hire prosthetists and orthotists. These include hospitals, clinics, government agencies, and private companies. Your school placement office can give you job information. The want ads in newspapers, Internet job banks, and professional publications may also list job openings.

Advancement Possibilities and Employment Outlook

The possibilities for advancement depend on education, experience, and skill. In large hospitals or clinics, prosthetists and orthotists can become department heads. They can also begin their own practices or move on to positions in research, sales, or teaching.

The employment outlook is good. The field is growing due to a increasing elderly population and greater access to medical and rehabilitation care brought by public and private insurance companies. Also, advancements in technology are allowing more people to have new devices designed for them.

Working Conditions

Most prosthetists and orthotists work in a combination shop-laboratory. Shops can volunteer to be inspected by the American Board for Certification in Orthotics and Prosthetics.

Prosthetists and orthotists must be skilled at using their hands and machinery. They must also be able to deal sympathetically with their patients and to cooperate with doctors and therapists.

Earnings and Benefits

Salaries vary depending on education, experience, and place of employment. Beginning workers who have a bachelor's degree earn about $27,500 a year. Experienced certified prosthetists and orthotists earn from $36,000 to $59,000 a year. Benefits generally include paid holidays and vacations, health insurance, and pension plans. Self-employed prosthetists and orthotists must provide their own benefits.

Where to Go for More Information

American Academy of Orthotists and Prosthetists
1650 King Street, Suite 500
Alexandria, VA 22314
(703) 836-7118
www.oandp.com

International Society for Prosthetics and Orthotics, United States National Member Society
1650 King Street, Suite 500
Alexandria, VA 22314
(708) 836-7114

Psychiatrist

Education and Training

Advanced degree; license

Salary Range

Average—$131,300

Employment Outlook

Very good

Definition and Nature of the Work

Psychiatrists are physicians who specialize in the prevention, diagnosis, and treatment of mental disorders. They often work with other mental health workers, such as psychologists, occupational therapists, psychiatric nurses, and psychiatric social workers. Psychiatrists treat many kinds of mental problems ranging from mild cases of anxiety to severe disorders that may cause dangerous and bizarre behavior. Psychiatrists work with patients who cannot distinguish reality from fantasy and with those who suffer excessive mood changes. Psychiatrists may also diagnose mental retardation and treat alcoholism.

Psychiatrists talk with patients to examine them and to learn about their mental and related physical problems. Psychiatrists also use information provided by patients' families or by other mental health workers. They may order laboratory tests or other kinds of diagnostic tests. Psychiatrists are trained to recognize the connection between physical and mental disorders. Their training helps them to decide on the proper treatment for each patient.

Psychiatrists use several types of treatment. They can prescribe drugs and use shock therapy and psychotherapy. In psychotherapy, psychiatrists use their special training to talk with one or more patients. They help the patients to understand and cope with their problems.

Psychiatrists may work with patients in private offices or in hospitals or clinics. They may also do research, studying the causes and treatment of mental illness. Some psychiatrists teach in medical schools or in special psychiatric institutes. Others write or edit psychiatric books or journals. Most psychiatrists combine some of these areas in their work.

Psychiatrists are often confused with psychologists and psychoanalysts. Psychiatrists are physicians who have advanced training in psychiatry. As physicians, they can prescribe medication. Psychologists have either a master's degree or a doctoral degree in psychology. They are not physicians and cannot prescribe drugs or perform surgery. Psychologists are basically scientists who study the reactions of people to their environment. Psychoanalysts are specially trained to practice long-term therapy that investigates the subconscious or hidden causes of emotional disturbances. Most psychoanalysts are psychiatrists, while those known as lay analysts are not.

Education and Training Requirements

Psychiatrists need extensive training after high school. They generally spend 4 years in college and another 4 years in medical school. Psychiatrists must also have 3 years of psychiatric training as a resident in a hospital. Usually after 1 or 2 years of residency, psychiatrists must take an examination to be licensed. All states require licensing. Psychiatrists also need additional experience before they are eligible to take an examination for certification as a psychiatrist.

Getting the Job

Psychiatrists who have completed their training work either in a private practice or at an institution. They can also combine the two types of work. Setting up a private practice is not expensive, but it takes time for a beginning psychiatrist to build a full-time schedule. Many new psychiatrists start by working with an established psychiatrist. Professional associations can provide information about setting up a practice or getting a salaried position.

Advancement Possibilities and Employment Outlook

Psychiatrists usually advance by building their practices. Some specialize in fields such as child psychology, educational psychiatry, or legal psychiatry. Others become teachers, researchers, or administrators in colleges, hospitals, or other institutions.

The job outlook is very good through the year 2008. Currently there is a shortage of psychiatrists, especially in rural areas and public facilities. A growing population and increasing life span, as well as higher incomes and educational levels, are all spurring the demand for psychiatrists.

Working Conditions

Psychiatrists in private practice work in pleasant surroundings. They try to create a quiet, peaceful setting so their patients can feel at ease. However, the emotional strain of the work is considerable because of the suffering that psychiatrists see every day. In addition, psychiatrists in private practice must be available to their patients whenever they need help. This makes their working hours somewhat irregular.

Psychiatrists who work in hospitals and clinics often have more regular hours than private practitioners do. This is because they divide the hours that they are on call with the other staff psychiatrists. However, working in mental hospitals and psychiatric clinics can be very difficult. To do the work well, psychiatrists must be well-balanced and well-disciplined. Psychiatrists need high intelligence and the ability to deal with many kinds of patients. They should enjoy the study and research that are needed to prepare for and to continue in this demanding profession.

Earnings and Benefits

Psychiatrists' earnings are similar to those of other physicians. Residents in this field of medicine earn between $38,000 and $77,000 a year. The average salary for an experienced psychiatrist is $131,300 a year. Those in private practice may earn as much as $200,000 or more a year. Psychiatrists in private practice must provide their own benefits. Salaried psychiatrists receive paid holidays and vacations, health insurance, and pension plans.

Where to Go for More Information

American College of Psychiatrists
732 Addison Street, Suite B
Berkeley, CA 94710
(510) 704-8020

The American Medical Association
515 North State Street
Chicago, IL 60610-4320
(312) 464-5000
www.ama-assn.org

The American Psychiatric Association
1400 K Street, NW
Washington, DC 20005
(202) 682-6138
www.psych.org

Psychologist

Education and Training
Advanced degree

Salary Range
Median—$48,050

Employment Outlook
Good

Definition and Nature of the Work

Psychologists are scientists who study behavior. They usually work in jobs that involve teaching, research, or social service. They work in a wide variety of places including schools, colleges, clinics, government agencies, and private industry. Some have their own private practices. Psychologists use scientific methods to learn about the behavior of humans and animals. These methods may include tests, laboratory experiments, case histories, and surveys. Psychologists use their research to develop theories to help explain the reactions of people to their environment. They use their knowledge to help emotionally or mentally disturbed people adjust to life, and may help medical and surgical patients deal with their illnesses and injuries.

There are several areas of specialization within the broad field of psychology. In experimental psychology, for example, psychologists carry out research projects that help them to develop theories about learning, motivation, hearing, or other aspects of animal or human behavior. Developmental psychology concerns the growth and development that takes place throughout life. Developmental psychologists may concentrate on one particular stage of development, such as adolescence or old age. Educational psychology pertains to learning and teaching and tries to improve the process of education. Other areas of specialization include comparative psychology, social psychology, and psychometrics.

Just as there are many areas of specialization, there are also many kinds of psychologists. The largest group is made up of clinical psychologists. They usually help people with emotional problems. They may interview these people, give them tests, and help them to understand and cope with their problems. School psychologists work with students in schools. They often give tests to identify gifted, handicapped, and emotionally disturbed students. They develop programs

Clinical psychologists help emotionally or mentally disturbed people to understand and cope with their problems. They constitute the largest area of specialization within the field of psychology. *(Martha Tabor.)*

to educate all types of students within a school system. Industrial and organizational psychologists study problems of motivation and morale in offices and factories. They often conduct surveys and give tests to employees, customers, and others. They may advise the company on personnel, management, or marketing problems. Other kinds of psychologists include engineering psychologists, counseling psychologists, and environmental psychologists.

Education and Training Requirements

To be a psychologist, you should first earn a bachelor's degree from a 4-year college. You can major in psychology or in a related field. Then you will need at least a master's degree to qualify for a limited number of assistant or school counseling jobs. To be employed as a psychologist, you should have a doctoral degree, which usually takes from 3 to 5 years of study after college. To practice clinical or counseling psychology, you generally must have an additional year or more of internship. Unlike psychiatrists, psychologists are not physicians.

All states require that you be certified or licensed to start a private practice. To become licensed, you usually need a doctoral degree plus 2 years of experience. The American Board of Professional Psychology awards diplomas in clinical, counseling, school, and industrial and organizational psychology. Candidates must have doctoral degrees, 5 years' experience, and professional endorsements.

Getting the Job

Your university placement office can help you to find a job. Want ads in newspapers, job banks on the Internet, and professional journals list openings for psychologists. You can also apply directly to the agency for which you want to work. Professional associations can provide information about opening a practice.

Advancement Possibilities and Employment Outlook

Advancement depends on many factors, including education, experience, and other personal qualities. Psychologists with a doctoral degree can move into high-level jobs in research, teaching, counseling, or administration. Those with private practices can expand their practices. Some psychologists advance by serving as consultants to government or industry or by writing about their special field.

The employment of psychologists is expected to grow as fast as the average for all occupations through the year 2008. Job opportunities in health care should increase slightly in health care provider networks, such as health maintenance and preferred provider organizations, and in nursing homes and alcohol and drug abuse programs. More opportunities will arise in businesses, nonprofit organizations, and research and computer firms for psychologists working as consultants. Companies will use psychologists to help design, analyze, and research surveys. They will also be needed to help employees with personal problems in employee assistance programs. For psychologists with doctoral degrees, opportunities will be best in clinical and counseling psychology.

Working Conditions

Working conditions vary widely. Psychologists in private practice usually have comfortable offices. Their schedules may include some evening and Saturday hours. Most psychologists work 40 hours a week. Hours can be flexible, however, depending on the type of work and the needs of the individual psychologist. School psychologists, for example, often have the same hours as teachers.

Psychologists usually need to spend time studying the latest developments in their field. They need high intelligence and emotional stability. The ability to deal with a wide variety of people is an asset in clinical and counseling psychology. Psychologists involved in research need to be self-disciplined people who are able to do detailed and careful work.

Earnings and Benefits

Salaries vary depending on education, experience, and type of work. Experienced psychologists earn a median salary of $48,050 a year. Psychologists in private practice must provide their own benefits, such as health insurance and pension plans. Benefits for salaried psychologists include paid holidays and vacations, health insurance, and pension plans.

Where to Go for More Information

The American Psychological Association
750 First Street, NE
Washington, DC 20002-4242
(800) 374-2721
www.apa.org

Public Health Educator

Education and Training
Advanced degree

Salary Range
Starting—$22,000 to $25,000 Average—$28,000 to $35,000

Employment Outlook
Very good

Definition and Nature of the Work

Public health educators plan, organize, and direct health education programs for communities and groups such as civic organizations and labor unions. They work with other health professionals, civic groups, and community officials to determine health needs, develop desirable health goals, and evaluate the availability of health services. They focus on promoting good health and preventing disease, but they must also deal with social, behavioral, legal, and economic issues.

Public health educators prepare and distribute educational and informational materials on public health issues such as smoking, immunization, drug abuse, and AIDS. They may plan exhibits and health fairs, and may conduct forum discussions to motivate their audiences to understand health issues so they can

Public health educators conduct classes on public health issues such as violence prevention, immunization, drug abuse, and smoking. *(Martha Tabor.)*

act in ways that promote good health. Public health educators may also be involved in health-related issues, such as traffic safety and the design of community health facilities. Their goals are to help people adopt healthier lifestyles, make the most efficient use of health services, and practice self-care.

Education and Training Requirements

To be a public health educator, you should have a master of public health (M.P.H.) or a master of science (M.S.) degree, preferably from one of the accredited schools of public health or an accredited graduate public health program offered at other educational institutions. Study for the M.P.H. or M.S. involves courses in public health practice and program management, behavioral sciences, and health education, among others.

Most prospective public health educators also have a medical degree and have worked in the medical field. Others have a bachelor's degree in a related field, such as sociology or anthropology, as well as related work experience. Practicing public health educators must continue to take courses to maintain and improve their skills, and many go on to earn doctoral degrees.

Getting the Job

Graduates can consult the college placement office for job openings. Many entry-level jobs are available with federal, state, and local governments; health agencies; and volunteer health organizations.

Advancement Possibilities and Employment Outlook

A public health educator for a town or county can become the director of health education for a state's Department of Health and Human Services or, at the federal level, a director of the National Institutes of Health or the Health Resources and Services Administration. A public health educator can also advance by becoming a specialist in a particular area-such as international health issues-and by working for the Centers for Disease Control and Prevention.

Employment opportunities for public health educators are expected to increase faster than the average through the year 2008. The rise of communicable diseases such as AIDS, the need for prenatal and child health care programs, and the increasing complexity of medical technology have all contributed to this growing demand. Community-oriented health care is also becoming increasingly important.

Working Conditions

Public health educators generally work in comfortable offices. When they are conducting forums or giving presentations, they may have to work some evenings and weekends. Public health educators also frequently travel to other communities or states to explore health education programs.

Educators must have good communication skills and be comfortable working with people. They must also be able to adapt ideas to suit various situations.

Earnings and Benefits

Starting salaries for public health educators range between $22,000 and $25,000 a year. Experienced health educators average between $28,000 and $35,000 a year, with some earning $50,000 or more. Salaried educators usually receive health insurance, paid holidays and vacations, and a pension plan.

Where to Go for More Information

American Health Care Association
1201 L Street, NW
Washington, DC 20005
(202) 842-4444
www.ahca.org

Recreation Therapist

Education and Training
College

Salary Range
Average—$13.98 an hour

Employment Outlook
Very good

Definition and Nature of the Work

Recreation therapists conduct specialized games, sports, crafts, and other leisure activities geared to help people with mental, emotional, and physical disabilities. The recreation programs they provide help the participants overcome or adjust to their difficulties. Therapeutic recreation is offered to individuals of all ages with all types of problems, from children hospitalized for minor surgery to wheelchair-bound elderly people. Recreation therapists are also known as play therapists. In nursing homes, recreation therapists are often classified as activities directors.

Mental health facilities, hospitals, correctional institutions, nursing homes, rehabilitation centers and specialized schools, training centers, camps, and residential centers for the disabled all employ recreation therapists. Some therapists develop, as well as conduct, therapeutic recreation programs, and many specialize in particular types of recreation, such as music, art, dance, drama, or sports.

Education and Training Requirements

Therapist positions require at least a bachelor's degree and sometimes a master's degree. Many colleges and universities offer undergraduate and graduate degree programs in therapeutic recreation or therapeutic education. Some offer programs in music, art, drama, and physical education therapy.

Recreation therapists plan and participate in specialized games, sports, crafts, and other leisure activities to help people overcome mental, emotional, and physical disabilities. *(Earl Dotter.)*

Some facilities require certification in some form of therapeutic recreation. Others hire recreation, physical education, and arts majors with experience in therapeutic activities.

Getting the Job

Job notifications are often posted in the special education departments of colleges, and some may be listed in civil service bulletins. Larger facilities often hire aides to work with therapists, and these positions usually do not require a college degree. Often you can work as an aide while pursuing a degree. This may give you the added training, experience, and contacts you need to find a job.

Advancement Possibilities and Employment Outlook

With further education, recreation therapists may become program developers, supervisors, and directors of special recreation programs. The job outlook for therapists is expected to be very good through the year 2008. Expansion in long-term care, physical and psychiatric rehabilitation, and services for people with disabilities will spur demand for therapists. Growth and aging of the population and growth of the number of people with disabilities should also increase the demand for qualified recreation therapists.

Working Conditions

Recreation therapists frequently must work evenings and weekends, and those who specialize in sports or outdoor games can anticipate extensive physical activity. Other conditions will depend largely on the size and type of the facility, the kind of recreation provided, and the individuals in the program. Therapists may work alone or as part of a professional team. They may work with one client at a time in a close, one-on-one relationship, or they may work with groups of clients. The work can be demanding and usually requires patience, creativity, and good judgment.

Earnings and Benefits

Salaries vary widely among facilities that employ recreation therapists. The average salary for all recreation therapists is $13.98 an hour. Benefits may include paid vacations, holidays, and sick leave, as well as health insurance and pension plans.

Where to Go for More Information

National Therapeutic Recreation Society
22377 Belmont Ridge Road
Ashburn, VA 20148-4501
(800) 626-6772
www.nrpa.org/branches/ntrs.htm

Registered Nurse

Education and Training
Varies—see profile

Salary Range
Median—$40,690

Employment Outlook
Very good

Definition and Nature of the Work

Registered nurses (RNs) work to promote good health and prevent illness. They use considerable judgment in providing a wide variety of patient-care services. Registered nurses observe and record the conditions of patients, and administer medications under the direction of a physician. They also advise patients and help in their rehabilitation.

Registered nurses work in various settings. Most work in hospitals, while others work in nursing homes, rehabilitation centers, and long-term care facilities. Many nurses are general duty nurses, who focus on the overall care of the patient. They administer medications and keep records of symptoms and progress. General duty nurses also provide reports to doctors and supervise practical nurses, nurse's aides, and orderlies.

In hospitals, nurses may work in special units, such as critical care, cardiac and burn units, and maternity care. This work often requires special training. Other hospital nurses may be operating room nurses, who help out before, during, and after surgery, and often stay with patients in the recovery room after operations. Some experienced hospital nurses are head nurses or directors of nursing services. Registered nurses also work as nurse educators or as researchers in hospitals. Other nurses who work in hospitals are private duty nurses. They are hired to attend to patients who need special care. Private duty nurses also work in patients' homes and in nursing homes.

Many registered nurses work in private doctors' offices or clinics. These office nurses may assist physicians such as obstetricians and dental surgeons. They may do some office or laboratory work in addition to their nursing duties.

Registered nurses also work in the community. Public health nurses generally work in clinics and help to teach the public about good health practices. They may also care for patients and their families under the supervision of a doctor. Visiting nurses treat patients in their homes. School nurses and industrial nurses promote good health in schools and industries, respectively.

Education and Training Requirements

After you graduate from high school, you can prepare for a career as a registered nurse in one of three ways. You can take a 2-year nursing program in a community college that will lead to an associate degree. Or you can enroll in a diploma program offered by a hospital or independent school of nursing. Diploma programs generally take 3 years to complete. You can also enroll in a college

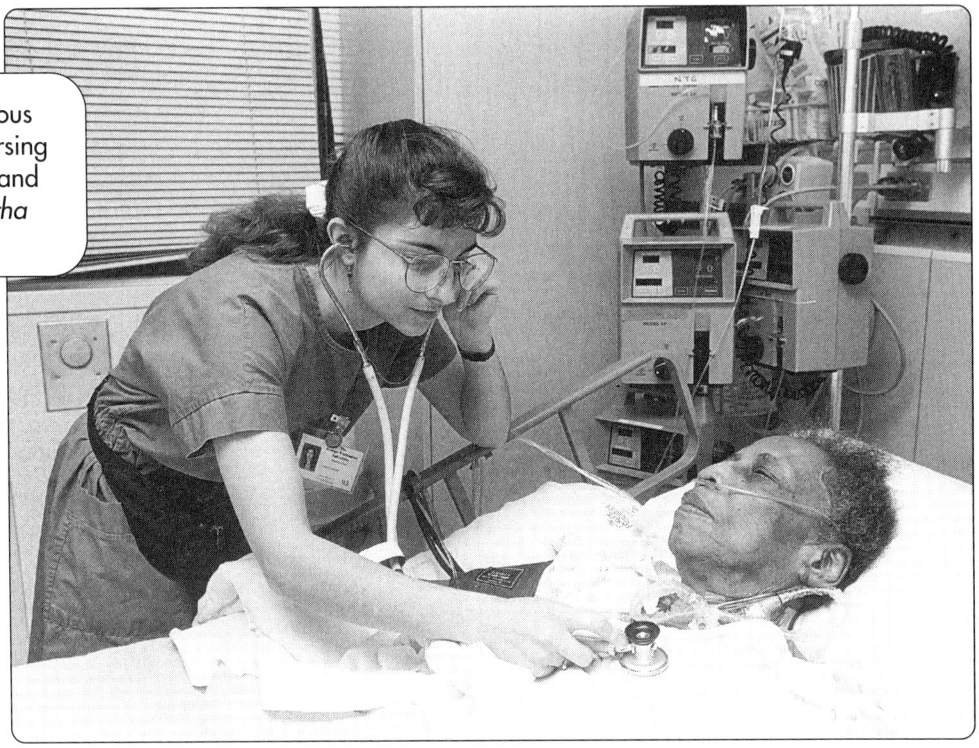

Registered nurses work in various settings including hospitals, nursing homes, rehabilitation centers, and long-term care facilities. *(Martha Tabor.)*

program that leads to a bachelor of science degree. College programs usually take 4 or 5 years to complete. They combine liberal arts courses with scientific and technical training. All programs include practical experience. There is a move toward two levels of nursing: technical nursing, which will require an associate degree, and professional nursing, which will require a bachelor's degree. Only nurses with a bachelor's degree will be eligible for RN licensing. You should check current requirements before deciding on a program.

After you have completed an approved program, you will be eligible to take the national written licensing exam, which is administered by each state. All states require licensing.

Getting the Job

Nursing school and college placement services can help you find a job. You can also apply directly to hospitals, clinics, nursing homes, and doctors' offices. For community health jobs, contact public health departments, home health agencies, and visiting nurse associations. The armed services also have openings for nurses. In addition, there are professional nurse registries for private duty nurses.

Advancement Possibilities and Employment Outlook

Advancement in nursing depends on education, experience, and place of employment. Registered nurses can become supervisors of departments or specialists in a particular field of nursing, such as pediatrics or psychiatry. Nurse practitioners need a master's degree. Those with a bachelor's or a master's degree are more likely to move into the higher-level jobs in these areas. Many positions in research, teaching, and administration require a master's or even a doctoral degree in nursing.

The employment outlook is very good through the year 2008. Increases in demand are partly due to technological advances in patient care, which permit a greater number of medical problems to be treated. In addition, the number of elderly people is projected to grow rapidly, which also spurs demand for RNs, especially in nursing homes. Employment in home health care is expected to increase the fastest, while employment in hospitals is expected to increase the slowest. This is because more patients are being released earlier from hospitals to reduce costs, and more prefer care in their homes. Also, technological progress is making it possible to bring complex treatments to the home.

Working Conditions

Although particular working conditions vary with the place of employment, nearly all nursing jobs involve close contact with people. Nurses are required to deal with all kinds of people. Good health and emotional stability are also valuable assets. Nurses must be careful workers who take their responsibilities seriously. They must follow rigid guidelines to ensure the safety of themselves and their patients against infectious diseases.

Registered nurses generally work 40 hours a week. This usually includes some night and weekend shifts, especially for hospital nurses. Many nurses are able to work part-time if they choose to do so.

Earnings and Benefits

Salaries for nurses vary depending on education, experience, and area of specialization. The median annual income for all registered nurses is $40,690. The highest paid nurses can earn up to $70,000 a year. Benefits include paid holidays and vacations, health insurance, and pension plans. Private duty nurses generally charge a daily fee and must provide their own benefits.

Where to Go for More Information

American Assembly for Men in Nursing
CO-NYSNA11 Cornell Road
Latham, NY 12110
(518) 782-9400
email: AAMN@nysna.org

American Association of Colleges of Nursing
1 Dupont Circle, NW, Suite 530
Washington, DC 20036-1110
(202) 463-6930
www.aacn.nche.edu

National League for Nursing
61 Broadway
New York, NY 10014
(800) 669-9656
www.nln.org

Speech Pathologist and Audiologist

Education and Training
Advanced degree

Salary Range
Median—$43,080

Employment Outlook
Excellent

Definition and Nature of the Work

Speech pathologists and audiologists help people who have speech, language, and hearing problems. Speech pathologists are trained in speech and language problems. Audiologists are trained in hearing problems. Many jobs require training in both fields.

Speech pathologists and audiologists evaluate and work with people who have speech and hearing problems. These problems may be a result of injury, illness, or emotional difficulties. Speech pathologists and audiologists may treat brain-damaged and mentally retarded patients and people who have a deformity, such as a cleft palate. Many patients are children who lisp or stutter. Adult patients may be victims of strokes or of cerebral palsy. Speech pathologists and audiologists often work closely with doctors, psychologists, physical therapists, or classroom teachers. They plan and carry out treatments that take into account the unique needs of each patient.

A speech pathologist works with children who have speech problems that result from injury, illness, or emotional difficulties. *(Martha Tabor.)*

The majority of speech pathologists and audiologists work in public schools. Some have private practices, and others work in colleges and universities, clinics, hospitals, special speech and hearing centers, government agencies, and private industry. Some speech pathologists and audiologists work on research projects to design and develop new equipment or methods for treating speech and hearing problems.

Education and Training Requirements

You usually need a master's degree in speech-language pathology or audiology to work in this field. Some states require you to have a teaching certificate to work in public schools. Some states also require a license to work in private practice, clinics, or other nonschool settings. Certification and licensing requirements vary from state to state.

Certification by the American Speech-Language-Hearing Association is recommended for those who want to advance. You must have a master's degree or its equivalent and a year of work experience. After passing an examination, you will receive a Certificate of Clinical Competence.

Getting the Job

You can apply directly to the school, clinic, or other institution in which you would like to work. Your school placement office or the American Speech-Language-Hearing Association can give you information about job openings. You can also check job listings in the want ads in newspapers and on the Internet.

Advancement Possibilities and Employment Outlook

Advancement depends on education and experience. Speech pathologists and audiologists can become supervisors or heads of clinics. They can set up private practices. Those with the necessary training can work as consultants, do research, and write books or articles on speech and hearing problems.

The employment outlook for speech pathologists and audiologists is excellent through the year 2008. Employment in health and rehabilitation services will increase as a result of advances in medical technology and growth in the elderly population. Hearing loss is associated with aging, and baby boomers are now entering middle age, when the possibility of hearing and speaking impairments increases. In addition, as awareness of the importance of the early recognition and treatment of hearing and speech problems increases, so will the demand for professionals in elementary and secondary schools.

Working Conditions

Working conditions are usually pleasant. Speech pathologists and audiologists are part of a health care team and interact with a wide variety of people. They should be patient and able to work well with others.

Many speech pathologists and audiologists work more than 40 hours a week. Their hours are often flexible, and there are part-time jobs available. Speech pathologists and audiologists working in public schools usually have the same schedule that classroom teachers have.

Earnings and Benefits

Salaries vary widely depending on education, experience, and location. The median salary for experienced speech pathologists and audiologists is $43,080 a year. Benefits usually include paid holidays and vacations, health insurance, and pension plans.

Where to Go for More Information

American Speech-Language-Hearing Association
10801 Rockville Pike
Rockville, MD 20852-3226
(800) 498-2071
www.asha.org

National Student Speech-Language-Hearing Association
10801 Rockville Pike
Rockville, MD 20852
(301) 897-5700
www.nsslha.org

Surgeon

Education and Training
Advanced degree; license

Salary Range
Median—$217,000

Employment Outlook
Very good

Definition and Nature of the Work

Surgeons are medical specialists who operate to repair injuries, correct deformities, prevent diseases, and generally improve the health of patients. They examine patients to determine if surgery is necessary, evaluate the risks involved, and select the appropriate surgical procedure.

Many surgeons are general surgeons, who perform many kinds of operations. Others specialize in one type of operation or one medical area. Neurosurgeons operate on the brain, spinal cord, and nervous system. Thoracic surgeons operate on lungs and other organs in the chest cavity. Diseases of bones and joints, such as arthritis, as well as the treatment of broken bones, are the focus of orthopedic surgeons. Plastic surgeons correct facial and body disfigurements and improve a person's appearance.

Education and Training Requirements

Becoming a surgeon requires many years of study as well as board certification and licensure. Most prospective surgeons graduate from college with a course concentration in the physical sciences and apply to one of the 142 accredited

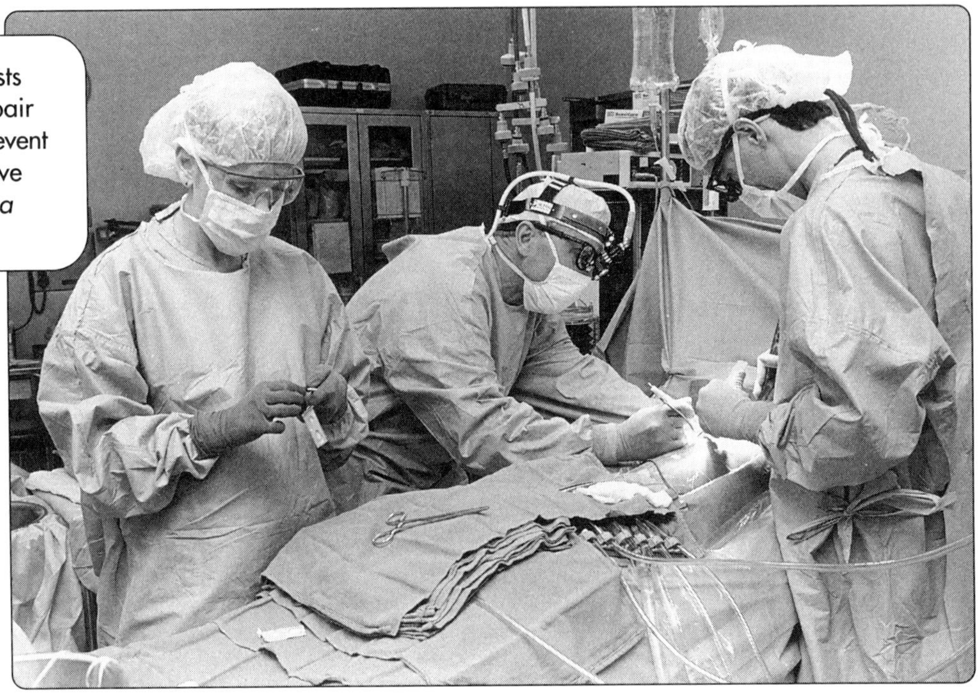

Surgeons are medical specialists who operate on patients to repair injuries, correct deformities, prevent diseases, and generally improve the health of patients. *(Martha Tabor.)*

medical schools in the United States. Competition for acceptance is very intense. Applicants must have a high scholastic average, submit letters of recommendation, score well on the Medical College Admission Test (MCAT), and demonstrate such desirable qualities as integrity, emotional stability, reliability, and a desire to serve others.

Medical students spend the first 2 years of medical school in laboratories and classrooms, taking courses in anatomy, biochemistry, pathology, and medical ethics, among others. During the last 2 years, students work with patients in a hospital under an experienced physician's supervision. Students also move from one medical specialty to another, gaining experience in each area.

After achieving the degree of doctor of medicine (M.D.), prospective surgeons must take an examination, administered through the Board of Medical Examiners in each state, to be licensed to practice. After they are licensed, doctors are required to complete graduate medical programs known as internships and residencies. Surgeons seeking certification by the American Board of Medical Specialists (ABMS) in a specialty may spend up to 7 years-depending on the specialty-in residency training.

Individuals who want to be surgeons must be self-motivated and have the physical and mental stamina to handle the pressure and long hours of a medical education. Surgeons also must be willing to continue studying throughout their careers to keep current in their field.

Getting the Job

Surgeons must meet these established requirements: an M.D. degree, a licensing exam, an internship, a residency, and board certification in the area of specialization. Beginning surgeons may enter private practice or group practice, with affiliations with one or more hospitals. Some surgeons choose to work for the federal government in veterans hospitals or the military.

Advancement Possibilities and Employment Outlook

Surgeons advance by gaining more skill and knowledge and by increasing their income and number of patients. General surgeons may move into areas of specialty. In some large urban hospitals, a surgeon may become head of surgery. Surgeons may also teach or do research after acquiring additional training and education.

Employment of surgeons will increase faster than the average for all occupations through the year 2008 due to continued expansion of the health industry. The growing and aging population will drive overall growth, and new technologies will permit more tests and more procedures for conditions that were once untreatable. Competition for specialists will be keen in urban and suburban areas that are attractive to surgeons for various reasons, such as higher earning potential and continued contact with colleagues.

Working Conditions

Surgeons spend much of their time at the hospital, operating on patients or visiting pre- or postsurgery patients. Surgeons frequently perform emergency surgery on short notice. Most surgeons maintain an office outside the hospital where they see patients by appointment. Surgeons usually work long hours.

Earnings and Benefits

Although surgeons have among the highest earnings of any profession, these earnings vary according to specialty, geographic location, years in practice, and reputation. The median salary for all surgeons is $217,000 a year.

Where to Go for More Information

American Medical Association
515 North State Street
Chicago, IL 60610-4320
(312) 464-5000
www.ama-assn.org

Association of American Medical Colleges
Section for Student Services
2450 N Street, NW
Washington, DC 20037-1127
(202) 828-0400
www.aamc.org

Resources General Career Information

Books

Exploring the Working World

The Adams Job Almanac. Holbrook, MA: Adams Media Corp., annual.

American Almanac of Jobs and Salaries, John W. Wright. New York: Avon Books, biennial.

American Salaries and Wages, 5th ed., Helen S. Fisher. Detroit, MI: Gale Research, Inc., 1999.

America's Top Jobs for College Graduates, 5th ed., J. Michael Farr. Indianapolis, IN: JIST Publishing, 2000.

America's Top Jobs for People Without a Four-Year Degree, 5th ed., J. Michael Farr. Indianapolis, IN: JIST Publishing, 2000.

The Big Book of Jobs. U.S. Dept. of Labor. Lincolnwood, IL: VGM Career Horizons, 2000.

Career Discovery Encyclopedia, 4th ed., Holli Cosgrove, ed., 6 vols. Chicago: Ferguson, 2000.

CareerSmarts: Jobs with a Future, Martin Yate. New York: Ballantine Books, 1999.

The Complete Guide to Public Employment, 3rd ed., Ronald Krannich and Caryl Rae Krannich. Manassas Park, VA: Impact Publications, 1995.

The Harvard Guide to Careers, 5th ed., Martha P. Leape and Susan M. Vacca. Cambridge, MA: Harvard University Press, 1995.

Job Hunter's Sourcebook. Detroit, MI: Gale Group, biennial.

Jobscape: Career Survival in the Global Economy, Colin Campbell. Indianapolis, IN: JIST Publishing, 1998.

Jobs '98 (title changes annually), Kathryn Petras, Ross Petras, and George Petras. New York: Simon & Schuster, annual.

Jobs Rated Almanac, Les Krantz. New York: St. Martin's Press, 2000.

Joyce Lain Kennedy's Career Book, Joyce Lain Kennedy and Darryl Laramore. Lincolnwood, IL: VGM Career Horizons, 1997.

The National JobBank, 2001 (title changes annually). Holbrook, MA: Adams Media Corp., annual. (The *JobBank* series also includes editions for several major U.S. cities and regions.)

Occupational Outlook series. Washington, DC: United States Government Printing Office. Briefs, separately published.

Occupational Outlook Quarterly. Washington, DC: Occupational Outlook Service, Bureau of Labor Statistics. Quarterly publication.

Professional Careers Sourcebook, 6th ed. Detroit, MI: Gale Research, Inc., 1999.

Recommended

Occupational Outlook Handbook, United States Department of Labor. Washington, DC: United States Government Printing Office, revised biennially. Expands on the *Dictionary of Occupational Titles.* Groups jobs into similar categories. Discusses the nature of the work, the employment outlook, and earnings.

VGM's Careers Encyclopedia, 4th ed. Lincolnwood, IL: VGM Career Horizons, 1997. A one-volume guide to 180 careers.

The Quick Internet Guide to Career and College Information, 2001 Edition, Anne Wolfinger. Indianapolis, IN: JIST Publishing, 2000.

A Student's Guide to Career Exploration on the Internet, Elizabeth H. Oakes. Chicago: Ferguson, 1998.

Vocational Careers Sourcebook, 4th ed., Detroit, MI: Gale Research, Inc., 1999.

Volunteer America, 4th ed., Harriet Clyde Kipps. Chicago: Ferguson, 1997.

Education and Training Opportunities

American Universities and Colleges, 15th ed. Hawthorne, NY: De Groyter, 1997.

America's Lowest Cost Colleges, Nicholas A. Roes. Barryville, NY: NAR Publications, biennial.

America's Top Internships, Mark Oldman and Samer Hamadeh. New York: Random House, annual.

Barron's Guide to Graduate Business Schools, Eugene Miller, ed. Hauppauge, NY: Barron's Educational Series, revised regularly.

Barron's Guide to Law Schools. Hauppauge, NY: Barron's Educational Series, revised regularly.

Barron's Guide to Medical and Dental Schools, Saul Wischnitzer and Edith Wischnitzer, eds. Hauppauge, NY: Barron's Educational Series, revised regularly.

Bear's Guide to Earning College Degrees Non-Traditionally, 11th ed., John Bear. Benicia, CA: C&B Publishing, 1994.

Chronicle Vocational School Manual. Moravia, NY: Chronicle Guidance Publications, annual.

College Applications and Essays, 3rd ed., Susan D. Van Raalte. New York: Macmillan, 1997.

The College Costs and Financial Aid Handbook, The College Board Staff. New York: The College Board, annual.

College Financial Aid for Dummies, 2nd ed., Herm Davis and Joyce Lain Kennedy. Foster City, CA: IDG Books Worldwide, 1999.

College Financial Aid Made Easy, Patrick L. Bellatoni. Berkeley, CA: Ten Speed Press, annual.

The College Guide for Parents, 3rd ed., Charles J. Shields. New York: The College Board, 1995.

The College Handbook. New York: The College Board, annual.

College Planning for Gifted Students, 2nd ed., Sandra L. Berger. Reston, VA: Council for Exceptional Children, 1998.

The Complete Book of Colleges. New York: Random House, annual.

Ferguson's Guide to Apprenticeship Programs, 2nd ed., 2 vols., C. J. Summerfield and Holli Cosgrove, eds. Chicago: Ferguson, 1998.

Free Money for College: A Guide to More Than 1000 Grants and Scholarships for Undergraduate Study, 5th ed., Laurie Blum. New York: Facts on File, 1999.

Recommended

The following four sources are basic directories of information on colleges and universities. They include general information on each school, its address, a list of the programs offered, the size of the institution, and costs for tuition.

Barron's Top 50: An Inside Look at America's Best Colleges, Tom Fischgrund, ed. Hauppauge, NY: Barron's Educational Series, revised regularly.

College Blue Book. New York: Macmillan Reference USA, revised annually.

Lovejoy's College Guide, Charles T. Straughn II and Barbarasue Lovejoy Straughn, eds. New York: ARCO, revised regularly.

Petersons Guide to Four-Year Colleges. Princeton, NJ: Petersons Guides, revised regularly.

Getting into College, Pat Orovensky. Princeton, NJ: Petersons, 1995.

The Gourman Report: A Rating of Undergraduate Programs in American and International Universities, Jack Gourman. Los Angeles, CA: National Education Standards, revised regularly.

Help Yourself: Handbook for College-Bound Students with Learning Disabilities, Erica-Lee Lewis. New York: Random House, 1996.

Index of Majors and Graduate Degrees. New York: The College Board, annual.

Insider's Guide to the Colleges, Yale Daily News Staff, ed. New York: St. Martin's Press, annual.

The Internship Bible. New York: Random House, annual.

Internships for 2-Year College Students. West Hartford, CT: Graduate Group, annual.

Internships Leading to Careers. West Hartford, CT: Graduate Group, annual.

Lovejoy's College Guide for the Learning Disabled, Charles T. Straughn. New York: ARCO, revised regularly.

The National Guide to Educational Credit for Training Programs, American Council on Education. Phoenix, AZ: ACE/Oryx Press, annual.

The 100 Best Colleges for African-American Students, Erlene B. Wilson. New York: Plume, 1998.

Petersons College Money Handbook. Princeton, NJ: Petersons, annual.

Petersons Competitive Colleges. Princeton, NJ: Petersons, annual.

Petersons Game Plan for Getting Into College, K. Patricia Aviezero. Princeton, NJ: Petersons, 2000.

Petersons Guide to Graduate and Professional Programs: An Overview. Princeton, NJ: Petersons, annual.

Petersons Guide to Two-Year Colleges. Princeton, NJ: Petersons, annual.

Petersons Internships. Princeton, NJ: Petersons, annual.

A Student's Guide to College Admissions: Everything Your Guidance Counselor Has No Time to Tell You, 3rd ed., Harlow Unger. New York: Facts on File, 1995.

Career Goals

Adventure Careers, Alex Hiam and Susan Angle. Franklin Lakes, NJ: Career Press, 1995.

Career Anchors: Discovering Your Real Values, Edgar H. Schein. San Diego, CA: Pfeiffer & Co., rev. 1993.

The Career Atlas, Gail Kuenstler. Franklin Lakes, NJ: Career Press, 1996.

The Career Guide for Creative and Unconventional People, 2nd ed., Carol Eikleberry. Berkeley, CA: Ten Speed Press, 1999.

Careers XRoads 2000: Where Talent and Opportunity Connect on the Internet, Jerry Crispin and Mark Mahler. Indianapolis, IN: JIST Publishing, 2000.

Recommended

What Color Is Your Parachute? Richard N. Bolles. Berkeley, CA: Ten Speed Press, revised annually. One of the best sources for career changers and job hunters. Workbook style with exercises to identify skills and interests. Provides comprehensive list of sources including books, agencies, and associations.

Careers for the Year 2000 and Beyond: Everything You Need to Know to Find the Right Career. Piscataway, NJ: Research and Education Association, 1997.

Choices for the High School Graduate: A Survival Guide for the Information Age, 3rd ed., Bryna J. Fireside. Chicago: Ferguson, 2000.

Choosing a Career Made Easy, Patty Marler and Jan Bailey Mattia. Lincolnwood, IL: VGM Career Horizons, 1997.

The College Board Guide to Jobs and Career Planning, 2nd ed., Joyce Slayton Mitchell. New York: The College Board, 1994.

College Majors and Careers: A Resource Guide for Effective Life Planning, 4th ed., Phil Phifer. Chicago: Ferguson, 1999.

Finding Your Perfect Work: The New Career Guide to Making a Living, Creating a Life, Paul Edwards and Sarah Edwards. New York: Putnam, 1997.

Graduate to Your Perfect Job in Six Easy Steps, Jason R. Dorsey. Austin, TX: Golden Ladder Productions, 1997.

Green at Work: Finding a Business Career that Works for the Environment, Susan Cohn. Washington, DC: Island Press, 1995.

The Job Seeker's Guide to Socially Responsible Companies, Katherine Jankowski. Detroit, MI: Gale Research, Inc., 1995.

Jobs for People who Love Travel: Opportunities at Home and Abroad, 3rd ed., Ronald L. Krannich and Caryl Rae Krannich. Manassas Park, VA: Impact Publications, 1999.

The Off-the-Beaten-Path Job Book: You Can Make a Living and Have a Life!, Sandra Gurvis. Secaucus, NJ: Carol Publishing Group, 1995.

The Parent's Crash Course in Career Planning: Helping Your College Student Succeed, Marcia B. Harris and Sharon L. Jones. Lincolnwood, IL: VGM Career Horizons, 1996.

The PIE Method for Career Success: A Unique Way to Find Your Ideal Job, Daniel Porot. Indianapolis, IN: JIST Publishing, 1996.

The Right Job for You: An Interactive Career Planning Guide, J. Michael Farr. Indianapolis, IN: JIST Publishing, 1997.

Success 2000: Moving into the Millennium with Purpose, Power, and Prosperity, Vicki Spina. New York: Wiley, 1997.

Getting the Job and Getting Ahead

The Adams Electronic Job Search Almanac 2000. Holbrook, MA: Adams Media Corp., 1999.

Almanac of American Employers, Jack W. Plunkett. Galveston, TX: Plunkett Research, Ltd., biennial.

CareerXroads: The Directory to Jobs, Resumes, and Career Management on the World Wide Web. 4th ed., Kendall Park, NJ: MMC Group, 1998.

The Complete Idiot's Guide to Getting the Job You Want, 2nd ed., Robert Bly. Indianapolis, IN: Alpha Books, 1999.

Getting Hired: A Guide for Managers and Professionals, Richard J. Pinsker. Menlo Park, CA: Crisp Publications, 1994.

Great Jobs Abroad, Arthur H. Bell. New York, McGraw Hill, 1997.

The Guide to Internet Job Searching, 2000–2001, Margaret Dikel, ed. Lincolnwood, IL: NTC/Contemporary Publishing, 2000.

Hoover's Directory of Human Resources Executives. Austin, TX: The Reference Press, revised regularly.

How to Get a Job in . . . (series for major U.S. cities). Chicago: Surrey Books, Inc., annual.

How to Hit the Ground Running in Your New Job, Lynda Pritchard Clemens and Andrea Trulson Dolph. Lincolnwood, IL: VGM Career Horizons, 1995.

International Job Finder: Where the Jobs are Worldwide, Daniel Lauber. River Forest, IL: Planning/Communications, 2000.

Job Savvy, How to be a Success at Work, 2nd ed., LaVerne L. Ludden. Indianapolis, IN: JIST Publishing, 1998.

Job Search 101: Getting Started on Your Career Path, Monica R. Fox and Pat Morton, eds. Indianapolis, IN: JIST Publishing, 1997.

Job Search Organizer, Hal Weatherman. Lincolnwood, IL: VGM Career Horizons, 1997.

Job Seeker's Guide to Private-Public Companies, Charity A. Dorgan, ed. Detroit, MI: Gale Research, Inc., 1995.

Jobsmarts for Twentysomethings, Bradley G. Richardson. New York: Vintage Books, 1995.

National Job Hotline Directory, Sue A. Cubbage. River Forest, IL: Planning/Communications, annual.

Non-Profits & Education Job Finder, 1997–2000, Daniel Lauber. River Forest, IL: Planning/Communications, 1997.

Petersons Hidden Job Market. Princeton, NJ: Petersons, annual.

Professional's Job Finder, 1997–2000, Daniel Lauber. River Forest, IL: Planning/Communications, 1997.

Resumes in Cyberspace: Your Guide to a Computerized Job Search, 2nd ed., Pat Criscito. Hauppage, NY: Barron's Educational Series, 2000.

Using the Internet and the World Wide Web in Your Job Search, Fred Edmund Jandt and Mary B. Nemnich. Indianapolis, IN: JIST Publishing, 1996.

The Very Quick Job Search: Get a Better Job in Half the Time, J. Michael Farr. Indianapolis, IN: JIST Publishing, 1996.

The Work-At-Home Sourcebook, 7th ed., Lynie Arden. Boulder, CO: Live Oak Publications, 1996.

Resumes and Interviews

Better Resumes for Executives and Professionals, 4th ed., Robert F. Wilson. Hauppauge, NY: Barron's Educational Series, 2000.

The Complete Idiot's Guide to the Perfect Resume, 2nd ed., Susan Ireland. Indianapolis, IN: Alpha Books, 2000.

Cover Letters for Dummies, 2nd ed., Joyce Lain Kennedy. Foster City, CA: IDG Books Worldwide, 2000.

Recommended

Knock 'Em Dead: The Ultimate Job Seeker's Handbook, Martin J. Yate. Holbrook, MA: Adams Media Corp., 1997. Helps job seekers identify their strengths and improve their interview techniques. Also gives practical advice on networking, handling tough interview questions, and negotiating salaries.

Cover Letters: Proven Techniques for Writing Letters that Will Help You Get the Job You Want, Taunee Besson and National Business Employment Weekly. New York: Wiley, 1995.

Developing a Professional Vita or Resume, 3rd ed., Carl McDaniels. Chicago: Ferguson, 1997.

Get Hired!: Winning Strategies to Ace the Interview, Paul C. Green. Austin, TX: Bard Books, 1996.

Information Interviewing, 2nd ed., Martha Stoodley. Chicago: Ferguson, 1997.

Interviewing, Arlene S. Hirsch and National Business Employment Weekly. New York: Wiley, 1997.

Job Interviews That Mean Business, 3rd ed., David R. Eyler. New York: Random House, 1999.

The Resume Handbook, 3rd ed., Arthur Rosenberg and David Hizer. Boston: Adams Media Corp., 1996.

The Resume Kit, 4th ed., Richard H. Beatty. New York: John Wiley & Sons, 2000.

Resume Power: Selling Yourself on Paper, 6th ed., Tom Washington. Bellevue, WA: Mount Vernon Press, 2000.

Resume Writing Made Easy, 6th ed., Lola M. Coxford. Scottsdale, AZ: Gorsuch Scarisbrick, 1997.

Resumes for Dummies, 3rd ed., Joyce Lain Kennedy. Foster City, CA: IDG Books Worldwide, 2000.

Resumes that Knock 'Em Dead, 4th ed., Martin Yate. Holbrook, MA: Adams Media Corp., 2000.

Your Resume: Key to a Better Job, 6th ed., Leonard Corwen. New York: Macmillan, 1995.

Recommended

Damn Good Resume Guide, 3rd ed., Yana Parker. Berkeley, CA: Ten Speed Press, 1996. Describes how to write a functional resume.

The New Perfect Resume, Tom Jackson and Ellen Jackson. New York: Doubleday, 1996. A CD-ROM version is also available.

Mid-Career Options

Beat the Odds: Career Buoyancy Tactics for Today's Turbulent Job Market, Martin Yate. New York: Ballantine Books, 1995.

The Career Trap: Breaking Through the 10-Year Barrier to Get the Job You Really Want, Jeffrey G. Allen. New York: AMACOM, 1995.

The Complete Idiot's Guide to Changing Careers, William Charland. Indianapolis, IN: Alpha Books, 1998.

The Complete Idiot's Guide to Freelancing, Laurie Rozakis. Indianapolis IN: Alpha Books, 1997.

How to Hold it All Together When You've Lost Your Job, Townsend Albright. Lincolnwood, IL: VGM Career Horizons, 1996.

Kiplinger's Survive and Profit from a Mid-Career Change, Daniel Moreau. Washington, DC: Kiplinger Books, 1994.

Out of Uniform: A Career Transition Guide for Ex-Military Personnel, Harry N. Drier. Lincolnwood, IL: VGM Career Horizons, 1995.

Recommended

Career Change: Everything You Need to Know to Meet New Challenges and Take Control of Your Career, David P. Helford. Lincolnwood, IL: VGM Career Horizons, 1995.

Change Your Job, Change Your Life: High Impact Strategies for Finding Great Jobs into the 21st Century, Ronald L. Krannich. Manassas Park, VA: Impact Publications, 1997.

Toxic Work: How to Overcome Stress, Overload, and Burnout and Revitalize Your Career, Barbara Bailey Reinhold. New York: Plume, 1997.

Equality of Opportunity

Cracking the Corporate Closet, Daniel B. Baker, Sean O'Brien Strub, and Bill Henning. New York: HarperBusiness, 1995.

Equal Opportunity. Hauppauge, NY: Equal Opportunity Publications, published 3 times a year.

Financial Aid for the Disabled and Their Families, 2000–2002, Gail A. Schlachter and R. David Weber. San Carlos, CA: Reference Services Press, 2000.

Financial Aid for Minorities. Garrett Park, MD: Garrett Park Press, 1994.

Successful Job Search Strategies for the Disabled: Understanding the ADA, Jeffrey G. Allen. New York: Wiley, 1994.

Women and Work, Susan Bullock. Atlantic Highlands, NJ: Humanities Press, 1994.

Lists and Indexes of Career and Vocational Information

The Career Guide: Dun's Employment Opportunities Directory. Parsippany, NJ: Dun and Bradstreet Information Services, annual.

Dictionary of Holland Occupational Codes (DHOC), 3rd ed., Gary D. Gottfredson and John L. Holland. Lutz, FL: Psychological Assessment Resources, 1996.

Dictionary of Instructional Programs and Careers. Indianapolis, IN: JIST Publishing, 2000.

Recommended

The Big Book of Minority Opportunities, 6th ed., Willis L. Johnson, ed. Chicago: Ferguson, 1995. Directory of organizations that have special programs to help minorities meet their educational and career goals.

The Big Book of Opportunities for Women, Elizabeth A. Olson, ed. Chicago: Ferguson, 1996. Directory of organizations that have special programs to help women meet their educational and career goals.

Coping with Sexual Harassment, Beryl Black, ed. New York: The Rosen Publishing Group, rev. 1992. Helpful in giving direct ways to respond to and prevent sexual harassment at work.

Internet Sites

Sites with Extensive Links

About.com
www.careerplanning.about.com

Catapult
www.jobweb.org/catapult/catapult.htm

JIST Publishing
www.jist.com

Job Hunt: A Meta-List of On-Line Job-Search Resources and Services
www.job-hunt.org

The Job Resource
www.thejobresource.com

The Riley Guide: Employment Opportunities and Job Resources on the Internet
www.dbm.com/jobguide

Career Development Resources

Career Magazine
www.careermag.com

Princeton Review
www.review.com

Online Information and References

AT&T Toll-Free Internet Directory
www.tollfree.att.net

Beatrice's Web Guide—Careers
www.bguide.com/webguide/careers

The Best Jobs in the USA Today
www.bestjobsusa.com

CareerMart
www.careermart.com

Federal Jobs Digest
www.fedworld.gov/jobs/jobsearch.html

Job Finders Online
jobfindersonline.com

Monster Career Center
content.monster.com

Occupational Outlook Handbook
stats.bls.gov/ocohome.htm

U.S. Bureau of Labor Statistics Home Page
stats.bls.gov/blshome.htm

US News Online Colleges and Career Center
www.usnews.com

Wall Street Journal Interactive Division
careers.wsj.com

Yahoo! Business and Economy
www.yahoo.com/business

Job Databases and Resume Posting

America's Job Bank
www.ajb.org

Career Builder
www.careerbuilder.com

CareerCity
www.careercity.com

CareerPath
www.careerpath.com

Career Site
www.careersite.com

CareerWeb
www.careerweb.com

Headhunter
www.headhunter.net

Idealist Nonprofit Career Center
www.idealist.org

JobBank USA
www.jobbankusa.com

Job Options
www.joboptions.com

Job Trak
www.jobtrak.com

Job Web
www.jobweb.org

The Monster Board
www.monster.com

World Wide Web Employment Office
www.employmentoffice.net

Audiovisual Materials

The following titles include, where possible, the developer's name and location or else the name and location of a distributor. Audiovisual titles may be available through several distributors.

Exploring the Working World

The Career Builders series. Video. New York: Educational Design, Inc.

Career Cluster Decisions. Video; guide. South Charleston, WV: Meridian Education Corp.

Career Exploration: A Job Seeker's Guide to the OOH, DOT, and GOE. Video. South Charleston, WV: Meridian Education Corp.

Career Plan. Video; guide. South Charleston, WV: Meridian Education Corp.

Career Plan: Putting Your Skills to Work. Video; guide. Mt. Kisco, NY: Guidance Associates.

Career S.E.L.F. Assessment: Designing a Self-Directed Job Search. Video. Charleston, WV: Cambridge Educational.

Career Self-Assessment: Where Do You Fit? Video; guide. Mt. Kisco, NY: Guidance Associates.

Careers for the 21st Century series. Video; guide. South Charleston, WV: Meridian Education Corp.

Careers Without College. Video. Charleston, WV: Cambridge Educational.

Connect on the Net: Finding a Job on the Internet. Video. Charleston, WV: Cambridge Educational.

Educational Planning for Your Career. Video. South Charleston, WV: Meridian Education Corp.

The JIST Video Guide for Occupational Exploration series. Video. Indianapolis, IN: JIST Publishing.

Jobs for the 21st Century. Video; guide. Mt. Kisco, NY: Guidance Associates.

Learning for Earning. Video; guide. South Charleston, WV: Meridian Education Corp.

Mapping Your Career. Video. South Charleston, WV: Meridian Education Corp.

School-to-Work Transition. Video; guide. South Charleston, WV: Meridian Education Corp.

Skills Identification: Discovering Your Skills. Video. Indianapolis, IN: JIST Publishing.

Working Towards a Career. Video. South Charleston, WV: Meridian Education Corp.

Your Aptitudes: Related to Learning Job Skills. Video. South Charleston, WV: Meridian Education Corp.

Your First Cruise: A Beginner's Guide to the Internet. Video. Charleston, WV: Cambridge Educational.

Your Future: Planning Through Career Exploration. Video. South Charleston, WV: Meridian Education Corp.

Your Interests: Related to Work Activities. Video. South Charleston, WV: Meridian Education Corp.

Your Life's Work series. Video. Indianapolis, IN: JIST Publishing.

Your Temperaments: Related to Work Situations. Video. South Charleston, WV: Meridian Education Corp.

Your 21st Century Employability Skills series. Video. Calhoun, KY: NIMCO.

Getting the Job and Getting Ahead

Ace the Interview. Video. Columbus, OH: Career Paths/MarkED.

The Art of Effective Communication. Video; guide. Indianapolis, IN: JIST Publishing.

Dialing for Jobs: Using the Phone in the Job Search. Video. Indianapolis, IN: JIST Publishing.

Extraordinary Answers to Common Interview Questions. Video. Charleston, WV: Cambridge Educational.

First Impressions: The Key to Successful Interviews. Video. Indianapolis, IN: JIST Publishing.

From Pink Slip to Paycheck: The Road to Reemployment series. Video. Indianapolis, IN: Park Avenue/JIST Publishing.

Getting a Job series. Video. New York: Educational Design, Inc.

How to Be a Success at Work series. Video. Indianapolis, IN: JIST Publishing.

How to Find a Job on the Internet. Video. Indianapolis, IN: JIST Publishing.

Interview Power. Video. Columbus, OH: Career Paths/MarkED.

Job Search and Job Survival series. Video. New York: Educational Design, Inc.

Job Survival Kit. Video. Charleston, WV: Cambridge Educational.

Job Survival Skills: Working with Others. Video. Mt. Kisco, NY: Guidance Associates.

Mastering Change: How to Be "Change Skilled" and Thrive in Turbulent Times series. Video; workbook. Harleysville, PA: Career Communications Inc.

Maximizing Your Public Image. Video. Hinesburg, VT: Image Vision.

The Resume Remedy. Video. Indianapolis, IN: JIST Publishing.

Shhh! I'm Finding a Job: The Library and Your Self-Directed Job Search. Video; workbook. Charleston, WV: Cambridge Educational.

Strategy: Planning Your Job Search. Video. Indianapolis, IN: JIST Publishing.

Survival Skills for the World of Work series. Video. New York: Educational Design, Inc.

Take This Job and Love It. Video. Charleston, WV: Cambridge Educational.

Ten Ways to Get a Great Job. Video. Charleston, WV: Cambridge Educational.

Tough Time: Finding the Jobs. Video. Charleston, WV: Cambridge Educational.

The Very Quick Job Search Video, 2nd ed. Indianapolis, IN: JIST Publishing.

The Video Guide to JIST's Self-Directed Job Search series. Video. Indianapolis, IN: JIST Publishing.

Video Guide to Summer Jobs and Part-Time Jobs. Video. Indianapolis, IN: JIST Publishing.

Your Public Image: Conducting Yourself in the Business World. Video. Hinesburg, VT: Image Vision.

Computer Software

The following titles include, where possible, the developer's name and location or else the name and location of a distributor. Software titles may be available through several distributors.

Ace the Interview: The Multimedia Job Interview Guide. CD-ROM for Macintosh or Windows. Charleston, WV: Cambridge Educational.

Adams JobBank FastResume Suite. CD-ROM for Windows. Holbrook, MA: Adams Media Corp.

Barron's Profiles of American Colleges on CD-ROM. Windows or Macintosh. Hauppauge, NY: Barron's.

The Cambridge Career Counseling System. Diskettes for IBM. Charleston, WV: Cambridge Educational.

Career Area Interest Checklist. Diskettes for IBM or Apple. South Charleston, WV: Meridian Education Corp.

Career Counselor. CD-ROM for Windows. New York: Kaplan Educational Centers.

Career Finder. Diskettes for IBM DOS, Windows, or Macintosh. Itasca, IL: Riverside Publishing.

Career Match. Diskettes for IBM or Macintosh. Charleston, WV: Cambridge Educational.

CD-ROM Version of the Occupational Outlook Handbook. Charleston, WV: Cambridge Educational.

Create Your Dream Job. CD-ROM for Windows or Macintosh. Columbus, OH: Career Paths/MarkED.

Discovering Careers and Jobs. CD-ROM. Detroit, MI: Gale Research, Inc.

Encyclopedia of Careers and Vocational Guidance. CD-ROM for Windows or Macintosh. Chicago: Ferguson.

Exploring Work, CD-Rom for Mac or Windows. Madison, WI: Career Development Systems.

Getting into College (U.S. News and World Report). CD-ROM. Portland, OR: Creative Multimedia.

Hoover's Company and Industry Database on CD-ROM. Austin, TX: The Reference Press.

*JIST's Electronic O*Net Dictionary of Occupational Titles.* CD-ROM for Windows. Indianapolis, IN: JIST Publishing.

JIST's Multimedia Occupational Outlook Handbook. CD-ROM for Windows. Indianapolis, IN: JIST Publishing.

Job Search Skills for the 21st Century. CD-ROM for Windows or Macintosh. Charleston, WV: Cambridge Educational.

MSPI: Exploring Career Goals and College Courses. Diskettes for IBM or Macintosh. Charleston, WV: Cambridge Educational.

Multimedia Career Center. CD-ROM for Windows or Macintosh. Charleston, WV: Cambridge Educational.

The Multimedia Career Path. CD-ROM for Windows or Macintosh. Charleston, WV: Cambridge Educational.

The Multimedia Guide to Occupational Exploration. CD-ROM for Windows or Macintosh. Charleston, WV: Cambridge Educational.

Multimedia Job Search. CD-ROM for Windows. Charleston, WV: Cambridge Educational.

Multimedia Take this Job and Love It. CD-ROM for Windows or Macintosh. Charleston, WV: Cambridge Educational.

OOH MultiMedia Hyper-Handbook. CD-ROM for Windows. Itasca, IL: Riverside Publishing.

The Perfect Resume. CD-ROM for Windows. Torrance, CA: Davidson.

Resume Express: The Multimedia Guide. CD-ROM for Windows or Macintosh. Charleston, WV: Cambridge Educational.

Resume Revolution: The Software Solution. Diskettes for Windows or Macintosh. Charleston, WV: Cambridge Educational.

What Color Is Your Parachute? CD-ROM for Windows. Boston: BumbleBee Technology.

Young Person's Electronic Occupational Outlook Handbook (OOH). CD-ROM for Windows, Macintosh, or Network. Indianapolis, IN: JIST Publishing.

Resources Health

General

Books

AHA Guide to the Health Care Field. Washington, DC: American Hospital Association, annual.

America's Top Medical, Education, and Human Services Jobs, 3rd ed., J. Michael Farr. Indianapolis, IN: JIST Publishing, 1996.

Brief Introduction to Health Occupations, 2nd ed. Shirley Badasch and Doreen S. Chesebro. Upper Saddle River, NJ: Prentice-Hall, 1999.

Career Opportunities in Health Care, Shelly Field. New York: Facts on File, 1997.

Careers in Aging: Opportunities and Options. Washington, DC: Association for Gerontology in Higher Education.

Careers in Alternative Medicine, Alan Steinfeld. New York: The Rosen Publishing Group, 1999.

Careers in Health Care, Barbara Swanson. Lincolnwood, IL: VGM Career Horizons, 1994.

Careers Inside the World of Health Care, Beth Wilkinson. New York: The Rosen Publishing Group, 1995.

Diversified Health Occupations, 5th ed., Louise Simmers. Albany, NY: Delmar Publishers, 2000.

Exploring Health Care Careers: Real People Tell You What You Need to Know, David Hayes, ed. Chicago: Ferguson, 1997.

Exploring Health Careers, 2nd ed., Maureen McCutcheon. Albany, NY: Delmar, 1998.

Health Care Career Starter, Cheryl Hancock. Sewickley, PA: LearningExpress, 1998.

Health Careers Today, Judith Gerdin. St. Louis, MO: Mosby-Year Book, 1996.

Health Occupations: Excerpts from the Occupational Outlook Handbook. Upper Saddle River, NJ: Prentice-Hall, 1994.

Introduction to the Health Professions, 3rd ed., Peggy Stanfield and Y. H. Hui. Sudbury, MA: Jones & Bartlett, 1998.

Job Opportunities in Health Care. Princeton, NJ: Petersons, annual.

Opportunities in Hospital Administration Careers, Donald Snook. Lincolnwood, IL: VGM Career Horizons, 1997.

Petersons Job Opportunities for Health and Science Majors. Princeton, NJ: Petersons, annual.

Tyler's Guide: The Healthcare Executive's Job Search, 2nd ed., J. Larry Tyler. Chicago: Health Administration Press, 1998.

VGM's Handbook of Health Care Careers, 2nd ed., Carla S. Rogers, ed. Lincolnwood, IL: VGM Career Horizons, 1997.

Working in Health Care and Wellness, Barbara Lee. Minneapolis, MN: Lerner Publications Co., 1996.

Internet Sites

Allied Health Opportunities
www.gvpub.com

American Dental Hygienists Association: Career Information
www.adha.org/careerinfo/index.html

Association of Operating Room Nurses Perioperative Referral Service
www.aorn.org/jobs/index.htm

Call24Online
www.healthcaresource.com

The Center for Health Careers
chc.hcwp.org

Edphysician.com
www.edphysician.com

HealthCareerWeb
www.healthcareerweb.com

HealthWeb Nursing!
http://healthweb.org

MedZilla
www.chemistry.com

Monster Healthcare
healthcare.monster.com

Nurse Options USA
www.nurseoptions.com

Pharmaceutical Online
www.pharmaceuticalonline.com

Pharmacy Week
www.pweek.com

Physicians Employment
www.physemp.com

PracticeLink
www.practicelink.com

Professional Information from the Journal of Nurse-Midwifery
www.midwife.org

PsychWeb
www.psywww.com

RadWork.com (radiologists)
radwork.com

RehabWorld
www.rehabworld.com

Yahoo!: Health/Employment/Jobs
www.yahoo.com/Health/Employment/Jobs/

Audiovisual Materials

Careers in Health. Video. S. Charleston, WV: Meridian Education Corp.

Careers in Health Services: Opportunities for You. Video. Calhoun, KY: NIMCO, Inc.

Enter Here: Health and Biomedical Services. Video. S. Charleston, WV: Meridian Education Corp.

Exploring Health Occupations. 10 videos. S. Charleston, WV: Meridan Education Corp.

Health and Hospitals (*Tech Prep* series). Video. S. Charleston, WV: Meridian Education Corp.

Health Occupations (*School to Work* series). Video. Charleston, WV: Cambridge Educational.

Health-Related Cluster (*Vocational Visions* series). Video. Mount Kisco, NY: Vocational Media Associates.

Humanitarian Careers. Video. Indianapolis, IN: JIST Publishing.

Innerview: Health Care. Video. Fresno, CA: Edgepoint Productions.

Innerview: Medical Professionals. Video. Fresno, CA: Edgepoint Productions.

Medicine (*Career Builders* series). Video. New York: Educational Design, Inc.

Medicine and Related Fields. Video. Bloomington, IL: Meridian Education Corp.

Physicians. (*Career Encounters* Series.) Video. S. Charleston, WV: Meridian Education Corp.

Scientific Careers. Video. Indianapolis, IN: JIST Publishing.

Tech Prep and Health Occupations. Video. Bloomington, IL: Meridian Education Corp.

Dentists, Dental Assistants, and Dental Technicians

Books

Career Directions for Dental Hygienists, Regina D. Thomas. Holmdel, NJ: Career Directions Press, 1992.

Careers Without College: Dental Hygienist, Charnan Simon and E. Russell Primm. Mankato, MN: Capstone Press, 1998.

Dentists, Robert James. Vero Beach, FL: The Rourke Book Co., 1995.

Exploring Careers in Dentistry, Jessica A. Rickert. New York: The Rosen Publishing Group, 1996.

Not Just the Cleaning Lady: A Hygienist's Guide to Survival, Catherine A. Schmidt. Nashville, TN: Pennywell Press, 1999.

Opportunities in Dental Care Careers, Bonnie Kendall. Lincolnwood, IL: VGM Career Horizons, 1999.

Audiovisual Materials

Innerview: Dentistry. Video. Fresno, CA: Edgepoint Productions.

Medical Assistants, Technicians, and Technologists

Books

Careers Without College: Medical Assistant, E. Russell Primm. Mankato, MN: Capstone Press, 1998.

Medical Technologists and Technicians Career Directory: A Practical One-Stop Guide to Getting a Job in Medical Technology, Bradley J. Morgan, Joseph M. Palmisano, and Diane M. Sawinski, eds. Detroit, MI: Visible Ink Press, 1994.

Opportunities in Medical Imaging Careers, Clifford J. Sherry. Lincolnwood, IL: VGM Career Horizons, 1999.

Opportunities in Medical Technology Careers: Clinical Laboratory Science, Karen J. Karni. Lincolnwood, IL: VGM Career Horizons, 1996.

Opportunities in Paramedical Careers, Alex Kacen. Lincolnwood, IL: VGM Career Horizons, 1994.

Opportunities in Physician Assistant Careers, Terence J. Sacks. Lincolnwood, IL: VGM Career Horizons, 1994.

Audiovisual Materials

Clinical Lab Science. (*Career Encounters* Series). Video. S. Charleston, WV: Meridian Education Corp.

Innerview: Medical Technicians. Video. Fresno, CA: Edgepoint Productions.

Radiology. (*Career Encounters* Series). Video. S. Charleston, WV: Meridian Education Corp.

X-Ray Technologist (*Day in a Career* series). Video. Charleston, WV: Cambridge Educational.

Nursing

Books

Advancing Your Career: Concepts of Professional Nursing, Rose Kearney Nunnery. Philadephia: F.A. Davis Co., 1997.

Career Planning for Nurses, Bette Case, ed. Albany, NY: Delmar, 1997.

Careers in Midwifery, Jennifer Croft. New York: The Rosen Publishing Group, 1995.

Developing Your Career in Nursing, Robert Newell, ed. Herndon, VA: Cassell Academic, 1996.

Guide to Surviving Nursing School, 2nd ed., Joan M. Regan. Springhouse, PA: Springhouse Publishing Co., 1996.

How to Get into the Right Nursing Program, Carla S. Rogers. Lincolnwood, IL: NTC Publishing Group, 1998.

LPN to RN Transitions, Nicki Harrington, Nancy E. Smith, and Wanda E. Spratt. Philadelphia: Lippincott-Raven Publishers, 1996.

Managing Your Career in Nursing, 2nd ed., Frances C. Henderson and Barbara O. McGettigan. New York: National League for Nursing, 1994.

Mosby's Tour Guide to Nursing School: A Student's Road Survival Kit, 3rd ed., Melodie Chenevert. St. Louis, MO: Mosby-Year Book, 1995.

The Nurse's Career Guide: Discovering New Horizons in Health Care, Zardoya E. Eagles. San Luis Obispo, CA: Sovereignty Press, 1997.

Nurses: People Who Care for our Health, Robert James. Vero Beach, FL: The Rourke Book Co., 1995.

Nursing, Blythe Camenson. Lincolnwood, IL: NTC Publishing Group, 1995.

Nursing: The Career of a Lifetime, Shirley H. Fondiller and Barbara J. Nerone. New York: National League for Nursing, 1995.

The Nursing Experience: Trends, Challenges, and Transitions, 3rd ed., Lucie Young Kelly and Lucille A. Joel. New York: McGraw-Hill, 1996.

Opportunities in Nursing Careers, 2nd ed. Keville Frederickson. Lincolnwood, IL: NTC Publishing Group, 1996.

Reinventing Your Nursing Career: A Handbook for Success in the Age of Managed Care, Michael Newell and Mario Pinardo. Gaithersburg, MD: Aspen Publishing, 1998.

Resumes for Nursing Careers, editors of VGM Career Horizons. Lincolnwood, IL: NTC Publishing Group, 1996.

Audiovisual Materials

Advanced Practical Nursing. (*Career Encounters* Series). S. Charleston, WV: Meridian Education Corp.

Innerview: Nursing. Video. Fresno, CA: Edgepoint Productions.

Medical Home Health Aide (*Day in a Career* series). Video. Charleston, WV: Cambridge Educational.

Nursing (*Career Builders* series). Video. New York: Educational Design, Inc.

Nursing (*Career Encounters* series). Video. Charleston, WV: Cambridge Educational.

Nursing (*Day in a Career* series). Video. Charleston, WV: Cambridge Educational.

Nursing: Oportunities Unlimited. Video. Lubbock, TX: CEV Multimedia.

Pharmacy

Books

Discovering New Medicines: Careers in Pharmaceutical Research and Development, Peter D. Stonier, ed. New York: John Wiley & Sons, 1995.

Opportunities in Pharmacy Careers, Fred B. Gable. Lincolnwood, IL: NTC Publishing Group, 1997.

Pharmacists: People Who Care for our Health, Robert James. Vero Beach, FL: The Rourke Book Co., 1995.

Pharmacy Education and Careers: Your Road Map to Pharmacy Education and Careers, 2nd ed., Daniel H. Albrant and Linda R. Harteker. Washington, DC: American Pharmaceutical Association, 1997.

Audiovisual Materials

Health and Pharmaceuticals. Video. Charleston, WV: Cambridge Educational.

Innerview: Pharmacology. Video. Fresno, CA: Edgepoint Productions.

Physicians and Specialized Practitioners

Books

Barron's Guide to Medical and Dental Schools, 9th ed., Saul Wischnitzer. Hauppauge, NY: Barron's Educational Series, 2000.

Becoming a Physician: A Practical and Creative Guide to Planning a Career in Medicine, Jennifer Danek and Marita Danek. New York: John Wiley & Sons, 1997.

Career Paths in Psychology: Where Your Degree Can Take You, Robert J. Sternberg, ed. Washington, DC: American Psychological Association, 1997.

Careers in Medicine, Carolyn Simpson and Penelope Hall. New York: The Rosen Publishing Group, 1994.

Doctors: People Who Care for our Health, Robert James. Vero Beach, FL: The Rourke Book Co., 1995.

Great Jobs for Psychology Majors, 2nd ed. Stephen E. Lambert and Julie Ann Degalan. Lincolnwood, IL: VGM Career Horizons, 2000.

How to Get into the Right Medical School, Carla S. Rogers. Lincolnwood, IL: NTC Publishing Group, 1996.

Life After Medical School: Thirty-Two Doctors Describe How They Shaped Their Medical Careers, Leonard Laster, ed. New York: W.W. Norton & Co., 1996.

Medical School Companion: The Ultimate Guide to Excelling in Medical School and Launching Your Career, Mary Ross-Dolen, Keith Berkowitz, and Ali Eyad. New York: The Princeton Review, 1996.

Mental Health and Social Work Career Directory : A Practical, One-Stop Guide to Getting a Job in the Helping Professions, Bradley J. Morgan, Joseph M. Palmisano, and Diane M. Sawinski, eds. Detroit, MI: Visible Ink Press, 1993.

Office and Career Management for the Eye Care Paraprofessional, Bill Borover and Tammy Langley. Thorofare, NJ: Slack, Inc., 1997.

Opportunities in Chiropractic Health-Care Careers, Lois Sportelli and R. C. Shafer. Lincolnwood, IL: NTC Publishing Group, 1994.

Opportunities in Eye Care Careers, Kathleen M. Belikoff. Lincolnwood, IL: NTC Publishing Group, 1998.

Opportunities in Physician Careers, Jan Sugar-Webb. Lincolnwood, IL: NTC Publishing Group, 1999.

Opportunities in Psychology Careers, Donald E. Super and Charles M. Super. Lincolnwood, IL: NTC Publishing Group, 1994.

What You Never Learned in Graduate School: A Survival Guide for Therapists, Jeffrey A. Kottler and Richard J. Hazler. New York: W.W. Norton & Co., 1997.

Audiovisual Materials

Clinical Lab Science (*Career Encounters* series). Video. S. Charleston, WV: Meridian Education Corp.

Exploring Careers in Psychology. Video. Mount Kisco, NY: Guidance Associates.

Innerview: Optical Services. Video. Fresno, CA: Edgepoint Productions.

Innerview: Psychology and Counseling. Video. Fresno, CA: Edgepoint Productions.

Physician (*Career Encounters* series). S. Charleston, WV: Meridian Education Corp.

Podiatric Medicine (*Career Encounters* series). S. Charleston, WV: Meridian Education Corp.

Radiology (*Career Encounters* series). Video. S. Charleston, WV: Meridian Education Corp.

Rehabilitation Therapists

Books

Opportunities in Fitness Careers, Mary Miller and Lewis Baratz. Lincolnwood, IL: NTC Publishing Group, 1997.

Opportunities in Occupational Therapy Careers, Marie-Louise Franciscus, Marguerite Abbot, and Zona R. Weeks. Lincolnwood, IL: NTC Publishing Group, 1994.

Opportunities in Physical Therapy Careers, Bernice Krumhansl. Lincolnwood, IL: NTC Publishing Group, 1993.

Opportunities in Speech-Language Pathology Careers, Patricia Larkins Hicks. Lincolnwood, IL: NTC Publishing Group, 1995.

Physical Therapists, Robert James. Vero Beach, FL: The Rourke Book Co., 1995.

Your Career in Physical Medicine, Roberta C. Weiss. Philadelphia: W.B. Saunders, 1997.

Audiovisual Materials

Occupational Therapist (*Day in a Career* series). Video. Charleston, WV: Meridian Education Corp.

Physical Therapist (*Day in a Career* series). Video. Charleston, WV: Meridian Education Corp.

Physical Therapist (*Vocational Visions* series). Video. Charleston, WV: Meridian Education Corp.

Related Health Careers

Books

Allied Health and Rehabilitation Professions Education Directory. Chicago: American Medical Association, revised regularly.

Allied Health Professions, Arco Editorial Board. New York: Macmillan General Reference, 1993.

Health Careers Today, Judith Gerdin. St. Louis, MO: Mosby-Year Book, 1996.

Health Careers: Undergraduate Careers in the Health Professions, Michael Beard and Yasmen Simonian. Dubuque, IA: Kendall-Hunt, 1994.

Your Career in Administrative Medical Services, Roberta C. Weiss. Philadelphia: W.B. Saunders, 1996.

Directory Directory Institutions Offering Career Training

The information in this directory was generated from the IPEDS (Integrated Postsecondary Education Data System) database of the U.S. Department of Education. It includes only regionally or nationally accredited institutions offering postsecondary occupational training in administration, business, and the office. Because college catalogs and directories of colleges and universities are readily available elsewhere, this directory does not include institutions that offer only bachelor's and advanced degrees.

Dental Assistant Technology

ALABAMA

Community College of the Air Force
130 West Maxwell Blvd.
Montgomery 36112-6613

ARIZONA

Apollo College
3870 North Oracle Rd.
Tucson 85705

Apollo College, Phoenix, Inc.
8503 North 27th Ave.
Phoenix 85051

Apollo College, Tri City, Inc.
630 West Southern Ave.
Mesa 85210

The Bryman School
4343 North 16th St.
Phoenix 85016

CALIFORNIA

Allan Hancock College
800 South College Dr.
Santa Maria 93454

Citrus College
1000 West Foothill Blvd.
Glendora 91741-1899

Concorde Career Institute
12412 Victory Blvd.
North Hollywood 91602

Concorde Career Institute
123 Camino De La Reina, Ste. E125
San Diego 92108

Concorde Career Institute
570 West Fourth St., Ste. 107
San Bernardino 92401

Diablo Valley College
321 Golf Club Rd.
Pleasant Hill 94523

Donald Vocational School
1833 West Eighth St., Ste. 200
Los Angeles 90057

Galen College of Medical and Dental Assistants
1325 North Wishon Ave.
Fresno 93728

Galen College of Medical and Dental Assistants
1604 Ford Ave.
Modesto 95350

Galen College of Medical and Dental Assistants
3908 West Coldwell, Ste. A
Visalia 93277

Huntington College of Dental Technology
250 Hospital Circle
Westminster 92683

Nova Institute of Health Technology
520 North Euclid Ave.
Ontario 91762

Nova Institute of Health Technology
12449 Putnam St.
Whittier 90602-1023

Nova Institute of Health Technology
3000 South Robertson Blvd.
Los Angeles 90034

Orange Coast College
2701 Fairview Rd.
Costa Mesa 92626

San Joaquin Valley College
201 New Stine Rd.
Bakersfield 93309

San Joaquin Valley College
295 East Sierra Ave.
Fresno 93710-3616

San Joaquin Valley College
8400 West Mineral King Ave.
Visalia 93291

Santa Rosa Junior College
1501 Mendocino Ave.
Santa Rosa 95401-4395

Western Career College
170 Bay Fair Mall
San Leandro 94578

COLORADO

Concorde Career Institute
770 Grant St.
Denver 80203

Front Range Community College
3645 West 112th Ave.
Westminster 80030

Heritage College of Health Careers
12 Lakeside Ln.
Denver 80212

CONNECTICUT

Huntington Institute, Inc.
193 Broadway
Norwich 06360

FLORIDA

Concorde Career Institute
7960 Arlington Expwy.
Jacksonville 32211

Concorde Career Institute
4202 West Spruce St.
Tampa 33607

Florida Community College at Jacksonville
501 West State St.
Jacksonville 32202

Palm Beach Community College
4200 Congress Ave.
Lake Worth 33461

Southern College
5600 Lake Underhill Rd.
Orlando 32807

GEORGIA

Albany Technical Institute
1021 Lowe Rd.
Albany 31708

Medix Schools
2108 Cobb Pkwy.
Smyrna 30080

IDAHO

American Institute of Health Technology, Inc.
6600 Emerald
Boise 83704

LLINOIS

Kaskaskia College
27210 College Rd.
Centralia 62801

Parkland College
2400 West Bradley Ave.
Champaign 61821

VIP Schools, Inc.
600N McClurg Ct., Ste. 304A
Chicago 60611-3044

INDIANA

Indiana University, Purdue University at Indianapolis
355 North Lansing
Indianapolis 46202

Professional Careers Institute
2611 Waterfront Pkwy., East Dr.
Indianapolis 46214-2028

LOUISIANA

Domestic Health Care Institute
4826 Jamestown Ave.
Baton Rouge 70808

Eastern College of Health Vocations
3321 Hessmer Ave., Ste. 200
Metairie 70002

MARYLAND

Medix Schools
1017 York Rd.
Towson 21204-9840

MASSACHUSETTS

Bryman Institute, a Corinthian School
323 Boylston St.
Brookline 02146

Northeastern University
360 Huntington Ave.
Boston 02115

MICHIGAN

Delta College
University Ctr.
University Center 48710

Ferris State University
901 South State St.
Big Rapids 49307

Grand Rapids Community College
143 Bostwick Ave. NE
Grand Rapids 49503-3295

Grand Rapids Educational Center
1750 Woodworth NE
Grand Rapids 49525

Grand Rapids Educational Center
5349 West Main
Kalamazoo 49009

Ross Medical Education Center
1036 Gilbert St.
Flint 48532

Ross Medical Education Center
1188 North West Ave.
Jackson 49202

Ross Medical Education Center
913 West Holmes, Ste. 260
Lansing 48910

Ross Medical Education Center
4054 Bay Rd.
Saginaw 48603

Ross Medical Education Center
26417 Hoover Rd.
Warren 48089

MINNESOTA

Century Community and Technical College
3300 Century Ave. N
White Bear Lake 55110

Hibbing Community College, a Technical and Community College
1515 East 25th St.
Hibbing 55746

Lakeland Medical and Dental Academy, Inc.
1402 West Lake St.
Minneapolis 55408

MISSISSIPPI

Hinds Community College, Raymond Campus
Raymond 39154

MISSOURI

Al-Med Academy
10963 Saint Charles Rock Rd.
Saint Louis 63074

Concorde Career Institute
3239 Broadway
Kansas City 64111

Missouri College
10121 Manchester Rd.
Saint Louis 63122

Saint Louis Community College, Forest Park
5600 Oakland Ave.
Saint Louis 63110

NEVADA

Heritage College
3305 Spring Mountain Rd., Ste. 7
Las Vegas 89120

NEW HAMPSHIRE

New Hampshire Technical Institute
11 Institute Dr.
Concord 03301

NEW JERSEY

Berdan Institute
265 Rte. 46
Totowa 07512

Camden County College
P.O. Box 200
Blackwood 08012

Empire Technical School of New Jersey
576 Central Ave.
East Orange 07018

NEW YORK

Continental Dental Assistant School
633 Jefferson Rd.
Rochester 14623

Mandl School
254 West 54th St.
New York 10019

New York School for Medical and Dental Assistants
116-16 Queens Blvd.
Forest Hills 11375

NORTH CAROLINA

Alamance Community College
P.O. Box 8000
Graham 27253

Guilford Technical Community College
Box 309
Jamestown 27282

OHIO

Akron Medical-Dental Institute, Inc., DBA Akron Institute
1625 Portage Tr.
Cuyahoga Falls 44223

Cleveland Institute of Dental-Medical Assistants
1836 Euclid Ave.
Cleveland 44115

Cleveland Institute of Dental-Medical Assistants
5564 Mayfield Rd.
Lyndhurst 44124

Cleveland Institute of Dental-Medical Assistants
5733 Hopkins Rd.
Mentor 44060

Eastland Career Center
4465 South Hamilton Rd.
Groveport 43125

Institute of Medical-Dental Technology
375 Glensprings Dr., Ste. 201
Cincinnati 45246

OKLAHOMA

Kiamichi Area Vocational Technical School SD 7, Talihina Campus
Rte. 2, Hwy. 63A
Talihina 74571

Metro Area Vocational Technical School District 22
1900 Springlake Dr.
Oklahoma City 73111

OREGON

Apollo College, Portland, Inc.
2600 Southeast 98th Ave.
Portland 97266

Lane Community College
4000 East 30th Ave.
Eugene 97405

Portland Community College
P.O. Box 19000
Portland 97280-0990

PENNSYLVANIA

Academy of Medical Arts and Business
2301 Academy Dr.
Harrisburg 17112

Career Training Academy
703 Fifth Ave.
New Kensington 15068

Community College of Philadelphia
1700 Spring Garden St.
Philadelphia 19130

Delaware Valley Academy of Medical and Dental Assistants
3330 Grant Ave.
Philadelphia 19114

Median School of Allied Health Careers
125 Seventh St.
Pittsburgh 15222-3400

RHODE ISLAND

Community College of Rhode Island
400 East Ave.
Warwick 02886-1807

TENNESSEE

Chattanooga State Technical Community College
4501 Amnicola Hwy.
Chattanooga 37406

Tennessee Technology Center at Memphis
550 Alabama Ave.
Memphis 38105-3604

Tennessee Technology Center at Shelbyville
1405 Madison St.
Shelbyville 37160

TEXAS

Allied Health Careers
5424 Hwy. 290 W, Ste. 105
Austin 78735

Career Centers of Texas El Paso
8375 Burnham Dr.
El Paso 79907

San Antonio College of Medical and Dental Assistants, Central
4205 San Pedro Ave.
San Antonio 78212-1899

San Antonio College of Medical and Dental Assistants, South
3900 North 23rd
McAllen 78501

Texas State Technical College, Waco
3801 Campus Dr.
Waco 76705

UTAH

American Institute of Medical-Dental Technology
1675 North 200 West, Bldg. 4
Provo 84604

Provo College
1450 West 820 North
Provo 84601

Utah Career College
1144 West 3300 South
Salt Lake City 84119-3330

VIRGINIA

Medical Careers Institute
605 Thimble Shoals
Newport News 23606

National Business College
1813 East Main St.
Salem 24153

Riverside Regional Medical Center, School of Professional Nursing
500 J Clyde Morris Blvd.
Newport News 23601

WASHINGTON

Bates Technical College
1101 South Yakima Ave.
Tacoma 98405

Bellingham Technical College
3028 Lindbergh Ave.
Bellingham 98225

Eton Technical Institute
209 East Casino Rd.
Everett 98208

Eton Technical Institute
31919 Sixth Ave. S
Federal Way 98003

Eton Technical Institute
3649 Frontage Rd., St. A
Port Orchard 98366

Lake Washington Technical College
11605 132nd Ave. NE
Kirkland 98034

Seattle Vocational Institute
315 22nd Ave. S
Seattle 98144

Spokane Community College
North 1810 Greene Ave.
Spokane 99207

WISCONSIN

Fox Valley Technical College at Appleton
1825 North Bluemound Dr.
Appleton 54913-2277

Western Wisconsin Technical College
304 North Sixth St., P.O. Box 908
La Crosse 54602-0908

Dental Laboratory Technology

CALIFORNIA

California Vocational College
3951 Balboa Ave.
San Francisco 94121

Huntington College of Dental Technology
250 Hospital Circle
Westminster 92683

Nova Institute of Health Technology
12449 Putnam St.
Whittier 90602-1023

Simi Valley Adult School
3192 Los Angeles Ave.
Simi Valley 93065

ILLINOIS

Midwest Institute of Technology, Inc.
3712 West Montrose Ave.
Chicago 60618

NEW YORK

Penaranda Institute of Dental Technology
40-17 82nd St.
Jackson Heights 11373

TENNESSEE

Tennessee Technology Center at Memphis
550 Alabama Ave.
Memphis 38105-3604

Dental Hygiene Technology

ARIZONA

Phoenix College
1202 West Thomas Rd.
Phoenix 85013

CALIFORNIA

Cabrillo College
6500 Soquel Dr.
Aptos 95003

Foothill College
12345 El Monte Rd.
Los Altos Hills 94022

Pasadena City College
1570 East Colorado Blvd.
Pasadena 91106

Riverside Community College
4800 Magnolia Ave.
Riverside 92506-1299

West Los Angeles College
4800 Freshman Dr.
Culver 90230

CONNECTICUT

Tunxis Community Technical College
Rtes. 6 and 177
Farmington 06032

University of Bridgeport
380 University Ave.
Bridgeport 06601

DELAWARE

Delaware Technical and Community College, Stanton-Wilmington
400 Stanton-Christiana Rd.
Newark 19702

FLORIDA

Miami-Dade Community College
300 Northeast Second Ave.
Miami 33132

Palm Beach Community College
4200 Congress Ave.
Lake Worth 33461

Pensacola Junior College
1000 College Blvd.
Pensacola 32504

Saint Petersburg Junior College
8580 66th St. N
Pinellas Park 34665

Santa Fe Community College
3000 Northwest 83rd St.
Gainesville 32606

GEORGIA

Darton College
2400 Gillionville Rd.
Albany 31707

Dekalb College
3251 Panthersville Rd.
Decatur 30034

Medical College of Georgia
1120 15th St.
Augusta 30912

ILLINOIS

Illinois Central College
One College Dr.
East Peoria 61635-0001

Parkland College
2400 West Bradley Ave.
Champaign 61821

Prairie State College
202 Halsted St.
Chicago Heights 60411

Southern Illinois University, Carbondale
Faner Hall 2179
Carbondale 62901-4512

William Rainey Harper College
1200 West Algonquin Rd.
Palatine 60067-7398

INDIANA

Indiana University, Northwest
3400 Broadway
Gary 46408

Indiana University, Purdue University, Indianapolis
355 North Lansing
Indianapolis 46202

KANSAS

Johnson County Community College
12345 College Blvd.
Overland Park 66210-1299

Wichita State University
1845 Fairmount
Wichita 67260

KENTUCKY

Lexington Community College
Cooper Dr.
Lexington 40506

LOUISIANA

Louisiana State University Medical Center
433 Bolivar St.
New Orleans 70112

MARYLAND

Allegany College of Maryland
12401 Willowbrook Rd. SE
Cumberland 21502

Baltimore City Community College
2901 Liberty Heights Ave.
Baltimore 21215

MASSACHUSETTS

Bristol Community College
777 Elsbree St.
Fall River 02720

Forsyth School for Dental Hygienists
140 the Fenway
Boston 02115

Middlesex Community College
Springs Rd.
Bedford 01730

MICHIGAN

Ferris State University
901 South State St.
Big Rapids 49307

Grand Rapids Community College
143 Bostwick Ave. NE
Grand Rapids 49503-3295

Mott Community College
1401 East Court St.
Flint 48503

Oakland Community College
2480 Opdyke Rd.
Bloomfield Hills 48304-2266

University of Detroit, Mercy
P.O. Box 19900
Detroit 48219-0900

MINNESOTA

Normandale Community College
9700 France Ave. S
Bloomington 55431

MISSOURI

Saint Louis Community College, Forest Park
5600 Oakland Ave.
Saint Louis 63110

NEW HAMPSHIRE

New Hampshire Technical Institute
11 Institute Dr.
Concord 03301

NEW JERSEY

Bergen Community College
400 Paramus Rd.
Paramus 07652

Camden County College
P.O. Box 200
Blackwood 08012

Middlesex County College
155 Mill Rd.
Edison 08818-3050

Union County College
1033 Springfield Ave.
Cranford 07016

NEW MEXICO

University of New Mexico, Main Campus
Albuquerque 87131

NEW YORK

Broome Community College
P.O. Box 1017
Binghamton 13902

CUNY New York City Technical College
300 Jay St.
Brooklyn 11201

Erie Community College, North Campus
Main St. and Youngs Rd.
Williamsville 14221

Hudson Valley Community College
80 Vandenburgh Ave.
Troy 12180

Monroe Community College
1000 East Henrietta Rd.
Rochester 14623

Onondaga Community College
4941 Onondaga Rd.
Syracuse 13215

SUNY College of Technology at Farmingdale
Melville Rd.
Farmingdale 11735-1021

NORTH CAROLINA

Central Piedmont Community College
P.O. Box 35009
Charlotte 28235-5009

Guilford Technical Community College
Box 309
Jamestown 27282

NORTH DAKOTA

North Dakota State College of Science
800 North Sixth St.
Wahpeton 58076

OHIO

Cuyahoga Community College District
700 Carnegie Ave.
Cleveland 44115-2878

Shawnee State University
940 Second St.
Portsmouth 45662

University of Cincinnati, Raymond Walters College
9555 Plainfield Rd.
Blue Ash 45236

Youngstown State University
One University Plaza
Youngstown 44555

OREGON

Lane Community College
4000 East 30th Ave.
Eugene 97405

PENNSYLVANIA

Community College of Philadelphia
1700 Spring Garden St.
Philadelphia 19130

Harcum College
750 Montgomery Ave.
Bryn Mawr 19010

ICS-International Correspondence Schools
Oak St. and Pawnee Ave.
Scranton 18515

Luzerne County Community College
1333 South Prospect St.
Nanticoke 18634

Northampton County Area Community College
3835 Green Pond Rd.
Bethlehem 18020-7599

Pennsylvania College of Technology
One College Ave.
Williamsport 17701

RHODE ISLAND

Community College of Rhode Island
400 East Ave.
Warwick 02886-1807

SOUTH CAROLINA

Greenville Technical College
P.O. Box 5616, Station B
Greenville 29606-5616

Midlands Technical College
P.O. Box 2408
Columbia 29202

Trident Technical College
P.O. Box 118067
Charleston 29423-8067

SOUTH DAKOTA

University of South Dakota
414 East Clark St.
Vermillion 57069-2390

TENNESSEE

East Tennessee State University
P.O. Box 70734
Johnson City 37614-0734

Tennessee State University
3500 John Merritt Blvd.
Nashville 37209-1561

TEXAS

Tyler Junior College
1327 South Baxter Ave.
Tyler 75711

The University of Texas Health Science Center
P.O. Box 20036
Houston 77225

The University of Texas Health Science Center, San Antonio
7703 Floyd Curl Dr.
San Antonio 78284

UTAH

American Institute of Medical-Dental Technology
1675 North 200 West, Bldg. 4
Provo 84604

Weber State University
3750 Harrison Blvd.
Ogden 84408

VIRGINIA

Wytheville Community College
1000 East Main St.
Wytheville 24382

WASHINGTON

Clark College
1800 East McLoughlin Blvd.
Vancouver 98663-3598

Shoreline Community College
16101 Greenwood Ave. N
Seattle 98133

WEST VIRGINIA

West Liberty State College
West Liberty 26074

WISCONSIN

Madison Area Technical College
3550 Anderson St.
Madison 53704

Northcentral Technical College
1000 Campus Dr.
Wausau 54401-1899

Northeast Wisconsin Technical College
2740 West Mason St., P.O. Box 19042
Green Bay 54307-9042

EEG and EKG Technology

CALIFORNIA

Institute of Computer Technology
3200 Wilshire Blvd.
Los Angeles 90010

Orange Coast College
2701 Fairview Rd.
Costa Mesa 92626

FLORIDA

Technical Career Institute
4299 Northwest 36th St., Ste. 300
Miami Springs 33166

Pasco-Hernando Community College
36727 Blanton Rd.
Dade City 33525-7599

ILLINOIS

Medical Careers Institute
116 South Michigan Ave.
Chicago 60603

MICHIGAN

Carnegie Institute
550 Stephenson Hwy.
Troy 48083

MISSOURI

Saint Louis College of Health Careers
4484 West Pine
Saint Louis 63108

NEW JERSEY

Hudson County Area Vocational Technical School, North Hudson Center
8511 Tonnelle Ave.
North Bergen 07047

NEW YORK

Niagara County Community College
3111 Saunders Settlement Rd.
Sanborn 14132

PENNSYLVANIA

American Center Technical Arts
1930 Chestnut St.
Philadelphia 19103

TEXAS

Career Centers of Texas El Paso
8375 Burnham Dr.
El Paso 79907

Laboratory Animal Care Technology

COLORADO

Institute for Nuclear Medical Education
5660 Airport Blvd., Ste. 101
Boulder 80301

CONNECTICUT

Huntington Institute, Inc.
193 Broadway
Norwich 06360

FLORIDA

Beacon Career Institute, Inc.
2900 Northwest 183rd St.
Miami 33056

Lee County High Vocational Technical Center, Central
3800 Michigan Ave.
Fort Myers 33916

Miriam Vocational School, Inc.
135 Southwest 57th Ave.
Miami 33144

Sarasota County Technical Institute
4748 Beneva Rd.
Sarasota 34233-1798

MINNESOTA

Saint Cloud Technical College
1540 Northway Dr.
Saint Cloud 56303

OHIO

Professional Skills Institute
20 Arco Dr.
Toledo 43607

PENNSYLVANIA

Allied Medical and Technical Careers
2901 Pittston Ave.
Scranton 18505

Allied Medical and Technical Careers
104 Woodward Hill Rd.
Edwardsville 18704

RHODE ISLAND

Community College of Rhode Island
400 East Ave.
Warwick 02886-1807

TENNESSEE

Nashville State Technical Institute
120 White Bridge Rd.
Nashville 37209

WISCONSIN

Saint Joseph's Hospital Histologic Technician Program
611 Saint Joseph's Ave.
Marshfield 54449

Licensed Practical Nursing

ALABAMA

Bessemer State Technical College
1100 Ninth Ave.
Bessemer 35021

Bevill State Community College
100 State St.
Sumiton 35148

Central Alabama Community College
1675 Cherokee Rd.
Alexander City 35010

Douglas MacArthur State Technical College
1708 North Main St.
Opp 36467

Gadsden State Community College
1001 George Wallace Dr.
Gadsden 35902-0227

George C Wallace State Community College, Selma
3000 Earl Goodwin Pkwy.
Selma 36702

George C Wallace State Community College, Dothan
Rte. 6, Box 62
Dothan 36303-9234

George C Wallace State Community College, Hanceville
801 Main St. NW
Hanceville 35077-2000

Harry M Ayers State Technical College
1801 Coleman Rd.
Anniston 36202

Jefferson Davis Community College
220 Alco Dr.
Brewton 36426

J F Drake State Technical College
3421 Meridian St. N
Huntsville 35811

John C Calhoun State Community College
Hwy. 31 N
Decatur 35602

Northwest Shoals Community College
800 George Wallace Blvd.
Muscle Shoals 35662

Reid State Technical College
I65 and Hwy. 83
Evergreen 36401

Shelton State Community College
9500 Old Greensboro Rd.
Tuscaloosa 35405

Southern Union State Junior College
P.O. Box 1000
Wadley 36276

Trenholm State Technical College
1225 Air Base Blvd.
Montgomery 36108

ARIZONA

Central Arizona College
8470 North Overfield Rd.
Coolidge 85228-9778

Gateway Community College
108 North 40th St.
Phoenix 85034

Mesa Community College
1833 West Southern Ave.
Mesa 85202

Mohave Community College
1971 Jagerson Ave.
Kingman 86401

Pima Community College
2202 West Anklam Rd.
Tucson 85709-0001

ARKANSAS

Arkansas Valley Technical Institute
P.O. Box 506, Hwy. 23 N
Ozark 72949

Baptist Schools of Nursing and Allied Health
11900 College Glenn Rd., Ste. 1000
Little Rock 72210-2820

Black River Technical College
Box 468, Hwy. 304
Pocahontas 72455

Cossatot Technical College
183 Hwy. 399
De Queen 71832

Cotton Boll Technical Institute
I55 and Hwy. 148
Burdette 72321

Crowley's Ridge Technical School
140 Crowleys Ridge Rd.
Forrest City 72336-0925

Foothills Technical Institute
1800 East Moore St.
Searcy 72143

Northwest Technical Institute
709 South Old Missouri Rd.
Springdale 72764

Pulaski Technical College
3000 West Scenic Dr.
North Little Rock 72118

Quapaw Technical Institute
201 Mid-America Blvd.
Hot Springs 71913

Southeast Arkansas Technical College
1900 Hazel
Pine Bluff 71603

Westark College
P.O. Box 3649
Fort Smith 72913

CALIFORNIA

Butte College
3536 Butte Campus Dr.
Oroville 95965

Casa Loma College
14445 Olive View Dr.
Sylmar 91342

Casa Loma College, Los Angeles
3761 Stocker
Los Angeles 90008

Cerro Coso Community College
3000 College Heights Blvd.
Ridgecrest 93555-7777

Citrus College
1000 West Foothill Blvd.
Glendora 91741-1899

Concorde Career Institute
12412 Victory Blvd.
North Hollywood 91606

Concorde Career Institute
570 West Fourth St., Ste. 107
San Bernardino 92401

Crafton Hills College
11711 Sand Canyon Rd.
Yucaipa 92399-1799

El Camino College
16007 Crenshaw Blvd.
Torrance 90506

Glendale Community College
1500 North Verdugo Rd.
Glendale 91208-2894

Hacienda La Puente Unified School District, Adult Education
P.O. Box 60002
City of Industry 91716-0002

Lassen College
Hwy. 139
Susanville 96130

Los Angeles Trade Technical College
400 West Washington Blvd.
Los Angeles 90015-4181

Maric College of Medical Careers
3666 Kearny Villa Rd., Ste. 100
San Diego 92123

Maric College of Medical Careers
2030 University Dr.
Vista 92083

Merced College
3600 M St.
Merced 95348-2898

Mission College
3000 Mission College Blvd.
Santa Clara 95054-1897

Mount San Jacinto College
1499 North State St.
San Jacinto 92383

Napa Valley College
2277 Napa Vallejo Hwy.
Napa 94558

Porterville College
100 East College Ave.
Porterville 93257

Sacramento City College
3835 Freeport Blvd.
Sacramento 95822

San Diego City College
1313 12th Ave.
San Diego 92101

Santa Barbara City College
721 Cliff Dr.
Santa Barbara 93109-2394

Sierra College
5000 Rocklin Rd.
Rocklin 95677

Yuba College
2088 North Beale Rd.
Marysville 95901

COLORADO

Community College of Denver
P.O. Box 173363
Denver 80217

Front Range Community College
3645 West 112th Ave.
Westminster 80030

Northeastern Junior College
100 College Dr.
Sterling 80751

Otero Junior College
1802 Colorado Ave.
La Junta 81050

Pikes Peak Community College
5675 South Academy Blvd.
Colorado Springs 80906-5498

Pueblo Community College
900 West Orman Ave.
Pueblo 81004

Red Rocks Community College
13300 West Sixth Ave.
Lakewood 80228

San Juan Basin Area Vocational School
Box 970
Cortez 81321

T H Pickens Technical Center
500 Airport Blvd.
Aurora 80011

Trinidad State Junior College
600 Prospect St.
Trinidad 81082

Trinidad State Junior College, San Luis Valley Education Center
1011 Main St.
Alamosa 81101

DELAWARE

Delaware Technical and Community College, Owens
Box 610
Georgetown 19947

Delaware Technical and Community College, Terry Campus
1832 North Dupont Pkwy.
Dover 19901

DISTRICT OF COLUMBIA

Harrison Center for Career Education
624 Ninth St. NW, 4th Fl.
Washington 20001

FLORIDA

Atlantic Vocational Technical Center
4700 Coconut Creek Pkwy.
Coconut Creek 33063

Brevard Community College, Cocoa Campus
1519 Clearlake Rd.
Cocoa 32922

Central Florida Community College
3001 Southwest College Rd.
Ocala 34474

Charlotte Vocational Technical Center
18300 Toledo Blade Blvd.
Port Charlotte 33948-3399

Daytona Beach Community College
1200 Volusia Ave.
Daytona Beach 32114

Florida Community College at Jacksonville
501 West State St.
Jacksonville 32202

Indian River Community College
3209 Virginia Ave.
Fort Pierce 34981

Lake City Community College
Rte. 19, Box 1030
Lake City 32025

Lake County Area Vocational-Technical Center
2001 Kurt St.
Eustis 32726

Lee County High Technical Center, Central
3800 Michigan Ave.
Fort Myers 33916

Lindsey Hopkins Technical Education Center
750 Northwest 20th St.
Miami 33127

Lively Technical Center
500 North Appleyard Dr.
Tallahassee 32304

Lorenzo Walker Institute of Technology
3702 Estey Ave.
Naples 34104

Manatee Vocational Technical Center
5603 34th St. W
Bradenton 34210

Miami Lakes Technical Education Center
5780 Northwest 158th St.
Miami Lakes 33169

North Florida Community College
Turner Davis Dr.
Madison 32340

North Technical Education Center
7071 Garden Rd.
Riviera Beach 33404

Pasco-Hernando Community College
36727 Blanton Rd.
Dade City 33525-7599

Pensacola Junior College
1000 College Blvd.
Pensacola 32504

Pinellas Technical Education Center, Clearwater
6100 154th Ave. N
Clearwater 34620

Pinellas Technical Education Center
901 34th St. S
Saint Petersburg 33711

Robert Morgan Vocational Technical Center
18180 Southwest 122nd Ave.
Miami 33177

Saint Augustine Technical Center
2980 Collins Ave.
Saint Augustine 32095-1919

Santa Fe Community College
3000 Northwest 83rd St.
Gainesville 32606

Sarasota County Technical Institute
4748 Beneva Rd.
Sarasota 34233-1798

Seminole Community College
100 Weldon Blvd.
Sanford 32773-6199

Sheridan Vocational Center
5400 Sheridan St.
Hollywood 33021

South Florida Community College
600 West College Dr.
Avon Park 33825

South Technical Education Center
1300 Southwest 30th Ave.
Boynton Beach 33426-9099

Washington-Holmes Area Vocational-Technical Center
757 Hoyt St.
Chipley 32428

William T McFatter Vocational Technical Center
6500 Nova Dr.
Davie 33317

Withlacoochee Technical Institute
1201 West Main St.
Inverness 32650

GEORGIA

Albany Technical Institute
504 College Dr.
Albany 31705

Athens Area Technical Institute
U.S. Hwy. 29 N
Athens 30610-0399

Atlanta Area Technical School
1560 Stewart Ave. SW
Atlanta 30310

Augusta Technical Institute
3116 Deans Bridge Rd.
Augusta 30906

Bainbridge College
2500 East Shotwell St.
Bainbridge 31717

Carroll Technical Institute
997 South Hwy. 16
Carrollton 30117

Chattahoochee Technical Institute
980 South Cobb Dr.
Marietta 30060-3398

Columbus Technical Institute
928 45th St.
Columbus 31904-6572

Coosa Valley Technical Institute
785 Cedar Ave.
Rome 30161

Dekalb Technical Institute
495 North Indian Creek Dr.
Clarkston 30021

East Central Technical Institute
667 Perry House Rd.
Fitzgerald 31750

Flint River Technical Institute
1533 Hwy. 19 S
Thomaston 30286

Griffin Technical Institute
501 Varsity Rd.
Griffin 30223

Heart of Georgia Technical Institute
560 Pinehill Rd.
Dublin 31021

Macon Technical Institute
3300 Macon Tech Dr.
Macon 31206

Middle Georgia Technical Institute
1311 Corder Rd.
Warner Robins 31088

Moultrie Area Technical Institute
361 Industrial Dr.
Moultrie 31768

North Georgia Technical Institute
Georgia Hwy. 197, P.O. Box 65
Clarkesville 30523

Pickens Technical Institute
100 Pickens Tech Dr.
Jasper 30143

Savannah Technical Institute
5717 White Bluff Rd.
Savannah 31405-5594

South College
709 Mall Blvd.
Savannah 31406

South Georgia Technical Institute
728 Souther Field Rd.
Americus 31709

Swainsboro Technical Institute
346 Kite Rd.
Swainsboro 30401

Thomas Technical Institute
15689 US Hwy. 19N
Thomasville 31792

Valdosta Technical Institute
4089 Valtech Rd.
Valdosta 31602-9796

HAWAII

Kapiolani Community College
4303 Diamond Head Rd.
Honolulu 96816

IDAHO

Boise State University
1910 University Dr.
Boise 83725

College of Southern Idaho
P.O. Box 1238
Twin Falls 83301

Idaho State University
741 South Seventh Ave.
Pocatello 83209

ILLINOIS

Black Hawk College, Quad-Cities
6600 34th Ave.
Moline 61265

Capital Area School of Practical Nursing
2201 Toronto Rd.
Springfield 62707-8645

Carl Sandburg College
2232 South Lake Storey Rd.
Galesburg 61401

City Colleges of Chicago, Central Office
226 West Jackson
Chicago 60606

Danville Area Community College
2000 East Main St.
Danville 61832

Decatur School of Practical Nursing
300 East Eldorado St.
Decatur 62523

Elgin Community College
1700 Spartan Dr.
Elgin 60123

F W Olin Vocational School of Practical Nursing
4200 Humbert Rd.
Alton 62002

Highland Community College
2998 West Pearl City Rd.
Freeport 61032-9341

Illinois Eastern Community Colleges, Olney Central College
305 North West St.
Olney 62450

Illinois Valley Community College
815 North Orlando Smith Ave.
Oglesby 61348-9692

Jacksonville School of Practical Nursing
32 North Central Park Plaza
Jacksonville 62650

John A Logan College
700 Logan College Rd.
Carterville 62918

John Wood Community College
150 South 48th St.
Quincy 62301-9147

Joliet Townwship High School Practical Nursing
201 East Jefferson St.
Joliet 60432

Kankakee Community College
P.O. Box 888
Kankakee 60901

Kaskaskia College
27210 College Rd.
Centralia 62801

Lake Land College
5001 Lake Land Blvd.
Mattoon 61938

Rend Lake College
468 North Ken Graz Pkwy.
Ina 62846

Shawnee Community College
8364 Shawnee College Rd.
Ullin 62992

Southeastern Illinois College
3575 College Rd.
Harrisburg 62946

South Suburban College
15800 South State St.
South Holland 60473

Spoon River College
23235 North CO 22
Canton 61520

Triton College
2000 Fifth Ave.
River Grove 60171

William Rainey Harper College
1200 West Algonquin Rd.
Palatine 60067-7398

INDIANA

Ebbert Education Center
325 West 38th St.
Anderson 46013

Ivy Tech State College, Central Indiana
One West 26th St.
Indianapolis 46206-1763

Ivy Tech State College, Columbus
4475 Central Ave.
Columbus 47203

Ivy Tech State College, East Central
4301 South Cowan Rd., Box 3100
Muncie 47302

Ivy Tech State College, Lafayette
3101 South Creasy Ln., P.O. Box 6299
Lafayette 47903

Ivy Tech State College, North Central
1534 West Sample St.
South Bend 46619

Ivy Tech State College, Northeast
3800 North Anthony Blvd.
Fort Wayne 46805

Ivy Tech State College, Northwest
1440 East 35th Ave.
Gary 46409

Ivy Tech State College, South Central
8204 Hwy. 311
Sellersburg 47172

Ivy Tech State College, Southeast
590 Ivy Tech Dr.
Madison 47250

Ivy Tech State College, Southwest
3501 First Ave.
Evansville 47710

Ivy Tech State College, Wabash Valley
7999 U.S. Hwy. 41
Terre Haute 47802-4898

Ivy Tech State College, Whitewater
P.O. Box 1145
Richmond 47374

J Everett Light Career Center
1901 East 86th St.
Indianapolis 46240

Vincennes University
1002 North First St.
Vincennes 47591

IOWA

Des Moines Community College
2006 Ankeny Blvd.
Ankeny 50021

Eastern Iowa Community College District
306 West River Dr.
Davenport 52801-1221

Hawkeye Institute of Technology
1501 East Orange Rd.
Waterloo 50704

Indian Hills Community College
525 Grandview
Ottumwa 52501

Iowa Central Community College
330 Ave. M
Fort Dodge 50501

Iowa Lakes Community College
19 South Seventh St.
Estherville 51334

Iowa Valley Community College District
Box 536
Marshalltown 50158

Iowa Western Community College
2700 College Rd., Box 4C
Council Bluffs 51502

Northeast Iowa Community College, Calmar
Box 400, Hwy. 150 S
Calmar 52132-0400

North Iowa Area Community College
500 College Dr.
Mason City 50401

Saint Luke's College of Nursing and Health Sciences
2720 Stone Park Blvd.
Sioux City 51104-0263

Southeastern Community College
Drawer F, 1015 South Gear Ave.
West Burlington 52655-0605

Southwestern Community College
1501 Townline
Creston 50801

Western Iowa Technical Community College
4647 Stone Ave., P.O. Box 5199
Sioux City 51102-5199

KANSAS

Barton County Community College
245 Northeast 30th Rd.
Great Bend 67530

Colby Community College
1255 South Range
Colby 67701

Dodge City Community College
2501 North 14th Ave.
Dodge City 67801

Flint Hills Technical School
3301 West 18th St.
Emporia 66801

Kansas City Area Vocational Technical School
2220 North 59th St.
Kansas City 66104

KAW Area Technical School
5724 Huntoon
Topeka 66604

Manhattan Area Technical Center
3136 Dickens Ave.
Manhattan 66503

Neosho County Community College
800 West 14th St.
Chanute 66720

North Central Kansas Technical College
Box 507, Hwy. 24
Beloit 67420

Northeast Kansas Area Vocational Technical School
1501 West Riley St., P.O. Box 277
Atchison 66002

Seward County Community College
Box 1137
Liberal 67905-1137

KENTUCKY

Galen Health Institutes
612 South Fourth St., Ste. 400
Louisville 40202

Kentucky Tech, Ashland Regional Technology Center
4818 Roberts Dr.
Ashland 41102

Kentucky Tech, Central Kentucky AVTS
308 Vo Tech Rd.
Lexington 40511-2626

Kentucky Technical, Hazard Regional Technology Center
101 Vo-Tech Dr.
Hazard 41701

Kentucky Technical, Jefferson Vocational Technical School
727 West Chestnut St.
Louisville 40203-2036

Kentucky Technical, Somerset Regional Technology Center
230 Airport Rd.
Somerset 42501

Kentucky Tech, Letcher County Technology Center
610 Circle Dr.
Whitesburg 41858

Mayo Regional Technology Center
Third St.
Paintsville 41240

Spencerian College
4627 Dixie Hwy.
Louisville 40216

West Kentucky Tech
5200 Blandville Rd.
Paducah 42002

LOUISIANA

Cameron College
2740 Canal St.
New Orleans 70119

Delta-Ouachita Regional Technical Institute
609 Vocational Pkwy.
West Monroe 71291

Huey P Long Technical Institute
303 South Jones St.
Winnfield 71483

Louisiana Technical College, Alexandria Campus
4311 South MacArthur Dr.
Alexandria 71302-3137

Louisiana Technical College, Bastrop Campus
Kammell St.
Bastrop 71221-1120

Louisiana Technical College, Florida Parishes
P.O. Box 130
Greensburg 70441

Louisiana Technical College, Gulf Area Campus
1115 Clover St.
Abbeville 70510

Louisiana Technical College, Jefferson Davis Campus
P.O. Box 1327
Jennings 70546

Louisiana Technical College, Jefferson Campus
5200 Blair Dr.
Metairie 70001

Louisiana Technical College, Lafayette Campus
1101 Bertrand Dr.
Lafayette 70502-4909

Louisiana Technical College, Lamar Salter Campus
15014 Lake Charles Hwy.
Leesville 71446

Louisiana Technical College, Northwest Louisiana
P.O. Box 835
Minden 71058-0835

Louisiana Technical College, Ruston Campus
1010 James St.
Ruston 71273-1070

Louisiana Technical College, Shreveport-Bossier
2010 North Market St.
Shreveport 71137

Louisiana Technical College, Sidney N Collier
3727 Louisa St.
New Orleans 70126

Louisiana Technical College, Slidell Campus
1000 Canulette Rd.
Slidell 70459

Louisiana Technical College, Sowela Campus
3820 J Bennet Johnston Ave.
Lake Charles 70615

Louisiana Technical College, Sullivan Campus
1710 Sullivan Dr.
Bogalusa 70427

Louisiana Technical College, T H Harris Campus
337 East South St.
Opelousas 70570

Louisiana Technical College, West Jefferson Campus
475 Manhattan Blvd.
Harvey 70058

Louisiana Tech College System, Young Memorial
900 Youngs Rd.
Morgan City 70380

Our Lady of the Lake College of Medical Technology
5345 Brittany Dr.
Baton Rouge 70808

MAINE

Central Maine Medical Center School of Nursing
300 Main St.
Lewiston 04240

Eastern Maine Technical College
354 Hogan Rd.
Bangor 04401

Northern Maine Technical College
33 Edgemont Dr.
Presque Isle 04769

Southern Maine Technical College
Fort Rd.
South Portland 04106

MARYLAND

Harford Community College
401 Thomas Run Rd.
Bel Air 21015

Johnston School of Practical Nursing
201 East University Pkwy.
Baltimore 21218-2895

Wor-Wic Community College
32000 Campus Dr.
Salisbury 21801-7131

MASSACHUSETTS

Assabet Valley Regional Vocational Technical School
215 Fitchburg St.
Marlborough 01752

Becker College, Worcester
61 Sever St.
Worcester 01615-0071

Berkshire Community College
1350 West St.
Pittsfield 01201-5786

Blue Hills Regional Technical School
800 Randolph St.
Canton 02021

Bristol Community College
777 Elsbree St.
Fall River 02720

Diman Regional Technical Institute
Stonehaven Rd.
Fall River 02723

Essex Agricultural Technical Institute
562 Maple St.
Hathorne 01937

Fisher College
118 Beacon St.
Boston 02116

Lemuel Shattuck Hospital School of Practical Nursing
180 Morton St.
Jamaica Plain 02130

Massachusetts Bay Community College
50 Oakland St.
Wellesley Hills 02181

Massachusetts Soldiers Home School of Practical Nursing
91 Crest Ave.
Chelsea 02150

Northern Essex Community College
Elliott Way
Haverhill 01830-2399

Quincy College
34 Coddington St.
Quincy 02169

Southeastern Technical Institute
250 Foundry St.
South Easton 02375

Tewksbury Hospital School of Practical Nursing
365 East St.
Tewksbury 01876

Upper Cape Cod Regional Vocational Technical School
220 Sandwich Rd.
Bourne 02532

Worcester Technical Institute
251 Belmont St.
Worcester 01605

Youville Hospital School of Practical Nursing
15 Walnut Park at Aquinas College
Newton 02158

MICHIGAN

Alpena Community College
666 Johnson St.
Alpena 49707

Bay De Noc Community College
2001 North Lincoln Rd.
Escanaba 49289

Delta College
University Ctr.
University Center 48710

Gogebic Community College
East 4946 Jackson Rd.
Ironwood 49938

Grand Rapids Community College
143 Bostwick Ave. NE
Grand Rapids 49503-3295

Jackson Community College
2111 Emmons Rd.
Jackson 49201-8399

Kalamazoo Valley Community College
6767 West O Ave.
Kalamazoo 49009

Kirtland Community College
10775 North Saint Helen Rd.
Roscommon 48653

Mid Michigan Community College
1375 South Clare Ave.
Harrison 48625

Montcalm Community College
2800 College Dr.
Sidney 48885

Mott Community College
1401 East Court St.
Flint 48503

Muskegon Community College
221 South Quarterline Rd.
Muskegon 49442

Northern Michigan University
1401 Presque Isle
Marquette 49855

Oakland Community College
2480 Opdyke Rd.
Bloomfield Hills 48304-2266

Saint Clair County Community College
P.O. Box 5015, 323 Erie
Port Huron 48061-5015

Schoolcraft College
18600 Haggerty Rd.
Livonia 48152

West Shore Community College
3000 North Stiles Rd.
Scottville 49454

MINNESOTA

Alexandria Technical College
1601 Jefferson St.
Alexandria 56308

Central Lakes College, Brainerd
501 West College Dr.
Brainerd 56401

Dakota County Technical College
1300 East 145th St.
Rosemount 55068

Fergus Falls Community College
1414 College Way
Fergus Falls 56537

Hennepin Technical College
9000 Brooklyn Blvd.
Plymouth 55445

Lake Superior College
2101 Trinity Rd.
Duluth 55811

Minneapolis Community and Technical College
1501 Hennepin Ave.
Minneapolis 55403-1779

Minnesota West Community and Technical College
1450 College Way
Worthington 56187

Northwest Community and Technical College
Hwy. 1 E
Thief River Falls 56701

Northwest Technical College, Detroit Lakes
900 Hwy. 34 E
Detroit Lakes 56501

Northwest Technical College, East Grand Forks
Hwy. 220 N
East Grand Forks 56721

Rainy River Community College
1501 Hwy. 71
International Falls 56649

Red Wing-Winona Technical College, Red Wing Campus
308 Pioneer Rd.
Red Wing 55066

Red Wing-Winona Technical College, Winona Campus
1250 Homer Rd., P.O. Box 409
Winona 55987

Ridgewater College, A Community and Technical College, Willmar
P.O. Box 1097
Willmar 56201

Riverland Community College
1900 Eighth Ave. NW
Austin 55912

Saint Cloud Technical College
1540 Northway Dr.
Saint Cloud 56303

Saint Paul Technical College
235 Marshall Ave.
Saint Paul 55102

South Central Technical College, Faribault
1225 Southwest Third St.
Faribault 55021

South Central Technical College, Mankato
1920 Lee Blvd.
North Mankato 56003

MISSISSIPPI

East Mississippi Community College
P.O. Box 158
Scooba 39358

Hinds Community College, Raymond Campus
Raymond 39154

Holmes Community College
Hill St.
Goodman 39079

Jones County Junior College
900 South Court St.
Ellisville 39437

Meridian Community College
910 Hwy. 19 N
Meridian 39307

Mississippi Delta Community College
P.O. Box 668
Moorhead 38761

Mississippi Gulf Coast Community College
Central Office, P.O. Box 67
Perkinston 39573

Northeast Mississippi Community College
Cunningham Blvd.
Booneville 38829

Northwest Mississippi Community College
510 North Panola, Hwy. 51 N
Senatobia 38668

Pearl River Community College
Station A
Poplarville 39470

Southwest Mississippi Community College
College Dr.
Summit 39666

MISSOURI

Columbia Area Vocational Technical School
4203 South Providence Rd.
Columbia 65203

Cox Health Systems School of Radiologic Technology
3801 South National Ave.
Springfield 65807

Gibson Technical Center
P.O. Box 169
Reeds Spring 65737

Hannibal Area Vocational Technical School
4550 McMasters Ave.
Hannibal 63401

Jefferson College
1000 Viking Dr.
Hillsboro 63050

Lutheran Medical Center School of Nursing
3547 South Jefferson Ave.
Saint Louis 63118

Mexico Public School Practical Nursing
620 East Monroe
Mexico 65265

Mineral Area College
P.O. Box 1000
Flat River 63601-1000

Nichols Career Center
609 Union
Jefferson City 65101

North Central Missouri College
1301 Main St.
Trenton 64683

Northwest Missouri Area Vocational Technical School
1515 South Munn
Maryville 64468

Poplar Bluff School District Practical Nurse Program
P.O. Box 47
Poplar Bluff 63901

Rolla Technical Institute
1304 East Tenth St.
Rolla 65401

Saint Charles County Community College
4601 Mid Rivers Mall Dr.
Saint Peters 63376

Saint Louis Board of Education, Practical Nursing Program
3815 McCausland Ave.
Saint Louis 63109

Saint Louis College of Health Careers
4484 West Pine
Saint Louis 63108

Sanford-Brown College
12006 Manchester Rd.
Des Peres 63131

Sikeston Area Vocational Technical School
1002 Virginia St.
Sikeston 63801

State Fair Community College
3201 West 16th
Sedalia 65301-2199

Waynesville Technical Academy
810 Roosevelt
Waynesville 65583

MONTANA

Helena College of Technology of University of Montana
1115 North Roberts St.
Helena 59601

Montana State University, College of Technology, Billings
3803 Central Ave.
Billings 59102

Montana State University, College of Technology, Great Falls
2100 16th Ave. S
Great Falls 59405

NEBRASKA

Central Community College Area
P.O. Box 4903
Grand Island 68802

Metropolitan Community College Area
5300 North 30th St.
Omaha 68111

Mid Plains Community College
416 North Jeffers
North Platte 69101

Northeast Community College
801 East Benjamin, P.O. Box 469
Norfolk 68702-0469

Southeast Community College Area
1111 O St., Ste. 111
Lincoln 68520

Western Nebraska Community College
1601 East 27th St. NE
Scottsbluff 69361-1899

NEVADA

Community College of Southern Nevada
3200 East Cheyenne Ave.
Las Vegas 89030

NEW HAMPSHIRE

Saint Joseph's Hospital School of Practical Nursing
Five Woodward Ave.
Nashua 03060

NEW JERSEY

Bergen Pines County Hospital School of Practical Nursing
230 East Ridgewood Ave.
Paramus 07652

Charles E Gregory School of Nursing
Old Bridge Medical Arts. Bldg. 1 Hospital
Old Bridge 08857

Mountainside Hospital School of Nursing
One Bay Ave.
Montclair 07042

Salem Community College
460 Hollywood Ave.
Carneys Point 08069

Union County College
1033 Springfield Ave.
Cranford 07016

NEW MEXICO

Clovis Community College
417 Schepps Blvd.
Clovis 88101

Northern New Mexico Community College
1002 North Onate St.
Espanola 87532

NEW YORK

Iona College
715 North Ave.
New Rochelle 10801

Isabella G Hart School of Practical Nursing
1425 Portland Ave.
Rochester 14621

Marion S Whelan School of Nursing of Geneva General Hospital
196-198 North St.
Geneva 14456

Niagara County Community College
3111 Saunders Settlement Rd.
Sanborn 14132

North Country Community College
20 Winona Ave., P.O. Box 89
Saranac Lake 12983

Oswego County Boces
179 Colorado Rte. 64
Mexico 13114

Saint Francis School of Practical Nursing
2221 West State St.
Olean 14760-1984

SUNY Westchester Commmunity College
75 Grasslands Rd.
Valhalla 10595

NORTH CAROLINA

Asheville Buncombe Technical Community College
340 Victoria Rd.
Asheville 28801

Caldwell Community College and Technical Institute
Box 600
Lenoir 28645

Carteret Community College
3505 Arendell St.
Morehead City 28557

Central Carolina Community College
1105 Kelly Dr.
Sanford 27330

Durham Technical Community College
1637 Lawson St.
Durham 27703

Forsyth Technical Community College
2100 Silas Creek Pkwy.
Winston-Salem 27103

Montgomery Community College
P.O. Box 787
Troy 27371

Richmond Community College
P.O. Box 1189
Hamlet 28345

Rockingham Community College
P.O. Box 38, Hwy 65 W, County Home Rd.
Wentworth 27375-0038

Rowan-Cabarrus Community College
Box 1595
Salisbury 28145-1595

Surry Community College
P.O. Box 304
Dobson 27017-0304

NORTH DAKOTA

Dickinson State University
Third St. and Eighth Ave. W
Dickinson 58601

North Dakota State College of Science
800 North Sixth St.
Wahpeton 58076

OHIO

Akron Adult Vocational Services
147 Park St.
Akron 44308

Akron School of Practical Nursing
619 Sumner St.
Akron 44311

Apollo Career Center
3325 Shawnee Rd.
Lima 45806-1454

Ashtabula County Joint Vocational School
1565 State Rte. 167
Jefferson 44047

Belmont Technical College
120 Fox Shannon Place
Saint Clairsville 43950

Butler County JVS District, D Russel Lee Career Center
3603 Hamilton Middletown Rd.
Hamilton 45011

Canton City School Practical Nurse Program
1253 Third St. SE
Canton 44707-4798

Central School of Practical Nursing
4600 Carnegie Ave.
Cleveland 44103

Choffin Career Center
200 East Wood St.
Youngstown 44503

Clark State Community College
570 East Leffel Ln.
Springfield 45505

Ehove School of Practical Nursing, Ehove Career Center
316 West Mason Rd.
Milan 44846

Gallia Jackson Vinton JUSD
Box 157
Rio Grande 45674

Hannah E Mullins School of Practical Nursing
1200 East Sixth St.
Salem 44460-1757

Health Occupations Program, Columbus Public School
100 Arcadia Ave.
Columbus 43202

Hocking Technical College
3301 Hocking Pkwy.
Nelsonville 45764

Jefferson Community College
4000 Sunset Blvd.
Steubenville 43952-3598

Lorain County Community College
1005 Abbe Rd. N
Elyria 44035

Marymount School of Practical Nursing
12300 McCracken Rd.
Garfield Heights 44125

North Central Technical College
2441 Kenwood Circle, P.O. Box 698
Mansfield 44901

Northwest State Community College
22-600 South Rte. 34
Archbold 43502-9542

Ohio Hi Point Joint Vocational School District
2280 SR 540
Bellefontaine 43311-9594

Parma School of Practical Nursing
6726 Ridge Rd.
Parma 44129

Pickaway Ross Joint Vocational School District
895 Crouse Chapel Rd.
Chillicothe 45601-9010

Portage Lakes Career Center
4401 Shriver Rd.
Greensburg 44232-0248

Scioto County Joint Vocational School District
P.O. Box 766
Lucasville 45648

Toledo School of Practical Nursing
1602 Washington St., Whitney Building
Toledo 43624

Upper Valley Joint Vocational School
8811 Career Dr.
Piqua 45356

W Howard Nicol School of Practical Nursing
4401 Shriver Rd.
Green 44232-0248

Walsh University
2020 Easton St. NW
North Canton 44720-3396

Washington State Community College
710 Colegate Dr.
Marietta 45750

Wayne Adult School of Practical Nursing
518 West Prospect St.
Smithville 44677-0378

OKLAHOMA

Caddo-Kiowa Area Vocational Technical School
P.O. Box 190
Fort Cobb 73038

Francis Tuttle Area Vocational Technical Center
12777 North Rockwell Ave.
Oklahoma City 73142-2789

Gordon Cooper Area Vocational Technical School
One John C Bruton Blvd.
Shawnee 74801

Great Plains Area Vocational Technical School
4500 West Lee Blvd.
Lawton 73505

Kiamichi AVTS SD #7, Hugo
107 South 15th
Hugo 74743

Kiamichi AVTS SD #7, McCurtain Campus
Box 177, Rte. 3, Hwy. 70 N
Idabel 74745

Kiamichi AVTS SD #7, Poteau
1509 South McKenna
Poteau 74953

Metro Area Vocational Technical School District 22
1900 Springlake Dr.
Oklahoma City 73111

Pioneer Area Vocational Technical School
2101 North Ash
Ponca City 74601

Pontotoc Area Vocational Technical School
601 West 33rd
Ada 74820

Red River Area Vocational Technical School
3300 West Bois Darc
Duncan 73533

Southwest Area Vocational Technical Center
711 West Tamarack
Altus 73521

OREGON

Blue Mountain Community College
P.O. Box 100
Pendleton 97801

Central Oregon Community College
2600 Northwest College Way
Bend 97701

Chemeketa Community College
4000 Lancaster Dr. NE
Salem 97305

Clackamas Community College
19600 Molalla Ave.
Oregon City 97045

Lane Community College
4000 East 30th Ave.
Eugene 97405

PENNSYLVANIA

Altoona Area Vocational Technical School
1500 Fourth Ave.
Altoona 16602

Fayette County Area Vocational Technical School of Practical Nursing
RD 2, Box 122A
Uniontown 15401

Frankford Hospital School of Nursing
4918 Penn St.
Philadelphia 19124

Franklin County Career and Technology Center
2463 Loop Rd.
Chambersburg 17201

Gannon University
109 West Sixth St.
Erie 16541

Harrisburg Area Community College, Harrisburg
One Hacc Dr.
Harrisburg 17110

Lawrence County Vocational Technical School Practical Nursing
750 Phelps Way
New Castle 16101-5099

Lehigh Carbon Community College
4525 Education Park Dr.
Schnecksville 18078-2598

Mercer County Area Vocational Technical School
776 Greenville Rd.
Mercer 16137-0152

Northampton County Area Community College
3835 Green Pond Rd.
Bethlehem 18017-7599

Pennsylvania College of Technology
One College Ave.
Williamsport 17701

Roxborough Memorial Hospital School of Nursing
5800 Ridge Ave.
Philadelphia 19128

Saint Francis Medical Center School of Nursing
400 45th St.
Pittsburgh 15201

Saint Luke's Hospital School of Nursing
801 Ostrum
Bethlehem 18015

Schuylkill County Area Vocational Technical School
101 Technology Dr.
Frackville 17931

Western Area Career and Technology Center
688 Western Ave.
Canonsburg 15317

Wilkes-Barre Area Vocational-Technical School of Practical Nursing
P.O. Box 1699, North End Station Jumper Rd.
Wilkes-Barre 18705-0699

RHODE ISLAND

Community College of Rhode Island
400 East Ave.
Warwick 02886-1807

SOUTH CAROLINA

Greenville Technical College
P.O. Box 5616, Station B
Greenville 29606-5616

Midlands Technical College
P.O. Box 2408
Columbia 29202

Orangeburg Calhoun Technical College
3250 Saint Matthew's Rd.
Orangeburg 29118

Piedmont Technical College
P.O. Drawer 1467
Greenwood 29648

Spartanburg Technical College
Business I-85
Spartanburg 29305

Trident Technical College
P.O. Box 118067
Charleston 29423-8067

SOUTH DAKOTA

Lake Area Technical Institute
230 11th St. NE
Watertown 57201

Western Dakota Vocational Technical Institute
800 Mickelson Dr.
Rapid City 57701

TENNESSEE

Chattanooga State Technical Community College
4501 Amnicola Hwy.
Chattanooga 37406

Tennessee Technology Center at Athens
P.O. Box 848, 1635 Vo Tech Dr.
Athens 37371-0848

Tennessee Technology Center at Covington
P.O. Box 249
Covington 38019

Tennessee Technology Center at Crossville
P.O. Box 2959
Crossville 38557

Tennessee Technology Center at Dickson
740 Hwy. 46
Dickson 37055

Tennessee Technology Center at Elizabethton
1500 Arney St.
Elizabethton 37643

Tennessee Technology Center at Harriman
P.O. Box 1109
Harriman 37748

Tennessee Technology Center at Jacksboro
Rte. 1
Jacksboro 37757

Tennessee Technology Center at Jackson
2468 Westover Rd.
Jackson 38301

Tennessee Technology Center at Knoxville
1100 Liberty St.
Knoxville 37919

Tennessee Technology Center at Livingston
740 High Tech Dr.
Livingston 38570

Tennessee Technology Center at McMinnville
241 Vo Tech Dr.
McMinnville 37110

Tennessee Technology Center at Memphis
550 Alabama Ave.
Memphis 38105-3604

Tennessee Technology Center at Morristown
821 West Louise Ave.
Morristown 37813

Tennessee Technology Center at Nashville
100 White Bridge Rd.
Nashville 37209

Tennessee Technology Center at Paris
312 South Wilson St.
Paris 38242

Tennessee Technology Center at Shelbyville
1405 Madison St.
Shelbyville 37160

Tennessee Technology Center at Whiteville
P.O. Box 489
Whiteville 38075

TEXAS

Amarillo College
P.O. Box 447
Amarillo 79178

Austin Community College
5930 Middle Fiskville Rd.
Austin 78752

Baptist Hospital System, Institute of Health Education
111 Dallas St.
San Antonio 78205

Bee County College
3800 Charco Rd.
Beeville 78102

Blinn College
902 College Ave.
Brenham 77833

Central Texas College
P.O. Box 1800
Killeen 76540-1800

Cisco Junior College
Rte. 3, Box 3
Cisco 76437

Clarendon College
P.O. Box 968
Clarendon 79226

Del Mar College
101 Baldwin
Corpus Christi 78404-3897

Delta Career Institute
1310 Pennsylvania Ave.
Beaumont 77701

El Centro College
Main and Lamar
Dallas 75202

Galveston College
4015 Ave. Q
Galveston 77550

Hill College
P.O. Box 619
Hillsboro 76645

Houston Community College System
22 Waugh Dr.
Houston 77270-7849

Howard County Junior College District
1001 Birdwell Ln.
Big Spring 79720

Huntsville Memorial Hospital School Vocational Nursing
3000 IH-45
Huntsville 77340

Kilgore College
1100 Broadway
Kilgore 75662-3299

Lamar University, Orange
410 Front St.
Orange 77630-5899

Lamar University, Port Arthur
1500 Proctor St.
Port Arthur 77640

Laredo Community College
West End Washington St.
Laredo 78040

Lee College
200 Lee Dr.
Baytown 77520-4703

McLennan Community College
1400 College Dr.
Waco 76708

Memorial Hospital, Memoral City School of Vocational Nursing
920 Frostwood
Houston 77024-2434

Navarro College
3200 West Seventh
Corsicana 75110

Northeast Texas Community College
FM 1735
Mount Pleasant 75456

North Harris Montgomery Community College District
250 North Sam Houston Pkwy. E, Ste. 300
Houston 77060

Odessa College
201 West University
Odessa 79764

Panola College
1109 West Panola St.
Carthage 75633

Paris Junior College
2400 Clarksville St.
Paris 75460

PCI Health Training Center
8101 John Carpenter Fwy.
Dallas 75247

Ranger College
College Circle
Ranger 76470

Saint Philip's College
1801 Martin Luther King Dr.
San Antonio 78203

San Jacinto College, North Campus
5800 Uvalde
Houston 77049

San Jacinto College, South Campus
13735 Beamer Rd.
Houston 77089-6009

Schreiner College
2100 Memorial Blvd.
Kerrville 78028

South Plains College
1401 College Ave.
Levelland 79336

Tarleton State University
Tarleton Station
Stephenville 76402

Temple College
2600 South First St.
Temple 76504-7435

Texarkana College
2500 North Robison Rd.
Texarkana 75599

Texas Southmost College
80 Fort Brown
Brownsville 78520

Texas State Technical College, Sweetwater
300 College Dr.
Sweetwater 79556

Trinity Valley Community College
500 South Prairieville
Athens 75751

Vernon Regional Junior College
4400 College Dr.
Vernon 76384-4092

Victoria College
2200 East Red River
Victoria 77901

Weatherford College
308 East Park Ave.
Weatherford 76086

Western Texas College
6200 College Ave.
Snyder 79549-9502

Wharton County Junior College
911 Boling Hwy.
Wharton 77488

UTAH

College of Eastern Utah
400 East 400 North
Price 84501

Davis Applied Technology Center
550 East 300 South
Kaysville 84037

Salt Lake Community College
P.O. Box 30808
Salt Lake City 84130

Uintah Basin Applied Technology Center
1100 East Lagoon St. (124-5)
Roosevelt 84066

Utah Valley State College
800 West 1200 South
Orem 84058

Weber State University
3750 Harrison Blvd.
Ogden 84408

VIRGINIA

Computer Dynamics Institute, Inc.
5361 Virginia Beach Blvd.
Virginia Beach 23462

Medical Careers Institute
605 Thimble Shoals
Newport News 23606

Petersburg Public Schools Practical Nursing Program
Blandford School, 816 East Bank St.
Petersburg 23803

Richmond Memorial Hospital School of Practical Nursing
1300 Westwood Ave.
Richmond 23227

Tidewater Technical
616 Denbigh Blvd.
Newport News 23608

WASHINGTON

Bates Technical College
1101 South Yakima Ave.
Tacoma 98405

Bellingham Technical College
3028 Lindbergh Ave.
Bellingham 98225

Centralia College
600 West Locust St.
Centralia 98531

Clark College
1800 East McLoughlin Blvd.
Vancouver 98663-3598

Columbia Basin College
2600 North 20th Ave.
Pasco 99301

Everett Community College
801 Wetmore Ave.
Everett 98201

Grays Harbor College
1620 Edward P Smith Dr.
Aberdeen 98520

Green River Community College
12401 Southeast 320th St.
Auburn 98092

Lower Columbia College
P.O. Box 3010
Longview 98632

Olympic College
1600 Chester Ave.
Bremerton 98310-1699

Seattle Community College, North Campus
9600 College Way N
Seattle 98103

Skagit Valley College
2405 College Way
Mount Vernon 98273

South Puget Sound Community College
2011 Mottman Rd. SW
Olympia 98512

Spokane Community College
North 1810 Greene Ave.
Spokane 99207

Walla Walla Community College
500 Tausick Way
Walla Walla 99362

Wenatchee Valley College
1300 Fifth St.
Wenatchee 98801

Yakima Valley Community College
P.O. Box 1647
Yakima 98907

WEST VIRGINIA

B M Spurr School of Practical Nursing
800 Wheeling Ave.
Glen Dale 26038

Fred W Eberle School of Practical Nursing
Rte. 5, Box 2
Buckhannon 26201

James Rumsey Technical Institute
Rte. 6, Box 268
Martinsburg 25401

Logan-Mingo School of Practical Nursing
Box 1747, Three Mile Curve
Logan 25601

Mercer County Technical Education Center
1397 Stafford Dr.
Princeton 24740

Roane-Jackson Technical Center
4800 Spencer Rd.
Leroy 25252-9700

Wood County Vocational School of Practical Nursing
1515 Blizzard Dr.
Parkersburg 26101-6424

WISCONSIN

Chippewa Valley Technical College
620 West Clairemont Ave.
Eau Claire 54701

Fox Valley Technical College at Appleton
1825 North Bluemound Dr.
Appleton 54913-2277

Madison Area Technical College
3550 Anderson St.
Madison 53704

Milwaukee Area Technical College
700 West State St.
Milwaukee 53233-1443

Moraine Park Technical College
235 North National Ave.
Fond Du Lac 54936-1940

WYOMING

Central Wyoming College
2660 Peck Ave.
Riverton 82501

Sheridan College
3059 Coffeen Ave.
Sheridan 82801

Western Wyoming Community College
2500 College Dr.
Rock Springs 82902

Medical Assistant Technology

ALABAMA

Capps College
3100 Cottage Hill Rd., Bldg. 5
Mobile 36606

Community College of the Air Force
130 West Maxwell Blvd.
Montgomery 36112-6613

Gadsden Business College
750 Forrest Ave.
Gadsden 35901

Gadsden Business College, Anniston
P.O. Box 1559
Anniston 36202-1575

George C Wallace State Community College, Dothan
Rte. 6, Box 62
Dothan 36303-9234

ARIZONA

Apollo College
3870 North Oracle Rd.
Tucson 85705

Apollo College, Phoenix, Inc.
8503 North 27th Ave.
Phoenix 85051

Apollo College, Tri City, Inc.
630 West Southern Ave.
Mesa 85210

The Bryman School
4343 North 16th St.
Phoenix 85016

Gateway Community College
108 North 40th St.
Phoenix 85034

Long Medical Institute
4126 North Black Canyon Hwy.
Phoenix 85017

Occupational Training Center
4136 North 75th Ave., Ste. 200
Phoenix 85033

Pima Medical Institute
3350 East Grant Rd.
Tucson 85716

Tucson College
7302-10 East 22nd St.
Tucson 85710

ARKANSAS

Eastern College of Health Vocations
6423 Forbing Rd.
Little Rock 72209

CALIFORNIA

American School of X-Ray
13723-1/2 Harvard Place
Gardena 90249

Andon College
1700 McHenry Village Way
Modesto 95354

Andon College
1201 North El Dorado St.
Stockton 95202

Assert, Inc.
16745 Saticoy St.
Van Nuys 91406

California Paramedical and Technical College
4550 La Sierra Ave.
Riverside 92505

Chabot College
25555 Hesperian Blvd.
Hayward 94545

Citrus College
1000 West Foothill Blvd.
Glendora 91741-1899

City College of San Francisco
50 Phelan Ave.
San Francisco 94112

Concorde Career Institute
12412 Victory Blvd.
North Hollywood 91606

Concorde Career Institute
123 Camino De La Reina, Ste. E125
San Diego 92108

Concorde Career Institute
570 West Fourth St., Ste. 107
San Bernardino 92401

Donald Vocational School
1833 West Eighth St., Ste. 200
Los Angeles 90057

Educorp Career College
230 East Third St.
Long Beach 90802

Foothill College
12345 El Monte Rd.
Los Altos Hills 94022

Galen College of Medical and Dental Assistants
1325 North Wishon Ave.
Fresno 93728

Galen College of Medical and Dental Assistants
1604 Ford Ave.
Modesto 95350

Galen College of Medical and Dental Assistants
3908 West Coldwell, Ste. A
Visalia 93277

Hacienda La Puente Unified School District, Adult Education
P.O. Box 60002
City of Industry 91716-0002

Institute for Business and Technology
2550 Scott Blvd.
Santa Clara 95050

Institute of Computer Technology
3200 Wilshire Blvd.
Los Angeles 90010

Maric College of Medical Careers
3666 Kearny Villa Rd., Ste. 100
San Diego 92120

Maric College of Medical Careers, Vista Campus
2030 University Dr.
Vista 92083

McKinnon Institute of Professional Massage and Bodywork
3798 Grand Ave.
Oakland 94610-1594

Modern Technology School
1232 East Katella Ave.
Anaheim 92805

Modern Technology School of X-Ray
6180 Laurel Canyon Blvd.
North Hollywood 91606

MTI Business College, Inc.
6006 North El Dorado St.
Stockton 95207-4349

National Career Education
6060 Sunrise Vista Dr.
Citrus Heights 95610

Newbridge College
1840 East 17th St., Ste. 140
Santa Ana 92705

Nova Institute of Health Technology
3000 South Robertson Blvd.
Los Angeles 90034

Nova Institute of Health Technology
520 North Euclid Ave.
Ontario 91762

Nova Institute of Health Technology
12449 Putnam St.
Whittier 90602-1023

Platt College, San Diego
6250 El Cajon Blvd.
San Diego 92115

San Joaquin Valley College
201 New Stine Rd.
Bakersfield 93309

San Joaquin Valley College
295 East Sierra Ave.
Fresno 93710-3616

San Joaquin Valley College
8400 West Mineral King Ave.
Visalia 93291

Santa Barbara Business College
211 South Real Rd.
Bakersfield 93309

Santa Barbara Business College
4333 Hansen Ave.
Fremont 94536

Santa Barbara Business College, Santa Maria Branch
303 East Plaza Dr., Ste. 1
Santa Maria 93454

Sawyer College, A Corinthian School
8475 Jackson Rd.
Sacramento 95826

Shasta College
P.O. Box 496006
Redding 96049

Simi Valley Adult School
3192 Los Angeles Ave.
Simi Valley 93065

Skadron College
295 East Caroline St., Ste. D
San Bernardino 92408

Travel and Trade Career Institute
3635 Atlantic Ave.
Long Beach 90807

United Education Institute
3727 West Sixth St., Ste. 317
Los Angeles 90020

Watterson College
150 South Los Robles Blvd., Ste. 100
Pasadena 91101

Western Career College
8909 Folsom Blvd.
Sacramento 95826

Western Career College
170 Bay Fair Mall
San Leandro 94578

COLORADO

Blair College
828 Wooten Rd.
Colorado Springs 80915

Concorde Career Institute
770 Grant St.
Denver 80203

Denver Technical College at Colorado Springs
225 South Union Blvd.
Colorado Springs 80910

Heritage College of Health Careers
12 Lakeside Ln.
Denver 80212

PPI Health Careers School
2345 North Academy Blvd.
Colorado Springs 80909

CONNECTICUT

Branford Hall Career Institute
One Summit Pl.
Branford 06405

Huntington Institute, Inc.
193 Broadway
Norwich 06360

Stone Academy
1315 Dixwell Ave.
Hamden 06514

DELAWARE

Star Technical Institute
Graystone Plaza, 631 West Newport Pike
Wilmington 19804

DISTRICT OF COLUMBIA

Harrison Center for Career Education
624 Ninth St. NW, 4th Fl.
Washington 20001

FLORIDA

Career Training Institute
3326 Edgewater Dr.
Orlando 32804

Concorde Career Institute
7960 Arlington Expwy.
Jacksonville 32211

Concorde Career Institute
4000 North State Rd. 7
Lauderdale Lakes 33319

Concorde Career Institute
285 Northwest 199th St.
Miami 33169

Concorde Career Institute
4202 West Spruce St.
Tampa 33607

Keiser College
1500 Northwest 49th St.
Fort Lauderdale 33309

Miami Lakes Technical Education Center
5780 Northwest 158th St.
Miami Lakes 33169

Miami Technical College
14701 Northwest Seventh Ave.
North Miami 33168

Miriam Vocational School, Inc.
135 Southwest 57th Ave.
Miami 33144

National School of Technology, Inc.
4410 West 16th Ave., Ste. 52
Hialeah 33012

National School of Technology, Inc.
16150 Northeast 17th Ave.
North Miami Beach 33162

Orlando College
5421 Diplomat Circle
Orlando 32810

Politechnical Institute of Florida
500 West 29th St.
Hialeah 33012

Ross Technical Institute
1490 South Military Trail
West Palm Beach 33415-9141

Santa Fe Community College
3000 Northwest 83rd St.
Gainesville 32606

Tampa College
3924 Coconut Palm Dr.
Tampa 33619

Technical Career Institute
4299 Northwest 36th St., Ste. 300
Miami Springs 33166

Webster College, Inc.
2127 Grand Blvd.
Holiday 34691

William T McFatter Vocational Technical Center
6500 Nova Dr.
Davie 33317

GEORGIA

Atlanta Area Technical School
1560 Stewart Ave. SW
Atlanta 30310

Augusta Technical Institute
3116 Deans Bridge Rd.
Augusta 30906

Gwinnett Technical Institute
5150 Sugarloaf Pkwy.
Lawrenceville 30043

Georgia Medical Institute
40 Marietta St. NW, Ste. 1333
Atlanta 30303

Medix Schools
2108 Cobb Pkwy.
Smyrna 30008

Valdosta Technical Institute
4089 Valtech Rd.
Valdosta 31602-9796

HAWAII

Medical Assistant School of Hawaii, Inc.
33 South King, Ste. 223
Honolulu 96813

IDAHO

American Institute of Health Technology, Inc.
6600 Emerald
Boise 83704

College of Southern Idaho
P.O. Box 1238
Twin Falls 83301

Ricks College
Rexburg 83460-4107

INDIANA

Davenport College, Merrillville
8200 Georgia St.
Merrillville 46410

International Business College
3811 Illinois Rd.
Fort Wayne 46804

Ivy Tech State College, North Central
1534 West Sample St.
South Bend 46619

Ivy Tech State College, Northeast
3800 North Anthony Blvd.
Fort Wayne 46805

Ivy Tech State College, South Central
8204 Hwy. 311
Sellersburg 47172

Ivy Tech State College, Southwest
3501 First Ave.
Evansville 47710

Michiana College
1030 East Jefferson Blvd.
South Bend 46617

Professional Careers Institute
2611 Waterfront Pkwy., East Dr.
Indianapolis 46214-2028

IOWA

Des Moines Community College
2006 Ankeny Blvd.
Ankeny 50021

Kirkwood Community College
P.O. Box 2068
Cedar Rapids 52406

Palmer College of Chiropractic
1000 Brady St.
Davenport 52803

KANSAS

Johnson County Community College
12345 College Blvd.
Overland Park 66210-1299

Southwest Kansas Technical School
2215 North Kansas
Liberal 67905-1599

Topeka Technical College
1620 Northwest Gage
Topeka 66618

KENTUCKY

Kentucky College of Business
628 East Main St.
Lexington 40508

Owensboro Junior College of Business
1515 East 18th St., Box 1350
Owensboro 42302

RETS Medical and Business Institute
1102 South Virginia St.
Hopkinsville 42240

Spencerian College
4627 Dixie Hwy.
Louisville 40216

LOUISIANA

Ayers Institute, Inc.
2924 Knight St., Ste. 318
Shreveport 71105

Cameron College
2740 Canal St.
New Orleans 70119

Coastal College, Hammond
4304 Yokum Rd.
Hammond 70403

Domestic Health Care Institute
4826 Jamestown Ave.
Baton Rouge 70808

Eastern College of Health Vocations
3321 Hessemer Ave., Ste. 200
Metairie 70002

Remington College
303 Rue Louis XIV
Lafayette 70508

MAINE

Andover College
901 Washington Ave.
Portland 04103

Beal College
629 Main St.
Bangor 04401

Mid-State College
88 East Hardscrabble Rd.
Auburn 04210

MARYLAND

Essex Community College
7201 Rossville Blvd.
Baltimore 21237

Medix Schools
1017 York Rd.
Towson 21204-9840

MASSACHUSETTS

Aquinas College at Newton
15 Walnut Park
Newton 02158

Bunker Hill Community College
250 New Rutherford Ave.
Boston 02129

Fisher College
118 Beacon St.
Boston 02116

The Salter School
1243 Main St.
Springfield 01103

The Salter School
155 Ararat St.
Worcester 01606

MICHIGAN

Carnegie Institute
550 Stephenson Hwy.
Troy 48083

Delta College
University Ctr.
University Center 48710

Detroit Business Institute
1249 Washington Blvd., Ste. 1200
Detroit 48226

Detroit Business Institute, Downriver
19100 Fort St.
Riverview 48192

Grand Rapids Educational Center
1750 Woodworth NE
Grand Rapids 49525

Grand Rapids Educational Center
5349 West Main
Kalamazoo 49009

Lansing Community College
419 North Capitol Ave.
Lansing 48901-7210

Macomb Community College
14500 Twelve Mile Rd.
Warren 48093-3896

Payne-Pulliam School of Trade and Commerce, Inc.
2345 Cass Ave.
Detroit 48201-3305

Ross Business Institute
37065 South Gratiot
Clinton Township 48036

Ross Business Institute
22293 Eureka
Taylor 48180

Ross Medical Education Center
1036 Gilbert St.
Flint 48532

Ross Medical Education Center
2035 28th St. SE
Grand Rapids 49508

Ross Medical Education Center
1188 North West Ave.
Jackson 49202

Ross Medical Education Center
913 West Holmes, Ste. 260
Lansing 48910

Ross Medical Education Center
Park Row Mall, 950 Norton Ave.
Roosevelt Park 49441

Ross Medical Education Center
4054 Bay Rd.
Saginaw 48603

Ross Medical Education Center
26417 Hoover Rd.
Warren 48089

Ross Medical Education Center
2495 Elizabeth Lake Rd.
Waterford 48328

Ross Technical Institute
4703 Washtenaw
Ann Arbor 48108-1411

Ross Technical Institute
5757 Whitmore Lake Rd., Ste. 800
Brighton 48116

Ross Technical Institute
20820 Greenfield Rd., Ste. 101
Oak Park 48237

Schoolcraft College
18600 Haggerty Rd.
Livonia 48152

MINNESOTA

Duluth Business University, Inc.
412 West Superior St.
Duluth 55802

Globe College of Business
175 Fifth St. E, Ste. 201, Box 60
Saint Paul 55101-2901

Lakeland Medical and Dental Academy, Inc.
1402 West Lake St.
Minneapolis 55408

Medical Institute of Minnesota
5503 Green Valley Dr.
Bloomington 55437

Northwest Technical College, East Grand Forks
Hwy. 220 N
East Grand Forks 56721

Rochester Community and Technical College
851 30th Ave. SE
Rochester 55904-4999

MISSISSIPPI

Northeast Mississippi Community College
Cunningham Blvd.
Booneville 38829

MISSOURI

Al-Med Academy
10963 Saint Charles Rock Rd.
Saint Louis 63074

Concorde Career Institute
3239 Broadway
Kansas City 64111

Metro Business College
1407 Southwest Blvd.
Jefferson City 65109

Metro Business College
1202 East Hwy. 72
Rolla 65401

Metro Business College of Cape Girardeau
1732 North Kings Hwy.
Cape Girardeau 63701

Midwest Institute for Medical Assistants
112 West Jefferson
Kirkwood 63122

Missouri College
10121 Manchester Rd.
Saint Louis 63122

Saint Louis College of Health Careers
4484 West Pine
Saint Louis 63108

Springfield College
1010 West Sunshine
Springfield 65807

Tad Technical Institute
7910 Troost Ave.
Kansas City 64131

NEBRASKA

Institute of Computer Science
808 South 74th Place, 7400 Court Building
Omaha 68114

Omaha College of Health Careers
10845 Harney St.
Omaha 68154

Southeast Community College Area
1111 O St., Ste. 111
Lincoln 68520

NEVADA

Canterbury Career Schools
2215C Renaissance Dr.
Las Vegas 89119

NEW JERSEY

American Business Academy
66 Moore St.
Hackensack 07601

Berdan Institute
265 Rte. 46
Totowa 07512

Business Training Institute
Four Forest Ave.
Paramus 07652

Dover Business College
15 East Blackwell St.
Dover 07801

Dover Business College
East 81 & Rte. 4 W
Paramus 07652

Drake College of Business
125 Broad St.
Elizabeth 07201

Ho-Ho-Kus School
50 South Franklin Tpke.
Ramsey 07446

Omega Institute
7050 Rte. 38 E
Pennsauken 08109

Star Technical Institute
4313 RR 130 S
Edgewater Park 08010

Star Technical Institute
1255 Rte. 70
Lakewood 08701

Star Technical Institute
1386 South Delsea Dr.
Vineland 08360

Star Technical Institute, Deptford
1450 Clements Bridge Rd.
Deptford 08096

NEW MEXICO

Franklin College
2400 Louisiana Blvd. NE, Ste. 200
Albuquerque 87110

Pima Medical Institute
2201 San Pedro NE, Bldg. 3, Ste. 100
Albuquerque 87110

NEW YORK

Bayley Seton Hospital School Physicians Assistant
75 Vanderbilt Ave.
Staten Island 10304-3850

Bryant and Stratton Business Institute, Buffalo
1028 Main St.
Buffalo 14202

Hudson Valley Community College
80 Vandenburgh Ave.
Troy 12180

Mandl School
254 West 54th St.
New York 10019

New York School for Medical and Dental Assistants
116-16 Queens Blvd.
Forest Hills 11375

Suburban Technical School
175 Fulton Ave.
Hempstead 11550

NORTH CAROLINA

Central Piedmont Community College
P.O. Box 35009
Charlotte 28235-5009

Miller-Motte Business College
606 South College Rd.
Wilmington 28403

NORTH DAKOTA

Interstate Business College
520 East Main Ave.
Bismarck 58501

Interstate Business College
2720 32nd Ave. SW
Fargo 58103

OHIO

Akron Medical-Dental Institute, Inc. DBA Akron Institute
1625 Portage Tr.
Cuyahoga Falls 44223

American School of Technology
2100 Morse Rd., Bldg. 4599
Columbus 43229

Aristotle Institute of Medical-Dental Technology
5900 Westerville Rd.
Westerville 43081

Belmont Technical College
120 Fox Shannon Place
Saint Clairsville 43950

Boheckers Business College, Ravenna
326 East Main St.
Ravenna 44266

Cleveland Institute of Dental-Medical Assistants
1836 Euclid Ave.
Cleveland 44115

Cleveland Institute of Dental-Medical Assistants
5564 Mayfield Rd.
Lyndhurst 44124

Cleveland Institute of Dental-Medical Assistants
5733 Hopkins Rd.
Mentor 44060

Columbus Paraprofessional Institute
1900 East Grandville Rd., Bldg. A, Ste. 210
Columbus 43229

Cuyahoga Community College District
700 Carnegie Ave.
Cleveland 44115-2878

Institute of Medical-Dental Technology
4452 Eastgate Blvd., Ste. 209
Cincinnati 45245

Institute of Medical-Dental Technology
375 Glensprings Dr., Ste. 201
Cincinnati 45246

Knox County Career Center
306 Martinsburg Rd.
Mount Vernon 43050

Mahoning County Joint Vocational School District
7300 North Palmyra Rd.
Canfield 44406

Professional Skills Institute
20 Arco Dr.
Toledo 43607

RETS Technical Center
116 Westpark Rd.
Centerville 45459

Sawyer College of Business
3150 Mayfield Rd.
Cleveland Heights 44118

Southwestern College of Business
225 West First St.
Dayton 45402

Stautzenberger College
5355 Southwyck Blvd.
Toledo 43614

Technology Education College
288 South Hamilton Rd.
Columbus 43213

Tri-County Vocational School
15675 St. Rte. 691
Nelsonville 45764

Trumbull County Joint Vocational School District
528 Educational Hwy.
Warren 44483

University of Toledo
2801 West Bancroft
Toledo 43606

Warren County Career Center
3525 North St. Rte. 48
Lebanon 45036-1099

OKLAHOMA

Central Oklahoma Area Vocational Technical School
1720 South Main
Sapulpa 74066

De Marge College North
3608 Northwest 58th
Oklahoma City 73112

Francis Tuttle Area Vocational Technical Center
12777 North Rockwell Ave.
Oklahoma City 73142-2789

Platt College
309 South Ann Arbor
Oklahoma City 73128

Southern Oklahoma Technology Center
2610 Sam Noble Pkwy.
Ardmore 73401

Wright Business School
2219 Southwest 74th St., Ste. 124
Oklahoma City 73159

OREGON

Apollo College, Portland, Inc.
2600 Southeast 98th Ave.
Portland 97266

Pioneer Pacific College
25195 Southwest Parkway Ave.
Wilsonville 97070

Western Business College
425 Southwest Washington
Portland 97204

PENNSYLVANIA

Academy of Medical Arts and Business
2301 Academy Dr.
Harrisburg 17112

Allied Medical and Technical Careers
2901 Pittston Ave.
Scranton 18505

Allied Medical and Technical Careers
104 Woodward Hill Rd.
Edwardsville 18704

Altoona Area Vocational Technical School
1500 Fourth Ave.
Altoona 16602

Antonelli Medical and Professional Institute
1700 Industrial Hwy.
Pottstown 19464

Berks Technical Institute
2205 Ridgewood Rd.
Wyomissing 19610-1168

Career Training Academy
105 Mall Blvd., Ste. 300 W
Monroeville 15146

Career Training Academy
703 Fifth Ave.
New Kensington 15068

Delaware Valley Academy of Medical and Dental Assistants
3300 Grant Ave.
Philadelphia 19114

Duffs Business Institute
110 Ninth St.
Pittsburgh 15222

ICM School of Business and Medical Careers
10-14 Wood St.
Pittsburgh 15222

J H Thompson Academies
2910 State St.
Erie 16508

Median School of Allied Health Careers
125 Seventh St.
Pittsburgh 15222-3400

North Hills School of Health Occupations
1500 Northway Mall
Pittsburgh 15237

Sawyer School
717 Liberty Ave.
Pittsburgh 15222

Thompson Institute
5650 Derry St.
Harrisburg 17111

Thompson Institute
3440 Market St.
Philadelphia 19104

SOUTH CAROLINA

Central Carolina Technical College
506 North Guignard Dr.
Sumter 29150

Trident Technical College
P.O. Box 118067
Charleston 29423-8067

TENNESSEE

Draughons Junior College
1860 Wilma Rudolph Blvd.
Clarksville 37040

Fugazzi College
5042 Linbar Dr., Ste. 200
Nashville 37211

TEXAS

The Academy of Health Care Professions
1919 Northloop W, Ste. 170
Houston 77008

Bradford School of Business
4669 Southwest Fwy., Ste. 300
Houston 77027

Career Centers of Texas El Paso
8375 Burnham Dr.
El Paso 79907

PCI Health Training Center
8101 John Carpenter Fwy.
Dallas 75247

San Antonio College of Medical and Dental Assistants, Central
4205 San Pedro Ave.
San Antonio 78212-1899

San Antonio College of Medical and Dental Assistants, South
3900 North 23rd
McAllen 78501

Southern Careers Institute, Inc.
2301 South Congress, Ste. 27
Austin 78704

Southern Careers Institute, South Texas
1414 North Jackson Rd.
Pharr 78577

Southwest School of Business and Technical Careers
602 West South Cross
San Antonio 78221

Western Technical Institute
4710 Alabama St.
El Paso 79930

UTAH

American Institute of Medical-Dental Technology
1675 North 200 West, Bldg. 4
Provo 84604

Stevens-Henager College of Business, Ogden
2168 Washington Blvd.
Ogden 84401

Stevens-Henager College of Business, Provo
25 East 1700 South
Provo 84606-6157

Utah Career College
1144 West 3300 South
Salt Lake City 84119-3330

VIRGINIA

Commonwealth College, Virginia Beach
301 Centre Pointe Dr.
Virginia Beach 23462

Dominion Business School
4142-1 Melrose Ave.
Roanoke 24017

Medical Careers Institute
605 Thimble Shoals
Newport News 23606

Tidewater Technical
1760 East Little Creek Rd.
Norfolk 23518

Tidewater Technical
2697 Dean Dr., Ste. 100
Virginia Beach 23452

WASHINGTON

Eton Technical Institute
209 East Casino Rd.
Everett 98208

Eton Technical Institute
31919 Sixth Ave. S
Federal Way 98003

Eton Technical Institute
3649 Frontage Rd., Ste. A
Port Orchard 98366

Pima Medical Institute
1627 Eastlake Ave. E
Seattle 98102

Seattle Vocational Institute
315 22nd Ave. S
Seattle 98144

Spokane Community College
North 1810 Greene Ave.
Spokane 99207

WEST VIRGINIA

Boone County Career & Technical Center
HC 81, Box 50B
Danville 25053

Huntington Junior College
900 Fifth Ave.
Huntington 25701

Opportunities Industrialization Center, North Central West Virginia
120 Jackson St.
Fairmont 26554

West Virginia Career College
148 Willey St.
Morgantown 26505

WISCONSIN

Blackhawk Technical College
P.O. Box 5009
Janesville 53547

Madison Area Technical College
3550 Anderson St.
Madison 53704

Mid-State Technical College, Main Campus
500 32nd St. N
Wisconsin Rapids 54494

Milwaukee Area Technical College
700 West State St.
Milwaukee 53233-1443

Northeast Wisconsin Technical College
2740 West Mason St., P.O. Box 19042
Green Bay 54307-9042

Waukesha County Technical College
800 Main St.
Pewaukee 53072

Western Wisconsin Technical College
304 North Sixth St., P.O. Box 908
La Crosse 54602-0908

Wisconsin Indianhead Technical College
505 Pine Ridge Dr.
Shell Lake 54871

Medical and Biological Laboratory Technology

ALABAMA

Capps College
3100 Cottage Hill Rd., Bldg. 5
Mobile 36606

Community College of the Air Force
130 West Maxwell Blvd.
Montgomery 36112-6613

Jefferson State Community College
2601 Carson Rd.
Birmingham 35215-3098

University of Alabama at Birmingham
Administration Bldg., Ste. 1070-2010
Birmingham 35294-0110

ARIZONA

Apollo College
3870 North Oracle Rd.
Tucson 85705

Apollo College, Phoenix, Inc.
8503 North 27th Ave.
Phoenix 85051

Long Medical Institute
4126 North Black Canyon Hwy.
Phoenix 85017

Occupational Training Center
4136 North 75th Ave., Ste. 200
Phoenix 85033

Phoenix College
1202 West Thomas Rd.
Phoenix 85013

Tucson College
7302-10 East 22nd St.
Tucson 85710

ARKANSAS

Arkansas Valley Technical Institute
P.O. Box 506, Hwy. 23 N
Ozark 72949

Carti School of Radiation Therapy Technology
P.O. Box 55050
Little Rock 72215

CALIFORNIA

American School of X-Ray
13723-1/2 Harvard Place
Gardena 90249

Associated Technical College
1670 Wilshire Blvd.
Los Angeles 90017

Butte College
3536 Butte Campus Dr.
Oroville 95965

El Camino College
16007 Crenshaw Blvd.
Torrance 90506

Glendale Career College
1015 Grandview Ave.
Glendale 91201

Grossmont College
8800 Grossmont College Dr.
El Cajon 92020

Hacienda La Puente Unified School District, Adult Education
P.O. Box 60002
City of Industry 91716-0002

Ila Polytechnic Institute
202 West Lincoln Ave., Ste. H
Orange 92665-1058

Institute for Business and Technology
2550 Scott Blvd.
Santa Clara 95050

Loma Linda University
Loma Linda 92350

McKinnon Institute of Professional Massage and Bodywork
3798 Grand Ave.
Oakland 94610-1594

Modern Technology School
1232 East Katella Ave.
Anaheim 92805

Modern Technology School of X-Ray
6180 Laurel Canyon Blvd., Ste. 101
North Hollywood 91606

National Career Education
6060 Sunrise Vista Dr.
Citrus Heights 95610

Newbridge College
1840 East 17th St., Ste. 140
Santa Ana 92705

Nova Institute of Health Technology
3000 South Robertson Blvd.
Los Angeles 90034

Nova Institute of Health Technology
12449 Putnam St.
Whittier 90602-1023

Orange Coast College
2701 Fairview Rd.
Costa Mesa 92626

Simi Valley Adult School
3192 Los Angeles Ave.
Simi Valley 93065

COLORADO

PPI Health Careers School
2345 North Academy Blvd.
Colorado Springs 80909

Regis University
3333 Regis Blvd.
Denver 80221-1099

CONNECTICUT

Department of Education Hartford Hospital School of Allied Health
312 Conklin Blvd., 80 Seymour St.
Hartford 06115

Gateway Community Technical College
60 Sargent Dr.
New Haven 06511

Housatonic Community Technical College
900 Lafayette Blvd.
Bridgeport 06604

Huntington Institute, Inc.
193 Broadway
Norwich 06360

DELAWARE

Delaware Technical and Community College, Owens
Box 610
Georgetown 19947

Delaware Technical and Community College, Stanton, Wilmington
400 Stanton-Christiana Rd.
Newark 19702

DISTRICT OF COLUMBIA

Harrison Center for Career Education
624 Ninth St. NW, 4th Fl.
Washington 20001

FLORIDA

Beacon Career Institute, Inc.
2900 Northwest 183rd St.
Miami 33056

Brevard Community College, Cocoa Campus
1519 Clearlake Rd.
Cocoa 32922

Brewster Technical Center
2222 North Tampa St.
Tampa 33602-2196

Florida Community College at Jacksonville
501 West State St.
Jacksonville 32202

Keiser College
1500 Northwest 49th St.
Fort Lauderdale 33309

Lake City Community College
Rte. 19, Box 1030
Lake City 32025

Lee County Technical Center, Central
3800 Michigan Ave.
Fort Myers 33916

Miami-Dade Community College
300 Northeast Second Ave.
Miami 33132

Miriam Vocational School, Inc.
135 Southwest 57th Ave.
Miami 33144

National School of Technology, Inc.
4410 West 16th Ave., Ste. 52
Hialeah 33012

National School of Technology, Inc.
16150 Northeast 17th Ave.
North Miami Beach 33162

Pasco-Hernando Community College
36727 Blanton Rd.
Dade City 33525-7599

Santa Fe Community College
3000 Northwest 83rd St.
Gainesville 32606

Sarasota County Technical Institute
4748 Beneva Rd.
Sarasota 34233-1798

Sheridan Vocational Center
5400 Sheridan St.
Hollywood 33021

Ultrasound Diagnostic School
10199 Southside Blvd., Ste. 106
Jacksonville 32256

Ultrasound Diagnostic School
9950 Princess Palm Ave., Reg 11, Ste. 120
Tampa 33619

William T McFatter Vocational Technical Center
6500 Nova Dr.
Davie 33317

GEORGIA

Columbus State University
4225 University Ave.
Columbus 31907-5645

Dekalb Technical Institute
495 North Indian Creek Dr.
Clarkston 30021

Grady Health System Professional Schools
80 Butler St.
Atlanta 30335-3801

ILLINOIS

Medical Careers Institute
116 South Michigan Ave.
Chicago 60603

Methodist Medical Center of Illinois, School of Nursing
221 Northeast Glen Oak Ave.
Peoria 61636

Oakton Community College
1600 East Golf Rd.
Des Plaines 60016

Swedish American Hospital School of Medical Technology
1400 Charles St.
Rockford 61104-2298

Triton College
2000 Fifth Ave.
River Grove 60171

INDIANA

Vincennes University
1002 North First St.
Vincennes 47591

IOWA

Des Moines Community College
2006 Ankeny Blvd.
Ankeny 50021

Iowa Methodist Medical Center, School of Radiologic Technology
1200 Pleasant St.
Des Moines 50309-1453

Palmer College of Chiropractic
1000 Brady St.
Davenport 52803

Saint Luke's College of Nursing and Health Sciences
2720 Stone Park Blvd.
Sioux City 51104-0263

KANSAS

Seward County Community College
Box 1137
Liberal 67905-1137

Wichita Area Technical College
201 North Water
Wichita 67202-1292

KENTUCKY

Spencerian College
4627 Dixie Hwy.
Louisville 40216

University of Louisville
2301 South Third St.
Louisville 40292-0001

LOUISIANA

Delgado Community College
501 City Park Ave.
New Orleans 70119

Eastern College of Health Vocations
3321 Hessmer Ave., Ste. 200
Metairie 70002

MARYLAND

Hagerstown Business College
18618 Crestwood Dr.
Hagerstown 21742

Ultrasound Diagnostic School
1320 Fenwick Ln., Ste. 206
Silver Spring 20910

MASSACHUSETTS

Middlesex Community College
Springs Rd.
Bedford 01730

Northeastern University
360 Huntington Ave.
Boston 02115

Springfield Technical Community College
One Armory Square
Springfield 01105

Ultrasound Diagnostic School
33 Boston Post Rd. W, Ste. 140
Marlborough 01752

MICHIGAN

Carnegie Institute
550 Stephenson Hwy.
Troy 48083

Krainz Woods Academy of Medical Laboratory Technology
4327 East Seven Mile Rd.
Detroit 48234

Marygrove College
8425 West McNichols Rd.
Detroit 48221

Northern Michigan University
1401 Presque Isle
Marquette 49855

Oakland Community College
2480 Opdyke Rd.
Bloomfield Hills 48304-2266

Schoolcraft College
18600 Haggerty Rd.
Livonia 48152

MINNESOTA

Fergus Falls Community College
1414 College Way
Fergus Falls 56537

Hibbing Community College, a Technical and Community College
1515 East 25th St.
Hibbing 55746

Lakeland Medical and Dental Academy, Inc.
1402 West Lake St.
Minneapolis 55408

Lake Superior College
2101 Trinity Rd.
Duluth 55811

Mayo School of Health-Related Sciences
200 First St. SW
Rochester 55905

Medical Institute of Minnesota
5503 Green Valley Dr.
Bloomington 55437

North Hennepin Community College
7411 85th Ave. N
Brooklyn Park 55445

Northwest Technical College, East Grand Forks
Hwy. 220 N
East Grand Forks 56721

Saint Cloud Technical College
1540 Northway Dr.
Saint Cloud 56303

Saint Paul Technical College
235 Marshall Ave.
Saint Paul 55102

MISSISSIPPI

Mississippi Gulf Coast Community College
Central Office, P.O. Box 67
Perkinston 39573

MISSOURI

Al-Med Academy
10963 Saint Charles Rock Rd.
Saint Louis 63074

Saint John's Regional Health Center School of Radiologic Technology
1235 East Cherokee
Springfield 65804

Saint Louis Community College, Forest Park
5600 Oakland Ave.
Saint Louis 63110

NEW JERSEY

Bergen Community College
400 Paramus Rd.
Paramus 07652

Drake College of Business
125 Broad St.
Elizabeth 07201

Omega Institute
7050 Rte. 38 E
Pennsauken 08109

Star Technical Institute
1255 Rte. 70
Lakewood 08701

Ultrasound Diagnostic School
675 Rte. 1, Second Fl.
Iselin 08830

University of Medicine and Dentistry of New Jersey
30 Bergen St.
Newark 07107

NEW MEXICO

Albuquerque Technical Vocational Institute
525 Buena Vista SE
Albuquerque 87106

New Mexico Junior College
5317 Lovington Hwy.
Hobbs 88240

Pima Medical Institute
2201 San Pedro NE, Bldg. 3, Ste. 100
Albuquerque 87110

NEW YORK

Dutchess Community College
53 Pendell Rd.
Poughkeepsie 12601

Hudson Valley Community College
80 Vandenburgh Ave.
Troy 12180

Institute of Allied Medical Professions
405 Park Ave., Ste. 501
New York 10022

Mandl School
254 West 54th St.
New York 10019

Monroe Community College
1000 East Henrietta Rd.
Rochester 14623

New York School for Medical and Dental Assistants
116-16 Queens Blvd.
Forest Hills 11375

NYU Medical Center Allied Health Education
483 First Ave.
New York 10016

SUNY College of Technology at Farmingdale
Melville Rd.
Farmingdale 11735-1021

SUNY Westchester Commmunity College
75 Grasslands Rd.
Valhalla 10595

Syrit College
1760 53rd St.
Brooklyn 11204

Ultrasound Diagnostic School
One Old Country Rd.
Carle Place 11514

Ultrasound Diagnostic School
2269 Saw Mill River Rd.
Elmsford 10523

Ultrasound Diagnostic School
120 East 16th St., Second Fl.
New York 10003

NORTH CAROLINA

Alamance Community College
P.O. Box 8000
Graham 27253

Caldwell Community College and Technical Institute
Box 600
Lenoir 28645

Halifax Community College
P.O. Drawer 809
Weldon 27890

Northern Hospital of Surry County School of Medical Laboratory Technology
830 Rockford St., P.O. Box 1101
Mount Airy 27030

Pitt Community College
Hwy. 11 S, P.O. Drawer 7007
Greenville 27835-7007

Southwestern Community College
447 College Dr.
Sylva 28779

Wake Technical Community College
9101 Fayetteville Rd.
Raleigh 27603-5696

NORTH DAKOTA

Trinity School of Clinical Laboratory Science
Three Burdick Expwy.
Minot 58701

OHIO

Akron Medical-Dental Institute, Inc., DBA Akron Institute
1625 Portage Tr.
Cuyahoga Falls 44223

Cincinnati State Technical and Community College
3520 Central Pkwy.
Cincinnati 45223

Cleveland Institute of Dental-Medical Assistants
1836 Euclid Ave.
Cleveland 44115

Cleveland Institute of Dental-Medical Assistants
5564 Mayfield Rd.
Lyndhurst 44124

Cleveland Institute of Dental-Medical Assistants
5733 Hopkins Rd.
Mentor 44060

Columbus State Community College
550 East Spring St.
Columbus 43216

Cuyahoga Community College District
700 Carnegie Ave.
Cleveland 44115-2878

Kettering College Medical Arts
3737 Southern Blvd.
Kettering 45429-1299

Marion Technical College
1467 Mount Vernon Ave.
Marion 43302-5694

Owens Community College
30335 Oregon Rd.
Toledo 43699-1947

Professional Skills Institute
20 Arco Dr.
Toledo 43607

Riverside School of Medical Technology
1600 North Superior St.
Toledo 43604

Tri-Rivers Career Center
2222 Marion Mount Gilead Rd.
Marion 43302

Trumbull County Joint Vocational School District
528 Educational Hwy.
Warren 44483

OKLAHOMA

Tulsa Community College
6111 East Skelly Dr.
Tulsa 74135

OREGON

Concorde Career Institute
1827 Northeast 44th Ave.
Portland 97213

PENNSYLVANIA

Abington Memorial Hospital Medical Technology Program
1200 Old York Rd.
Abington 19001

Allied Medical and Technical Careers
2901 Pittston Ave.
Scranton 18505

Allied Medical and Technical Careers
104 Woodward Hill Rd.
Edwardsville 18704

Chambersburg Hospital Medical Laboratory Technical School
112 North Seventh St.
Chambersburg 17201

Community College of Allegheny County, Pittsburgh
800 Allegheny Ave.
Pittsburgh 15233-1895

Community College of Philadelphia
1700 Spring Garden St.
Philadelphia 19130

Conemaugh Valley Memorial Hospital
1086 Franklin St.
Johnstown 15905-4398

Divine Providence Hospital School of Medical Technology
1100 Grampian Blvd.
Williamsport 17754

Edinboro University of Pennsylvania
Edinboro 16444

Gwynedd-Mercy College
Sumneytown Pike
Gwynedd Valley 19437

Johnson Technical Institute
3427 North Main Ave.
Scranton 18508-1495

Mount Aloysius College
7373 Admiral Peary Hwy.
Cresson 16630-1999

North Hills School of Health Occupations
1500 Northway Mall
Pittsburgh 15237

Pennsylvania State University, New Kensington
3550 Seventh Street Rd.
New Kensington 15068

Ultrasound Diagnostic School
5830 Ellsworth Ave., Ste. 102
Pittsburgh 15232

Western School of Health & Business Careers
411 Seventh Ave.
Pittsburgh 15219

RHODE ISLAND

Community College of Rhode Island
400 East Ave.
Warwick 02886-1807

SOUTH CAROLINA

Central Carolina Technical College
506 North Guignard Dr.
Sumter 29150

Midlands Technical College
P.O. Box 2408
Columbia 29202

Orangeburg Calhoun Technical College
3250 Saint Matthew's Rd.
Orangeburg 29118

Trident Technical College
P.O. Box 118067
Charleston 29423-8067

SOUTH DAKOTA

Presentation College
1500 North Main
Aberdeen 57401

Southeast Technical Institute
2301 Career Place
Sioux Falls 57107

TENNESSEE

Nashville State Technical Institute
120 White Bridge Rd.
Nashville 37209

Roane State Community College
276 Patton Ln.
Harriman 37748

Shelby State Community College
P.O. Box 40568
Memphis 38174-0568

TEXAS

The Academy of Health Care Professions
1919 Northloop W, Ste. 170
Houston 77008

Austin Community College
5930 Middle Fiskville Rd.
Austin 78752

Del Mar College
101 Baldwin
Corpus Christi 78404-3897

El Centro College
Main and Lamar
Dallas 75202

El Paso Community College
P.O. Box 20500
El Paso 79998

Houston Community College System
22 Waugh Dr.
Houston 77270-7849

Microcomputer Technology Institute
7277 Regency Square Blvd.
Houston 77036

Saint Philip's College
1801 Martin Luther King Dr.
San Antonio 78203

San Antonio College of Medical and Dental Assistants, Central
4205 San Pedro Ave.
San Antonio 78212-1899

Texas State Technical College, Waco
3801 Campus Dr.
Waco 76705

Ultrasound Diagnostic School
1333 Corporate Dr., Ste. 200
Irving 75038

Wadley Regional Medical Center School of Medical Technology
1000 Pine St.
Texarkana 75501

WASHINGTON

Pima Medical Institute
1627 Eastlake Ave. E
Seattle 98102

Shoreline Community College
16101 Greenwood Ave. N
Seattle 98133

Spokane Community College
North 1810 Greene Ave.
Spokane 99207

WEST VIRGINIA

Boone County Career & Technical Center
HC 81, Box 50B
Danville 25053

West Virginia University Hospital School of Radiation Technology
Medical Center Dr., P.O. Box 8062
Morgantown 26506-8062

WISCONSIN

Chippewa Valley Technical College
620 West Clairemont Ave.
Eau Claire 54701

Madison Area Technical College
3550 Anderson St.
Madison 53704

Milwaukee Area Technical College
700 West State St.
Milwaukee 53233-1443

Saint Joseph's Hospital Histologic Technician Program
611 Saint Joseph's Ave.
Marshfield 54449

Saint Luke's Medical Center, School of Diagnostic Medical Sonography
2900 West Oklahoma Ave.
Milwaukee 53215

Western Wisconsin Technical College
304 North Sixth St., P.O. Box 908
La Crosse 54602-0908

Medical Emergency Technology

ALABAMA

Bessemer State Technical College
1100 Ninth Ave.
Bessemer 35021

George C Wallace State Community College, Hanceville
801 Main St. NW
Hanceville 35077-2000

University of Alabama at Birmingham
Administration Bldg., Ste. 1070-2010
Birmingham 35294-2010

University of Alabama in Huntsville
301 Sparkman Dr.
Huntsville 35899

University of South Alabama
307 North University Blvd.
Mobile 36688-0002

ARIZONA

Phoenix College
1202 West Thomas Rd.
Phoenix 85013

Pima Community College
2202 West Anklam Rd.
Tucson 85709-0001

CALIFORNIA

Crafton Hills College
11711 Sand Canyon Rd.
Yucaipa 92399-1799

Daniel Freeman Hospital Paramedic School
333 North Prairie Ave.
Inglewood 90301-4514

Imperial Valley College
P.O. Box 158
Imperial 92251-0158

Pacoima Skills Center, Los Angeles Unified School District
13545 Van Nuys Blvd.
Pacoima 91331

Simi Valley Adult School
3192 Los Angeles Ave.
Simi Valley 93065

Skyline College
3300 College Dr.
San Bruno 94066

COLORADO

Aims Community College
Box 69
Greeley 80632

Colorado Mountain College
P.O. Box 10001
Glenwood Springs 81602

Morgan Community College
17800 County Rd. 20
Fort Morgan 80701

San Juan Basin Area Vocational School
Box 970
Cortez 81321

FLORIDA

Brevard Community College, Cocoa Campus
1519 Clearlake Rd.
Cocoa 32922

Broward Community College
225 East Las Olas Blvd.
Fort Lauderdale 33301

Central Florida Community College
3001 Southwest College Rd.
Ocala 34474

Daytona Beach Community College
1200 Volusia Ave.
Daytona Beach 32114

Hillsborough Community College
P.O. Box 31127
Tampa 33631-3127

Indian River Community College
3209 Virginia Ave.
Fort Pierce 34981

Lake City Community College
Rte. 19, Box 1030
Lake City 32025

Lake County Area Vocational Technical Center
2001 Kurt St.
Eustis 32726

Manatee Vocational Technical Center
5603 34th St. W
Bradenton 34210

Palm Beach Community College
4200 Congress Ave.
Lake Worth 33461

Pasco-Hernando Community College
36727 Blanton Rd.
Dade City 33525-7599

Pensacola Junior College
1000 College Blvd.
Pensacola 32504

Saint Petersburg Junior College
8580 66th St. N
Pinellas Park 34665

Santa Fe Community College
3000 Northwest 83rd St.
Gainesville 32606

Seminole Community College
100 Weldon Blvd.
Sanford 32773-6199

South Florida Community College
600 West College Dr.
Avon Park 33825

Tallahassee Community College
444 Appleyard Dr.
Tallahassee 32304-2895

Valencia Community College
P.O. Box 3028
Orlando 32802

GEORGIA

Dekalb Technical Institute
495 North Indian Creek Dr.
Clarkston 30021

Gwinnett Technical Institute
5150 Sugarloaf Pkwy.
Lawrenceville 30043

ILLINOIS

City Colleges of Chicago, Central Office
226 West Jackson
Chicago 60606

Southeastern Illinois College
3575 College Rd.
Harrisburg 62946

INDIANA

Sawyer College, Hammond
6040 Hohman Ave.
Hammond 46320

IOWA

North Iowa Area Community College
500 College Dr.
Mason City 50401

KANSAS

Allen County Community College
1801 North Cottonwood
Iola 66749

Cloud County Community College
2221 Campus Dr., Box 1002
Concordia 66901-1002

Colby Community College
1255 South Range
Colby 67701

Johnson County Community College
12345 College Blvd.
Overland Park 66210-1299

Salina Area Vocational Technical School
2562 Scanlan Ave.
Salina 67401

LOUISIANA

Huey P Long Technical Institute
303 South Jones St.
Winnfield 71483

Louisiana Technical College, Hammond Area Campus
111 Pride Ave.
Hammond 70404

MARYLAND

Baltimore City Community College
2901 Liberty Heights Ave.
Baltimore 21215

MICHIGAN

Davenport College Career Center
3030 Easter SE
Grand Rapids 49508

Lansing Community College
419 North Capitol Ave.
Lansing 48901-7210

MINNESOTA

Century Community and Technical College
3300 Century Ave. N
White Bear Lake 55110

MISSISSIPPI

University of Mississippi Medical Center
2500 North State St.
Jackson 39216

MISSOURI

Cape Girardeau Area Vocational Technical School
301 North Clark Ave.
Cape Girardeau 63701

Rolla Area Vocational-Technical School
1304 East Tenth St.
Rolla 65401

MONTANA

Montana State University, College of Technology, Great Falls
2100 16th Ave. S
Great Falls 59405

NEW HAMPSHIRE

New Hampshire Technical Institute
11 Institute Dr.
Concord 03301

NEW YORK

Hudson Valley Community College
80 Vandenburgh Ave.
Troy 12180

NORTH DAKOTA

Med Center One EMS Education
Box 5525
Bismarck 58505

OHIO

Akron Adult Vocational Services
147 Park St.
Akron 44308

Butler County JVS District, D Russel Lee Career Center
3603 Hamilton Middletown Rd.
Hamilton 45011

Columbus State Community College
550 East Spring St.
Columbus 43216

Lima Technical College
4240 Campus Dr.
Lima 45804

Tri-Rivers Career Center
2222 Marion Mount Gilead Rd.
Marion 43302

OKLAHOMA

Oklahoma City Community College
7777 South May Ave.
Oklahoma City 73159

TENNESSEE

Shelby State Community College
P.O. Box 40568
Memphis 38174-0568

Walters State Community College
500 South Davy Crockett Pkwy.
Morristown 37813-6899

TEXAS

Texas State Technical College, Sweetwater
300 College Dr.
Sweetwater 79556

UTAH

Bridgerland Applied Technology Center
1301 North 600 West
Logan 84321

WISCONSIN

Blackhawk Technical College
P.O. Box 5009
Janesville 53547

Fox Valley Technical College at Appleton
1825 North Bluemound Dr.
Appleton 54913-2277

Gateway Technical College
3520 30th Ave.
Kenosha 53144-1690

Lakeshore Technical College
1290 North Ave.
Cleveland 53015

Madison Area Technical College
3550 Anderson St.
Madison 53704

Mid-State Technical College
500 32nd St. N
Wisconsin Rapids 54494

Moraine Park Technical College
235 North National Ave.
Fond Du Lac 54936-1940

Northcentral Technical College
1000 Campus Dr.
Wausau 54401-1899

Northeast Wisconsin Technical College
2740 West Mason St., P.O. Box 19042
Green Bay 54307-9042

Waukesha County Technical College
800 Main St.
Pewaukee 53072

Medical Illustrating

ARIZONA

Pima Medical Institute
957 South Dobson
Mesa 85202

CALIFORNIA

West Hills Community College
300 Cherry Ln.
Coalinga 93210

MICHIGAN

Muskegon Community College
221 South Quarterline Rd.
Muskegon 49442

OHIO

Ohio State University, Main Campus
1800 Cannon Dr., Rm. 1210
Columbus 43210

Medical Record Technology

ALABAMA

Capps College
3100 Cottage Hill Rd., Bldg. 5
Mobile 36606

Community College of the Air Force
130 West Maxwell Blvd.
Montgomery 36112-6613

University of Alabama at Birmingham, Walker College
1411 Indiana Ave.
Jasper 35501

ARIZONA

Arizona Institute of Business and Technology
925 South Gilbert Rd., Ste. 201
Mesa 85204

Arizona Institute of Business and Technology
6049 North 43rd Ave.
Phoenix 85019

The Bryman School
4343 North 16th St.
Phoenix 85016

Gateway Community College
108 North 40th St.
Phoenix 85034

Tucson College
7302-10 East 22nd St.
Tucson 85710

ARKANSAS

Foothills Technical Institute
1800 East Moore St.
Searcy 72143

CALIFORNIA

Allan Hancock College
800 South College Dr.
Santa Maria 93454

California College for Health Science
222 West 24th St.
National City 91950

California Paramedical and Technical College
4550 La Sierra Ave.
Riverside 92505

Career Development Center
255 East Bonita Ave.
Pomona 91767

Concorde Career Institute
570 West Fourth St., Ste. 107
San Bernardino 92401

Concorde Career Institute
123 Camino De La Reina, Ste. E25
San Diego 92108

Empire College School of Business
3033 Cleveland Ave.
Santa Rosa 95403

Hacienda La Puente Unified School District, Adult Education
P.O. Box 60002
City of Industry 91716-0002

Institute for Business and Technology
2550 Scott Blvd.
Santa Clara 95050

Larson Training Centers, Inc.
2041 West Orangewood Ave.
Orange 92668

Maric College of Medical Careers
3666 Kearny Villa Rd., Ste. 100
San Diego 92123

Maric College of Medical Careers
2030 University Dr.
Vista 92083

Mount Saint Mary's College
12001 Chalon Rd.
Los Angeles 90049

MTI Business College, Inc.
6006 North El Dorado St.
Stockton 95207-4349

National Career Education
6060 Sunrise Vista Dr.
Citrus Heights 95610

Sawyer College A Corinthian School
8475 Jackson Rd.
Sacramento 95826

Newbridge College
1840 East 17th St., Ste. 140
Santa Ana 92705

Nova Institute of Health Technology
12449 Putnam St.
Whittier 90602-1023

San Joaquin Valley College
8400 West Mineral King Ave.
Visalia 93291

Santa Barbara Business College
211 South Real Rd.
Bakerfield 93309

Summit Career College
1330 East Cooley Dr.
Colton 92324

COLORADO

Arapahoe Community College
2500 West College Dr.
Littleton 80160-9002

Concorde Career Institute
770 Grant St.
Denver 80203

Denver Academy of Court Reporting, Main Campus
7920 Samuel Dr., Ste. 200
Denver 80221-2792

Heritage College of Health Careers
12 Lakeside Ln.
Denver 80212

DELAWARE

Star Technical Institute
Graystone Plaza, 631 West Newport Pike
Wilmington 19804

FLORIDA

Atlantic Vocational Technical Center
4700 Coconut Creek Pkwy.
Coconut Creek 33063

Beacon Career Institute, Inc.
2900 Northwest 183rd St.
Miami 33056

Brewster Technical Center
2222 North Tampa St.
Tampa 33602-2196

Concorde Career Institute
7960 Arlington Expwy.
Jacksonville 32211

Concorde Career Institute
4202 West Spruce St.
Tampa 33607

Daytona Beach Community College
1200 Volusia Ave.
Daytona Beach 32114

Miami-Dade Community College
300 Northeast Second Ave.
Miami 33132

Pasco-Hernando Community College
36727 Blanton Rd.
Dade City 33525-7599

Pensacola Junior College
1000 College Blvd.
Pensacola 32504

Sarasota County Technical Institute
4748 Beneva Rd.
Sarasota 34233-1798

Sheridan Vocational Center
5400 Sheridan St.
Hollywood 33021

Withlacoochee Technical Institute
1201 West Main St.
Inverness 32650

GEORGIA

Medix Schools
2108 Cobb Pkwy.
Smyrna 30080

HAWAII

Heald College School of Business and Technology
1500 Kapiolani Blvd.
Honolulu 96816

Medical Assistant School of Hawaii, Inc.
33 South King, Ste. 223
Honolulu 96813

IDAHO

American Institute of Health Technology, Inc.
6600 Emerald
Boise 83704

ILLINOIS

American Health Information Management Association
919 North Michigan Ave., Ste. 1400
Chicago 60611

Belleville Area College
2500 Carlyle Rd.
Belleville 62221

Lewis and Clark Community College
5800 Godfrey Rd.
Godfrey 62035

Medical Careers Institute
116 South Michigan Ave.
Chicago 60603

INDIANA

Indiana University, Northwest
3400 Broadway
Gary 46408

Professional Careers Institute
2611 Waterfront Pkwy., East Dr.
Indianapolis 46214-2028

Saint Margaret Hospital Medical Technology Program
5454 Hohman Ave.
Hammond 46320

IOWA

Indian Hills Community College
525 Grandview
Ottumwa 52501

KANSAS

Dodge City Community College
2501 North 14th Ave.
Dodge City 67801

KENTUCKY

Eastern Kentucky University
Lancaster Ave.
Richmond 40475

Interactive Learning Systems
11 Spiral Dr., Bldg. 13, Ste. 8
Florence 41042

LOUISIANA

American School of Business
702 Professional Dr. N
Shreveport 71105

Ayers Institute, Inc.
2924 Knight St., Ste. 318
Shreveport 71105

MARYLAND

Essex Community College
7201 Rossville Blvd.
Baltimore 21237

Medix Schools
1017 York Rd.
Towson 21204-9840

MASSACHUSETTS

Bryman Institute, A Corinthian School
323 Boylston St.
Brookline 02146

MICHIGAN

Baker College of Flint
G1050 West Bristol Rd.
Flint 48507

Baker College of Muskegon
1903 Marquette Ave.
Muskegon 49442

Carnegie Institute
550 Stephenson Hwy.
Troy 48083

Davenport College, Kalamazoo
4123 West Main St.
Kalamazoo 49006-2791

Dorsey Business Schools
31542 Gratiot
Roseville 48066

Dorsey Business Schools
15755 Northline Rd.
Southgate 48195

Dorsey Business Schools
34841 Veterans Plaza
Wayne 48184

Ferris State University
901 South State St.
Big Rapids 49307

Grand Rapids Educational Center
1750 Woodworth NE
Grand Rapids 49525

Grand Rapids Educational Center
5349 West Main
Kalamazoo 49009

Henry Ford Community College
5101 Evergreen Rd.
Dearborn 48128

Lawton School
20755 Greenfield Rd., Ste. 300
Southfield 48075

SER Business and Technical Insti tute
9301 Michigan Ave.
Detroit 47210-2095

MINNESOTA

Hennepin Technical College
9000 Brooklyn Blvd.
Plymouth 55445

Northwest Technical College, East Grand Forks
Hwy. 220 N
East Grand Forks 56721

Saint Paul Technical College
235 Marshall Ave.
Saint Paul 55102

MISSISSIPPI

Amherst Career Center
201 West Park Ave.
Greenwood 38930

MISSOURI

Concorde Career Institute
3239 Broadway
Kansas City 64111

Miss Vanderschmidt's Secretarial School
4625 Lindell Blvd.
Saint Louis 63108

Missouri College
10121 Manchester Rd.
Saint Louis 63122

Penn Valley Community College
3201 Southwest Trafficway
Kansas City 64111

Saint Louis College of Health Careers
4484 West Pine
Saint Louis 63108

Sikeston Area Vocational Technical School
1002 Virginia St.
Sikeston 63801

NEBRASKA

College of Saint Mary
1901 South 72nd St.
Omaha 68124

NEVADA

Nevada School of Insurance, Las Vegas
3305 Spring Mountain Rd., Ste. 50
Las Vegas 89102

NEW JERSEY

Berdan Institute
265 Rte. 46
Totowa 07512

Business Training Institute
Four Forest Ave.
Paramus 07652

Star Technical Institute
1255 Rte. 70
Lakewood 08701

NEW MEXICO

Albuquerque Technical Vocational Institute
525 Buena Vista SE
Albuquerque 87106

NEW YORK

CUNY Borough of Manhattan Community College
199 Chambers St.
New York 10007

Monroe Community College
1000 East Henrietta Rd.
Rochester 14623

NORTH CAROLINA

Central Piedmont Community College
P.O. Box 35009
Charlotte 28235-5009

Kings College
322 Lamar Ave.
Charlotte 28204

Pitt Community College
Hwy. 11 S, P.O. Drawer 7007
Greenville 27835-7007

OHIO

Chase School of Medical Transcription
Ten West Streetsboro St., Ste. 101-303
Hudson 44236

Cincinnati State Technical and Community College
3520 Central Pkwy.
Cincinnati 45223

Cleveland Institute of Dental-Medical Assistants
1836 Euclid Ave.
Cleveland 44115

Cleveland Institute of Dental-Medical Assistants
5564 Mayfield Rd.
Lyndhurst 44124

Cleveland Institute of Dental-Medical Assistants
5733 Hopkins Rd.
Mentor 44060

Pioneer Career and Technical Center, A Vocational School District
27 Ryan Rd.
Shelby 44875

Remington College
14445 Broadway Ave.
Cleveland 44125

OKLAHOMA

De Marge College North
3608 Northwest 58th
Oklahoma City 73112

Francis Tuttle Area Vocational-Technical Center
12777 North Rockwell Ave.
Oklahoma City 73142-2789

Pontotoc Area Vocational Technical School
601 West 33rd
Ada 74820

Wright Business School
2219 Southwest 74th St., Ste. 124
Oklahoma City 73159

OREGON

Chemeketa Community College
4000 Lancaster Dr. NE
Salem 97305

Concorde Career Institute
1827 Northeast 44th Ave.
Portland 97213

Portland Community College
P.O. Box 19000
Portland 97280-0990

PENNSYLVANIA

Allied Medical and Technical Careers
2901 Pittston Ave.
Scranton 18505

Allied Medical and Technical Careers
104 Woodward Hill Rd.
Edwardsville 18704

Antonelli Medical and Professional Institute
1700 Industrial Hwy.
Pottstown 19464

Bidwell Training Center, Inc.
1815 Metropolitan St.
Pittsburgh 15233

Community College of Allegheny County, Pittsburgh
800 Allegheny Ave.
Pittsburgh 15233-1895

Computer Learning Network
2900 Fairway Dr.
Altoona 16602

Delaware County Community College
901 South Media Line Rd.
Media 19063-1094

Median School of Allied Health Careers
125 Seventh St.
Pittsburgh 15222-3400

National Education Center, Allentown Business School Campus
1501 Lehigh St.
Allentown 18103

Thompson Institute
3440 Market St.
Philadelphia 19104

RHODE ISLAND

New England Institute of Technology
2500 Post Rd.
Warwick 02886

SOUTH DAKOTA

National American University
321 Kansas City St.
Rapid City 57701

TENNESSEE

Fugazzi College
5042 Linbar Dr., Ste. 200
Nashville 37211

Nashville State Technical Institute
120 White Bridge Rd.
Nashville 37209

Roane State Community College
276 Patton Ln.
Harriman 37748

TEXAS

The Academy of Health Care Professions
1919 Northloop W, Ste. 170
Houston 77008

American Commercial College
3177 Executive Dr.
San Angelo 76904

Career Centers of Texas El Paso
8375 Burnham Dr.
El Paso 79907

PCI Health Training Center
8101 John Carpenter Fwy.
Dallas 75247

Saint Philip's College
1801 Martin Luther King Dr.
San Antonio 78203

San Antonio College of Medical and Dental Assistants, Central
4205 San Pedro Ave.
San Antonio 78212-1899

Texas School of Business, Inc.
711 Airtex Dr.
Houston 77073

Texas School of Business, Southwest, Inc.
10250 Bissonnet
Houston 77036

Texas State Technical College, Harlingen
2424 Boxwood
Harlingen 78550-3697

UTAH

Bridgerland Applied Technology Center
1301 North 600 West
Logan 84321

Provo College
1450 West 820 N
Provo 84601

VIRGINIA

Computer Dynamics Institute, Inc.
5361 Virginia Beach Blvd.
Virginia Beach 23462

Medical Careers Institute
605 Thimble Shoals
Newport News 23606

WASHINGTON

Clark College
1800 East McLoughlin Blvd.
Vancouver 98663-3598

Eton Technical Institute
209 East Casino Rd.
Everett 98208

Eton Technical Institute
31919 Sixth Ave. S
Federal Way 98003

Eton Technical Institute
3649 Frontage Rd., St. A
Port Orchard 98366

Lower Columbia College
P.O. Box 3010
Longview 98632

Spokane Community College
North 1810 Greene Ave.
Spokane 99207

Tacoma Community College
5900 South 12th St.
Tacoma 98465

WEST VIRGINIA

Marshall University
400 Hal Greer Blvd.
Huntington 25755

West Virginia Business College
1052 Main St.
Wheeling 26003

WISCONSIN

Chippewa Valley Technical College
620 West Clairemont Ave.
Eau Claire 54701

Gateway Technical College
3520 30th Ave.
Kenosha 53144-1690

Mid-State Technical College
500 32nd St. N
Wisconsin Rapids 54494

Milwaukee Area Technical College
700 West State St.
Milwaukee 53233-1443

Northeast Wisconsin Technical College
2740 West Mason St., P.O. Box 19042
Green Bay 54307-9042

Waukesha County Technical College
800 Main St.
Pewaukee 53072

Western Wisconsin Technical College
304 North Sixth St., P.O. Box 908
La Crosse 54602-0908

Nurse's Aide

ALABAMA

Bevill State Community College
100 State St.
Sumiton 35148

Reid State Technical College
I65 and Hwy. 83
Evergreen 36401

Trenholm State Technical College
1225 Air Base Blvd.
Montgomery 36108

ARIZONA

Eastern Arizona College
Church St.
Thatcher 85552-0769

Gateway Community College
108 North 40th St.
Phoenix 85034

Pima Community College
2202 West Anklam Rd.
Tucson 85709-0001

Pima Medical Institute
3350 East Grant Rd.
Tucson 85716

Tucson College
7302-10 East 22nd St.
Tucson 85710

ARKANSAS

Arkansas Valley Technical Institute
P.O. Box 506, Hwy. 23 N
Ozark 72949

Black River Technical College
Box 468, Hwy. 304
Pocahontas 72455

Crowley's Ridge Technical Institute
140 Crowleys Ridge Rd.
Forrest City 72335-0925

Eastern College of Health Vocations
6423 Forbing Rd.
Little Rock 72209

Great Rivers Vocational Technical School
P.O. Box 747, Hwy. One NE
McGehee 71654

University of Arkansas Community College, Batesville
P.O. Box 3350
Batesville 72503

CALIFORNIA

Allan Hancock College
800 South College Dr.
Santa Maria 93454

American School of X-Ray
13723-1/2 Harvard Place
Gardena 90249

Butte College
3536 Butte Campus Dr.
Oroville 95965

Educorp Career College
230 East Third St.
Long Beach 90802

Hacienda La Puente Unified School District, Adult Education
P.O. Box 60002
City of Industry 91716-0002

Mission College
3000 Mission College Blvd.
Santa Clara 95054-1897

Nova Institute of Health Technology
520 North Euclid Ave.
Ontario 91762

Santa Rosa Junior College
1501 Mendocino Ave.
Santa Rosa 95401-4395

Simi Valley Adult School
3192 Los Angeles Ave.
Simi Valley 93065

COLORADO

Colorado Mountain College
P.O. Box 10001
Glenwood Springs 81602

PPI Health Careers School
2345 North Academy Blvd.
Colorado Springs 80909

Trinidad State Junior College, San Luis Valley Education Center
1011 Main St.
Alamosa 81101

FLORIDA

Atlantic Vocational Technical Center
4700 Coconut Creek Pkwy.
Coconut Creek 33063

Beacon Career Institute, Inc.
2900 Northwest 183rd St.
Miami 33056

Brevard Community College, Cocoa Campus
1519 Clearlake Rd.
Cocoa 32922

Brewster Technical Center
2222 North Tampa St.
Tampa 33602-2196

Charlotte Vocational Technical Center
18300 Toledo Blade Blvd.
Port Charlotte 33948-3399

Daytona Beach Community College
1200 Volusia Ave.
Daytona Beach 32114

Florida Community College at Jacksonville
501 West State St.
Jacksonville 32202

Lorenzo Walker Institute of Technology
3702 Estey Ave.
Naples 33942

Lee County High Technical Center, Central
3800 Michigan Ave.
Fort Myers 33916

Lindsey Hopkins Technical Education Center
750 Northwest 20th St.
Miami 33127

Manatee Vocational Technical Center
5603 34th St. W
Bradenton 34210

Miriam Vocational School, Inc.
135 Southwest 57th Ave.
Miami 33144

Pensacola Junior College
1000 College Blvd.
Pensacola 32504

Pinellas Technical Education Centers
901 34th St. S
Saint Petersburg 33711

Radford M Locklin Vocational Technical Center
5330 Berryhill Rd.
Milton 32570

Robert Morgan Vocational Technical Center
18180 Southwest 122nd Ave.
Miami 33177

Santa Fe Community College
3000 Northwest 83rd St.
Gainesville 32606

Sarasota County Technical Institute
4748 Beneva Rd.
Sarasota 34233-1798

Seminole Community College
100 Weldon Blvd.
Sanford 32773-6199

South Florida Community College
600 West College Dr.
Avon Park 33825

Suwannee-Hamilton Area Vocational and Adult Center
415 Southwest Pinewood Dr.
Live Oak 32060

U.S. Schools
100 North Plaza
Miami 33147

Washington-Holmes Area Vocational-Technical Center
757 Hoyt St.
Chipley 32428

Withlacoochee Technical Institute
1201 West Main St.
Inverness 32650

GEORGIA

Kerr Business College
2528 Centerwest Pkwy., Bldg. A
Augusta 30909

Meadows Junior College
1170 Brown Ave.
Columbus 31906

ILLINOIS

Belleville Area College
2500 Carlyle Rd.
Belleville 62221

Career Academy
20 North Michigan Ave., Ste. 302
Chicago 60601

City Colleges of Chicago, Central Office
226 West Jackson Blvd.
Chicago 60606

John Wood Community College
150 South 48th St.
Quincy 62301-9147

Kishwaukee College
21193 Malta Rd.
Malta 60150

Lake Land College
5001 Lake Land Blvd.
Mattoon 61938

Lewis and Clark Community College
5800 Godfrey Rd.
Godfrey 62035

McHenry County College
8900 U.S. Hwy. 14
Crystal Lake 60012

Rock Valley College
3301 North Mulford Rd.
Rockford 61114

Sauk Valley Community College
173 Illinois Rte. 2
Dixon 61021

Shawnee Community College
8364 Shawnee College Rd.
Ullin 62992

Waubonsee Community College
IL Rte. 47 at Harter Rd.
Sugar Grove 60554-0901

IOWA

North Iowa Area Community College
500 College Dr.
Mason City 50401

KANSAS

Cloud County Community College
2221 Campus Dr., Box 1002
Concordia 66901-1002

Colby Community College
1255 South Range
Colby 67701

KAW Area Technical School
5724 Huntoon
Topeka 66604

Southwest Kansas Technical School
P.O. Box 1599
Liberal 67905-1599

Salina Area Vocational Technical School
2562 Scanlan Ave.
Salina 67401

KENTUCKY

Kentucky Tech, Ashland Regional Technology Center
4818 Roberts Dr.
Ashland 41102

LOUISIANA

Ascension College
320 East Ascension St.
Gonzales 70737

Cameron College
2740 Canal St.
New Orleans 70119

Charles B Coreil Technical Institute
Industrial Park Ward I
Ville Platte 70586

Coastal College, Hammond
4304 Yokum Rd.
Hammond 70403

Domestic Health Care Institute
4826 Jamestown Ave.
Baton Rouge 70808

Eastern College of Health Vocations
3321 Hessmer Ave., Ste. 200
Metairie 70002

Elaine P Nunez Community College
3710 Paris Rd.
Chalmette 70043

Huey P Long Technical Institute
303 South Jones St.
Winnfield 71483

Louisiana Technical College, Ascension Campus
P.O. Box 38
Sorrento 70778

Louisiana Technical College, Avoyelles Campus
508 Choupique St.
Cottonport 71327

Louisiana Technical College, Baton Rouge Campus
3250 North Acadian Twy. E
Baton Rouge 70805

Louisiana Technical College, Claiborne Campus
3001 Minden Rd.
Homer 71040

Louisiana Technical College, Evangeline Campus
P.O. Box 68
Saint Martinville 70582

Louisiana Technical College, Mansfield Campus
943 Oxford Rd.
Mansfield 71052

Louisiana Technical College, Sabine Valley Campus
1255 Fisher Rd.
Many 71449

Louisiana Technical College, T H Harris Campus
337 East South St.
Opelousas 70570

Louisiana Technical College, Thibodaux Lafourche Campus
1425 Tiger Dr.
Thibodaux 70302

MASSACHUSETTS

Assabet Valley Regional Vocational Technical School
215 Fitchburg St.
Marlborough 01752

MICHIGAN

Detroit Business Institute
1249 Washington Blvd., Ste. 1200
Detroit 48226

Ross Medical Education Center
1036 Gilbert St.
Flint 48532

Ross Medical Education Center
913 West Holmes, Ste. 260
Lansing 48910

Ross Medical Education Center
Park Row Mall, 950 Norton Ave.
Roosevelt Park 49441

Ross Medical Education Center
4054 Bay Rd.
Saginaw 48603

Ross Technical Institute
20820 Greenfield Rd., Ste. 101
Oak Park 48237

MINNESOTA

Century Community and Technical College
3300 Century Ave. N
White Bear Lake 55110

Itasca Community College
1851 Hwy. 169 E
Grand Rapids 55744

Lake Superior College
2101 Trinity Rd.
Duluth 55811

MISSISSIPPI

Northwest Mississippi Community College
510 North Panola, Hwy. 51 N
Senatobia 38668

MISSOURI

Cape Girardeau Area Vocational Technical School
301 North Clark Ave.
Cape Girardeau 63701

Saint Louis College of Health Careers
4484 West Pine
Saint Louis 63108

Sikeston Area Vocational Technical School
1002 Virginia St.
Sikeston 63801

MONTANA

Dawson Community College
300 College Dr.
Glendive 59330

Montana State University, College of Technology, Great Falls
2100 16th Ave. S
Great Falls 59405

NEBRASKA

Opportunity Industrialization Center Omaha
2725 North 24th St.
Omaha 68110

NEW MEXICO

Albuquerque Technical Vocational Institute
525 Buena Vista SE
Albuquerque 87106

Crownpoint Institute of Technology
P.O. Box 849
Crownpoint 87313

Franklin College
2400 Louisiana Blvd. NE, Ste. 200
Albuquerque 87110

Pima Medical Institute
2201 San Pedro NE, Bldg. 3, Ste. 100
Albuquerque 87110

NEW YORK

Municipal Training Center
44 Court St., 7th Fl.
Brooklyn 11201

Silhouette
3187 Steinway St.
Long Island City 11103

Suburban Technical School
175 Fulton Ave.
Hempstead 11550

Superior Career Institute, Inc.
254 West 29th St., 3rd Fl.
New York 10011

Travel Institute
15 Park Row
New York 10038

NORTH CAROLINA

Brunswick Community College
P.O. Box 30
Supply 28462

Coastal Carolina Community College
444 Western Blvd.
Jacksonville 28546-6877

Craven Community College
800 College Ct.
New Bern 28562

Piedmont Community College
P.O. Box 1197
Roxboro 27573

Roanoke-Chowan Community College
Rte. 2, Box 46A
Ahoskie 27910

Robeson Community College
P.O. Box 1420
Lumberton 28359

OHIO

Gallia Jackson Vinton JUSD
Box 157
Rio Grande 45674

Madison Local Schools, Madison Adult Education
600 Esley Ln.
Mansfield 44905

Tri-Rivers Career Center
2222 Marion Mount Gilead Rd.
Marion 43302

OKLAHOMA

Southwest Area Vocational Technical Center
711 West Tamarack
Altus 73521

Tulsa Colorado Area Vocational Technical School District 18, Peoria
3850 North Peoria
Tulsa 74106

OREGON

Southwestern Oregon Community College
1988 Newmark Ave.
Coos Bay 97420

PENNSYLVANIA

Advanced Career Training
McClatchy Bldg., 2nd Fl., Southwest Corner 69th
Upper Darby 19082

Allied Medical and Technical Careers
2901 Pittston Ave.
Scranton 18505

Allied Medical and Technical Careers
104 Woodward Hill Rd.
Edwardsville 18704

American Center for Technical Arts and Sciences
1616 Orthodoy St.
Philadelphia 19124

Antonelli Medical and Professional Institute
1700 Industrial Hwy.
Pottstown 19464

McKeesport Hospital School of Nursing Assistants
1500 Fifth Ave.
McKeesport 15132

Pennsylvania State University, Lehigh Valley Berks, Lehigh
6090 Mohr Ln.
Fogelsville 18051-9733

Presbyterian Home Nurse Assistant School
P.O. Box 551
Philipsburg 16866

SOUTH CAROLINA

Trident Technical College
P.O. Box 118067
Charleston 29423-8067

TENNESSEE

Davidson Technical College
212 Pavilion Blvd.
Nashville 37217-1002

Draughons Junior College
1860 Wilma Rudolph Blvd.
Clarksville 37040

Tennessee Technology Center at Elizabethton
1500 Arney St.
Elizabethton 37643

Tennessee Technology Center at Hohenwald
813 West Main
Hohenwald 38462-2201

Tennessee Technology Center at Knoxville
1100 Liberty St.
Knoxville 37919

Tennessee Technology Center at Memphis
550 Alabama Ave.
Memphis 38105-3604

Tennessee Technology Center at Paris
312 South Wilson St.
Paris 38242

TEXAS

Delta Career Institute
1310 Pennsylvania Ave.
Beaumont 77701

Houston Medical Career Training, Inc.
2420 Garland Dr.
Houston 77087

Southwest School of Business and Technical Careers
602 West South Cross
San Antonio 78221

Texas State Technical College, Harlingen
2424 Boxwood
Harlingen 78550-3697

Transworld Academy, Inc.
6220 West Park, Ste. 110
Houston 77057

UTAH

Bridgerland Applied Technology Center
1301 North 600 West
Logan 84321

Salt Lake Community College, Skills Center
South City Campus, 1575 South State St.
Salt Lake City 84115

VIRGINIA

Blue Ridge Nursing Home School
Commerce St., P.O. Box 459
Stuart 24171

Medical Careers Institute
605 Thimble Shoals
Newport News 23606

Southside Training Skill Center Nottoway County
P.O. Box 258
Crewe 23930

Tidewater Technical
616 Denbigh Blvd.
Newport News 23602

Tidewater Technical
1760 East Little Creek Rd.
Norfolk 23518

Tidewater Technical
2697 Dean Dr., Ste. 100
Virginia Beach 23452

WASHINGTON

Bates Technical College
1101 South Yakima Ave.
Tacoma 98405

Lower Columbia College
P.O. Box 3010
Longview 98632

Yakima Valley Community College
P.O. Box 1647
Yakima 98907

WEST VIRGINIA

Opportunities Industrialization Center, North Central West Virginia
120 Jackson St.
Fairmont 26554

WISCONSIN

Blackhawk Technical College
P.O. Box 5009
Janesville 53547

Fox Valley Technical College at Appleton
1825 North Bluemound Dr.
Appleton 54913-2277

Gateway Technical College
3520 30th Ave.
Kenosha 53144-1690

Lakeshore Technical College
1290 North Ave.
Cleveland 53015

Madison Area Technical College
3550 Anderson St.
Madison 53704

Mid-State Technical College, Main Campus
500 32nd St. N
Wisconsin Rapids 54494

Milwaukee Area Technical College
700 West State St.
Milwaukee 53233-1443

Moraine Park Technical College
235 North National Ave.
Fond Du Lac 54936-1940

Nicolet Area Technical College
Hwy. G South
Rhinelander 54501

Northcentral Technical College
1000 Campus Dr.
Wausau 54401-1899

Northeast Wisconsin Technical College
2740 West Mason St., P.O. Box 19042
Green Bay 54307-9042

Southwest Wisconsin Technical College
1800 Bronson Blvd.
Fennimore 53809

Waukesha County Technical College
800 Main St.
Pewaukee 53072

Western Wisconsin Technical College
304 North Sixth St., P.O. Box 908
La Crosse 54602-0908

Wisconsin Indianhead Technical College
505 Pine Ridge Dr.
Shell Lake 54871

Occupational Therapy Technology

CALIFORNIA

Imperial Valley College
P.O. Box 158
Imperial 92251-0158

COLORADO

Aims Community College
Box 69
Greeley 80632

CONNECTICUT

Manchester Community Technical College
60 Bidwell St.
Manchester 06040-1046

FLORIDA

Charlotte Vocational Technical Center
18300 Toledo Blade Blvd.
Port Charlotte 33948-3399

ILLINOIS

College of Du Page
425 22nd St.
Glen Ellyn 60137-6599

IOWA

Kirkwood Community College
P.O. Box 2068
Cedar Rapids 52406

KANSAS

Allen County Community College
1801 North Cottonwood
Iola 66749

Cloud County Community College
2221 Campus Dr., Box 1002
Concordia 66901-1002

Colby Community College
1255 South Range
Colby 67701

Kansas City Area Vocational Technical School
2220 North 59th St.
Kansas City 66104

KAW Area Technical School
5724 Huntoon
Topeka 66604

Neosho County Community College
800 West 14th St.
Chanute 66720

North Central Kansas Technical College
Box 507, Hwy. 24
Beloit 67420

Salina Area Vocational Technical School
2562 Scanlan Ave.
Salina 67401

Wichita Area Technical College
201 North Water
Wichita 67202-1292

LOUISIANA

Northeast Louisiana University
700 University Ave.
Monroe 71209

MASSACHUSETTS

Quinsigamond Community College
670 West Boylston St.
Worcester 01606

MICHIGAN

Grand Rapids Community College
143 Bostwick Ave. NE
Grand Rapids 49503-3295

Schoolcraft College
18600 Haggerty Rd.
Livonia 48152

Wayne County Community College
801 West Fort St.
Detroit 48226

MINNESOTA

Century Community and Technical College
3300 Century Ave. N
White Bear Lake 55110

Hibbing Community College, A Technical and Community College
1515 East 25th St.
Hibbing 55746

Lake Superior College
2101 Trinity Rd.
Duluth 55811

MISSOURI

Jefferson College
1000 Viking Dr.
Hillsboro 63050

Saint Louis Community College, Forest Park
5600 Oakland Ave.
Saint Louis 63110

NEW YORK

CUNY La Guardia Community College
31-10 Thomson Ave.
Long Island City 11101

Erie Community College, North Campus
Main St. and Youngs Rd.
Williamsville 14221

Herkimer County Community College
Reservoir Rd.
Herkimer 13350-1598

Rockland Community College
145 College Rd.
Suffern 10901

NORTH DAKOTA

North Dakota State College of Science
800 North Sixth St.
Wahpeton 58076

OKLAHOMA

Metro Area Vocational Technical School District 22
1900 Springlake Dr.
Oklahoma City 73111

Oklahoma City Community College
7777 South May Ave.
Oklahoma City 73159

PENNSYLVANIA

Community College of Allegheny County, Pittsburgh
800 Allegheny Ave.
Pittsburgh 15233-1895

Harcum College
750 Montgomery Ave.
Bryn Mawr 19010

Median School of Allied Health Careers
125 Seventh St.
Pittsburgh 15222-3400

Mount Aloysius College
7373 Admiral Peary Hwy.
Cresson 16630-1999

TENNESSEE

Shelby State Community College
P.O. Box 40568
Memphis 38174-0568

TEXAS

Houston Community College System
22 Waugh Dr.
Houston 77270-7849

WASHINGTON

Green River Community College
12401 Southeast 320th St.
Auburn 98092

Spokane Falls Community College
West 3410 Fort George Wright Dr.
Spokane 99224

WISCONSIN

Fox Valley Technical College at Appleton
1825 North Bluemound Dr.
Appleton 54913-2277

Madison Area Technical College
3550 Anderson St.
Madison 53704

Milwaukee Area Technical College
700 West State St.
Milwaukee 53233-1443

Optical Technology

ARIZONA

The Bryman School
4343 North 16th St.
Phoenix 85016

CALIFORNIA

National Career Education
6060 Sunrise Vista Dr.
Citrus Heights 95610

FLORIDA

Miami-Dade Community College
300 Northeast Second Ave.
Miami 33132

MASSACHUSETTS

Worcester Technical Institute
251 Belmont St.
Worcester 01605

MICHIGAN

Detroit Institute of Ophthalmology
15415 East Jefferson Ave.
Grosse Pointe Park 48230

Ferris State University
901 South State St.
Big Rapids 49307

NEW YORK

Allied Health Program in Orthoptics & Opthalmic Technology
310 East 14th St.
New York 10003

CUNY New York City Technical College
300 Jay St.
Brooklyn 11201

Erie Community College, North Campus
Main St. and Youngs Rd.
Williamsville 14221

Interboro Institute
450 West 56th St.
New York 10019

TEXAS

San Antonio College of Medical and Dental Assistants, Central
4205 San Pedro Ave.
San Antonio 78212-1899

UTAH

American Institute of Medical-Dental Technology
1675 North 200 West, Bldg. 4
Provo 84604

WISCONSIN

Lakeshore Technical College
1290 North Ave.
Cleveland 53015

Pharmaceutical Technology

ALABAMA

Community College of the Air Force
130 West Maxwell Blvd.
Montgomery 36112-6613

ARIZONA

Apollo College
3870 North Oracle Rd.
Tucson 85705

Long Medical Institute
4126 North Black Canyon Hwy.
Phoenix 85017

Pima Community College
2202 West Anklam Rd.
Tucson 85709-0001

CALIFORNIA

American Career College
4021 Rosewood Ave., First Fl.
Los Angeles 90004

California Paramedical and Technical College
4550 La Sierra Ave.
Riverside 92505

California Paramedical and Technical College
3745 Long Beach Blvd.
Long Beach 90807

Concorde Career Institute
570 West Fourth St., Ste. 107
San Bernardino 92401

Donald Vocational School
1833 West Eighth St., Ste. 200
Los Angeles 90057

Healthstaff Training Institute, Inc.
1505 East 17th St., Ste. 122
Santa Ana 92705

Western Career College
170 Bay Fair Mall
San Leandro 94578

COLORADO

Concorde Career Institute
770 Grant St.
Denver 80203

FLORIDA

Beacon Career Institute, Inc.
2900 Northwest 183rd St.
Miami 33056

Technical Career Institute
4299 Northwest 36th St., Ste. 300
Miami Springs 33166

IDAHO

American Institute of Health Technology, Inc.
6600 Emerald
Boise 83704

MICHIGAN

Ferris State University
901 South State St.
Big Rapids 49307

MINNESOTA

Century Community and Technical College
3300 Century Ave. N
White Bear Lake 55110

MISSOURI

Al-Med Academy
10963 Saint Charles Rock Rd.
Saint Louis 63074

Saint Louis College of Health Careers
4484 West Pine
Saint Louis 63108

OREGON

Apollo College, Portland, Inc.
2600 Southeast 98th Ave.
Portland 97266

PENNSYLVANIA

Allied Medical and Technical Careers
2901 Pittston Ave.
Scranton 18505

Allied Medical and Technical Careers
104 Woodward Hill Rd.
Edwardsville 18704

Bidwell Training Center, Inc.
1815 Metropolitan St.
Pittsburgh 15233

North Hills School of Health Occupations
1500 Northway Mall
Pittsburgh 15237

TEXAS

Amarillo College
P.O. Box 447
Amarillo 79178

WASHINGTON

Seattle Community College, North Campus
9600 College Way N
Seattle 98103

WISCONSIN

Milwaukee Area Technical College
700 West State St.
Milwaukee 53233-1443

Physical Therapy Technology

ALABAMA

Community College of the Air Force
130 West Maxwell Blvd.
Montgomery 36112-6613

George C Wallace State Community College, Hanceville
801 Main St. NW
Hanceville 35077-2000

University of Alabama at Birmingham
Administration Bldg., Ste. 1070-2010
Birmingham 35294-0110

ARIZONA

Long Medical Institute
4126 North Black Canyon Hwy.
Phoenix 85017

ARKANSAS

University of Central Arkansas
201 Donaghey Ave.
Conway 72035-0001

CALIFORNIA

Cerritos College
11110 Alondra Blvd.
Norwalk 90650

De Anza College
21250 Stevens Creek Blvd.
Cupertino 95014

Imperial Valley College
P.O. Box 158
Imperial 92251-0158

Loma Linda University
Loma Linda 92350

Watterson College Pacific
150 South Los Robles Blvd., Ste. 100
Pasadena 91101

COLORADO

Aims Community College
Box 69
Greeley 80632

CONNECTICUT

Manchester Community Technical College
60 Bidwell St.
Manchester 06040-1046

FLORIDA

Broward Community College
225 East Las Olas Blvd.
Fort Lauderdale 33301

Charlotte Vocational Technical Center
18300 Toledo Blade Blvd.
Port Charlotte 33948-3399

Miami-Dade Community College
300 Northeast Second Ave.
Miami 33132

Saint Petersburg Junior College
8580 66th St.
Pinellas Park 34665

GEORGIA

Gwinnett Technical Institute
5150 Sugarloaf Pkwy.
Lawrenceville 30043

IDAHO

American Institute of Health Technology, Inc.
6600 Emerald
Boise 83704

ILLINOIS

Belleville Area College
2500 Carlyle Rd.
Belleville 62221

Morton College
3801 South Central Ave.
Cicero 60804

KANSAS

Allen County Community College
1801 North Cottonwood
Iola 66749

Cloud County Community College
2221 Campus Dr., Box 1002
Concordia 66901-1002

Colby Community College
1255 South Range
Colby 67701

Kansas City Area Technical School
2220 North 59th St.
Kansas City 66104

KAW Area Technical School
5724 Huntoon
Topeka 66604

Neosho County Community College
800 West 14th St.
Chanute 66720

North Central Kansas Technical College
Box 507, Hwy. 24
Beloit 67420

Salina Area Vocational Technical School
2562 Scanlan Ave.
Salina 67401

Wichita Area Technical College
201 North Water
Wichita 67202-1292

MARYLAND

Baltimore City Community College
2901 Liberty Heights Ave.
Baltimore 21215

MASSACHUSETTS

Becker College, Worcester
61 Sever St.
Worcester 01615-0071

Newbury College, Inc.
129 Fisher Ave.
Brookline 02146

MICHIGAN

Delta College
University Ctr.
University Center 48710

Macomb Community College
14500 Twelve Mile Rd.
Warren 48093-3896

MINNESOTA

Anoka-Ramsey Community College
11200 Mississippi Blvd.
Coon Rapids 55433-3470

College of Saint Catherine, Minneapolis
601 25th Ave. S
Minneapolis 55454

MISSOURI

Jefferson College
1000 Viking Dr.
Hillsboro 63050

NEW JERSEY

University of Medicine and Dentistry of New Jersey
30 Bergen St.
Newark 07107

NEW YORK

CUNY Kingsborough Community College
2001 Oriental Blvd.
Brooklyn 11235

CUNY La Guardia Community College
31-10 Thomson Ave.
Long Island City 11101

Genesee Community College
One College Rd.
Batavia 14020

Nassau Community College
One Education Dr.
Garden City 11530

Suffolk County Community College, Ammerman Campus
533 College Rd.
Selden 11784

NORTH CAROLINA

Central Piedmont Community College
P.O. Box 35009
Charlotte 28235-5009

OHIO

Cuyahoga Community College District
700 Carnegie Ave.
Cleveland 44115-2878

Kent State University, East Liverpool Regional Campus
400 East Fourth St.
East Liverpool 43920

Stark State College of Technology
6200 Frank Ave. NW
Canton 44720

OKLAHOMA

Metro Area Vocational Technical School District 22
1900 Springlake Dr.
Oklahoma City 73111

OREGON

Mount Hood Community College
26000 Southeast Stark St.
Gresham 97030

PENNSYLVANIA

Community College of Allegheny County, Pittsburgh
800 Allegheny Ave.
Pittsburgh 15233-1895

Harcum College
750 Montgomery Ave.
Bryn Mawr 19010

Lehigh Carbon Community College
4525 Education Park Dr.
Schnecksville 18078-2598

Pennsylvania State University, Hazleton
Highacres
Hazleton 18201

SOUTH CAROLINA

Trident Technical College
P.O. Box 118067
Charleston 29423-8067

TENNESSEE

Volunteer State Community College
1480 Nashville Pike
Gallatin 37066-3188

TEXAS

Amarillo College
P.O. Box 447
Amarillo 79178

Houston Community College System
22 Waugh Dr.
Houston 77270-7849

Tarrant County Junior College
1500 Houston St.
Fort Worth 76102

Transworld Academy, Inc.
6220 West Park, Ste. 110
Houston 77057

VIRGINIA

Northern Virginia Community College
4001 Wakefield Chapel Rd.
Annandale 22003

WASHINGTON

Green River Community College
12401 Southeast 320th St.
Auburn 98092

WISCONSIN

Milwaukee Area Technical College
700 West State St.
Milwaukee 53233-1443

Northeast Wisconsin Technical College
2740 West Mason St., P.O. Box 19042
Green Bay 54307-9042

Psychiatric and Mental Health Technology

ALABAMA

Chauncey Sparks State Technical College
Hwy. 431 S
Eufaula 36027

Gadsden State Community College
1001 George Wallace Dr.
Gadsden 35902-0227

George C Wallace State Community College, Hanceville
801 Main St. NW
Hanceville 35077-2000

ALASKA

University of Alaska, Anchorage
3211 Providence Dr.
Anchorage 99508

University of Alaska, Fairbanks
Signers Hall
Fairbanks 99775

ARIZONA

Apollo College
3870 North Oracle Rd.
Tucson 85705

Apollo College, Tri City, Inc.
630 West Southern Ave.
Mesa 85210

Glendale Community College
6000 West Olive Ave.
Glendale 85302

Maricopa Skill Center
1245 East Buckeye
Phoenix 85034-4101

Phoenix College
1202 West Thomas Rd.
Phoenix 85013

Pima Community College
2202 West Anklam Rd.
Tucson 85709-0001

Rio Salado Community College
2323 West 14th St.
Tempe 85281

CALIFORNIA

Allan Hancock College
800 South College Dr.
Santa Maria 93454

American River College
4700 College Oak Dr.
Sacramento 95841

American School of X-Ray
13723-1/2 Harvard Place
Gardena 90249

Butte College
3536 Butte Campus Dr.
Oroville 95965

California Paramedical and Technical College
4550 La Sierra Ave.
Riverside 92505

California Paramedical and Technical College
3745 Long Beach Blvd.
Long Beach 90807

Citrus College
1000 West Foothill Blvd.
Glendora 91741-1899

Cypress College
9200 Valley View
Cypress 90630

De Anza College
21250 Stevens Creek Blvd.
Cupertino 95014

Foothill College
12345 El Monte Rd.
Los Altos Hills 94022

Fresno City College
1101 East University Ave.
Fresno 93741

Glendale Community College
1500 North Verdugo Rd.
Glendale 91208-2894

Hacienda La Puente Unified School District, Adult Education
P.O. Box 60002
City of Industry 91716-0002

Hypnosis Motivation Institute
18607 Ventura Blvd., Ste. 310
Tarzana 91356

Hypnotism Training Institute of Los Angeles
700 South Central
Glendale 91204

Imperial Valley College
P.O. Box 158
Imperial 92251-0158

L & P School of Professional Hypnotherapy
12941 Gilbert, Ste. D
Garden Grove 92841

Marin Regional Occupational Program
P.O. Box 4925
San Rafael 94913

Merced College
3600 M St.
Merced 95348-2898

Mission College
3000 Mission College Blvd.
Santa Clara 95054-1897

Mount San Antonio College
1100 North Grand
Walnut 91789

Mueller College of Holistic Studies
4607 Park Blvd.
San Diego 92116

Napa Valley College
2277 Napa Vallejo Hwy.
Napa 94558

Pacific College of Oriental Medicine
7445 Mission Valley Rd., Ste. 105
San Diego 92108

Pacific Oaks College
Five Westmoreland Place
Pasadena 91103

Porterville College
100 East College Ave.
Porterville 93257

Santa Rosa Junior College
1501 Mendocino Ave.
Santa Rosa 95401-4395

Simi Valley Adult School
3192 Los Angeles Ave.
Simi Valley 93065

Ventura College
4667 Telegraph Rd.
Ventura 93003

Yuba College
2088 North Beale Rd.
Marysville 95901

COLORADO

Aims Community College
Box 69
Greeley 80632

Community College of Denver
P.O. Box 173363
Denver 80217

Modern Institute of Reflexology
7043 West Colfax Ave.
Lakewood 80215

Morgan Community College
17800 County Rd. 20
Fort Morgan 80701

Red Rocks Community College
13300 West Sixth Ave.
Lakewood 80228

CONNECTICUT

Asnuntuck Community Technical College
170 Elm St.
Enfield 06082

Housatonic Community Technical College
900 Lafayette Blvd.
Bridgeport 06604

Manchester Community Technical College
60 Bidwell St.
Manchester 06040-1046

Middlesex Community Technical College
100 Training Hill Rd.
Middletown 06457

Mitchell College
437 Pequot Ave.
New London 06320

Northwestern Connecticut Community Technical College
Park Place E
Winsted 06098

Norwalk Community Technical College
188 Richards Ave.
Norwalk 06854

Tunxis Community Technical College
Rtes. 6 and 177
Farmington 06032

DELAWARE

Delaware Technical and Community College, Owens
Box 610
Georgetown 19947

Delaware Technical and Community College, Terry
1832 North Dupont Pkwy.
Dover 19901

Delaware Technical and Community College Stanton, Wilmington
400 Stanton-Christiana Rd.
Newark 19702

DISTRICT OF COLUMBIA

Howard University
2400 Sixth St. NW
Washington 20059

FLORIDA

Charlotte Vocational Technical Center
18300 Toledo Blade Blvd.
Port Charlotte 33948-3399

Daytona Beach Community College
1200 Volusia Ave.
Daytona Beach 32114

Florida Community College at Jacksonville
501 West State St.
Jacksonville 32202

Lee County High Technical Center, Central
3800 Michigan Ave.
Fort Myers 33916

Sarasota County Technical Institute
4748 Beneva Rd.
Sarasota 34233-1798

Seminole Community College
100 Weldon Blvd.
Sanford 32773-6199

Sheridan Vocational Center
5400 Sheridan St.
Hollywood 33021

GEORGIA

Dekalb College
3251 Panthersville Rd.
Decatur 30034

ILLINOIS

City Colleges of Chicago, Harold Washington College
30 East Lake St.
Chicago 60601

College of Du Page
425 22nd St.
Glen Ellyn 60137-6599

Elgin Community College
1700 Spartan Dr.
Elgin 60123

Moraine Valley Community College
10900 South 88th Ave.
Palos Hills 60465-0937

Prairie State College
202 Halsted St.
Chicago Heights 60411

Swedish American Hospital School of Radiography
1400 Charles St.
Rockford 61104-2298

Triton College
2000 Fifth Ave.
River Grove 60171

Waubonsee Community College
IL Rte. 47 at Harter Rd.
Sugar Grove 60554-0901

William Rainey Harper College
1200 West Algonquin Rd.
Palatine 60067-7398

INDIANA

Indiana University, Purdue University, Fort Wayne
2101 Coliseum Blvd. E
Fort Wayne 46805

IOWA

Iowa Lakes Community College
19 South Seventh St.
Estherville 51334

KANSAS

Allen County Community College
1801 North Cottonwood
Iola 66749

Cloud County Community College
2221 Campus Dr., Box 1002
Concordia 66901-1002

Colby Community College
1255 South Range
Colby 67701

Cowley County Community College
125 South Second St.
Arkansas City 67005

Kansas City Area Technical School
2220 North 59th St.
Kansas City 66104

KAW Area Technical School
5724 Huntoon
Topeka 66604

Neosho County Community College
800 West 14th St.
Chanute 66720

North Central Kansas Technical College
Box 507, Hwy. 24
Beloit 67420

Salina Area Vocational Technical School
2562 Scanlan Ave.
Salina 67401

Washburn University of Topeka
1700 College Ave.
Topeka 66621

Wichita Area Technical College
201 North Water
Wichita 67260

KENTUCKY

Northern Kentucky University
University Dr.
Highland Heights 41099

LOUISIANA

Southern University, New Orleans
6400 Press Dr.
New Orleans 70126

MAINE

University of Maine at Augusta
46 University Dr.
Augusta 04330-9410

MARYLAND

Allegany College of Maryland
12401 Willowbrook Rd. SE
Cumberland 21502

Anne Arundel Community College
101 College Pkwy.
Arnold 21012

Baltimore City Community College
2901 Liberty Heights Ave.
Baltimore 21215

Dundalk Community College
7200 Sollers Point Rd.
Dundalk 21222

Essex Community College
7201 Rossville Blvd.
Baltimore 21237

MASSACHUSETTS

Bristol Community College
777 Elsbree St.
Fall River 02720

Bunker Hill Community College
250 New Rutherford Ave.
Boston 02129

Lawrence Memorial Hospital School of Nursing
170 Governors Ave.
Medford 02155

Middlesex Community College
Springs Rd.
Bedford 01730

Mount Wachusett Community College
444 Green St.
Gardner 01440

Northern Essex Community College
Elliott Way
Haverhill 01830-2399

North Shore Community College
One Ferncroft Rd.
Danvers 01923

Quinsigamond Community College
670 West Boylston St.
Worcester 01606

Springfield Technical Community College
One Armory Square
Springfield 01105

Stonehill College
Washington St.
North Easton 02357

MICHIGAN

Delta College
University Ctr.
University Center 48710

Lansing Community College
419 North Capitol Ave.
Lansing 48901-7210

Macomb Community College
14500 Twelve Mile Rd.
Warren 48093-3896

Mott Community College
1401 East Court St.
Flint 48503

Oakland Community College
2480 Opdyke Rd.
Bloomfield Hills 48304-2266

Wayne County Community College
801 West Fort St.
Detroit 48226

MINNESOTA

College of Saint Catherine, Minneapolis
601 25th Ave. S
Minneapolis 55454

Minneapolis Community and Technical College
1501 Hennepin Ave.
Minneapolis 55403-1779

Saint Cloud Technical College
1540 Northway Dr.
Saint Cloud 56303

University of Minnesota, Crookston
105 Selvig Hall
Crookston 56716

MISSOURI

Jefferson College
1000 Viking Dr.
Hillsboro 63050

NEBRASKA

Central Community College Area
P.O. Box 4903
Grand Island 68802

Omaha College of Health Careers
10845 Harney St.
Omaha 68154

Opportunity Industrialization Center Omaha
2725 North 24th St.
Omaha 68110

Southeast Community College Area
1111 O St., Ste. 111
Lincoln 68520

NEW HAMPSHIRE

Keene State College
229 Main
Keene 03431

New Hampshire Technical Institute
11 Institute Dr.
Concord 03301

NEW JERSEY

Camden County College
P.O. Box 200
Blackwood 08012

Star Technical Institute, Deptford
1450 Clements Bridge Rd.
Deptford 08096

NEW MEXICO

Hypnosis Career Institute
10701 Lomas NE, Ste. 216
Albuquerque 87112

Northern New Mexico Community College
1002 North Onate St.
Espanola 87532

NEW YORK

CUNY Kingsborough Community College
2001 Oriental Blvd.
Brooklyn 11235

Erie Community College, City Campus
121 Ellicott St.
Buffalo 14203

Mercy College, Main Campus
555 Broadway
Dobbs Ferry 10522

Rochester Institute of Technology
One Lamb Memorial Dr.
Rochester 14623-5603

Saint Joseph's College, Main Campus
245 Clinton Ave.
Brooklyn 11205-3688

Saint Joseph's College, Suffolk Campus
155 West Roe Blvd.
Patchogue 11772-2399

Sullivan County Community College
1000 Le Roy Rd.
Loch Sheldrake 12759-4002

NORTH CAROLINA

Duke University
103 Allen Building
Durham 27708

Southeastern Community College
4564 Chadburn Hwy.
Whiteville 28472

Wake Technical Community College
9101 Fayetteville Rd.
Raleigh 27603-5696

Wayne Community College
3000 Wayne Memorial Dr.
Goldsboro 27533-8002

Western Piedmont Community College
1001 Burkemont Ave.
Morganton 28655-9978

OHIO

Belmont Technical College
120 Fox Shannon Place
Saint Clairsville 43950

Columbus State Community College
550 East Spring St.
Columbus 43216

English Nanny and Governess School
30 South Franklin St.
Chagrin Falls 44022

Kettering College Medical Arts
3737 Southern Blvd.
Kettering 45429-1299

Muskingum Area Technical College
1555 Newark Rd.
Zanesville 43701

North Central Technical College
2441 Kenwood Circle, P.O. Box 698
Mansfield 44901

Sinclair Community College
444 West Third St.
Dayton 45402

University of Toledo
2801 West Bancroft
Toledo 43606

OKLAHOMA

Central Oklahoma Area Vocational Technical School
Three Court Circle
Drumright 74030

Kiamichi Area Vocational Technical School SD #7, McCurtain
Rte. 3, Box 177, Hwy. 70 N
Idabel 74745

Metro Area Vocational Technical School District 22
1900 Springlake Dr.
Oklahoma City 73111

OREGON

Chemeketa Community College
4000 Lancaster Dr. NE
Salem 97305

Mount Hood Community College
26000 Southeast Stark St.
Gresham 97030

PENNSYLVANIA

Bucks County Community College
Swamp Rd.
Newtown 18940

Community College of Allegheny County, Pittsburgh
800 Allegheny Ave.
Pittsburgh 15233-1895

Community College of Philadelphia
1700 Spring Garden St.
Philadelphia 19130

Edinboro University of Pennsylvania
Edinboro 16444

Harcum College
750 Montgomery Ave.
Bryn Mawr 19010

Manor Junior College
700 Fox Chase Rd.
Jenkintown 19046

Mercer County Area Vocational Technical School
776 Greenville Rd.
Mercer 16137-0152

Pennsylvania College of Technology
One College Ave.
Williamsport 17701

Pennsylvania State University, Main Campus
201 Old Main
University Park 16802

Reading Area Community College
P.O. Box 1706
Reading 19603-1706

Sawyer School
717 Liberty Ave.
Pittsburgh 15222

Seton Hill College
Seton Hill Dr.
Greensburg 15601

RHODE ISLAND

Community College of Rhode Island
400 East Ave.
Warwick 02886-1807

SOUTH CAROLINA

York Technical College
452 South Anderson Rd.
Rock Hill 29730

SOUTH DAKOTA

Lake Area Technical Institute
230 11th St. NE
Watertown 57201

TENNESSEE

Shelby State Community College
P.O. Box 40568
Memphis 38174-0568

TEXAS

Career Academy, Inc.
32 Oak Lawn Village
Texarkana 75501

Career Centers of Texas El Paso, Inc.
8375 Burnham Dr.
El Paso 79907

Cisco Junior College
Rte. 3, Box 3
Cisco 76437

Eastfield College
3737 Motley Dr.
Mesquite 75150

El Paso Community College
P.O. Box 20500
El Paso 79998

Houston Community College System
22 Waugh Dr.
Houston 77270-7849

Howard County Junior College District
1001 Birdwell Ln.
Big Spring 79720

McLennan Community College
1400 College Dr.
Waco 76708

PCI Health Training Center
8101 John Carpenter Fwy.
Dallas 75247

San Antonio College of Medical and Dental Assistants, Central
4205 San Pedro Ave.
San Antonio 78229

Tarrant County Junior College
1500 Houston St.
Fort Worth 76102

UTAH

Bridgerland Applied Technology Center
1301 North 600 West
Logan 84321

VERMONT

Community College of Vermont
Box 120
Waterbury 05676

VIRGINIA

Blue Ridge Community College
P.O. Box 80
Weyers Cave 24486

Central Virginia Community College
3506 Wards Rd.
Lynchburg 24502

Danville Community College
1008 South Main St.
Danville 24541

Eastern Shore Community College
29300 Lankford Hwy.
Melfa 23410

Germanna Community College
2130 Germanna Hwy.
Locust Grove 22508

J Sargeant Reynolds Community College
P.O. Box 85622
Richmond 23285-5622

John Tyler Community College
13101 Jefferson Davis Hwy.
Chester 23831-5399

Lord Fairfax Community College
173 Skirmisher Ln.
Middletown 22645

Mountain Empire Community College
Drawer 700
Big Stone Gap 24219

New River Community College
Drawer 1127
Dublin 24084-1127

Northern Virginia Community College
4001 Wakefield Chapel Rd.
Annandale 22003

Patrick Henry Community College
P.O. Box 5311
Martinsville 24115-5311

Paul D Camp Community College
P.O. Box 737, 100 North College Dr.
Franklin 23851

Rappahannock Community College
12745 College Dr.
Glenns 23149

Southside Virginia Community College
109 Campus Dr.
Alberta 23821

Southwest Virginia Community College
Box SVCC
Richlands 24641

Thomas Nelson Community College
P.O. Box 9407
Hampton 23670

Tidewater Community College
121 College Pl.
Norfolk 23510

Virginia Highlands Community College
P.O. Box 828
Abingdon 24210-0828

Virginia Western Community College
3095 Colonial Ave.
Roanoke 24015

WASHINGTON

Edmonds Community College
20000 68th Ave. W
Lynnwood 98036

Lake Washington Technical College
11605 132nd Ave. NE
Kirkland 98034

Pierce College
9401 Farwest Dr. SW
Tacoma 98498

Spokane Falls Community College
West 3410 Fort George Wright Dr.
Spokane 99224

Tacoma Community College
5900 South 12th St.
Tacoma 98465

Yakima Valley Community College
P.O. Box 1647
Yakima 98907

WEST VIRGINIA

Opportunities Industrialization Center, North Central West Virginia
120 Jackson St.
Fairmont 26554

WISCONSIN

C Ross Educational Center
2821 North Fourth St.
Milwaukee 53212

Chippewa Valley Technical College
620 West Clairemont Ave.
Eau Claire 54701

Lac Courte Oreilles Ojibwa Community College
Rte. 2, Box 2357
Hayward 54843

Waukesha County Technical College
800 Main St.
Pewaukee 53072

Western Wisconsin Technical College
304 North Sixth St., P.O. Box 908
La Crosse 54602-0908

Wisconsin Indianhead Technical College
505 Pine Ridge Dr.
Shell Lake 54871

Radiologic Technology

ALABAMA

Community College of the Air Force
130 West Maxwell Blvd.
Montgomery 36112-6613

Gadsden State Community College
1001 George Wallace Dr.
Gadsden 35902-0227

George C Wallace State Community College, Hanceville
801 Main St. NW
Hanceville 35077-2000

Jefferson State Community College
2601 Carson Rd.
Birmingham 35215-3098

University of Alabama at Birmingham
Administration Bldg., Ste. 1070-2010
Birmingham 35294-0110

University of South Alabama
307 North University Blvd.
Mobile 36688-0002

ARIZONA

The Bryman School
4343 North 16th St.
Phoenix 85016

Gateway Community College
108 North 40th St.
Phoenix 85034

ARKANSAS

Arkansas Valley Technical Institute
P.O. Box 506, Hwy. 23 N
Ozark 72949

Carti School of Radiation Therapy Technology
P.O. Box 55050
Little Rock 72215

Sparks Regional Medical Center School of Radiography
1311 South I St.
Fort Smith 72917-7006

CALIFORNIA

American School of X-Ray
13723-1/2 Harvard Place
Gardena 90249

Butte College
3536 Butte Campus Dr.
Oroville 95965

Cabrillo College
6500 Soquel Dr.
Aptos 95003

Chaffey Community College
5885 Haven Ave.
Rancho Cucamonga 91737-3002

Charles R Drew University of Medicine and Science
1730 East 118th St.
Los Angeles 90059

Cypress College
9200 Valley View
Cypress 90630

Educorp Career College
230 East Third St.
Long Beach 90802

Foothill College
12345 El Monte Rd.
Los Altos Hills 94022

Fresno City College
1101 East University Ave.
Fresno 93741

Loma Linda University
Loma Linda 92350

Long Beach City College
4901 East Carson St.
Long Beach 90808

Merced College
3600 M St.
Merced 95348-2898

Modern Technology School of X-Ray
6180 Laurel Canyon Blvd., Ste. 101
North Hollywood 91606

Mount San Antonio College
1100 North Grand
Walnut 91789

Nova Institute of Health Technology
3000 South Robertson Blvd.
Los Angeles 90034

Nova Institute of Health Technology
12449 Putnam St.
Whittier 90602-1023

Orange Coast College
2701 Fairview Rd.
Costa Mesa 92626

San Diego Mesa College
7250 Mesa College Dr.
San Diego 92111-4998

San Joaquin General Hospital School of Radiation Technology
P.O. Box 1020
Stockton 95201

Santa Barbara City College
721 Cliff Dr.
Santa Barbara 93109-2394

Santa Rosa Junior College
1501 Mendocino Ave.
Santa Rosa 95401-4395

Yuba College
2088 North Beale Rd.
Marysville 95901

COLORADO

Community College of Denver
P.O. Box 173363
Denver 80217

CONNECTICUT

Gateway Community Technical College
60 Sargent Dr.
New Haven 06511

Saint Vincent's College
2800 Main St.
Bridgeport 06606

DELAWARE

Delaware Technical and Community College, Stanton, Wilmington
400 Stanton-Christiana Rd.
Newark 19702

DISTRICT OF COLUMBIA

George Washington University
2121 Eye St. NW
Washington 20052

FLORIDA

Hillsborough Community College
P.O. Box 31127
Tampa 33631-3127

National School of Technology, Inc.
4410 West 16th Ave., Ste. 52
Hialeah 33012

Pensacola Junior College
1000 College Blvd.
Pensacola 32504

Saint Petersburg Junior College
8580 66th St. N
Pinellas Park 34665

Santa Fe Community College
3000 Northwest 83rd St.
Gainesville 32606

GEORGIA

De Kalb Medical Center School of Radiologic Technology
2701 North Decatur Rd.
Decatur 30033

Grady Health System Professional Schools
80 Butler St.
Atlanta 30335-3801

Medical Center, Inc., School of Radiologic Technology
710 Center St., Hospital Drawer 85
Columbus 31994-2299

Medical College of Georgia
1120 15th St.
Augusta 30912

HAWAII

Kapiolani Community College
4303 Diamond Head Rd.
Honolulu 96816

ILLINOIS

Belleville Area College
2500 Carlyle Rd.
Belleville 62221

College of Du Page
425 22nd St.
Glen Ellyn 60137-6599

Cook County Hospital School of X-Ray Technology
1825 West Harrison St.
Chicago 60612

Kaskaskia College
27210 College Rd.
Centralia 62801

Methodist Medical Center of Illinois, School of Nursing
221 Northeast Glen Oak Ave.
Peoria 61636

Moraine Valley Community College
10900 South 88th Ave.
Palos Hills 60465-0937

Rockford Memorial Hospital School of X-Ray Technology
2400 North Rockton Ave.
Rockford 61103

Southern Illinois University, Carbondale
Faner Hall 2179
Carbondale 62901-4512

Swedish American Hospital School of Medical Technology
1400 Charles St.
Rockford 61104-2298

Triton College
2000 Fifth Ave.
River Grove 60171

INDIANA

Ball State University
2000 University Ave.
Muncie 47306

Fort Wayne School of Radiography
700 Broadway
Fort Wayne 46802

Indiana University, Purdue University, Indianapolis
355 North Lansing
Indianapolis 46202

IOWA

University of Iowa
Jessup Hall
Iowa City 52242

KANSAS

Fort Hays State University
600 Park St.
Hays 67601-4099

Labette Community College
200 South 14th
Parsons 67357

Washburn University of Topeka
1700 College Ave.
Topeka 66621

KENTUCKY

Kentucky Technical, Bowling Green Regional Technical Center
845 Loop Dr.
Bowling Green 42101-3601

Lexington Community College
Cooper Dr.
Lexington 40506

Morehead State University
University Blvd.
Morehead 40351

LOUISIANA

Delgado Community College
501 City Park Ave.
New Orleans 70119

MAINE

Southern Maine Technical College
Fort Rd.
South Portland 04106

MARYLAND

Essex Community College
7201 Rossville Blvd.
Baltimore 21237

Prince Georges Community College
301 Largo Rd.
Largo 20774-2199

MASSACHUSETTS

Bunker Hill Community College
250 New Rutherford Ave.
Boston 02129

Holyoke Community College
303 Homestead Ave.
Holyoke 01040

Massasoit Community College
One Massasoit Blvd.
Brockton 02402

Northeastern University
360 Huntington Ave.
Boston 02115

Springfield Technical Community College
One Armory Square
Springfield 01105

MICHIGAN

Carnegie Institute
550 Stephenson Hwy.
Troy 48083

Ferris State University
901 South State St.
Big Rapids 49307

Grand Rapids Community College
143 Bostwick Ave. NE
Grand Rapids 49503-3295

Lansing Community College
419 North Capitol Ave.
Lansing 48901-7210

William Beaumont Hospital
3601 West 13 Mile Rd.
Royal Oak 48073-6769

MINNESOTA

Mayo School of Health-Related Sciences
200 First St. SW
Rochester 55905

Northwest Technical College, East Grand Forks
Hwy. 220 N
East Grand Forks 56721

Rochester Community and Technical College
851 30th Ave. SE
Rochester 55904-4999

MISSISSIPPI

University of Mississippi Medical Center
2500 North State St.
Jackson 39216

MISSOURI

Research Medical Center School of Nuclear Medical Technology
2316 East Meyer Blvd.
Kansas City 64132

Saint Louis Community College, Forest Park
5600 Oakland Ave.
Saint Louis 63110

Saint Luke's College
4426 Wornall Rd.
Kansas City 64111

NEW HAMPSHIRE

New Hampshire Technical Institute
11 Institute Dr.
Concord 03301

NEW JERSEY

Bergen Community College
400 Paramus Rd.
Paramus 07652

Hudson Area School of Radiologic Technology
29 East 29th St.
Bayonne 07002

Middlesex County College
155 Mill Rd.
Edison 08818-3050

University of Medicine and Dentistry of New Jersey
30 Bergen St.
Newark 07107

NEW YORK

Bellevue Hospital Center School of Radiation Technology
First Ave. and 27th St., Rm. D510
New York 10016

Broome Community College
P.O. Box 1017
Binghamton 13902

CUNY New York City Technical College
300 Jay St.
Brooklyn 11201

Hudson Valley Community College
80 Vandenburgh Ave.
Troy 12180

Institute of Allied Medical Professions
405 Park Ave., St. 501
New York 10022

Monroe Community College
1000 East Henrietta Rd.
Rochester 14623

Nassau Community College
One Education Dr.
Garden City 11530

Saint Luke's Memorial Hospital Center
Champlin Rd., P.O. Box 479
Utica 13503-0479

SUNY Health Science Center at Syracuse
750 East Adams St.
Syracuse 13210

SUNY Westchester Commmunity College
75 Grasslands Rd.
Valhalla 10595

Trocaire College
360 Choate Ave.
Buffalo 14220

NORTH CAROLINA

Edgecombe Community College
2009 West Wilson St.
Tarboro 27886

Forsyth Technical Community College
2100 Silas Creek Pkwy.
Winston-Salem 27103

Pitt Community College
Hwy. 11 S, P.O. Drawer 7007
Greenville 27835-7007

Southwestern Community College
447 College Dr.
Sylva 28779

OHIO

Cuyahoga Community College District
700 Carnegie Ave.
Cleveland 44115-2878

Kent State University, Salem Regional Campus
2491 South Rte. 45 S
Salem 44460

Kettering College Medical Arts
3737 Southern Blvd.
Kettering 45429-1299

Lima Technical College
4240 Campus Dr.
Lima 45804

Lorain County Community College
1005 Abbe Rd. N
Elyria 44035

Owens Community College
30335 Oregon Rd.
Toledo 43699-1947

Sinclair Community College
444 West Third St.
Dayton 45402

Tri-Rivers Career Center
2222 Marion Mount Gilead Rd.
Marion 43302

University of Cincinnati, Raymond Walters College
9555 Plainfield Rd.
Blue Ash 45236

OREGON

Concorde Career Institute
1827 Northeast 44th Ave.
Portland 97213

Oregon Health Science University
3181 Southwest Sam Jackson Park Rd.
Portland 97201

Portland Community College
P.O. Box 19000
Portland 97280-0990

PENNSYLVANIA

Community College of Allegheny County, Pittsburgh
800 Allegheny Ave.
Pittsburgh 15233-1895

Crozer-Chester Medical Center, Allied Health Program
One Medical Center Blvd.
Upland 19013

Gannon University
109 West Sixth St.
Erie 16541

Harrisburg Area Community College, Harrisburg
One Hacc Dr.
Harrisburg 17110

Northampton County Area Community College
3835 Green Pond Rd.
Bethlehem 18020-7599

North Hills School of Health Occupations
1500 Northway Mall
Pittsburgh 15237

Ohio Valley Hospital School of Nursing
25 Heckel Rd.
McKees Rocks 15136

RHODE ISLAND

Community College of Rhode Island
400 East Ave.
Warwick 02886-1807

Rhode Island Hospital School of Nuclear Medicine
593 Eddy St.
Providence 02903

Rhode Island Hospital School of Radiologic Technology
593 Eddy St.
Providence 02903

SOUTH CAROLINA

Greenville Technical College
P.O. Box 5616, Station B
Greenville 29606-5616

Horry-Georgetown Technical College
P.O. Box 1966
Conway 29526

Trident Technical College
P.O. Box 118067
Charleston 29423-8067

TENNESSEE

Chattanooga State Technical Community College
4501 Amnicola Hwy.
Chattanooga 37406

East Tennessee State University
P.O. Box 70734
Johnson City 37614-0734

Roane State Community College
276 Patton Ln.
Harriman 37748

Shelby State Community College
P.O. Box 40568
Memphis 38174-0568

TEXAS

Amarillo College
P.O. Box 447
Amarillo 79178

Austin Community College
5930 Middle Fiskville Rd.
Austin 78752

El Centro College
Main and Lamar
Dallas 75202

El Paso Community College
P.O. Box 20500
El Paso 79998

Galveston College
4015 Ave. Q
Galveston 77550

Houston Community College System
22 Waugh Dr.
Houston 77270-7849

Lamar University, Beaumont
P.O. Box 10001, 4400 Mlk
Beaumont 77710

McLennan Community College
1400 College Dr.
Waco 76708

Midwestern State University
3410 Taft Blvd.
Wichita Falls 76308-2099

Saint Philip's College
1801 Martin Luther King Dr.
San Antonio 78203

San Jacinto College, Central Campus
8060 Spencer Hwy.
Pasadena 77505

Ultrasound Diagnostic School
1333 Corporate Dr., Ste. 200
Irving 75038

UTAH

Utah Valley Hospital School of Radiogic Technology
1034 North Fifth West St.
Provo 84603

VIRGINIA

Tidewater Community College
121 College Pl.
Norfolk 23510

WASHINGTON

Bellevue Community College
3000 Landerholm Circle SE
Bellevue 98007-6484

Tacoma Community College
5900 South 12th St.
Tacoma 98465

Yakima Valley Community College
P.O. Box 1647
Yakima 98907

WEST VIRGINIA

West Virginia University Hospital School of Radiation Technology
Medical Center Dr., P.O. Box 8062
Morgantown 26506-8062

WISCONSIN

Mercy Medical Center School of Radiologic Technology
631 Hazel St.
Oshkosh 54902

Milwaukee Area Technical College
700 West State St.
Milwaukee 53233-1443

Saint Joseph's Hospital Histologic Technician Program
611 Saint Joseph's Ave.
Marshfield 54449

Saint Luke's Medical Center, School of Diagnostic Medical Sonography
2900 West Oklahoma Ave.
Milwaukee 53215

Registered Nursing

ALABAMA

Bishop State Community College
351 North Broad St.
Mobile 36608

Gadsden State Community College
1001 George Wallace Dr.
Gadsden 35902-0227

George C Wallace State Community College, Selma
3000 Earl Goodwin Pkwy.
Selma 36702

George C Wallace State Community College, Dothan
Rte. 6, Box 62
Dothan 36303-9234

George C Wallace State Community College, Hanceville
801 Main St. NW
Hanceville 35077-2000

Jefferson Davis Community College
220 Alco Dr.
Brewton 36426

Jefferson State Community College
2601 Carson Rd.
Birmingham 35215-3098

John C Calhoun State Community College
Hwy. 31 N
Decatur 35602

Northeast Alabama State Community College
Hwy. 35 W
Rainsville 35986

Samford University
800 Lakeshore Dr., Ste. 2240
Birmingham 35229-2240

Shelton State Community College
9500 Old Greensboro Rd.
Tuscaloosa 35405

Southern Union State Community College
P.O. Box 1000
Wadley 36276

Troy State University, Main Campus
University Ave.
Troy 36082

University of Alabama at Birmingham, Walker College
1411 Indiana Ave.
Jasper 35501

University of West Alabama
Station One
Livingston 35470

University of Mobile
P.O. Box 13220
Mobile 36663-0220

ALASKA

University of Alaska, Anchorage
3211 Providence Dr.
Anchorage 99508

ARIZONA

Arizona Western College
P.O. Box 929
Yuma 85366

Central Arizona College
8470 North Overfield Rd.
Coolidge 85228-9778

Cochise College
4190 West Hwy. 80
Douglas 85607-9724

Gateway Community College
108 North 40th St.
Phoenix 85034

Glendale Community College
6000 West Olive Ave.
Glendale 85302

Mesa Community College
1833 West Southern Ave.
Mesa 85202

Mohave Community College
1971 Jagerson Ave.
Kingman 86401

Phoenix College
1202 West Thomas Rd.
Phoenix 85013

Pima Community College
2202 West Anklam Rd.
Tucson 85709-0001

Scottsdale Community College
9000 East Chaparral Rd.
Scottsdale 85253

Yavapai College
1100 East Sheldon St.
Prescott 86301

ARKANSAS

Arkansas State University, Main Campus
P.O. Box 790
State University 72467

Arkansas Valley Technical Institute
P.O. Box 506, Hwy. 23 N
Ozark 72949

Baptist Schools of Nursing and Allied Health
11900 College Glenn Rd., Ste. 1000
Little Rock 72210-2820

East Arkansas Community College
1700 Newcastle Rd.
Forrest City 72335

Garland County Community College
100 College Dr.
Hot Springs 71913

Jefferson School of Nursing
1515 West 42nd Ave.
Pine Bluff 71603

Mississippi County Community College
P.O. Box 1109
Blytheville 72316-1109

North Arkansas College
1515 Pioneer Dr.
Harrison 72601

Phillips Community College of the University of Arkansas
Box 785
Helena 72342

Southern Arkansas University, Main Campus
SAU Box 1288
Magnolia 71753

University of Arkansas at Fayetteville
Administration Bldg. 422
Fayetteville 72701

University of Arkansas at Little Rock
2801 South University Ave.
Little Rock 72204

University of Arkansas at Monticello
P.O. Box 3598
Monticello 71656

Westark College
P.O. Box 3649
Fort Smith 72913

CALIFORNIA

Allan Hancock College
800 South College Dr.
Santa Maria 93454

American River College
4700 College Oak Dr.
Sacramento 95841

Antelope Valley College
3041 West Ave. K
Lancaster 93536

Bakersfield College
1801 Panorama Dr.
Bakersfield 93305-1299

Cabrillo College
6500 Soquel Dr.
Aptos 95003

Cerritos College
11110 Alondra Blvd.
Norwalk 90650

Chabot College
25555 Hesperian Blvd.
Hayward 94545

Chaffey Community College
5885 Haven Ave.
Rancho Cucamonga 91737-3002

City College of San Francisco
50 Phelan Ave.
San Francisco 94112

College of Marin
835 College Ave.
Kentfield 94904

College of San Mateo
1700 West Hillsdale Blvd.
San Mateo 94402

College of the Canyons
26455 Rockwell Canyon Rd.
Santa Clarita 91355

College of the Desert
43-500 Monterey St.
Palm Desert 92260

College of the Redwoods
7351 Tompkins Hill Rd.
Eureka 95501-9302

College of the Sequoias
915 South Mooney Blvd.
Visalia 93277

Compton Community College
1111 East Artesia Blvd.
Compton 90221

Contra Costa College
2600 Mission Bell Dr.
San Pablo 94806

Crafton Hills College
11711 Sand Canyon Rd.
Yucaipa 92399-1799

Cuesta College
P.O. Box 8106
San Luis Obispo 93403-8106

De Anza College
21250 Stevens Creek Blvd.
Cupertino 95014

El Camino College
16007 Crenshaw Blvd.
Torrance 90506

Fresno City College
1101 East University Ave.
Fresno 93741

Gavilan College
5055 Santa Teresa Blvd.
Gilroy 95020

Glendale Community College
1500 North Verdugo Rd.
Glendale 91208-2894

Golden West College
15744 Golden West
Huntington Beach 92647

Grossmont College
8800 Grossmont College Dr.
El Cajon 92020

Hartnell College
156 Homestead Ave.
Salinas 93901

Imperial Valley College
P.O. Box 158
Imperial 92251-0158

Loma Linda University
Loma Linda 92350

Long Beach City College
4901 East Carson St.
Long Beach 90808

Los Angeles County Medical Center School of Nursing
Muir Hall, Rm. 114
Los Angeles 90033-1084

Los Angeles Harbor College
1111 Figueroa Place
Wilmington 90744

Los Angeles Pierce College
6201 Winnetka Ave.
Woodland Hills 91371

Los Angeles Trade Technical College
400 West Washington Blvd.
Los Angeles 90015-4181

Los Angeles Valley College
5800 Fulton Ave.
Van Nuys 91401

Los Medanos College
2700 East Leland Rd.
Pittsburg 94565

Maric College of Medical Careers
3666 Kearny Villa Rd., Ste. 100
San Diego 92123

Merced College
3600 M St.
Merced 95348-2898

Merritt College
12500 Campus Dr.
Oakland 94619

Mira Costa College
One Barnard Dr.
Oceanside 92056-3899

Modesto Junior College
435 College Ave.
Modesto 95350-5800

Monterey Peninsula College
980 Fremont Blvd.
Monterey 93940-4799

Moorpark College
7075 Campus Rd.
Moorpark 93021

Mount Saint Mary's College
12001 Chalon Rd.
Los Angeles 90049

Mount San Antonio College
1100 North Grand
Walnut 91789

Napa Valley College
2277 Napa Vallejo Hwy.
Napa 94558

Ohlone College
43600 Mission Blvd.
Fremont 94539

Pacific Union College
One Angwin Ave.
Angwin 94508-9707

Palomar College
1140 West Mission
San Marcos 92069-1487

Pasadena City College
1570 East Colorado Blvd.
Pasadena 91106

Rancho Santiago College District
1530 West 17th St.
Santa Ana 92706

Rio Hondo College
3600 Workman Mill Rd.
Whittier 90601-1699

Riverside Community College
4800 Magnolia Ave.
Riverside 92506-1299

Sacramento City College
3835 Freeport Blvd.
Sacramento 95822

San Diego City College
1313 12th Ave.
San Diego 92101

San Joaquin Delta College
5151 Pacific Ave.
Stockton 95207

Santa Barbara City College
721 Cliff Dr.
Santa Barbara 93109-2394

Santa Monica College
1900 Pico Blvd.
Santa Monica 90405-1628

Santa Rosa Junior College
1501 Mendocino Ave.
Santa Rosa 95401-4395

Shasta College
P.O. Box 496006
Redding 96049

Sierra College
5000 Rocklin Rd.
Rocklin 95677

Solano County Community College District
4000 Suisun Valley Rd.
Suisun 94585-3197

Southwestern College
900 Otay Lakes Rd.
Chula Vista 92010

Ventura College
4667 Telegraph Rd.
Ventura 93003

Victor Valley College
18422 Bear Valley Rd.
Victorville 92392-9699

Yuba College
2088 North Beale Rd.
Marysville 95901

COLORADO

Arapahoe Community College
2500 West College Dr.
Littleton 80160-9002

Community College of Denver
P.O. Box 173363
Denver 80217

Front Range Community College
3645 West 112th Ave.
Westminster 80030

Mesa State College
P.O. Box 2647
Grand Junction 81502

Otero Junior College
1802 Colorado Ave.
La Junta 81050

Pikes Peak Community College
5675 South Academy Blvd.
Colorado Springs 80906-5498

Pueblo College of Business & Technology
330 Lake Ave.
Pueblo 81004

Pueblo Community College
900 West Orman Ave.
Pueblo 81004

Red Rocks Community College
13300 West Sixth Ave.
Lakewood 80228

Trinidad State Junior College
600 Prospect St.
Trinidad 81082

CONNECTICUT

Bridgeport Hospital School of Nursing
200 Mill Hill Ave.
Bridgeport 06610

Greater Hartford Community College
61 Woodland St.
Hartford 06105-2354

Mattatuck Community College
750 Chase Pkwy.
Waterbury 06708

Mohegan Community College
Mahan Dr., P.O. Box 629
Norwich 06360

Norwalk Community Technical College
188 Richards Ave.
Norwalk 06854

Quinnipiac College
Mount Carmel Ave.
Hamden 06518

St. Vincent's College
2800 Main St.
Bridgeport 06606

Wilcox College of Nursing
28 Crescent St.
Middletown 06457

DELAWARE

Delaware Technical and Community College, Owens
Box 610
Georgetown 19947

Delaware Technical and Community College, Stanton, Wilmington
400 Stanton-Christiana Rd.
Newark 19702

FLORIDA

Brevard Community College, Cocoa Campus
1519 Clearlake Rd.
Cocoa 32922

Broward Community College
225 East Las Olas Blvd.
Fort Lauderdale 33301

Central Florida Community College
3001 Southwest College Rd.
Ocala 34474

Daytona Beach Community College
1200 Volusia Ave.
Daytona Beach 32114

Edison Community College
8099 College Pkwy. SW
Fort Myers 33906-6210

Florida Community College at Jacksonville
501 West State St.
Jacksonville 32202

Florida Keys Community College
5901 West College Rd.
Key West 33040

Gulf Coast Community College
5230 West Hwy. 98
Panama City 32401

Hillsborough Community College
P.O. Box 31127
Tampa 33631-3127

Indian River Community College
3209 Virginia Ave.
Fort Pierce 34981

Lake City Community College
Rte. 19, Box 1030
Lake City 32025

Lake County Area Vocational-Technical Center
2001 Kurt St.
Eustis 32726

Lake-Sumter Community College
9501 U.S. Hwy. 441
Leesburg 34788-8751

Manatee Community College
5840 26th St. W
Bradenton 34207

Miami-Dade Community College
300 Northeast Second Ave.
Miami 33132

North Florida Community College
Turner Davis Dr.
Madison 32340

North Technical Education Center
7071 Garden Rd.
Riviera Beach 33404

Palm Beach Community College
4200 Congress Ave.
Lake Worth 33461

Pasco-Hernando Community College
36727 Blanton Rd.
Dade City 33525-7599

Pensacola Junior College
1000 College Blvd.
Pensacola 32504

Pinellas Technical Education Center
901 34th St. S
Saint Petersburg 33711

Polk Community College
999 Ave. H NE
Winter Haven 33881

Saint Petersburg Junior College
8580 66th St. N
Pinellas Park 34665

Santa Fe Community College
3000 Northwest 83rd St.
Gainesville 32606

Seminole Community College
100 Weldon Blvd.
Sanford 32773-6199

Tallahassee Community College
444 Appleyard Dr.
Tallahassee 32304-2895

Valencia Community College
P.O. Box 3028
Orlando 32802

GEORGIA

Abraham Baldwin Agricultural College
ABAC 9, 2802 Moore Hwy.
Tifton 31794-2601

Armstrong Atlantic State College
11935 Abercorn St.
Savannah 31419

Augusta State University
2500 Walton Way
Augusta 30904-2200

Clayton College and State University
5900 North Lee St.
Morrow 30260

Columbus State University
4225 University Ave.
Columbus 31907-5645

Dalton College
213 North College Dr.
Dalton 30720

Darton College
2400 Gillionville Rd.
Albany 31707

Dekalb College
3251 Panthersville Rd.
Decatur 30034

Floyd College
P.O. Box 1864
Rome 30162-1864

Georgia Southwestern State University
800 Wheatley St.
Americus 31709-4693

Gordon College
419 College Dr.
Barnesville 30204

Kennesaw State University
1000 Chastain Rd.
Marietta 30061

Lagrange College
601 Broad St.
La Grange 30240

Macon State College
100 College Station Dr.
Macon 31206

Middle Georgia College
1100 Second St. SE
Cochran 31014-1599

North Georgia College and State University
College Ave.
Dahlonega 30597

South Georgia College
100 West College Park Dr.
Douglas 31533

HAWAII

Hawaii Community College
200 West Kawili St.
Hilo 96720-4091

Kapiolani Community College
4303 Diamond Head Rd.
Honolulu 96816

Maui Community College
310 Kaahumanu Ave.
Kahului 96732

University of Hawaii at Manoa
2444 Dole St.
Honolulu 96822

IDAHO

Boise State University
1910 University Dr.
Boise 83725

College of Southern Idaho
P.O. Box 1238
Twin Falls 83301

Lewis-Clark State College
500 Eighth Ave.
Lewiston 83501

North Idaho College
1000 West Garden Ave.
Coeur D'Alene 83814

Ricks College
Rexburg 83460-4107

ILLINOIS

Belleville Area College
2500 Carlyle Rd.
Belleville 62221

Black Hawk College
6600 34th Ave.
Moline 61265

Carl Sandburg College
2232 South Lake Storey Rd.
Galesburg 61401

City Colleges of Chicago, Olive-Harvey College
10001 South Woodlawn Ave.
Chicago 60628

City Colleges of Chicago, Kennedy-King College
6800 South Wentworth Ave.
Chicago 60621

City Colleges of Chicago, Richard J Daley College
7500 South Pulaski Rd.
Chicago 60652

City Colleges of Chicago, Harry S Truman College
1145 Wilson Ave.
Chicago 60640

City Colleges of Chicago, Malcolm X College
1900 West Van Buren
Chicago 60612

College of Du Page
425 22nd St.
Glen Ellyn 60137-6599

College of Lake County
19351 West Washington St.
Grays Lake 60030-1198

Elgin Community College
1700 Spartan Dr.
Elgin 60123

Highland Community College
2998 West Pearl City Rd.
Freeport 61032-9341

Illinois Central College
One College Dr.
East Peoria 61635-0001

Illinois Eastern Community Colleges, Olney Central College
305 North West St.
Olney 62450

Illinois Valley Community College
815 North Orlando Smith Ave.
Oglesby 61348-9692

John A Logan College
700 Logan College Rd.
Carterville 62918

Joliet Junior College
1216 Houbolt Ave.
Joliet 60431

Kankakee Community College
P.O. Box 888
Kankakee 60901

Kaskaskia College
27210 College Rd.
Centralia 62801

Kishwaukee College
21193 Malta Rd.
Malta 60150

Lake Land College
5001 Lake Land Blvd.
Mattoon 61938

Lewis and Clark Community College
5800 Godfrey Rd.
Godfrey 62035

Lincoln Land Community College
Shepherd Rd.
Springfield 62194-9256

Methodist Medical Center of Illinois School of Nursing
221 Northeast Glen Oak Ave.
Peoria 61636

Moraine Valley Community College
10900 South 88th Ave.
Palos Hills 60465-0937

Morton College
3801 South Central Ave.
Cicero 60804

Oakton Community College
1600 East Golf Rd.
Des Plaines 60016

Parkland College
2400 West Bradley Ave.
Champaign 61821

Prairie State College
202 Halsted St.
Chicago Heights 60411

Ravenswood Hospital Medical Center School of Radiologic Technology
4550 North Winchester Ave.
Chicago 60640-5205

Rend Lake College
468 North Ken Graz Pkwy.
Ina 62846

Rock Valley College
3301 North Mulford Rd.
Rockford 61114

Saint Francis Hospital School of Nursing
319 Ridge Ave.
Evanston 60202

Shawnee Community College
8364 Shawnee College Rd.
Ullin 62992

Southeastern Illinois College
3575 College Rd.
Harrisburg 62946

South Suburban College
15800 South State St.
South Holland 60473

Trinity School of Surgical Technology
501 Tenth Ave.
Moline 61265

Triton College
2000 Fifth Ave.
River Grove 60171

Waubonsee Community College
IL Rte. 47 at Harter Rd.
Sugar Grove 60554-0901

William Rainey Harper College
1200 West Algonquin Rd.
Palatine 60067-7398

INDIANA

Ball State University
2000 University Ave.
Muncie 47306

Bethel College
1001 West McKinley Ave.
Mishawaka 46545

Indiana State University
210 North Seventh St.
Terre Haute 47809

Indiana University, East
2325 Chester Blvd.
Richmond 47374

Indiana University, Kokomo
2300 South Washington
Kokomo 46902

Indiana University, Northwest
3400 Broadway
Gary 46408

Indiana University, Purdue University, Fort Wayne
2101 Coliseum Blvd. E
Fort Wayne 46805

Indiana University, Purdue University, Indianapolis
355 North Lansing
Indianapolis 46202

Indiana University, South Bend
1700 Mishawaka Ave.
South Bend 46615

Ivy Tech State College, North Central
1534 West Sample St.
South Bend 46619

Ivy Tech State College, Southeast
590 Ivy Tech Dr.
Madison 47250

Ivy Tech State College, Southwest
3501 First Ave.
Evansville 47710

Ivy Tech State College, Whitewater
P.O. Box 1145
Richmond 47374

Lutheran College of Health Professions
3024 Fairfield Ave.
Fort Wayne 46807

Marian College
3200 Cold Spring Rd.
Indianapolis 46222-1997

Purdue University, Calumet Campus
2233 171st St.
Hammond 46323

Purdue University, North Central Campus
1401 South U.S. Hwy. 421
Westville 46391

Saint Elizabeth School of Nursing
1508 Tippecanoe St.
Lafayette 47904-2198

University of Indianapolis
1400 East Hanna Ave.
Indianapolis 46227

University of Southern Indiana
8600 University Blvd.
Evansville 47712

Vincennes University
1002 North First St.
Vincennes 47591

IOWA

Allen Memorial Hospital, School of Nursing
1825 Logan Ave.
Waterloo 50703

Des Moines Community College
2006 Ankeny Blvd.
Ankeny 50021

Eastern Iowa Community College District
306 West River Dr.
Davenport 52801-1221

Hawkeye Community College
1501 East Orange Rd.
Waterloo 50704

Indian Hills Community College
525 Grandview
Ottumwa 52501

Iowa Central Community College
330 Ave. M
Fort Dodge 50501

Iowa Lakes Community College
19 South Seventh St.
Estherville 51334

Iowa Methodist School of Nursing
1117 Pleasant St.
Des Moines 50309

Iowa Valley Community College District
Box 536
Marshalltown 50158

Iowa Western Community College
2700 College Rd., Box 4C
Council Bluffs 51502

Jennie Edmundson Memorial Hospital School of Nursing
933 East Pierce St., P.O. Box 2C
Council Bluffs 51502

Kirkwood Community College
P.O. Box 2068
Cedar Rapids 52406

Mercy College of Health Sciences
928 6th Ave.
Des Moines 50309

Northeast Iowa Community College, Calmar
Box 400, Hwy. 150 S
Calmar 52132-0400

North Iowa Area Community College
500 College Dr.
Mason City 50401

Saint Luke's College of Nursing and Health Sciences
2720 Stone Park Blvd.
Sioux City 51104-0263

Southeastern Community College
Drawer F, 1015 South Gear Ave.
West Burlington 52655-0605

Southwestern Community College
1501 Townline
Creston 50801

Western Iowa Technical Community College
4647 Stone Ave., P.O. Box 5199
Sioux City 51102-5199

KANSAS

Baker University College of Arts and Sciences
8th and Grove
Baldwin City 66006

Barton County Community College
245 Northeast 30th Rd.
Great Bend 67530

Butler County Community College
901 South Haverhill Rd.
El Dorado 67042

Cloud County Community College
2221 Campus Dr., Box 1002
Concordia 66901-1002

Colby Community College
1255 South Range
Colby 67701

Dodge City Community College
2501 North 14th Ave.
Dodge City 67801

Fort Scott Community College
2108 South Horton
Fort Scott 66701

Garden City Community College
801 Campus Dr.
Garden City 67846

Hesston College
Box 3000
Hesston 67062

Hutchinson Community College
1300 North Plum St.
Hutchinson 67501

Johnson County Community College
12345 College Blvd.
Overland Park 66210-1299

Kansas City Area Vocational Technical School
2220 North 59th St.
Kansas City 66104

Kansas City Kansas Community College
7250 State Ave.
Kansas City 66112

Kansas Newman College
3100 McCormick Ave.
Wichita 67213-2097

Kansas Wesleyan University
100 East Claflin
Salina 67401-6196

Labette Community College
200 South 14th
Parsons 67357

Neosho County Community College
800 West 14th St.
Chanute 66720

Seward County Community College
Box 1137
Liberal 67905-1137

KENTUCKY

Ashland Community College
1400 College Dr.
Ashland 41101

Eastern Kentucky University
Lancaster Ave.
Richmond 40475

Elizabethtown Community College
College Street Rd.
Elizabethtown 42701

Hazard Community College
Hazard 41701

Henderson Community College
2660 South Green St.
Henderson 42420

Hopkinsville Community College
North Dr.
Hopkinsville 42240

Jefferson Community College
109 East Broadway
Louisville 40202

Kentucky State University
East Main St.
Frankfort 40601

Kentucky Wesleyan College
3000 Frederica St.
Owensboro 42302-1039

Lexington Community College
Cooper Dr.
Lexington 40506

Madisonville Community College
University Dr.
Madisonville 42431

Maysville Community College
Maysville 41056

Midway College
512 Stephens St.
Midway 40347-1120

Morehead State University
University Blvd.
Morehead 40351

Northern Kentucky University
University Dr.
Highland Heights 41099

Paducah Community College
P.O. Box 7380
Paducah 42002-7380

Prestonsburg Community College
Bert Combs Dr.
Prestonsburg 41653

Somerset Community College
808 Monticello Rd.
Somerset 42501

Southeast Community College
300 College Rd.
Cumberland 40823

Western Kentucky University
One Big Red Way
Bowling Green 42101-3576

LOUISIANA

Baton Rouge General Medical Center School of Nursing
3616 North Blvd.
Baton Rouge 70806

Huey P Long Technical Institute
303 South Jones St.
Winnfield 71483

Louisiana State University, Alexandria
8100 Hwy. 71 S
Alexandria 71302-9121

Louisiana State University, Eunice
P.O. Box 1129
Eunice 70535

Louisiana State University Medical Center
433 Bolivar St.
New Orleans 70112

Louisiana Technical University
P.O. Box 3168, Tech Station
Ruston 71272

Nicholls State University
University Station, LA Hwy. 1
Thibodaux 70310

Northwestern State University of Louisiana
College Ave.
Natchitoches 71497

Our Lady of the Lake College
5345 Brittany Dr.
Baton Rouge 70808

MAINE

Central Maine Medical Center School of Nursing
300 Main St.
Lewiston 04240

Kennebec Valley Technical College
92 Western Ave.
Fairfield 04937-1367

Northern Maine Technical College
33 Edgemont Dr.
Presque Isle 04769

Southern Maine Technical College
Fort Rd.
South Portland 04106

University of Maine at Augusta
46 University Dr.
Augusta 04330-9410

MARYLAND

Allegany College of Maryland
12401 Willowbrook Rd. SE
Cumberland 21502

Anne Arundel Community College
101 College Pkwy.
Arnold 21012

Baltimore City Community College
2901 Liberty Heights Ave.
Baltimore 21215

Catonsville Community College
800 South Rolling Rd.
Catonsville 21228

Cecil Community College
1000 North East Rd.
North East 21901-1999

Charles County Community College
8730 Mitchell Rd.
La Plata 20646-0910

Essex Community College
7201 Rossville Blvd.
Baltimore 21237

Frederick Community College
7932 Opossumtown Pike
Frederick 21702

Hagerstown Junior College
11400 Robinwood Dr.
Hagerstown 21742-6590

Harford Community College
401 Thomas Run Rd.
Bel Air 21015

Howard Community College
10901 Little Patuxent Pkwy.
Columbia 21044

Montgomery College of Takoma Park
Takoma Ave. and Fenton St.
Takoma Park 20912

Prince Georges Community College
301 Largo Rd.
Largo 23774-2199

Wor-Wic Community College
32000 Campus Dr.
Salisbury 21801-7131

MASSACHUSETTS

Atlantic Union College
338 Main St.
South Lancaster 01561

Bay State Medical Center School of Nursing
759 Chestnut St.
Springfield 01199

Berkshire Community College
1350 West St.
Pittsfield 01201-5786

Bristol Community College
777 Elsbree St.
Fall River 02720

Bunker Hill Community College
250 New Rutherford Ave.
Boston 02129

Cape Cod Community College
2240 Iyanough Rd.
West Barnstable 02668-1599

Fisher College
118 Beacon St.
Boston 02116

Framingham Union School of Nursing, Merrowest Medical Center
85 Lincoln St.
Framingham 01702

Greenfield Community College
One College Dr.
Greenfield 01301-9739

Holyoke Community College
303 Homestead Ave.
Holyoke 01040

Laboure College
2120 Dorchester Ave.
Boston 02124-5698

Massachusetts Bay Community College
50 Oakland St.
Wellesley Hills 02181

Massasoit Community College
One Massasoit Blvd.
Brockton 02402

Middlesex Community College
Springs Rd.
Bedford 01730

Mount Wachusett Community College
444 Green St.
Gardner 01440

Northern Essex Community College
Elliott Way
Haverhill 01830-2399

North Shore Community College
One Ferncroft Rd.
Danvers 01923

Quincy College
34 Coddington St.
Quincy 02169

Quinsigamond Community College
670 West Boylston St.
Worcester 01606

Saint Elizabeth's Hospital School of Nursing
159 Washington St.
Brighton 02135

Somerville Hospital School of Nursing
125 Lowell St.
Somerville 02143

Springfield Technical Community College
One Armory Square
Springfield 01105

MICHIGAN

Alpena Community College
666 Johnson St.
Alpena 49707

Bay De Noc Community College
2001 North Lincoln Rd.
Escanaba 49289

Bronson Methodist Hospital
252 East Lovell St.
Kalamazoo 49007

Delta College
University Ctr.
University Center 48710

Ferris State University
901 South State St.
Big Rapids 49307

Grand Rapids Community College
143 Bostwick Ave. NE
Grand Rapids 49503-3295

Great Lakes Junior College of Business, Saginaw
310 South Washington Ave.
Saginaw 48607

Henry Ford Community College
5101 Evergreen Rd.
Dearborn 48128

Henry Ford Hospital School of Radiologic Technology
2799 West Grand Blvd.
Detroit 48202

Jackson Community College
2111 Emmons Rd.
Jackson 49201-8399

Kalamazoo Valley Community College
6767 West O Ave.
Kalamazoo 49009

Kellogg Community College
450 North Ave.
Battle Creek 49017

Kirtland Community College
10775 North Saint Helen Rd.
Roscommon 48653

Lake Michigan College
2755 East Napier Ave.
Benton Harbor 49022-8099

Lansing Community College
419 North Capitol Ave.
Lansing 48901-7210

Macomb Community College
14500 Twelve Mile Rd.
Warren 48093-3896

Mid Michigan Community College
1375 South Clare Ave.
Harrison 48625

Monroe County Community College
1555 South Raisinville Rd.
Monroe 48161

Montcalm Community College
2800 College Dr.
Sidney 48885

Mott Community College
1401 East Court St.
Flint 48503

Muskegon Community College
221 South Quarterline Rd.
Muskegon 49442

North Central Michigan College
1515 Howard St.
Petoskey 49770

Northwestern Michigan College
1701 East Front St.
Traverse City 49686

Oakland Community College
2480 Opdyke Rd.
Bloomfield Hills 48304-2266

Saint Clair County Community College
P.O. Box 5015, 323 Erie
Port Huron 48061-5015

Schoolcraft College
18600 Haggerty Rd.
Livonia 48152

Southwestern Michigan College
58900 Cherry Grove Rd.
Dowagiac 49047-9793

Suomi College
601 Quincy St.
Hancock 49930

University of Detroit, Mercy
P.O. Box 19900
Detroit 48219-0900

Washtenaw Community College
P.O. Drawer 1
Ann Arbor 48016-1610

Wayne County Community College
801 West Fort St.
Detroit 48226

West Shore Community College
3000 North Stiles Rd.
Scottville 49454

MINNESOTA

Anoka-Ramsey Community College
11200 Mississippi Blvd.
Coon Rapids 55433-3470

Central Lakes College, Brainerd
501 West College Dr.
Brainerd 56401

Century Community and Technical College
3300 Century Ave. N
White Bear Lake 55110

College of Saint Catherine, Minneapolis
601 25th Ave. S
Minneapolis 55454

Hibbing Community College, A Technical and Community College
1515 East 25th St.
Hibbing 55746

Inver Hills Community College
2500 80th St. E
Inver Grove Heights 55076

Minneapolis Community and Technical College
1501 Hennepin Ave.
Minneapolis 55403

Normandale Community College
9700 France Ave. S
Bloomington 55431

North Hennepin Community College
7411 85th Ave. N
Brooklyn Park 55445

Northland Community and Technical College
Hwy. 1 E
Thief River Falls 56701

Ridgewater College, A Community and Technical College, Willmar
P.O. Box 1097
Willmar 56201

Riverland Community College
1900 Eighth Ave. NW
Austin 55912

Rochester Community and Technical College
851 30th Ave. SE
Rochester 55904-4999

MISSISSIPPI

Alcorn State University
P.O. Box 359
Lorman 39096

Hinds Community College, Raymond Campus
Raymond 39154

Holmes Community College
Hill St.
Goodman 39079

Itawamba Community College
602 West Hill St.
Fulton 38843

Jones County Junior College
900 South Court St.
Ellisville 39437

Meridian Community College
910 Hwy. 19 N
Meridian 39307

Mississippi Delta Community College
P.O. Box 668
Moorhead 38761

Mississippi Gulf Coast Community College
Central Office, P.O. Box 67
Perkinston 39573

Mississippi University for Women
P.O. Box W1600
Columbus 39701

Northeast Mississippi Community College
Cunningham Blvd.
Booneville 38829

Northwest Mississippi Community College
510 North Panola, Hwy. 51 N
Senatobia 38668

Pearl River Community College
Station A
Poplarville 39470

Southwest Mississippi Community College
College Dr.
Summit 39666

MISSOURI

Barnes Jewish School of Radiologic Technology
One Barnes Hospital Plaza
Saint Louis 63110

Central Methodist College
411 Central Methodist Square
Fayette 65248

East Central College
P.O. Box 529
Union 63084

Hannibal-Lagrange College
2800 Palmyra Rd.
Hannibal 63401

Jefferson College
1000 Viking Dr.
Hillsboro 63050

Lincoln University
820 Chestnut
Jefferson City 65102-0029

Lutheran Medical Center School of Nursing
3547 South Jefferson Ave.
Saint Louis 63118

Mineral Area College
P.O. Box 1000
Park Hills 63601-1000

Missouri Baptist Medical Center School of Nursing
3015 North Ballas Rd.
Saint Louis 63131

Missouri Southern State College
3950 East Newman Rd.
Joplin 64801-1595

Moberly Area Community Co llege
101 College Ave.
Moberly 65270

North Central Missouri College
1301 Main St.
Trenton 64683

Park College
8700 River Park Dr.
Parkville 64152-3795

Penn Valley Community College
3201 Southwest Trafficway
Kansas City 64111

Saint Charles County Community College
4601 Mid Rivers Mall Dr.
Saint Peter's 63376

Saint John's School of Nursing
4431 South Fremont
Springfield 65804-2263

Saint Louis Community College, Forest Park
5600 Oakland Ave.
Saint Louis 63110

Saint Luke's College
4426 Wornall Rd.
Kansas City 64111

Sanford-Brown Business College
12006 Manchester Rd.
Des Peres 63131

Southeast Missouri State University
One University Plaza
Cape Girardeau 63701

Southwest Missouri State University, West Plains
128 Garfield
West Plains 65775

State Fair Community College
3201 West 16th
Sedalia 65301-2199

Three Rivers Community College
Three Rivers Blvd.
Poplar Bluff 63901

Waynesville Technical Academy
810 Roosevelt
Waynesville 65583

MONTANA

Miles Community College
2715 Dickinson
Miles City 59301

Montana State University, Northern
300 West 11th St.
Havre 59501

Salish Kootenai College
P.O. Box 117
Pablo 59855

NEBRASKA

Bryan Memorial Hospital School of Nursing
5000 Sumner St.
Lincoln 68506-1398

Central Community College Area
P.O. Box 4903
Grand Island 68802

College of Saint Mary
1901 South 72nd St.
Omaha 68124

Metropolitan Community College Area
5300 North 30th St.
Omaha 68111

Northeast Community College
801 East Benjamin, P.O. Box 469
Norfolk 68702-0469

Southeast Community College Area
1111 O St., Ste. 111
Lincoln 68520

NEVADA

Community College of Southern Nevada
3200 East Cheyenne Ave.
Las Vegas 89030

Truckee Meadows Community College
7000 Dandini Blvd.
Reno 89512

Western Nevada Community College
2201 West College Pkwy.
Carson City 89703

NEW HAMPSHIRE

New Hampshire Community Technical College, Berlin/Laco
2020 Riverside Dr.
Berlin 03570

New Hampshire Community Technical College, Manchester/Stratham
1066 Front St.
Manchester 03102

New Hampshire Technical Institute
11 Institute Dr.
Concord 03301

Rivier College
429 Main St.
Nashua 03060

NEW JERSEY

Ann May School of Nursing, Jersey Shore Medical Center
1945 Rte. 33
Neptune 07754

Atlantic Community College
5100 Black Horse Pike
Mays Landing 08330-2699

Bergen Community College
400 Paramus Rd.
Paramus 07652

Brookdale Community College
765 Newman Springs Rd.
Lincroft 07738-1599

Burlington County College
Rte. 530
Pemberton 08068

Camden County College
P.O. Box 200
Blackwood 08012

Charles E Gregory School of Nursing
Old Bridge Medical Arts. Bldg. 1
Hospital
Old Bridge 08857

County College of Morris
214 Center Grove Rd.
Randolph 07869

Cumberland County College
P.O. Box 517, College Dr.
Vineland 08360

Englewood Hospital Medical Center
School of Radiology
36 Engle St.
Englewood 07631

Essex County College
303 University Ave.
Newark 07102

Felician College
260 South Main St.
Lodi 07644

Gloucester County College
1400 Tanyard Rd.
Sewell 08080

Helene Fuld School of Nursing
832 Brunswick Ave.
Trenton 08638

Holy Name Hospital School of Nursing
690 Teaneck Rd.
Teaneck 07666

Mercer County Community College
1200 Old Trenton Rd.
Trenton 08690

Mercer Medical Center School of
Nursing
446 Bellevue Ave., Box 1658
Trenton 08607

Mountainside Hospital School of
Nursing
One Bay Ave.
Montclair 07042

Muhlenberg Regional Medical Center,
School of Nursing
Park Ave. and Randolph Rd.
Plainfield 07061

Ocean County College
College Dr.
Toms River 08753

Our Lady of Lourdes School of Nursing
1565 Vesper Blvd.
Camden 08103

Passaic County Community College
One College Blvd.
Paterson 07505-1179

Raritan Valley Community College
P.O. Box 3300, Lamington Rd.
Somerville 08876

Saint Francis Medical Center School of
Nursing
601 Hamilton Ave.
Trenton 08629-1986

Union County College
1033 Springfield Ave.
Cranford 07016

NEW MEXICO

Albuquerque Technical Vocational
Institute
525 Buena Vista SE
Albuquerque 87106

Clovis Community College
417 Schepps Blvd.
Clovis 88101

Eastern New Mexico University, Roswell
Campus
52 University Blvd., Administration Ctr.
Roswell 88202

New Mexico Junior College
5317 Lovington Hwy.
Hobbs 88240

New Mexico State University,
Alamogordo
Box 477, 2400 North Scenic Dr.
Alamogordo 88310

New Mexico State University, Carlsbad
1500 University Dr.
Carlsbad 88220

New Mexico State University, Main
Campus
Box 30001, Department 3Z, Weddell Dr.
Las Cruces 88003

San Juan College
4601 College Blvd.
Farmington 87402

University of New Mexico, Gallup
Campus
200 College Rd.
Gallup 87301

NEW YORK

Adirondack Community College
Bay Rd.
Queensbury 12804

Arnot-Ogden Medical Center School of
Nursing
600 Roe Ave.
Elmira 14905

Broome Community College
P.O. Box 1017
Binghamton 13902

Catholic Medical Center School of
Nursing
175-05 Horace Harding Expy.
Fresh Meadows 11365

Cayuga County Community College
Franklin St.
Auburn 13021

Clinton Community College
136 Clinton Point Dr.
Plattsburgh 12901

Cochran School of Nursing
967 North Broadway, Andrus Pavillion,
Saint John's Riverside Hospital
Yonkers 10701

Columbia-Greene Community College
4400 Rte. 23
Hudson 12534

Corning Community College
Spencer Hill
Corning 14830

Crouse Hospital School of Nursing
736 Irving Ave.
Syracuse 13210

CUNY Borough of Manhattan
Community College
199 Chambers St.
New York 10007

CUNY Bronx Community College
West 181st St. & University Ave.
Bronx 10453

CUNY College of Staten Island
2800 Victory Blvd.
Staten Island 10314

CUNY Kingsborough Community
College
2001 Oriental Blvd.
Brooklyn 11235

CUNY La Guardia Community College
31-10 Thomson Ave.
Long Island City 11101

CUNY New York City Technical College
300 Jay St.
Brooklyn 11201

CUNY Queensborough Community
College
56th Ave. Springfield Blvd.
New York 11364

Dorothea Hopfer School of Nursing,
Mount Vernon Hospital
53 Valentine St.
Mount Vernon 10550

Dutchess Community College
53 Pendell Rd.
Poughkeepsie 12601

Ellis Hospital School of Nursing
1101 Nott St.
Schenectady 12308

Erie Community College, City Campus
121 Ellicott St.
Buffalo 14203

Erie Community College, North
Campus
Main St. and Youngs Rd.
Williamsville 14221

Finger Lakes Community College
4355 Lake Shore Dr.
Canandaigua 14424

Fulton-Montgomery Community
College
2805 State Hwy. 67
Johnstown 12095

Genesee Community College
One College Rd.
Batavia 14020

Helene Fuld School of Nursing
1879 Madison Ave.
New York 10035

Hudson Valley Community College
80 Vandenburgh Ave.
Troy 12180

Iona College
715 North Ave.
New Rochelle 10801

Jamestown Community College
525 Falconer St.
Jamestown 14701

Jefferson Community College
Outer Coffeen St.
Watertown 13601

Long Island College Hospital School of
Nursing
397 Hicks St.
Brooklyn 11201

Maria College of Albany
700 New Scotland Ave.
Albany 12208

Millard Fillmore Hospital School of
Nursing
Three Gates Circle
Buffalo 14209

Mohawk Valley Community College,
Utica Branch
1101 Sherman Dr.
Utica 13501

Monroe Community College
1000 East Henrietta Rd.
Rochester 14623

Nassau Community College
One Education Dr.
Garden City 11530

Niagara County Community College
3111 Saunders Settlement Rd.
Sanborn 14132

North Country Community College
20 Winona Ave., P.O. Box 89
Saranac Lake 12983

Onondaga Community College
4941 Onondaga Rd.
Syracuse 13215

Orange County Community College
115 South St.
Middletown 10940

Pace University, Pleasantville Briarcliff
Bedford Rd.
Pleasantville 10570

Phillips Beth Israel School of Nursing
310 East 22nd St.
New York 10010

Regents College, University of the State
of New York
Seven Columbia Cir.
Albany 12203

Rockland Community College
145 College Rd.
Suffern 10901

Saint Elizabeth College of Nursing
2215 Genessee St.
Utica 13501

Saint Joseph's Hospital Health Center
School of Nursing
206 Prospect Ave.
Syracuse 13203

Samaritan Hospital School of Nursing
2215 Burdett Ave.
Troy 12180

Sisters of Charity Hospital School of
Nursing
2157 Main St.
Buffalo 14214

St. Vincent's Medical Center of
Richmond, School of Nursing
Two Gridley Ave.
Staten Island 10303

Suffolk County Community College,
Ammerman Campus
533 College Rd.
Selden 11784

Suffolk County Community College,
Western Campus
Crooked Hill Rd.
Brentwood 11717

Sullivan County Community College
1000 Le Roy Rd.
Loch Sheldrake 12759-4002

SUNY College of Agriculture &
Technology at Morrisville
Morrisville 13408

SUNY College of Technology at Alfred
Alfred 14802

SUNY College of Technology at Canton
Cornell Dr.
Canton 13617

SUNY College of Technology at Delhi
Delhi 13753

SUNY College of Technology at
Farmingdale
Melville Rd.
Farmingdale 11735-1021

SUNY Ulster County Community
College
Cottekill Rd.
Stone Ridge 12484

SUNY Westchester Commmunity
College
75 Grasslands Rd.
Valhalla 10595

Tompkins-Cortland Community
College
170 North St.
Dryden 13053

Trocaire College
360 Choate Ave.
Buffalo 14220

NORTH CAROLINA

Alamance Community College
P.O. Box 8000
Graham 27253

Asheville Buncombe Technical Community College
340 Victoria Rd.
Asheville 28801

Beaufort County Community College
Box 1069
Washington 27889

Caldwell Community College and Technical Institute
Box 600
Lenoir 28645

Cape Fear Community College
411 North Front St.
Wilmington 28401

Catawba Valley Community College
2550 Hwy. 70 SE
Hickory 28602-0699

Central Carolina Community College
1105 Kelly Dr.
Sanford 27330

Central Piedmont Community College
P.O. Box 35009
Charlotte 28235-5009

College of the Albemarle
1208 North Road St.
Elizabeth City 27906-2327

Craven Community College
800 College Ct.
New Bern 28562

Davidson County Community College
297 Davidson Community College Rd.
Lexington 27292

Durham Technical Community College
1637 Lawson St.
Durham 27703

Edgecombe Community College
2009 West Wilson St.
Tarboro 27886

Fayetteville Technical Community College
2201 Hull Rd.
Fayetteville 28303-0236

Forsyth Technical Community College
2100 Silas Creek Pkwy.
Winston-Salem 27103

Gardner-Webb University
Main St.
Boiling Springs 28017

Gaston College
201 Hwy. 321 S
Dallas 28034

Guilford Technical Community College
Box 309
Jamestown 27282

Halifax Community College
P.O. Drawer 809
Weldon 27890

James Sprunt Community College
P.O. Box 398
Kenansville 28349

Johnston Community College
P.O. Box 2350
Smithfield 27577-2350

Mayland Community College
P.O. Box 547
Spruce Pine 28777

Mercy School of Nursing
1921 Vail Ave.
Charlotte 28207

Mitchell Community College
500 West Broad
Statesville 28677

Nash Community College
P.O. Box 7488
Rocky Mount 27804

Piedmont Community College
P.O. Box 1197
Roxboro 27573

Pitt Community College
Hwy. 11 S, P.O. Drawer 7007
Greenville 27835-7007

Presbyterian Hospital School of Nursing
1901 East Fifth St.
Charlotte 28204

Randolph Community College
629 Industrial Park Ave.
Asheboro 27204

Robeson Community College
P.O. Box 1420
Lumberton 28359

Rockingham Community College
P.O. Box 38, Hwy. 65W, County Home Rd.
Wentworth 27375-0038

Rowan-Cabarrus Community College
Box 1595
Salisbury 28145-1595

Sampson Community College
P.O. Box 318
Clinton 28329-0318

Sandhills Community College
2200 Airport Rd.
Pinehurst 28374

Southeastern Community College
4564 Chadburn Hwy.
Whiteville 28472

Stanly Community College
141 College Dr.
Albemarle 28001

Surry Community College
P.O. Box 304
Dobson 27017-0304

Vance-Granville Community College
P.O. Box 917, State Rd. 1126
Henderson 27536

Wake Technical Community College
9101 Fayetteville Rd.
Raleigh 27603-5696

Watts School of Nursing
3643 North Roxboro St.
Durham 27704-2763

Wayne Community College
3000 Wayne Memorial Dr.
Goldsboro 27533-8002

Western Piedmont Community College
1001 Burkemont Ave.
Morganton 28655-9978

Wilson Technical Community College
902 Herring Ave.
Wilson 27893

OHIO

Ashtabula County Joint Vocational School
1565 State Rte. 167
Jefferson 44047

Aultman Hospital School of Nursing
2600 Sixth St. SW
Canton 44710-1797

Belmont Technical College
120 Fox Shannon Place
Saint Clairsville 43950

Central Ohio Technical College
1179 University Dr.
Newark 43055-1767

Christ Hospital School of Nursing
2139 Auburn Ave.
Cincinnati 45219

Cincinnati State Technical and Community College
3520 Central Pkwy.
Cincinnati 45223

Clark State Community College
570 East Leffel Ln.
Springfield 45505

Columbus State Community College
550 East Spring St.
Columbus 43216

Community Hospital School of Nursing
330 South Burnett Rd.
Springfield 45505

Cuyahoga Community College District
700 Carnegie Ave.
Cleveland 44115-2878

Edison State Community College
1973 Edison Dr.
Piqua 45356

Fairview General Hospital School of Nursing
18101 Lorain Ave.
Cleveland 44111

Good Samaritan Hospital School of Nursing
375 Dixmyth Ave.
Cincinnati 45220

Hocking Technical College
3301 Hocking Pkwy.
Nelsonville 45764

Kent State University, Ashtabula Regional Campus
3325 West 13th St.
Ashtabula 44004

Kent State University, East Liverpool Regional Campus
400 East Fourth St.
East Liverpool 43920

Kettering College of Medical Arts
3737 Southern Blvd.
Kettering 45429-1299

Knox County Career Center
306 Martinsburg Rd.
Mount Vernon 43050

Lakeland Community College
7700 Clocktower Dr.
Mentor 44060-5198

Lima Technical College
4240 Campus Dr.
Lima 45804

Lorain County Community College
1005 North Abbe Rd.
Elyria 44035

Mansfield General Hospital School of Nursing
335 Glessner Ave.
Mansfield 44903-2265

Marion Technical College
1467 Mount Vernon Ave.
Marion 43302-5694

Mercy College of Northwest Ohio
2238 Jefferson Ave.
Toledo 43624-1197

Meridia Huron School of Nursing
13951 Terrace Rd.
Cleveland 44112-4399

Miami University, Oxford
500 High St.
Oxford 45056

North Central Technical College
2441 Kenwood Circle, P.O. Box 698
Mansfield 44901

Northwest State Community College
22-600 South Rte. 34
Archbold 43502-9542

Ohio University, Zanesville Branch
1425 Newark Rd.
Zanesville 43701

Owens Community College
39335 Oregon Rd.
Toledo 43699-1947

Providence Hospital School of Nursing
1912 Hayes Ave.
Sandusky 44870-4788

Queen City Vocational Center
425 Ezzard Charles Dr.
Cincinnati 45203

Saint Elizabeth Health Center School of Nurse Anesthesiology Inc.
1044 Belmont Ave.
Youngstown 44501-1790

Saint Thomas Medical Center School of Nursing
41 Arch St.
Akron 44304

Saint Vincent Medical Center School of Nursing
2201 Cherry St.
Toledo 43608-2603

Shawnee State University
940 Second St.
Portsmouth 45662

Sinclair Community College
444 West Third St.
Dayton 45402

Southern State Community College
100 Hobart Dr.
Hillsboro 45133

University of Cincinnati, Raymond Walters College
9555 Plainfield Rd.
Blue Ash 45236

University of Rio Grande
North College St.
Rio Grande 45674

University of Toledo
2801 West Bancroft
Toledo 43606

Xavier University
3800 Victory Pkwy.
Cincinnati 45207-1092

OKLAHOMA

Bacone College
2299 Old Bacome Rd.
Muskogee 74403-1597

Cameron University
2800 Gore Blvd.
Lawton 73505

Carl Albert State College
1507 South McKenna
Poteau 74953-5208

Connors State College
Rte. 1, Box 1000
Warner 74469

Eastern Oklahoma State College
1301 West Main St.
Wilburton 74578

Murray State College
One Murray Campus
Tishomingo 73460

Northeastern Oklahoma Agricultural and Mechanical College
200 I St. NE
Miami 74354

Northern Oklahoma College
Box 310 Tonkawa
Tonkawa 74653

Oklahoma City Community College
7777 South May Ave.
Oklahoma City 73159

Oklahoma State University, Oklahoma City
900 North Portland
Oklahoma City 73107

Pontotoc Area Vocational Technical School
601 West 33rd
Ada 74820

Redlands Community College
1300 South Country Club Rd.
El Reno 73036-5304

Rogers University, Claremore
1701 West Will Rogers Blvd.
Claremore 74017

Rose State College
6420 Southeast 15th
Midwest City 73110

Seminole State College
2701 Boren Blvd.
Seminole 74868

Tulsa Community College
6111 East Skelly Dr.
Tulsa 74135

OREGON

Blue Mountain Community College
P.O. Box 100
Pendleton 97801

Central Oregon Community College
2600 Northwest College Way
Bend 97701

Chemeketa Community College
4000 Lancaster Dr. NE
Salem 97305

Clackamas Community College
19600 Molalla Ave.
Oregon City 97045

Clatsop Community College
1653 Jerome St.
Astoria 97103

Lane Community College
4000 East 30th Ave.
Eugene 97405

Linn-Benton Community College
6500 Southwest Pacific Blvd.
Albany 97321

Mount Hood Community College
26000 Southeast Stark St.
Gresham 97030

Portland Community College
P.O. Box 19000
Portland 97280-0990

Rogue Community College
3345 Redwood Hwy.
Grants Pass 97527

Southwestern Oregon Community College
1988 Newmark Ave.
Coos Bay 97420

Umpqua Community College
P.O. Box 967
Roseburg 97470

PENNSYLVANIA

Abington Memorial Hospital School of Nursing
2500 Maryland Rd., Ste. 200
Willow Grove 19090-1284

Altoona Hospital School of Medical Technology
620 Howard Ave.
Altoona 16601-4899

Alvernia College
400 St. Bernardine St.
Reading 19607

Brandywine Hospital School of Nursing
215 Reeceville Rd.
Coatesville 19320-1536

Bucks County Community College
Swamp Rd.
Newtown 18940

Butler County Community College
College Dr. Oak Hills
Butler 16003-1203

Chester County Hospital School of Nursing
701 East Marshall St.
West Chester 19380

Citizens General Hospital School of Nursing
651 Fourth Ave.
New Kensington 15068

Clarion University of Pennsylvania
Wood St.
Clarion 16214

Community College of Allegheny County, Pittsburgh
800 Allegheny Ave.
Pittsburgh 15233-1895

Community College of Beaver County
One Campus Dr.
Monaca 15061

Community College of Philadelphia
1700 Spring Garden St.
Philadelphia 19130

Delaware County Community College
901 South Media Line Rd.
Media 19063-1094

Episcopal Hospital, School of Nursing
100 East Lehigh Ave.
Philadelphia 19125-1098

Gwynedd-Mercy College
Sumneytown Pike
Gwynedd Valley 19437

Harrisburg Area Community College, Harrisburg
One Hacc Dr.
Harrisburg 17110

Jameson Memorial Hospital
1211 Wilmington Ave.
New Castle 16105-2595

Lancaster General Hospital, Lancaster Institute for Health Education
143 East Lemon St.
Lancaster 17602

Lehigh Carbon Community College
4525 Education Park Dr.
Schnecksville 18078-2598

Lock Haven University of Pennsylvania
North Fairview St.
Lock Haven 17745-2390

Luzerne County Community College
1333 South Prospect St.
Nanticoke 18634

Mercer County Area Vocational Technical School
776 Greenville Rd.
Mercer 16137-0152

Montgomery County Community College
340 Dekalb Pike
Blue Bell 19422

Mount Aloysius College
7373 Admiral Peary Hwy.
Cresson 16630-1999

Northampton County Area Community College
3835 Green Pond Rd.
Bethlehem 18020-7599

Northeastern Hospital School of Nursing
2301 East Allegheny Ave. S
Philadelphia 19134

Pennsylvania College of Technology
One College Ave.
Williamsport 17701

Pennsylvania State University, Main Campus
201 Old Main
University Park 16802

Pottsville Hospital School of Nursing
Washington and Jackson St.
Pottsville 17901

Reading Area Community College
P.O. Box 1706
Reading 19603-1706

Roxborough Memorial Hospital School of Nursing
5800 Ridge Ave.
Philadelphia 19128

Saint Francis Hospital School of Nursing
1100 South Mercer St.
New Castle 16101

Saint Luke's Hospital School of Nursing
801 Ostrum
Bethlehem 18015

Saint Vincent Health Center School of Nursing
P.O. Box 740
Erie 16544

Sewickley Valley Hospital School of Nursing
720 Blackburn Rd.
Sewickley 15143

Shadyside Hospital School of Nursing
5230 Centre Ave.
Pittsburgh 15232

Sharon Regional Health System School of Nursing
740 East State St.
Sharon 16146

University of Pittsburgh, Bradford
Campus Dr.
Bradford 16701

Washington Hospital School of Nursing
155 Wilson Ave.
Washington 15301

Western Pennsylvania Hospital School of Nursing
4900 Friendship Ave.
Pittsburgh 15224

Westmoreland County Community College
Youngwood 15697-1895

RHODE ISLAND

Community College of Rhode Island
400 East Ave.
Warwick 02886-1807

Saint Joseph Hospital School of Nursing
200 High Service Ave.
North Providence 02904

SOUTH CAROLINA

Florence Darlington Technical College
P.O. Box 100548
Florence 29501-0548

Greenville Technical College
P.O. Box 5616, Station B
Greenville 29606-5616

Midlands Technical College
P.O. Box 2408
Columbia 29202

Orangeburg Calhoun Technical College
3250 Saint Matthew's Rd.
Orangeburg 29118

Piedmont Technical College
P.O. Drawer 1467
Greenwood 29648

Tri-County Technical College
P.O. Box 587
Pendleton 29670

Trident Technical College
P.O. Box 118067
Charleston 29423-8067

University of South Carolina at Aiken
171 University Pkwy.
Aiken 29801

University of South Carolina at Spartanburg
800 University Way
Spartanburg 29303

SOUTH DAKOTA

Dakota Wesleyan University
1200 West University Ave.
Mitchell 57301-4398

Huron University
333 Ninth St. SW
Huron 57350

Presentation College
1500 North Main
Aberdeen 57401

University of South Dakota
414 East Clark St.
Vermillion 57069-2390

TENNESSEE

Baptist Memorial College of Health Sciences
1003 Monroe Ave.
Memphis 38104

Chattanooga State Technical Community College
4501 Amnicola Hwy.
Chattanooga 37406

Cleveland State Community College
P.O. Box 3570
Cleveland 37320-3570

Columbia State Community College
P.O. Box 1315
Columbia 38402

Dyersburg State Community College
1510 Lake Rd.
Dyersburg 38024

East Tennessee State University
P.O. Box 70734
Johnson City 37614-0734

Fort Sanders School of Nursing
1915 White Ave.
Knoxville 37916

Jackson State Community College
2046 North Pkwy.
Jackson 38301

Lincoln Memorial University
Cumberland Gap Pkwy.
Harrogate 37752

Methodist Hospital School of Nursing
251 South Claybrook
Memphis 38104

Motlow State Community College
P.O. Box 88100, Ledford Mill Rd.
Tullahoma 37388-8100

Roane State Community College
276 Patton Ln.
Harriman 37748

Saint Joseph Hospital School of Nursing
204 Overton Ave.
Memphis 38105

Shelby State Community College
P.O. Box 40568
Memphis 38174-0568

Southern Adventist University
Box 370, 4881 Taylor Circle
Collegedale 37315-0370

Tennessee State University
3500 John Merritt Blvd.
Nashville 37209-1561

Union University
1050 Union University Dr.
Jackson 38305-9901

Walters State Community College
500 South Davy Crockett Pkwy.
Morristown 37813-6899

TEXAS

Alvin Community College
3110 Mustang Rd.
Alvin 77511

Amarillo College
P.O. Box 447
Amarillo 79178

Angelina College
P.O. Box 1768
Lufkin 75902-1768

Angelo State University
2601 West Ave. N
San Angelo 76909

Austin Community College
5930 Middle Fiskville Rd.
Austin 78752

Baptist Hospital System, Institute of Health Education
111 Dallas St.
San Antonio 78205

Blinn College
902 College Ave.
Brenham 77833

Central Texas College
P.O. Box 1800
Killeen 76540-1800

College of the Mainland
1200 Amburn Rd.
Texas City 77591

Collin County Community College, Central Park
2200 West University Dr.
McKinney 75070

Del Mar College
101 Baldwin
Corpus Christi 78404-3897

El Centro College
Main and Lamar
Dallas 75202

El Paso Community College
P.O. Box 20500
El Paso 79998

Frank Phillips College
P.O. Box 5118
Borger 79008-5118

Galveston College
4015 Ave. Q
Galveston 77550

Grayson County College
6101 Grayson Dr.
Denison 75020

Houston Baptist University
7502 Fondren Rd.
Houston 77074

Houston Community College System
22 Waugh Dr.
Houston 77270-7849

Howard County Junior College District
1001 Birdwell Ln.
Big Spring 79720

John Peter Smith Healthcare Network
2400 Circle Dr.
Fort Worth 76104

Kilgore College
1100 Broadway
Kilgore 75662-3299

Lamar University, Beaumont
P.O. Box 10001, 4400 Mlk
Beaumont 77710

Lamar University, Orange
410 Front St.
Orange 77630-5899

Laredo Community College
West End Washington St.
Laredo 78040

Lee College
200 Lee Dr.
Baytown 77520-4703

McLennan Community College
1400 College Dr.
Waco 76708

Midland College
3600 North Garfield
Midland 79705

Navarro College
3200 West Seventh
Corsicana 75110

North Harris Montgomery Community College District
250 North Sam Houston Pkwy. E, Ste. 300
Houston 77060

Odessa College
201 West University
Odessa 79764

Paris Junior College
2400 Clarksville St.
Paris 75460

PCI Health Training Center
8101 John Carpenter Fwy.
Dallas 75247

San Antonio College
1300 San Pedro Ave.
San Antonio 78284

San Jacinto College, Central Campus
8060 Spencer Hwy.
Pasadena 77505

South Plains College
1401 College Ave.
Levelland 79336

Southwestern Adventist College
P.O. Box 567
Keene 76059

Southwest Texas Junior College
2401 Garner Field Rd.
Uvalde 78801

Tarrant County Junior College
1500 Houston St.
Fort Worth 76102

Texarkana College
2500 North Robison Rd.
Texarkana 75599

Texas Southmost College
80 Fort Brown
Brownsville 78520

Trinity Valley Community College
500 South Prairieville
Athens 75751

Tyler County Hospital School of Nursing
1100 West Bluff
Woodville 75979

Tyler Junior College
1327 South Baxter Ave.
Tyler 75711

The University of Texas, Pan American
1201 West University Dr.
Edinburg 78539-2999

Victoria College
2200 East Red River
Victoria 77901

Wharton County Junior College
911 Boling Hwy.
Wharton 77488

UTAH

Salt Lake Community College
P.O. Box 30808
Salt Lake City 84130

Utah Valley State College
800 West 1200 South
Orem 84058

Weber State University
3750 Harrison Blvd.
Ogden 84408

VERMONT

Norwich University
65 South Main St.
Northfield 05663

University of Vermont and State Agricultural College
223 Waterman Building, South Prospect
Burlington 05405-0160

VIRGINIA

Community Hospital of Roanoke Valley College of Health Sciences
920 South Jefferson St.
Roanoke 24016

Dabney S Lancaster Community College
P.O. Box 1000
Clifton Forge 24422-1000

Danville Community College
1008 South Main St.
Danville 24541

De Paul Medical Center School of Nursing
150 Kingsley Ln.
Norfolk 23505

Germanna Community College
2130 Germanna Hwy.
Locust Grove 22508

John Tyler Community College
13101 Jefferson Davis Hwy.
Chester 23831-5399

J Sargeant Reynolds Community College
P.O. Box 85622
Richmond 23285-5622

Mountain Empire Community College
Drawer 700
Big Stone Gap 24219

Norfolk State University
2401 Corprew Ave.
Norfolk 23504

Northern Virginia Community College
4001 Wakefield Chapel Rd.
Annandale 22003

Patrick Henry Community College
P.O. Box 5311
Martinsville 24115-5311

Piedmont Virginia Community College
501 College Dr.
Charlottesville 22902

Rappahannock Community College
12745 College Dr.
Glenns 23149

Sentara Norfolk General Hospital School of Nursing
600 Gresham Dr., Jenkins Hall
Norfolk 23507

Shenandoah University
1460 University Dr.
Winchester 22601

Southwest Virginia Community College
Box SVCC
Richlands 24641

Thomas Nelson Community College
P.O. Box 9407
Hampton 23670

Tidewater Community College
121 College Pl.
Norfolk 23510

Tidewater Technical
616 Denbigh Blvd.
Newport News 23608

Virginia Highlands Community College
P.O. Box 828
Abingdon 24212-0828

Virginia Western Community College
3095 Colonial Ave.
Roanoke 24015

Wytheville Community College
1000 East Main St.
Wytheville 24382

WASHINGTON

Bellevue Community College
3000 Landerholm Circle SE
Bellevue 98007-6484

Clark College
1800 East McLoughlin Blvd.
Vancouver 98663-3598

Columbia Basin College
2600 North 20th Ave.
Pasco 99301

Everett Community College
801 Wetmore Ave.
Everett 98201

Grays Harbor College
1620 Edward P Smith Dr.
Aberdeen 98520

Highline Community College
P.O. Box 98000
Des Moines 98198-9800

Lower Columbia College
P.O. Box 3010
Longview 98632

Olympic College
1600 Chester Ave.
Bremerton 98310-1699

Seattle Community College, Central Campus
1701 Broadway
Seattle 98122

Shoreline Community College
16101 Greenwood Ave. N
Seattle 98133

Skagit Valley College
2405 College Way
Mount Vernon 98273

South Puget Sound Community College
2011 Mottman Rd. SW
Olympia 98512

Spokane Community College
North 1810 Greene Ave.
Spokane 99207

Tacoma Community College
5900 South 12th St.
Tacoma 98465

Walla Walla Community College
500 Tausick Way
Walla Walla 99362

Wenatchee Valley College
1300 Fifth St.
Wenatchee 98801

Yakima Valley Community College
P.O. Box 1647
Yakima 98907

WEST VIRGINIA

Bluefield State College
219 Rock St.
Bluefield 24701

Cabell County Vocational Technical Center
1035 Norway Ave.
Huntington 25705

Davis and Elkins College
100 Campus Dr.
Elkins 26241-3996

Fairmont State College
1201 Locust Ave.
Fairmont 26554

Shepherd College
King St., Ikenberry Hall
Shepherdstown 25443

Southern West Virginia Community and Technical College
Box 2900
Mt. Gay 25637

University of Charleston
2300 MacCorkle Ave. SE
Charleston 25304

West Virginia Northern Community College
1704 Market St.
Wheeling 26003

West Virginia University at Parkersburg
300 Campus Dr.
Parkersburg 26101

WISCONSIN

Blackhawk Technical College
P.O. Box 5009
Janesville 53547

Chippewa Valley Technical College
620 West Clairemont Ave.
Eau Claire 54701

Fox Valley Technical College at Appleton
1825 North Bluemound Dr.
Appleton 54913-2277

Gateway Technical College
3520 30th Ave.
Kenosha 53144-1690

Lakeshore Technical College
1290 North Ave.
Cleveland 53015

Madison Area Technical College
3550 Anderson St.
Madison 53704

Milwaukee Area Technical College
700 West State St.
Milwaukee 53233-1443

Moraine Park Technical College
235 North National Ave.
Fond Du Lac 54936-1940

Nicolet Area Technical College
Hwy. G South
Rhinelander 54501

Northcentral Technical College
1000 Campus Dr.
Wausau 54401-1899

Northeast Wisconsin Technical College
2740 West Mason St., P.O. Box 19042
Green Bay 54307-9042

Southwest Wisconsin Technical College
1800 Bronson Blvd.
Fennimore 53809

Waukesha County Technical College
800 Main St.
Pewaukee 53072

Western Wisconsin Technical College
304 North Sixth St., P.O. Box 908
La Crosse 54602-0908

Wisconsin Indianhead Technical College
505 Pine Ridge Dr.
Shell Lake 54871

WYOMING

Casper College
125 College Dr.
Casper 82601

Central Wyoming College
2660 Peck Ave.
Riverton 82501

Laramie County Community College
1400 East College Dr.
Cheyenne 82007

Northwest Community College
231 West Sixth St.
Powell 82435

Sheridan College
3059 Coffeen Ave.
Sheridan 82801

Western Wyoming Community College
2500 College Dr.
Rock Springs 82902

Respiratory Technology

ALABAMA

George C Wallace State Community College, Hanceville
801 Main St. NW
Hanceville 35077-2000

University of Alabama at Birmingham
Administration Bldg., Ste. 1070-2010
Birmingham 35294-0110

ARIZONA

Apollo College, Phoenix, Inc.
8503 North 27th Ave.
Phoenix 85051

Apollo College, Tri City, Inc.
630 West Southern Ave.
Mesa 85210

Gateway Community College
108 North 40th St.
Phoenix 85034

Long Medical Institute
4126 North Black Canyon Hwy.
Phoenix 85017

Pima Community College
2202 West Anklam Rd.
Tucson 85709-0001

ARKANSAS

Arkansas Valley Technical Institute
P.O. Box 506, Hwy. 23 N
Ozark 72949

Black River Technical College
Box 468, Hwy. 304
Pocahontas 72455

Pulaski Technical College
3000 West Scenic Dr.
North Little Rock 72118

University of Arkansas for Medical Sciences
4301 West Markham, Slot 601
Little Rock 72205

CALIFORNIA

California College for Health Science
222 West 24th St.
National City 91950

California Paramedical and Technical College
4550 La Sierra Ave.
Riverside 92505

California Paramedical and Technical College
3745 Long Beach Blvd.
Long Beach 90807

Concorde Career Institute
12412 Victory Blvd.
North Hollywood 91606

Crafton Hills College
11711 Sand Canyon Rd.
Yucaipa 92399-1799

El Camino College
16007 Crenshaw Blvd.
Torrance 90506

Foothill College
12345 El Monte Rd.
Los Altos Hills 94022

Grossmont-Cuyamaca Community College District
8800 Grossmont College Dr.
El Cajon 92020

Hacienda La Puente Unified School District, Adult Education
P.O. Box 60002
City of Industry 91716-0002

Modesto Junior College
435 College Ave.
Modesto 95350-5800

Napa Valley College
2277 Napa Vallejo Hwy.
Napa 94558

San Joaquin Valley College
201 New Stine Rd.
Bakersfield 93309

San Joaquin Valley College
8400 West Mineral King Ave.
Visalia 93291

Simi Valley Adult School
3192 Los Angeles Ave.
Simi Valley 93065

Victor Valley College
18422 Bear Valley Rd.
Victorville 92392-9699

COLORADO

Front Range Community College
3645 West 112th Ave.
Westminster 80030

FLORIDA

ATI Health Education Center
1395 Northwest 167th St.
Miami 33169

Daytona Beach Community College
1200 Volusia Ave.
Daytona Beach 32114

Flagler College
74 Kings St.
St. Augustine 32085-1027

Manatee Community College
5840 26th St. W
Bradenton 34207

Miami-Dade Community College
300 Northeast Second Ave.
Miami 33132

Palm Beach Community College
4200 Congress Ave.
Lake Worth 33461

GEORGIA

Augusta Technical Institute
3116 Deans Bridge Rd.
Augusta 30906

HAWAII

Kapiolani Community College
4303 Diamond Head Rd.
Honolulu 96816

IDAHO

Boise State University
1910 University Dr.
Boise 83725

ILLINOIS

Belleville Area College
2500 Carlyle Rd.
Belleville 62221

College of Du Page
425 22nd St.
Glen Ellyn 60137-6599

Illinois Central College
One College Dr.
East Peoria 61635-0001

Moraine Valley Community College
10900 South 88th Ave.
Palos Hills 60465-0937

Rock Valley College
3301 North Mulford Rd.
Rockford 61114

Saint John's Hospital School of Respiratory Therapy
800 East Carpenter
Springfield 62769

Triton College
2000 Fifth Ave.
River Grove 60171

INDIANA

Ivy Tech State College, Central Indiana
One West 26th St.
Indianapolis 46206-1763

Ivy Tech State College, Northeast
3800 North Anthony Blvd.
Fort Wayne 46805

KANSAS

Seward County Community College
Box 1137
Liberal 67905-1137

Washburn University of Topeka
1700 College Ave.
Topeka 66621

KENTUCKY

Kentucky Tech, Central Kentucky AVTS
308 Vo Tech Rd.
Lexington 40510-2626

Kentucky Technical, Bowling Green Regional Technology Center
845 Loop Dr.
Bowling Green 42101-3601

Kentucky Technical, Rowan Regional Technology Center
609 Viking Dr.
Morehead 40351

LOUISIANA

Bossier Parish Community College
2719 Airline Dr. N
Bossier City 71111

Delgado Community College
615 City Park Ave.
New Orleans 70119

Louisiana Technical College, West Jefferson Campus
475 Manhattan Blvd.
Harvey 70058

Southeastern Louisiana University
100 West Dakota
Hammond 70402

MICHIGAN

Macomb Community College
14500 Twelve Mile Rd.
Warren 48093-3896

MINNESOTA

Northwest Technical College, East Grand Forks
Hwy. 220 N
East Grand Forks 56721

MISSISSIPPI

Hinds Community College, Raymond Campus
Raymond 39154

Mississippi Gulf Coast Community College
Central Office, P.O. Box 67
Perkinston 39573

University of Mississippi Medical Center
2500 North State St.
Jackson 39216

MISSOURI

Hannibal Area Vocational Technical School
4550 McMasters Ave.
Hannibal 63401

MONTANA

Montana State University, College of Technology, Great Falls
2100 16th Ave. S
Great Falls 59405

NEBRASKA

Metropolitan Community College Area
5300 North 30th St.
Omaha 68111

NEW JERSEY

Gloucester County College
1400 Tanyard Rd.
Sewell 08080

University of Medicine and Dentistry of New Jersey
30 Bergen St.
Newark 07107

NEW YORK

CUNY Borough of Manhattan Community College
199 Chambers St.
New York 10007

NYU Medical Center Allied Health Education
483 First Ave.
New York 10016

Onondaga Community College
4941 Onondaga
Syracuse 13215

NORTH CAROLINA

Carteret Community College
3505 Arendell St.
Morehead City 28557

Durham Technical Community College
1637 Lawson St.
Durham 27703

Edgecombe Community College
2009 West Wilson St.
Tarboro 27886

Stanly Community College
141 College Dr.
Albemarle 28001

OHIO

Columbus State Community College
550 East Spring St.
Columbus 43216

Lima Technical College
4240 Campus Dr.
Lima 45804

University of Toledo
2801 West Bancroft
Toledo 43606

OKLAHOMA

Francis Tuttle Area Vocational-Technical Center
12777 North Rockwell Ave.
Oklahoma City 73142-2789

OREGON

Apollo College, Portland, Inc.
2600 Southeast 98th Ave.
Portland 97266

PENNSYLVANIA

Lehigh Carbon Community College
4525 Education Park Dr.
Schnecksville 18078-2598

SOUTH CAROLINA

Greenville Technical College
P.O. Box 5616, Station B
Greenville 29606-5616

Midlands Technical College
P.O. Box 2408
Columbia 29202

Spartanburg Technical College
Business I-85
Spartanburg 29305

TENNESSEE

Tennessee Technology Center at Memphis
550 Alabama Ave.
Memphis 38105-3604

Roane State Community College
276 Patton Ln.
Harriman 37748

TEXAS

Alvin Community College
3110 Mustang Rd.
Alvin 77511

El Centro College
Main and Lamar
Dallas 75202

Houston Community College System
22 Waugh Dr.
Houston 77270-7849

North Harris Montgomery Community College District
250 North Sam Houston Pkwy. E, Ste. 300
Houston 77060

Saint Philip's College
1801 Martin Luther King Dr.
San Antonio 78203

San Jacinto College, Central Campus
8060 Spencer Hwy.
Pasadena 77505

Southwest Texas State University
601 University Dr.
San Marcos 78666

Temple College
2600 South First St.
Temple 76504-7435

Texas Southmost College
80 Fort Brown
Brownsville 78520

Tyler Junior College
1327 South Baxter Ave.
Tyler 75711

UTAH

Weber State University
3750 Harrison Blvd.
Ogden 84408

VIRGINIA

Northern Virginia Community College
4001 Wakefield Chapel Rd.
Annandale 22003

WASHINGTON

Tacoma Community College
5900 South 12th St.
Tacoma 98465

WEST VIRGINIA

West Virginia Northern Community College
1704 Market St.
Wheeling 26003

WYOMING

Western Wyoming Community College
2500 College Dr.
Rock Springs 82902

Surgical Technology

ALABAMA

Community College of the Air Force
130 West Maxwell Blvd.
Montgomery 36112-6613

ARIZONA

The Bryman School
4343 North 16th St.
Phoenix 85016

CALIFORNIA

California Paramedical and Technical College
3745 Long Beach Blvd.
Long Beach 90807

Newbridge College
1840 East 17th St., Ste. 140
Santa Ana 92705

COLORADO

Concorde Career Institute
770 Grant St.
Denver 80203

FLORIDA

Sheridan Vocational Center
5400 Sheridan St.
Hollywood 33021

ILLINOIS

Swedish American Hospital School of Medical Technology
1400 Charles St.
Rockford 61104-2298

KENTUCKY

Kentucky Tech, Central Kentucky AVTS
308 Vo Tech Rd.
Lexington 40511-2626

Kentucky Technical, Jefferson State Vocational Technical School
727 West Chestnut
Louisville 40203-2036

LOUISIANA

Delgado Community College
501 City Park Ave.
New Orleans 70119

MASSACHUSETTS

Quincy College
34 Coddington St.
Quincy 02169

MICHIGAN

Lansing Community College
419 North Capitol Ave.
Lansing 48901-7210

MINNESOTA

Northwest Technical College, East Grand Forks
Hwy. 220 N
East Grand Forks 56721

Saint Cloud Technical College
1540 Northway Dr.
Saint Cloud 56303

MISSISSIPPI

Itawamba Community College
602 West Hill St.
Fulton 38843

PENNSYLVANIA

Delaware County Community College
901 South Media Line Rd.
Media 19063-1094

Mount Aloysius College
7373 Admiral Peary Hwy.
Cresson 16630-1999

Saint Francis Medical Center School of Nursing
400 45th St.
Pittsburgh 15201

SOUTH CAROLINA

Midlands Technical College
P.O. Box 2408
Columbia 29202

York Technical College
452 South Anderson Rd.
Rock Hill 29730

TENNESSEE

Aquinas College
4210 Harding Rd.
Nashville 37205

Tennessee Technology Center at Knoxville
1100 Liberty St.
Knoxville 37919

Tennessee Technology Center at Memphis
550 Alabama Ave.
Memphis 38105-3604

TEXAS

Houston Community College System
22 Waugh Dr.
Houston 77270-7849

San Antonio College of Medical and Dental Assistants, Central
4205 San Pedro Ave.
San Antonio 78212-1899

South Plains College
1401 College Ave.
Levelland 79336

Temple College
2600 South First St.
Temple 76504-7435

Texas State Technical College, Harlingen
2424 Boxwood
Harlingen 78550-3697

VIRGINIA

NNPS RRMC School of Surgical Technology
12420 Warwick Blvd., Ste. 6G
Newport News 23606

WASHINGTON

Seattle Community College, Central Campus
1701 Broadway
Seattle 98122

WISCONSIN

Northeast Wisconsin Technical College
2740 West Mason St., P.O. Box 19042
Green Bay 54307-9042

Veterinarian's Assistant

ARIZONA

Long Medical Institute
4126 North Black Canyon Hwy.
Phoenix 85017

Pima Medical Institute
3350 East Grant Rd.
Tucson 85716

CALIFORNIA

San Diego Mesa College
7250 Mesa College Dr.
San Diego 92111-4998

Yuba College
2088 North Beale Rd.
Marysville 95901

COLORADO

Bel-Rea Institute of Animal Technology
1681 South Dayton St.
Denver 80231

FLORIDA

Saint Petersburg Junior College
8580 66th St. N
Pinellas Park 34665

IDAHO

American Institute of Health Technology, Inc.
6600 Emerald
Boise 83704

ILLINOIS

Parkland College
2400 West Bradley Ave.
Champaign 61821

KANSAS

Colby Community College
1255 South Range
Colby 67701

MINNESOTA

Duluth Business University, Inc.
412 West Superior St.
Duluth 55802

Globe College of Business
175 Fifth St. E, Ste. 201, P.O. Box 60
Saint Paul 55101-2901

MISSOURI

Maple Woods Community College
2601 Northeast Barry Rd.
Kansas City 64156

Midwest Institute for Medical Assistants
112 West Jefferson
Kirkwood 63122

NEW YORK

SUNY College of Technology at Canton
Cornell Dr.
Canton 13617

SUNY College of Technology at Delhi
Delhi 13753

SUNY College of Technology at Farmingdale
Melville Rd.
Farmingdale 11735-1021

NORTH CAROLINA

Central Carolina Community College
1105 Kelly Dr.
Sanford 27330

OHIO

Columbus State Community College
550 East Spring St.
Columbus 43216

PENNSYLVANIA

Allied Medical and Technical Careers
2901 Pittston Ave.
Scranton 18505

Allied Medical and Technical Careers
104 Woodward Hill Rd.
Edwardsville 18704

Median School of Allied Health Careers
125 Seventh St.
Pittsburgh 15222-3400

TEXAS

North Harris Montgomery Community College District
250 North Sam Houston Pkwy. E, Ste. 300
Houston 77060

WASHINGTON

Pima Medical Institute
1627 Eastlake Ave. E
Seattle 98102

Index

All jobs mentioned in this volume are listed and cross-referenced in the index. Entries that appear in all capital letters have separate occupational profiles. For example, ACUPUNCTURIST, ADMITTING CLERK, AIDS COUNSELOR, and so on are profiles in this volume. Entries that are not capitalized refer to jobs that do not have a separate profile but for which information is given.

Under some capitalized entries there is a section entitled "Profile includes." This lists jobs that are mentioned in the profile. For example, in the case of PHYSICIAN, jobs that are described in the profile are: General practitioner, Internist, and Pediatrician.

Some entries are followed by a job title in parentheses after the page number on which it can be found. This job title is the occupational profile in which the entry is discussed. For instance, the Obstetrician entry is followed by the profile title (Physician).